Virtue's Hero

Virtue's

Hero

Emerson,

Antislavery,

and Reform

Len Gougeon

The University of Georgia Press   Athens and London

Paperback edition, 2010
© 1990 by the University of Georgia Press
Preface to the 2010 Edition © 2010 by the University of Georgia Press
Athens, Georgia 30602
www.ugapress.org
All rights reserved

Designed by Sandra Strother Hudson
Set in Linotron 10 on 14 Pilgrim by
Tseng Information Systems, Inc.

Printed digitally in the United States of America

The Library of Congress has cataloged the hardcover
edition of this book as follows:

Gougeon, Len.
Virtue's hero : Emerson, antislavery, and reform / Len Gougeon.
xiii, 408 p. ; 25 cm.
Includes bibliographical references (p. 349–397) and index.
ISBN 0-8203-1193-6 (alk. paper)
1. Emerson, Ralph Waldo, 1803–1882. 2. Antislavery movements—
United States. 3. Authors, American—19th century—Biography.
4. Social reformers—United States—Biography. 5. Abolitionists—
United States—Biography. 6. Slavery in literature. I. Title.
PS1642.S56G68 1990
814'.3—dc20   89-37662

Paperback ISBN-13: 978-0-8203-3469-1
ISBN-10: 0-8203-3469-3

British Library Cataloging-in-Publication Data available

For Deborah

Contents

Preface to the 2010 Edition

When this book was first published nearly twenty years ago, almost no one was aware that Ralph Waldo Emerson had a lengthy and at times intense antislavery career. Most historians accepted Arthur Schlesinger Jr.'s assessment in his *The Age of Jackson* (Boston: Little, Brown and Company, 1945) that transcendentalists in general and Emerson in particular tended to be a rather reclusive bunch. Their emphasis on self-reliance, it was believed, led them to stand aloof from the frenetic reform activities that characterized the "era of reform" in which they lived. Stephen Whicher's classic study *Freedom and Fate: An Inner Life of Ralph Waldo Emerson* (Philadelphia: University of Pennsylvania Press, 1953) did much to reinforce this view. Whicher insisted that, after his bitter experience following his controversial Divinity School Address in 1838, Emerson disengaged from society and led an increasingly quiet and contemplative life. The ten years that I spent in numerous archives researching this study revealed a strikingly different picture. Rather than a reclusive philosopher, I found a deeply engaged activist who sought to reform American society through the moral and ethical dynamic of his transcendental philosophy. Far from being a detached abstractionist, this Emerson, who has recently been described as the first modern American public intellectual, was both socially and politically active. Throughout his long public career, he sought consistently to "put his creed into his deed" in order to insure that the foundational promise of America—freedom, equality, and justice—would finally be a reality for all.

The revelation of this new image of a socially engaged Emerson has largely displaced that of the aloof scholar. Studies of the American antislavery movement now routinely acknowledge the role that Emerson played. The same is true for general histories of the antebellum period. Additionally, a growing interest among literary scholars in the reform movements of that period has contributed to a remarkable growth in the number of publications over the past two decades that deal with Emerson and reform. Among these are many fine journal articles, but I will limit my discussion here to books, monographs, and collections. First of all, there have been important additions to the Emerson canon that serve to provide a more complete picture of the range, depth, and duration of his social engagement. Several of the antislavery addresses that I cite here in manuscript have since been published in a collection that I edited with Joel Myerson. They are now available, complete with scholarly annotations and variants, in *Emerson's Antislavery Writings* (New Haven, Conn.: Yale University Press, 1995, 2001). Other important lectures, including several from the Civil War period, can now be found in *The Later Lectures of Ralph Waldo Emerson*, published in two volumes and edited by Ronald A. Bosco and Joel Myerson (Athens: University of Georgia Press, 2001). The new *Collected Works of Ralph Waldo Emerson* from Harvard University Press (eight volumes to date) includes a good deal of valuable information that relates to Emerson's reformist career and its impact on his thought. Barbara Packer's excellent "Historical Introduction" to *Conduct of Life* (1860), for example, shows in detail how Emerson's antislavery activities in the turbulent decade of the 1850s had a significant influence on the essays included in that work. These editions, in turn, have prompted other collections that are focused specifically on Emerson's political thought. Notable among these are David Robinson's *The Political Emerson* (Boston: Beacon Press, 2004) and Kenneth Sacks's *Emerson: Political Writings* (New York: Cambridge University Press, 2008). Both of these collections have well-informed and helpful introductions. It is now clear that Emerson's political thinking was integral to his antislavery career. Indeed, Eduardo Cadava argues for a pervasive, even organic, political strain in Emerson in his *Emerson and the Climates of History* (Stanford, Calif.: Stanford University Press, 1997). Politics was, in many ways, the arena in which Emerson's commitment to transcendental philosophy, as well as the fundamental principles of American democracy, faced their most severe test. This tension provides the thematic focus for the several historically detailed essays that are included in *The Emerson Dilemma: Essays on Emerson and Social Reform* (Athens: University of Georgia Press, 2001), edited by T. Gregory

Preface to the 2010 Edition

Garvey. Garvey extends his work on transcendental politics considerably in his *Creating the Culture of Reform in Antebellum America* (Athens: University of Georgia Press, 2007), where the focus remains primarily on Emerson. Most recently, the roots of Emerson's liberal political thought are shown to reach back to his classical predecessors in Neal Dolan's comprehensive study, *Emerson's Liberalism* (Madison: University of Wisconsin Press, 2009).

In addition to an expansion of the Emerson canon and studies of his political thought, a number of works have come forth over the past two decades that enlarge considerably the picture of Emerson's social activism and its impact on both his life and writings. These include David M. Robinson's insightful and cogent *Emerson and the Conduct of Life: Pragmatism and Ethical Purpose in the Later Work* (New York: Cambridge University Press, 1993), Robert Richardson's monumental and definitive biography *Emerson: The Mind on Fire* (Berkeley: University of California Press, 1995), and Lawrence Buell's astute, biographically based treatment of the meaning and enduring relevance of Emerson's thought, *Emerson* (Cambridge, Mass.: Harvard University Press, 2003). It is this latter study that quite properly identifies Emerson as America's first modern public intellectual.

Emerson's antislavery career is also an important component in other studies of the man, his family, and his society. Kenneth Sacks shows the early influence of the antislavery controversy in Emerson's social environment in his revealing and detailed study *Understanding Emerson: "The American Scholar" and His Struggle for Self-Reliance* (Princeton, N.J.: Princeton University Press, 2003). Also, Albert J. von Frank presents a comprehensive overview of the overwhelming presence of slavery and antislavery as it evolved during the violent decade of the 1850s in *The Trials of Anthony Burns: Freedom and Slavery in Emerson's Boston* (Cambridge, Mass.: Harvard University Press, 1998). In this work and elsewhere von Frank makes a convincing argument that Emerson's transcendental philosophy provided a strong stimulus for social activism among his contemporaries. Laura Dassow Walls shows that it was this same transcendental faith in human equality that allowed Emerson to effectively discount the many pseudo-scientific claims of African American racial inferiority that were current in his environment in her definitive *Emerson's Life in Science: The Culture of Truth* (Ithaca, N.Y.: Cornell University Press, 2003). Phyllis Cole reveals the seminal influence of Emerson's brilliant and eccentric aunt on both the development of his transcendental philosophy as well as his social reform activism in her groundbreaking biography, *Mary Moody Emerson and the Origins of Transcendentalism* (New York: Oxford University Press, 1996).

Some scholars, while acknowledging that Emerson was both politically active and substantially involved in social reform, have argued that this activism was fundamentally at odds with his transcendental philosophy and therefore, by definition, "untranscendental." This is largely because of that philosophy's emphasis on self-reliance and personal transcendence. These studies include John Carlos Rowe's *At Emerson's Tomb: The Politics of Classic American Literature* (New York: Columbia University Press, 1997), Christopher Newfield's *The Emerson Effect: Individualism and Submission in America* (Chicago: University of Chicago Press, 1996), and George Kateb's *Emerson and Self-Reliance* (Thousand Oaks, Calif.: Sage Publications, 1995). This position, however, is challenged by several studies that argue for transcendentalism as an activist philosophy that stressed the individual's obligation to bring transcendental ideals to bear directly on social problems. In addition to von Frank's work, noted above, Sarah Wider, in her authoritative study of Emerson's reputation, *The Critical Reception of Emerson* (Rochester, N.Y.: Camden House, 2000), shows that his liberating philosophy was consistently perceived as a threat to the cultural and political establishment, both early and late in his career. Recent histories of the movement tend to affirm this radical element. Barbara Packer in *The Transcendentalists* (Athens: University of Georgia Press, 2007) and Philip Gura in *American Transcendentalism: A History* (New York: Hill and Wang, 2007) both demonstrate that active social reform was always a major concern for transcendentalists generally. Other studies have shown that transcendental idealism, especially as articulated by Emerson, had a significant influence on later social-reform activists and writers, especially those involved in the civil rights movement. These include Anita Patterson's *From Emerson to King: Democracy, Race, and the Politics of Protest* (New York: Oxford University Press, 1997), Greg Crane's *Race, Citizenship, and Law in American Literature* (New York: Cambridge University Press, 2002), and Michael

Preface to the 2010 Edition

Magee's *Emancipating Pragmatism: Emerson, Jazz, and Experimental Writing* (Tuscaloosa: University of Alabama Press, 2004). Lastly, my own recent study, *Emerson & Eros: The Making of a Cultural Hero* (Albany: State University of New York Press, 2007), which tracks the intellectual, psychological, and spiritual evolution of Emerson's thought, reveals a natural, necessary, and nearly seamless relationship between the development of his transcendental philosophy and his social reform activism.

Finally, many excellent collections of essays have appeared that include important discussions of Emerson, transcendentalism, and social reform, especially antislavery and the women's movement. Among these are *Emersonian Circles: Essays in Honor of Joel Myerson*, edited by Wesley T. Mott and Robert E. Burkholder (Rochester, N.Y.: University of Rochester Press, 1997), *Transient and Permanent: The Transcendental Movement and Its Contexts*, edited by Charles Capper and Conrad Wright (Boston: Massachusetts Historical Society, 1999), *Emerson Bicentennial Essays*, edited by Ronald A. Bosco and Joel Myerson (Boston: Massachusetts Historical Society, 2006), *New Morning: Emerson in the Twenty-first Century*, edited by Arthur S. Lothstein and Michael Brodrick (Albany: State University of New York Press, 2008), the *Oxford Handbook of Transcendentalism*, edited by Joel Myerson, Sandra Petrulionis, and Laura Dassow Walls (New York: Oxford University Press, 2010), and *Emerson for the Twenty-first Century: Global Perspectives on an American Icon*, edited by Barry Tharaud (Newark: University of Delaware Press, 2010).

The sheer bulk of these works, as well as related studies, testifies to the important role that Emerson played during his lifetime as an advocate for human rights and social justice and also to his continuing influence on the major social reform movements that followed. That influence continues today through the lives of many individuals, from the president of the United States to common people on the street, who point to Ralph Waldo Emerson as a personal source of inspiration in their efforts to make American society ever more just and humane.

Acknowledgments

I would like to take this opportunity to express my gratitude to the following individuals and institutions who, over the past several years, provided invaluable assistance in making this work possible.

The administration and staff of the Houghton Library, Harvard University, for their consistent help in locating and providing access to a huge number of items in the Emerson Family Papers and other collections; to Mr. Rodney Dennis and the Ralph Waldo Emerson Memorial Association for permission to quote from these documents; to the staff of the Department of Rare Books and Manuscripts of the Boston Public Library, who provided able assistance in facilitating my examination of the large collection of various abolitionists' materials in their collection, and to the Trustees of the Boston Public Library for permission to quote from these materials; to the staffs of the Boston Athenaeum, the Essex Institute in Salem, Massachusetts, the Rare Books and Manuscripts Division of the New York Public Library, and the Sophia Smith Collection of the Smith College Library in Northampton, Massachusetts, for providing me with a variety of materials related to the abolitionists and their activities in Boston, New York, and elsewhere, and to the trustees of these institutions for permission to quote from these materials; to the Library of Congress in Washington, D.C., for access to the Moorfield Storey, Oliver Wendell Holmes, Sr., and Ainsworth Spofford papers and other materials relating to abolitionists; to the American Antiquarian Society in Worcester, Massachusetts, for providing newspaper accounts of Emerson's Civil War lectures; to Mrs. Marcia Moss, curator, and the staff of the Concord Free Public Library for innumerable personal kindnesses and access to the Sanborn Papers, records of the Middlesex Abolition Society, and other essential materials, and for permission to quote from these documents.

Acknowledgments

I would also like to express my gratitude to A. W. Plumstead, editor of volumes 7 and 11 of the *Journal and Miscellaneous Notebooks of Ralph Waldo Emerson*, who, as mentor and friend, introduced me to Emerson when I was a graduate student at the University of Massachusetts; to David Porter, who acquainted me with the poetic soul of Emerson while at UMass; to Walter Harding, who brought me to Concord, Massachusetts, in 1977 for an NEH summer seminar and who shared unreservedly his unbounded enthusiasm for the study of the transcendentalists, and life; to Joel Myerson, who, as editor and friend, has been consistently helpful, supportive, and generous with his time, who painstakingly read through the various drafts of this work, and who made innumerable helpful comments based upon his nearly limitless knowledge of the period and the critical literature it has spawned; to Eleanor Tilton, who generously provided access to innumerable Emerson letters collected by her for publication in her new multivolume edition of the *Letters of Ralph Waldo Emerson;* Professor Tilton also shared with me the exhaustively detailed documentation and information she developed for this edition from her vast store of knowledge of the period; to Bill Rakauskas and Bob Hueston of my own institution, who provided invaluable advice that helped to improve both the style and the content of this work; to Mrs. Rose Pedley, whose help in typing and preparing this manuscript went well beyond what any departmental secretary should be expected to do; to my indefatigable graduate research assistant Bill Conlogue, who spent many more hours in the library than most graduate students because of me; to our research and interlibrary loan librarians, Kevin Norris and Helen Weiss, who exercised extraordinary ingenuity and persistence in locating the most esoteric items and information.

I am also grateful to the National Endowment for the Humanities, whose summer seminar took me to Concord in 1977, and whose six-month Fellowship for College Teachers in 1982 gave me the opportunity to develop the framework, and many of the resources, that made this work possible; to the Faculty Research Committee of the University of Scranton for providing me with innumerable travel and research grants over the years, which took me to the various archives, libraries, and collections necessary for this study.

Acknowledgments

And finally, I would like to express my gratitude to my wife Deborah and my children, without whose patience, enthusiasm, and love this work would never have been possible.

Over the years some elements of this study have appeared in the following journals: the *New England Quarterly* (September 1981 and 1989); *Studies in the American Renaissance* (1981 and 1985); *American Literature* (1982); the *Walt Whitman Quarterly Review* (1985); the *Historical Journal of Massachusetts* (1988); and *Modern Language Studies* (1989). I am grateful to the editors of these journals for permission to quote from my previous work.

Abbreviations

CEC *The Correspondence of Emerson and Carlyle*, edited by Joseph Slater. New York: Columbia University Press, 1964.

CW *The Collected Works of Ralph Waldo Emerson*. 4 vols. to date. Edited by Robert E. Spiller et al. Cambridge: The Belknap Press of Harvard University Press, 1971–.

EL *The Letters of Ellen Tucker Emerson*. 2 vols. Edited by Edith E. W. Gregg. Kent, Ohio: Kent State University Press, 1982.

JMN *The Journals and Miscellaneous Notebooks of Ralph Waldo Emerson*. 16 vols. Edited by William H. Gilman et al. Cambridge: Harvard University Press, 1960–82.

L *The Letters of Ralph Waldo Emerson*. 6 vols. Edited by Ralph L. Rusk. New York: Columbia University Press, 1939.

LL *The Selected Letters of Lidian Jackson Emerson*, edited by Delores Bird Carpenter. Columbia: University of Missouri Press, 1987.

W *The Complete Works of Ralph Waldo Emerson*. 12 vols. Edited by Edward Waldo Emerson. Boston: Houghton Mifflin, 1903–4.

Virtue's Hero

Chapter One

Abolition
and the Biographers

The relationship of Ralph Waldo Emerson to the abolition movement and the degree of his commitment to the cause of antislavery have been sources of disagreement and controversy among scholars and critics almost from the beginning of his biographical history. In the one hundred years or so since his death an enormous number of commentaries have been produced that take profoundly disparate stands on the issue, both in matters of fact and in interpretation. Contemporary scholarship has been greatly affected by this biographical legacy, and individuals have been free to choose among the numerous possibilities in order to establish a variety of critical theories regarding Emerson's attitude toward abolition in particular, and social reform in general.

At the present time interpretations of Emerson's life revolve around two strikingly different poles of thought. The first describes Emerson as an active social reformer, a public figure who was very much caught up in the major reform efforts of his age, and an individual who, while a scholarly intellectual, wrestled with the thorny issues of the day and insisted upon the importance of action from principle. The modern mainstay for this perspective is Ralph Rusk's monumental *Life of Ralph Waldo Emerson* (1949). The opposite polarity depicts a more withdrawn and philosophical Emerson, the transcendental philosopher who succes-

I

sively separated himself, intellectually and emotionally, from the various crises of the hour throughout the 1840s and 1850s, and who, trusting in the tendency of all things toward ultimate goodness, eventually surrendered to a serene acceptance of fate, that is, things as they are. The chief proponent of this view is Stephen Whicher, author of *Freedom and Fate: An Inner Life of Ralph Waldo Emerson* (1953), a seminal work that remains firmly established in the canon of Emerson scholarship.

Over the years, scholarly efforts to understand the relationship of Ralph Waldo Emerson to the abolition movement have been met with many difficulties.[1] Among the most prominent are the following. First, although Emerson frequently spoke on the abolition question, beginning in earnest in the mid-1840s and continuing through to the Civil War, many of the manuscripts for these speeches have apparently not been preserved. Second, other addresses for which manuscripts existed were not published until long after Emerson's death. The "Fugitive Slave Law Address" of 1851, for example, first appeared in Emerson's *Collected Works* in 1903. Others that exist in complete manuscript form, such as the important 1855 address "American Slavery," have never been published. A possible explanation for this situation is that, in the 1840s especially, Emerson looked upon these occasional discourses on specific social issues as largely ephemeral and therefore not indicative of the more philosophical and comprehensive treatment of the human condition that is reflected in the essays and lectures he chose to publish at the time. Emerson's earliest abolition addresses, which he delivered in 1837, 1844, 1845, 1846, and 1849, simply did not represent what he considered to be his best work, and, with the exception of the famous 1844 "Emancipation in the British West Indies" speech, over which he labored for some time, none of the addresses from this early period were ever published during his lifetime. Even the 1844 address, which stands as one of Emerson's most comprehensive statements on slavery and abolition in the period, he saw as a divergence from his proper role as poet and scholar. As he told Carlyle shortly after that experience, "Though I sometimes accept a popular call, & preach on Temperance or the abolition of Slavery, as lately on the First of August, I am sure to feel before I have done with it, what an intrusion it is into another sphere & so much loss of virtue in my own" (*CEC* 373).

As a result of this situation, early biographers and commentators were deprived of valuable sources of information regarding Emerson's earliest abolition activities, as well as his most articulate and detailed thinking regarding what was clearly the most pressing and important social reform movement of his time. Consequently, many of these critics were led to conclude that Emerson was uninterested in, or even opposed to, the abolition movement generally. In support of this position some writers pointed to critical remarks in Emerson's early and better-known works like "Self-Reliance" (1841) and "Man the Reformer" (1841) regarding what he considered to be the egotism and myopia of single-issue reformers. In this early period he also frequently emphasized the need to work toward reform through the promotion of individual self-culture rather than associated action. Those who chose to emphasize this aspect of Emerson's thinking on abolitionism usually cast him in the role of a social conservative or, in some cases, a reclusive hermit who developed radical philosophies but who was more than happy to delegate the actual application and implementation of his ideas to others. Perhaps the most influential of these conservative commentators was Oliver Wendell Holmes, whose 1884 biography *Ralph Waldo Emerson* was published by Houghton Mifflin in its *American Men of Letters* series. In this study Holmes depicts Emerson, in the words of one reviewer, as "a conservative like himself," and a considerable amount of controversy followed the publication of this work. Many old-time abolitionists like Thomas Wentworth Higginson, who had known Emerson to be very firmly in the abolition ranks, came forward to argue their case. Higginson and others like him had made the transition from abolition to civil rights in the period following the Civil War, and he was loath to see the name of one of America's most recent saints appropriated by the other side.

The political climate in America during the age of the captains of industry, laissez-faire economics, and imperialistic expansion also contributed a great deal to the flavor of the arguments on both sides. Unfortunately for Higginson and his cohorts—reformers like Wendell Phillips, William Lloyd Garrison II, and William J. Potter—a lack of biographical resources limited their arguments largely to Emerson's activities in the 1850s, where the record was reasonably well established. This, unfortunately, had the effect of suggesting to some that Emerson was indeed a reluctant latecomer to the cause, and so the debate was inconclusive and continues to this day.

An understanding, if not a resolution, of the development of this historical dichotomy is imperative to an accurate understanding of Emerson's relationship to the abolition movement. Even an "inner life" such as Stephen Whicher's, in order to be valid, must be predicated largely upon the evidence provided by an outer life. This would include not only what Emerson actually said and wrote on the subject of abolition but also the activities he undertook in the name of this reform. However, as the present study will show, some of the most deep-seated scholarly commonplaces regarding Emerson's relationship to the important reforms of his day are based upon assumptions that have obtained credibility almost solely on the basis of historical reiteration rather than historical fact.

Emerson's first major biographer and commentator, George Willis Cooke, in his *Ralph Waldo Emerson: His Life, Writings, and Philosophy* (1881) devotes a full chapter to the antislavery movement and maintains that "the real spirit and purpose of the man, [Emerson] are not likely to be understood without a knowledge of his relations to this agitation."[2] Cooke highlights the growth of Emerson's involvement in the antislavery cause beginning in 1831–32 when he allowed Samuel May and Arnold Buffum to deliver antislavery addresses from his pulpit in the Second Church in Boston. This was at a time "when all the pulpits were silent on the subject of slavery."[3] In his discussion Cooke also quotes extensively from Emerson's famous 1 August 1844 address, "Emancipation in the British West Indies," and other major speeches such as "American Slavery" (1855), "The Assault upon Mr. Sumner" (1856), and "John Brown" (1859), which were delivered throughout the 1850s. Overall, Cooke creates the impression of a very concerned and active Emerson who strongly supported abolitionism, and who, because he "had faith in the triumph of freedom and love, gave such aid as he could and all his sympathies, to those seeking the emancipation of the poor and oppressed."[4]

Cooke's work was followed in 1882 by Moncure Conway's *Emerson at Home and Abroad*. Conway, a former slave owner who became an abolitionist, was a personal friend of Emerson in his later years. His study devotes an entire chapter to an exposition of Emerson's anti-slavery activities. Indeed, his enthusiasm in depicting Emerson as an active reformer led him at times to make somewhat misleading statements. Among these, for example, are the assertions that "Emerson was the first American scholar to cast a dart at slavery,"[5] and that he was battling slavery "six years before even [William Ellery] Channing had committed himself to that side."[6] Despite such deficiencies, however, Conway does succeed in calling attention to some of Emerson's major abolition activities and furthers the idea suggested by Cooke of an early and constant commitment on Emerson's part to the principles of abolition.

Another important biographical study of Emerson was published in 1882 by a British writer, Alexander Ireland. Emerson had met Ireland on his first visit to England in 1833, and he maintained a cordial correspondence and friendship with him for the rest of his life. Ireland had first published *In Memoriam. Ralph Waldo Emerson: Recollections of His Visits to England in 1833, 1847–8, 1872–3 and Extracts from Unpublished Letters* in London early in 1882. Encouraged by the swift sale of the book, he soon added a biographical sketch and, later in 1882, published *Ralph Waldo Emerson: His Life, Genius, and Writings, A Biographical Sketch, to Which Are Added Personal Recollections of His Visits to England, Extracts from Unpublished Letters, and Miscellaneous Characteristic Records.*[7]

Ireland relied in part on Cooke's biography for the general outline of Emerson's life, to which he added details that he could uniquely provide based upon his correspondence with Emerson and his contact with him in England. In his biographical sketch he alludes to the first West Indian emancipation speech (misdating it as 1841) and also takes note of several of the antislavery speeches of the 1850s and 1860s. In general, Ireland is very clear in stressing Emerson's "sympathy with the Anti-Slavery Movement, and the priceless service he rendered to that cause."[8]

Later in the work, when discussing Emerson's lifelong commitment to freedom in all areas of human endeavor, Ireland notes approvingly the following comment on the bard from the British *Spectator* (6 May 1882): "He sympathized ardently with all the great practical movements of his own day, while Carlyle held contemptuously aloof. He was one of the first to strike a heavy blow at the institution of slavery. He came forward to encourage his country in the good cause, when slavery raised the flag of rebellion. He had a genuine desire to see all men free, while Carlyle only felt the desire to see all men strongly governed—which they might be, without being free at all."[9]

Last, perhaps in an effort to elaborate upon this contrast, Ireland also published in his volume several of Emerson's letters to Carlyle, including those of the Civil War period in which Emerson describes the sacrifices of young Union soldiers fighting to destroy the institution of slavery. "One lesson they all learn [is] to hate slavery, *teterrima causa*." In another of these letters Emerson identifies the slaveholders emphatically as the "enemies of mankind," and he seeks to enlist Carlyle's "thunderbolt on our part" and to discourage his unfortunate sympathy for the southern cause.[10]

Generally, this view of Emerson's activism was maintained in a variety of articles written about him in the early 1880s. Frequently he was ranked among the major reform activists of the pre–Civil War period. Thus, an article on "Emerson and Theodore Parker" published in the *Index* (a Boston weekly that served as the official voice of the Free Religious Association, a group Emerson helped to found in the early 1860s and in which he later served for some years nominally as vice president)[11] in August 1882 asserts that William Ellery Channing was "in a true and large sense the spiritual father of both Emerson and Parker." The author points out the numerous controversial reform movements in which the two were involved and suggests that by comparison the other Unitarian clergy of the time appeared to be "a petrified and asphyxiated set of men, as destitute of red blood as pre-Raphaelite saints."[12]

Moncure Conway also continued to produce articles on the subject, frequently repeating some of the material from his biography. For example, in an essay appearing in the *Fortnightly Review* (London) in June 1882, Conway discusses at length Emerson's antislavery involvement and asserts that "the destinies of hundreds of young men and women were determined by his lectures." Regarding the antislavery cause in particular, Conway asserts that Emerson "did more than he exacted from others, and recognized it as a far more important reform than others."[13]

It was with the publication of Oliver Wendell Holmes's highly influential and consistently popular biography, *Ralph Waldo Emerson* (1884), however, that the image of Emerson as an abolitionist and reformer became blurred both in matters of fact and interpretation. In a complete break with Cooke, Conway, and Ireland, Holmes states flatly that "Emerson had never been identified with the abolitionists" and implies that his sympathies for their cause were not strong.[14] This statement and others, as well as the generally conservative image of Emerson that the biography presents, infuriated many who had known Emerson as an abolitionist and reformer. However, there were also those who supported Holmes's view. This opposition led to a flurry of article writing arguing the issue both pro and con.

One of the earliest reviews of the work appeared in the 29 January 1885 issue of the *Nation*.[15] In this article the author indicates that about two-thirds of Holmes's work consists of "a detailed review of the *opera omnia* of one man of genius by another," which is acceptable as far as it goes, although "there is a good deal that suggests the scissors and paste" in its "running annotations [which are] grave, gay, learned and witty." However, the review becomes nearly vitriolic when the subject turns to Emerson's reform activities. "It is among the most conspicuous deficiencies of this memoir that it leaves us almost wholly uninformed as to two of the most important aspects of Emerson's earlier life—his relations to the antislavery agitation and to the so-called transcendental movement." It seems clear that "in both cases there is an obvious lack of personal knowledge, not filled by any assiduous inquiry." The author attributes this failing to the fact that Holmes was "simply bored" by transcendentalism and "toward the anti-slavery agitation he probably had the usual prejudices of his social and professional circle." Regarding Holmes's statement that Emerson "had never been identified with the abolitionists," the reviewer observes, "it is impossible to say what Doctor Holmes means by being identified; Emerson no more merged himself in any anti-slavery society than in the 'Saturday Club.'" The author goes on to note that "there is no doubt that from the day when [Emerson's] great address on West India Emancipation was delivered in Concord the abolitionists, who were not at all given to claiming or even recognizing any half-converts, always accounted Emerson as their own." Regarding the question of how satisfying the speech might have been to the abolitionists, Holmes could have answered the question himself "by stepping into the Boston Public Library and looking at a file of the *Liberator* for 1844," which, obviously, he chose not to do. After presenting several details regarding Emerson's antislavery activities, the author concludes this portion of his review with an affirmation of the significance of Emerson's early association with the abolitionists by noting bluntly, "Men with ropes around their necks generally know who their friends are."

The controversy soon spilled over onto the pages of the *Index*. William J. Potter, who had joined with Emerson in establishing the Free Religious Association, and who was then serving as editor of the *Index*, entered the fray in February 1885 with an article entitled "Mr. Holmes' Limitation as Emerson's Biographer."[16] In this highly critical article Potter points out that Dr. Holmes "has never shown himself specially interested in social and religious reform" and that, unfortunately, he has represented Emerson's views in these matters as "too much like his own." Unlike Holmes, Potter insists that "Emerson had that innate moral chivalry which took him without a question to the defense of the weak and the wronged. He was therefore to be found at certain public meetings, and was interested in objects, of which Dr. Holmes knew nothing except by hearsay or by highly colored reports of a hostile press." Echoing the *Nation*, Potter adds that this characteristic of Emerson was so marked that "any biography of him that treats it slightingly is fatally defective." The article closes with the statement that when the "complete biographer comes," Emerson will be seen not only as a "serene, scholarly philosopher" but also as "one of the leading heroic reformers of this nineteenth century."

Potter's article was followed by others, including a short note from Thomas Wentworth Higginson in August. Higginson had been for years an active and strong supporter of Garrisonian abolitionism, and as a young man he looked to Emerson as one who "had praised the zeal and enthusiasm of the best reformers." By the mid-1850s Higginson himself was known and highly regarded by Emerson personally, and on occasion he shared an abolition platform with him.[17] In later years Higginson would do much to memorialize Emerson's efforts in "the cause." In his article Higginson, like Potter and others, asserts unequivocally that Emerson was "thoroughly identified" with the abolitionists. However, as support for his claim he refers to a speech by an antiabolitionist, Caleb Cushing, delivered in December 1859, where Emerson was castigated along with Wendell Phillips, William Lloyd Garrison, Theodore Parker, and others as being one who "brooded" over the singular cause of abolition to the point of monomania.[18] Higginson's attempt at clarification thus tended to suggest to some that Emerson was a latecomer to the cause.

Indeed, Nathaniel Bowditch argued this very point in a rather vitriolic article that followed in the November *Index*. In this piece, entitled "Did Mr. Emerson Sympathize with the Abolitionists?" Bowditch, who had been an active Garrisonian abolitionist from 1835 on, insists that "Emerson never publicly showed the least interest in our proceedings," and that "he never spoke any ringing words in our behalf until long after the battle was half won; namely until 1854 . . . in a lecture on the Fugitive Slave Bill."[19] Bowditch goes on to analyze briefly Emerson's poem "Ode to W. H. Channing," which he felt expressed Emerson's "abhorrence of abolition methods." His piece concludes with the statement, "I have lately conversed with some of the old abolitionists, and I find all agree with me that Emerson was never known to be in our ranks, or to show any active sympathy for the slave. . . . No! Holmes is right, and his critics are wrong."

Potter and others responded to Bowditch's attack in later issues, and this controversy was finally brought to a close, largely without resolution, with the publication of two letters to the editor of the *Index* in late December 1885. The first of these letters was from Elizabeth Peabody, who, as an early and active advocate of a variety of reforms, had become by this time a Boston institution. The letter is remarkable both for its information and its misinformation. Peabody, for example, insists that "as far back as the publication of Lydia Maria Child's awakening book [undoubtedly *An Appeal in Favor of that Class of Americans Called Africans* (1833)], before he knew the present Mrs. Emerson (who was always an ardent professor of the doctrines afterwards published by Garrison in the *Liberator*), Mr. Emerson was uncompromisingly an abolitionist."[20] Peabody recounts the strong and positive influence of Aunt Mary Moody Emerson in this regard and even points out that when the Grimké sisters were in Concord lecturing against slavery in the 1830s, they stayed with the Emersons. However, in addition to supplying these valuable insights into Emerson's early abolition interests and activities, she also makes the egregious misstatement that Emerson's "first public activity [regarding abolition] was just after Webster's 7th of March speech, 1850," thus apparently ignoring all of the speeches and activities of the 1840s, including the well-known 1 August 1844 address.

The second letter to the editor, which was signed simply "C. K. W.," presents a reading of Emerson's "Ode to W. H. Channing" that refutes the somewhat lopsided interpretation of the work that Bowditch had offered. This writer insists that in the poem "Emerson is chastising, not the abolitionists, but the North" for its failure to act against the immorality of slavery. He concludes with the observation that while Emerson joined no antislavery society, "his constant upholding of justice and righteousness gave full assurance that his heart and his influence were with them."[21]

Returning now to the Holmes biography itself, a question arises regarding the basis for his blatant assertions regarding Emerson's alleged lack of sympathy with the abolitionists and his possible motivations in making such statements. Since the work has been reprinted several times and remains a significant Emerson biography, it is both appropriate and necessary to address the issue. A careful examination of the several "memoranda books" and note files that Holmes used in writing his biography (now on deposit at the Houghton Library, Harvard), as well as the later handwritten manuscript and related notes (now on deposit at the Library of Congress), yields some revealing insights.

The Houghton materials show that Holmes was thoroughly acquainted with the previous Emerson biographies noted above and the statements they make regarding Emerson's abolition activities. One notebook actually outlines in vertical columns, side by side, the chronological development of Emerson's life as presented in the studies by Cooke, Conway, and Ireland.[22] These outlines are actually detailed synopses of each work. From Ireland's study, for example, Holmes records "1855, 6, 9, 60 Antislavery speeches—Sumner Assault, etc. Speech at Anti-Slavery Soc. in Boston, Hisses, etc. etc.," and other such details. However, very little of this information got into the later manuscript. The papers at the Library of Congress consist of two large, bound volumes, one a late manuscript of the Emerson biography, and the other "notes" for the same work.[23] Perhaps the most conspicuous and compelling insight into the work is furnished by a recognition of what these documents do not contain, and that is any reference whatsoever to the subjects of antislavery and the abolition movement. Thus, within the pages of the manuscript volume Holmes includes discussions of major speeches like the "American Scholar" and "Divinity School" addresses and lesser presentations like "Man the Reformer" (1841), "Lecture on the Times" (1841), and "The Young American" (1844), but he says nothing about "Emancipation in the British West Indies," certainly one of Emerson's most important and well-known addresses. In fact, in the "Corrected Table of Contents" that appears in the front of the manuscript volume, Holmes had originally listed the address, in chapter 6, as "Emancipation in the *East* Indies," and he subsequently corrected the error.

The same is true for the later antislavery addresses of the 1850s. Nothing appears in the manuscript relative to them. When consulting the published work at the appropriate chronological junctures, one finds abbreviated interjections that suggest the quality of an afterthought. Thus, following a discussion of "The Young American," the reader finds a single-paragraph discussion of the "Emancipation in the West Indies Address," with no quotation from the work and the extraordinarily inaccurate statement that "this discourse would not have satisfied the Abolitionists."[24] Obviously, such a statement flies in the face of the ample testimony to the contrary rendered in the earlier biographies, especially Cooke's (which Holmes on occasion specifically refers to), and also contemporary newspaper accounts.

Regarding the later antislavery speeches of the 1850s, which are barely touched upon in the published work, Holmes offers facile and at times misleading obiter dicta such as "of course with notions like these he [Emerson] could not be hand in hand with the Abolitionists," or "he was never in the front rank of the aggressive Anti-Slavery men," or, as noted earlier, the totally erroneous statement that "Emerson had never been identified with the abolitionists."[25] And finally, in an index of topics that appears at the end of the manuscript volume, Holmes lists, among topics to be discussed, "character," "personality," and "Emerson as an American," but there are no entries regarding abolition or the antislavery question.

While admittedly somewhat conjectural, this seems to suggest at least two things. First, Potter's claim in the *Index* that Holmes's tendency was to depict Emerson in the light of his own conservative image and likeness appears accurate. And second, the observation in the *Nation* that Holmes's discussion of the antislavery agitation and the transcendental movement is characterized by "an obvious lack of personal knowledge, not filled by any assiduous inquiry" seems an apt description. In short, Holmes just wasn't interested in such things, and they did not fit his image of Emerson. Perhaps it is revealing that in a volume of typed notes that Holmes used in preparing his biography of Emerson, he recorded the following from Emerson's memorial lecture on Theodore Parker (W 11: 285): "I have the feeling that . . . biography is at his [the author's] own expense. He furnishes not only the facts but the report. I mean all biography is autobiography. It is only what he tells of himself that comes to be known and believed."[26]

The influence of the Holmes biography in projecting a distorted image of Emerson as a conservative in regard to abolition and other reforms was mitigated somewhat by the publication three years later of James Elliot Cabot's seminal work, *A Memoir of Ralph Waldo Emerson* (1887).

Cabot was Emerson's friend and literary executor, and he had the advantage of virtually unlimited access to Emerson's manuscripts, journals, and correspondence. Additionally, his project was enthusiastically supported by the Emerson family, who read the work in progress.[27] In his *Memoir* Cabot presents the most detailed account of all the early biographies regarding Emerson's abolition activities, and there is a possibility that Lidian Emerson, who had been an abolitionist and civil rights activist all her life, had some influence in this regard.

Cabot covers a broad spectrum of Emerson's abolition activities, quoting extensively from major speeches and other documents from 1837 through 1864. While still not a complete account of the matter by far, Cabot's work certainly contradicted significantly the implications and assertions of Holmes's study and was seen by many as a necessary corrective to that work. Thus, for example, Ebenezer Rockwood Hoar, a prominent squire of Concord, longtime friend of the Emerson family, and an early and consistent foe of slavery, noted the following in a letter to Cabot shortly after publication: "I cannot deny myself the pleasure of expressing to you the delight I have had in reading your life of Mr. Emerson—and my sense of how well done it is. I thought Dr. Holmes' memoir very good—for what he knew and understood of Mr. Emerson —and was even astounded that he knew so much—But there was a good deal that he did not know; in short, the minds were not commensurate."[28] The Emerson family was also delighted with the work. In another letter to Cabot, Emerson's daughter Edith insists that it is "more perfectly done—more faultless and satisfying than could have been written by anyone in the world," and that "it would satisfy Father's taste entirely." Ellen Emerson refers to it as "this perfect beautiful book, our delight and glory."[29]

The reviews of Cabot's biography were almost uniformly positive, and many reviewers took note of what they considered to be Emerson's longtime and consistent commitment to the abolition cause. The *Nation*, which had been so unhappy with Holmes's performance, praised the *Memoir* extravagantly and noted that now "no one could doubt where he [Emerson] stood on the issues involved in the slavery question and some other leading reforms of his period."[30] A writer in the *New Englander and Yale Review* noted that "it was impossible that Emerson should not have been from the first an opponent of the system of American slavery."[31] However, despite the general approval that greeted Cabot's *Memoir*, there were those who were less than satisfied with the work's treatment of Emerson's reform activity. Chief among these was Thomas Wentworth Higginson.

In an article entitled "Emerson as the Reformer," which appeared in the *Boston Advertiser* on 25 May 1903 in conjunction with the Emerson centenary, Higginson made his most direct assault upon the inadequacies of the biographical treatment of Emerson's reform activities up to that time. In the process he offers an interesting insight into the Cabot biography, which presented the most complete accounting in this matter.[32] In his article Higginson points out that "complaints are often made by those who knew Mr. Emerson in the light of a reformer, or who wished to regard him in that light, as to the want of information given in that direction by his biographers." These individuals "do not sufficiently allow for the fact that, of his two chief biographers, Dr. Holmes saw him but little on that side, and Mr. J. E. Cabot, though a most faithful and conscientious biographer, was, as he frankly admitted to me, constitutionally reticent, like Emerson himself, and in a general way shortened the chapters as much as he fairly could."[33] Clearly, the full story of Emerson as reformer and abolitionist had yet to be told.

There are several possible reasons for this early failure to address Emerson's abolitionism in a comprehensive and detailed fashion. Not the least of these was the lack of firsthand information on the topic. Many of the accounts of Emerson's abolition activity published before the turn of the century were written by abolitionists. Commentators like Conway, Higginson, Elizabeth Peabody, and Franklin Sanborn relied for the most part upon their own sometimes inaccurate memories for information, and they tended generally to date Emerson's involvement in the abolition movement to coincide with their personal contact with him, thus ignoring, in most cases, the numerous activities of the 1840s. Additionally, many relied on the published editions of Emerson's complete works as the primary source for information regarding his public addresses, even though the earliest antislavery speeches, with the exception of the 1 August 1844 address, are not reproduced there. The problem is compounded by the fact that the manuscripts for Emerson's antislavery addresses from 1837, 1845, 1846, and 1849 were either lost or destroyed. And last, there is the matter of biographical selectivity. James Elliot Cabot's *Memoir* offers one of the most detailed accountings of Emerson's abolition and other reform activities, and yet there is his statement to Higginson noted above that, as a conservative individual, he was "constitutionally reticent" in discussing such matters.

As the years passed following the Emerson centenary, the reform-ers who had actually known Emerson as an active abolitionist passed away.[34] Biographers, critics, and historians since that time have relied largely upon the established accounts and early biographies when dis-cussing Emerson and his relationship to the movement. As we have seen, there is a significant inconsistency regarding both factual accuracy and interpretative attitudes among these accounts, and not surprisingly, Emerson scholars have since taken a variety of positions on the matter.

The first significant biography of Emerson produced in the twentieth century was by an Englishman, George Edward Woodberry. Woodberry's work, which was written for the *English Men of Letters Series* in 1907, is noteworthy mainly as an examination of Emerson's ideas. However, the author does present a brief and selective overview of Emerson's anti-slavery activities, even while noting that, for the most part, "in the presence of the great miseries of the world he [Emerson] was dumb."[35] Woodberry points out Emerson's participation in "several [John] Brown meetings" and suggests that it was at this time (1859) that he was "classed by public opinion with the abolitionists." Throughout, Wood-berry stresses the "inertia of his [Emerson's] reluctant nature" regarding participation in social reform movements, but suggests that abolition eventually became the exception to this rule. He concludes his discus-sion with the assertion that "it is in his conduct as an opponent of slavery that Emerson revealed his height as a citizen and participant in the public affairs of his generation."

The publication by Houghton Mifflin of a ten-volume selected edi-tion of *The Journals of Ralph Waldo Emerson* (1909–14) offered scholars an abundance of new materials for consideration. This effort contributed to the development of a new biography by Oscar W. Firkins, which was issued by Houghton Mifflin in 1915. Firkins suggests that Emerson maintained a "relatively passive attitude" toward matters of reform from 1825 to 1850.[36] Eventually, however, came the "maturing of his hostility to slavery, a phase of his career for which his lovers are perennially grateful." Firkins, like Woodberry, feels that involvement in the anti-slavery movement was a singularly important phenomenon for Emerson because "the effect of his life is completed by this development." Unlike Woodberry, however, he offers considerably more evidence of the extent and nature of Emerson's activities and notes in passing at least some of the major events from the 1840s. Among these are Emerson's outspoken support of Wendell Phillips as a Concord Lyceum speaker in 1845, his public outrage in the same year at the expulsion of his Concord neighbor Samuel Hoar from South Carolina (as a result of his efforts to look after the interests of black citizens of Massachusetts who were being detained there), and his resistance to the annexation of Texas, which most assuredly would result in the extension of the slave powers. Firkins also offered some analysis of the 1 August 1844 address "Emancipation in the British West Indies," and utilized the *Journals* to supplement and reinforce his discussion.

Subsequent biographies over the next three decades contributed nothing new to the discussion of Emerson as reformer. The most important new insights into the matter came thirty-four years after Firkins's work. In 1949 Ralph Rusk published his monumental *Life of Ralph Waldo Emerson*. In editing his well-known six-volume edition of *The Letters of Ralph Waldo Emerson* a decade earlier, Rusk inevitably came across many letters that concerned Emerson's abolition activities, both great and small. This extensive effort provided Rusk with more substantive information on this often-obscured topic than any biographer since James Elliot Cabot had seen. Rusk's extensive and well-documented account of Emerson's life presented the most detailed and circumspect picture of Emerson's involvement in the abolition movement up to that time. Although by no means a complete accounting of the matter, Rusk does, for example, point out such previously unnoted facts as Emerson's refusal in 1845 to lecture before the New Bedford Lyceum because that organization "had excluded Negroes from regular membership"; his literary contributions to the antislavery annual the *Liberty Bell* in 1850; and his "sad but severe rebuke" of Oliver Wendell Holmes for his apparent support of slaveholders in 1855.[37] With the addition of these and many other such details, as well as Rusk's willingness to discuss the matter, the image of Emerson as a reformer and abolitionist is presented much more clearly here than in any previous biography.

Despite this development, however, the early 1950s saw the publication of a work that tended to revive the earlier image of Emerson as a withdrawn scholar who consistently chose to eschew involvement in public affairs in preference to the life of the mind. Stephen Whicher's *Freedom and Fate: An Inner Life of Ralph Waldo Emerson* (1953) has been described as "the most important study of Emerson's ideas in the twentieth century." Indeed, Emerson's most comprehensive bibliographers have pointed out that "nearly all subsequent criticism of Emerson argues for or against" the view Whicher presents.[38]

Whicher, while recognizing the importance of Rusk's "monument of thorough and discerning scholarship," offers what he considers to be "a complementary sketch of the inner life of Ralph Waldo Emerson, the life —so much more real to him—of which the only record is his works."[39] Whicher's study seems more paradoxical than complementary, however, because while Rusk's study documents specifically many of Emerson's numerous activities as an abolitionist and social reformer, and the acceleration of his involvement with such matters throughout the 1840s and 1850s, Whicher asserts that Emerson successively withdrew his interests from efforts at social reform after the "Divinity School Address" in 1838, and that after this time his "image of the hero-scholar, leading mankind to the promised land, steadily gave way to the solitary observer, unregarded and unregarding of the multitude."[40] Thus, paradoxically, just at the time when the external record shows that Emerson was increasing his involvement in reform and abolition efforts, Whicher insists that he was "formally repudiating the ideal of great action." In support of this position Whicher quotes selectively from such lectures as "The Times" (1841) and "The Conservative" (1841), where, he contends, the conservative "is portrayed with considerable sympathy."[41]

Pointedly, Whicher makes no note of any of Emerson's several abolition speeches in the detailed chronology of the "outer life" that precedes his study. Indeed, throughout the work he insists that Emerson's life overall was "an inner one, the poet's life of imagination, an adventure of the mind," and that we should "not be surprised to find . . . that it was outwardly a quiet life" and generally "uneventful."[42]

The most important development in modern Emerson studies was the publication for the first time of Emerson's complete journals in the sixteen-volume Harvard edition of the *Journals and Miscellaneous Notebooks of Ralph Waldo Emerson* (1960–82). This project laid the groundwork for a good deal of new Emerson study. As with the original publication of the *Journals* in 1909–14, this event also led to a new major biography, in this case Gay Wilson Allen's *Waldo Emerson* (1981). While admittedly an effort to present a more "intimate and personal life" of his subject, Allen does spend considerable time discussing Emerson's commitment to reform, especially abolition. Thus at the outset he points out that, initially, Emerson "tried to remain aloof from political and social reform . . . but his conscience inevitably drew him into movements promoting the abolition of slavery and the defense of a free society— more deeply than he usually gets credit for." Allen offers significant insights into the development of what he sees as a strong and consistent commitment on Emerson's part to the abolition movement. Thus he insists, unlike many of his predecessors, that Emerson was "emotionally involved with the antislavery movement" as early as 1844. By the 1850s Emerson was even experimenting "with poems that might encourage the slaves to rebel."[43] Interestingly enough, with the supporting evidence provided by the new journals and other sources, Allen's work projects an image of Emerson as reformer that is reminiscent of the earliest biographies, such as Cooke's, which was published some one hundred years before.

The most recent major biography of Emerson, John McAleer's *Ralph Waldo Emerson: Days of Encounter* (1984), presents a more conservative view of Emerson as reformer than Allen's work, and not surprisingly, McAleer defers to Holmes's position on the question. "Holmes assessed Emerson's role [in reform] correctly when he said: 'Nothing is plainer than that it was Emerson's calling to supply impulses and not methods. He was not an organizer, but a power behind many organizers, inspiring them with lofty motive, giving breath to their views.' "[44] And so it seems that the polarities that evolved over the past one hundred years remain very much with us.

The present study is based on a painstaking ten-year effort that involved the evaluation of over a thousand primary documents relating in one way or another to Emerson's abolition activities. The documents consulted include Emerson's unpublished antislavery speeches, as well as newspaper accounts of the same, the unpublished correspondence of abolitionists, records of abolition society meetings and annual reports, scrapbooks, giftbooks, newspaper and journal accounts of abolition meetings, and reports of abolition activities that appeared in Concord's local newspapers (the *Yeoman's Gazette* and the *Concord Freeman*) and the larger Boston papers like the *Advertiser* and the *Post*, as well as the venerable and exhaustively detailed *Liberator*, the *Anti-slavery Standard*, and Horace Greeley's *New York Tribune*. With the aid of these and other primary resources and the now complete Harvard edition of Emerson's *Journals and Miscellaneous Notebooks*, it is possible to provide a more complete, accurate, and detailed accounting of Emerson's abolitionism than was heretofore possible. In the process of rendering this account, a deliberate effort has been made to observe Emerson in the context of his time. This includes not only an evaluation of his formal addresses and presentations on the issues of the moment but also a consideration of the public and private influences that he felt regarding such matters. Within Emerson's own family, for example, as well as in the communities of Concord and Boston, there were individuals close to him who held very strong opinions on the issues of slavery and abolition. These individuals, as well as national and local political events, had a significant impact on Emerson's thinking regarding the important social reform questions of his time.

The image of Emerson that emerges from this study is that of a concerned, sometimes frustrated, but always committed social activist who was very much involved with, and interested in, the abolition of slavery as well as the other important social reforms of his day. Emerson did not, however, simply spring onto the American scene as an avowed abolitionist in the mid-1840s. As was the case with most major developments in his life, there was a lengthy and thoughtful prologue to the commencement of his public commitment to abolition and a substantial evolution thereafter. This study will show, among other things, that Emerson's thinking on the topics of abolition and social reform in general went through a substantial process of development and change. While certain philosophical guideposts remained fixed, his approach to the challenges of social reform and the unique evil represented by the institution of American slavery changed markedly, even dramatically, from 1837 to 1865. Unfortunately, most discussions of Emerson's views on reform have traditionally concentrated on the early lectures such as "Man the Reformer" (1841), "Lecture on the Times" (1841), "The Conservative" (1841), and "The Young American" (1844), which offer only a small part of the total picture.

A brief overview of the study, which follows, suggests that Emerson's initial attitude toward abolitionism, as reflected in his 1837 speech on the topic, was remarkably similar to that of William Ellery Channing. Channing's views, as reflected in such works as *Slavery* (1835), were considered painfully conservative by abolitionists like William Lloyd Garrison and Wendell Phillips, and painfully radical by his Unitarian cohorts. The emphasis at this time, for both Emerson and Channing, was on the need for moral suasion and the comprehensive reform of individuals. This, in turn, would result in a general reform of society. Furthermore, in the pursuit of this goal both believed that it was necessary to avoid concentrating on only one moral issue, as the abolitionists generally did, and to promote a free and open discussion of this volatile topic.

After 1844, however, as the prospect of Texas annexation brought with it a de facto end to the Compromise of 1820 and a potentially disastrous expansion of the slave powers, Emerson began to consider the need for a more aggressive response to the problem. Unlike Channing, who died in 1842, Emerson had always believed that politics could offer a vehicle for influencing the positive development of society, and after 1844 he was less reluctant to associate himself with organized abolitionists, who frequently provided him with a platform from which he addressed the specific issues of slavery and abolition. Consequently, he began appearing and speaking at abolition gatherings and anti-Texas "conventions" in the mid to late 1840s. Despite the prevalence of the scholarly notion that Emerson was largely removed from the everyday affairs of the world, his notebooks show that throughout the period he was vitally concerned with the slavery issue, in particular, and the national and state political developments that related to it.

This was an especially difficult time for Emerson, because it was during this same period that he began reading Oriental literature and philosophy, and lecturing about "fate" as a substantial influence in the lives of men. The power of fate, as Emerson understood the concept, could render foolish and nugatory all efforts to change the course of things for either better or worse. Ultimately, Emerson came to believe at this time in a "beautiful necessity" that moved all things toward goodness and contributed to the natural amelioration of all evils. At approximately this same time, however, he began reading and writing about the "Uses of Great Men," a development that would culminate with the publication in 1850 of one of his most important works, *Representative Men*. The emphasis in this instance was just the opposite of the "beautiful necessity." Emerson could see the possibility of individuals influencing substantially the world around them, a view that would tend in turn to emphasize the importance of individual as well as collective efforts at reform. The conflict between these opposing forces of "freedom" and "fate," along with the generally negative trend of national events following the annexation of Texas and the Mexican War, culminated in a substantial depression for Emerson. This condition was aggravated by his concern at this time with determining the proper role that a "poet" like himself might play in furthering specific social reforms, and the obligation he felt to personally address pressing social problems, especially slavery. The question of Negro inferiority, which was a topic of general debate even among abolitionists at the time, gave him further cause for concern.

These and other anxieties helped to precipitate Emerson's decision to depart for England in May 1847. His spirits were bolstered somewhat by his experiences there, and not long after his return to this country he accepted an invitation from William Lloyd Garrison to speak once again at an abolition gathering, the annual celebration of West Indian emancipation in August 1849. Emerson's remarks on this occasion suggest the nature of the philosophical "compromise" that he had apparently reached concerning the conflict between freedom and fate. His brief presentation articulates his support for the abolitionists who had been so long in the lists, because "they have anticipated this triumph which I look upon as inevitable, and which it is not in man to retard." But at the same time, active and diligent effort is required of all good persons in order to promote this cause because, despite its inevitability, "it is the order of Providence that we should conspire heartily in this work." Emerson sums up this curious equipoise of freedom and fate by calling to mind, appropriately enough, an "old eastern verse."

> Fool thou must be, though wisest of the wise,
> Then be the fool of virtue, not of vice.

This delicate balance, which Emerson was able to maintain throughout the later 1840s, came to a crashing end with the passage of the Fugitive Slave Law in the fall of 1850 and the rendition of the first victims of that law in the spring of 1851. The outrage that Emerson felt at this "quadraped law," which was passed by "men who could read and write," reflected his bitter disappointment that the forces of culture and progress had failed to improve the moral status of American society, or even to prevent a retrograde movement toward outright barbarism. Consequently, throughout the period of the 1850s Emerson became more and more militant in his attacks upon slavery as the outrages of the southern slave owners and their northern apologists became ever more blatant. The bloody attack on Charles Sumner, the war in Kansas, the Dred Scott decision, the execution of John Brown, and other such provocative events elicited from Emerson a variety of responses, including an outspoken condemnation of the Constitution, exhortations to civil disobedience, active efforts to raise money to purchase Sharpe's rifles for Kansas partisans, and even his first stump campaign for a congressional candidate, John Gorham Palfrey, who ran on the Free Soil ticket in Emerson's own Middlesex District in the spring of 1851. From 1844 onward, despite his recurring concern about the myopia of associated reform efforts, Emerson maintained a durable public alliance with organized abolitionists and, although never joining an abolition organization, he effectively became an abolitionist, in the eyes of both his friends and his enemies.

Emerson welcomed the outbreak of the Civil War, a development that took him by surprise. He felt that the war was sent by God to provide a necessary cleansing for the nation. As the war dragged on, however, with a mighty cost in lives and suffering, Emerson sometimes became depressed with events, but he never wavered in his faith that goodness would eventually triumph. In Emerson's opinion the war was being waged to free the slaves and to reestablish the moral integrity of the nation, not simply to preserve the Union. He contributed to the cause in many ways, from providing moral leadership and supplying occasional verses to mark major events to providing help in organizing the Union army's first all-black regiment, the Massachusetts Fifty-fourth.

The end of the Civil War did not bring with it an end to Emerson's concern with social justice and "equal opportunity." He recognized clearly how vital Reconstruction would be in securing the rights of the newly freed slaves. Thus he was a consistent supporter of Senator Charles Sumner, and he told Carlyle of his efforts to protect the "newly won rights of the slave, & the new measures we had contrived to keep the planter from sucking his blood" (*CEC* 548). Virtually until the time of his death, Emerson and his wife Lidian would continue to make their contributions to the efforts to secure firmly the civil rights of all people in America, especially the poor, blacks, and Indians. These efforts influenced the next generation of reformers, who would draw from Emerson's example, both in his writings and in his life, the principles that would help to inspire some of the major reform movements of the twentieth century.

While the debate regarding Emerson's conservatism or radicalism in social affairs will no doubt continue as long as there are people reading him, I hope that the following study will provide at the very least some of the factual evidence necessary to inform that debate.

Chapter Two

Early Concerns:
1821–1837

The plight of blacks had long concerned the Emerson family. Despite his modest income, Emerson's father, William, had helped to maintain the Smith School in Boston, which provided free education "for colored children of both sexes," from 1798 until his death in 1811.[1] Mary Moody Emerson, William's colorful and somewhat eccentric sister, and the Reverend Ezra Ripley, his stepfather and probably Concord's most distinguished clergyman, were prominently involved in the antislavery agitation of the 1830s and 1840s. An early account of an abolitionist gathering in Concord in 1835 reveals something of the essential attitudes of these two toward the cause. The narrative appears in a letter from Charles Burleigh, an agent and lecturer for the Middlesex County Anti-slavery Society, to R. W. Emerson's friend and former Unitarian colleague, Samuel J. May.

> On repairing to the house at the hour (we met in Mr. Wilder's,) we found it well filled with a very respectable looking assembly, & soon proceeded to business. Two hymns were sung, & a prayer offered before the lecture, I then talked an hour & a half, & the assembly was dismissed with the benediction. Dr Ripley was present & sat full in front of the pulpit, listening apparently with the most fixed attention. Though I never saw him before yet almost as soon as my eye fell upon him, I said to myself, that is Dr

Ripley. After the meeting he told me he should call on me in the morning & ask me some questions. So about 10 the next day, the old gentleman made his appearance, & forthwith we fell into quite an animated discussion—his only difficulty being what he could do—what we could any of us do to forward the liberation of the slaves.

The following day, the correspondent continued with an account of a certain lady whose acquaintance he had made in Concord.

I don't know but you are somewhat acquainted with the lady I have introduced to your notice. Whether you are or not she bade me give her love to you whenever I should see you. She is an elderly lady—say sixty—unmarried I think. Her name is Mary Emerson, and she . . . has been very much prejudiced . . . against Abolitionists & particularly against Garrison. . . . I answered all Miss Emerson's questions as well as I could, & do believe I removed some of her prejudices. She seems to be a good hearted woman, easily excited, inclined too hastily to take up wrong opinions, but willing to abandon them as soon as the error is clearly pointed out to her.

Burleigh then went on to defend Garrison and "the cause" with the following result. "Her countenance brightened as I proceeded, & before I could complete my narrative she exclaimed 'he ought to be *canonized*.' She said she had written to her friends in Maine, to have nothing to do with Garrison's paper, but says she 'I must write again, & tell them better.' In fact, her feelings toward Mr. G. seemed to be totally revolutionized." This portion of the letter concludes with "I have reason to be very grateful for the uniform kindness & politeness with which I was treated in Concord, & I think there are indications decidedly favorable to our cause."[2]

Dr. Ripley was consistent in supporting the antislavery cause until his death in 1841. The records of the Middlesex County Anti-slavery Society indicate that the first quarterly meeting of the group for the year 1835 took place in the Reverend Ripley's Unitarian meetinghouse.[3] Later that same year, when the famous British abolitionist George Thompson spoke at a meeting of the Middlesex society, Ripley was in attendance and after the meeting "complimented [Thompson] for his eloquent discourse, commended the sentiments and said that charity compelled him to acknowledge that he was engaged in a good cause."[4] Although apparently not a member, Ripley frequently attended meetings of the Middlesex society, and on those occasions when he could not attend he usually sent a laudatory note of encouragement. The meeting of 24 January 1837 was typical. Ripley generously provided his church for the occasion, and the records indicate that "a letter from Rev. Ripley was read, giving reasons for his non attendance and wishing success to the Abolition of Slavery throughout our Country & the world."[5]

Following her conversion, Aunt Mary Moody Emerson's commitment to the abolition movement was a durable one. In 1835 she somewhat clandestinely arranged a breakfast for George Thompson at the home of nephew Ralph Waldo.[6] The purpose of the meeting was probably to encourage a more active sympathy for the cause on Emerson's part. The strategy, however, did not work out quite as planned. Emerson found Thompson to be unbearably egocentric and closed minded. A journal entry dated 10 October records, "This morning Mr May & Mr George Thompson breakfasted with me. I bade them defend their cause as a thing too sacred to be polluted with any personal feelings." Apparently the defense offered was far from satisfying to the bard, and he goes on to conclude from his interview the following, which also expresses Emerson's concerns about abolitionists in general at this time: "Thompson the Abolitionist is inconvertible; what you say or what might be said would make no impression on him. He belongs I fear to that great class of the Vanity-stricken. An inordinate thirst for notice can not be gratified until it has found in its gropings what is called a Cause that men will bow to; tying him self fast to that, the small man is then at liberty to consider all objections made to him as proofs of folly & the devil in the objector, & under that screen, if he gets a rotten egg or two, yet his name sounds through the world and he is praised & praised" (*JMN* 5:90–91).

In the mid-1830s the most outspoken member of the Emerson family on the subject of slavery was Ralph Waldo's younger brother, Charles. The two brothers enjoyed a close relationship and found themselves, by Waldo's account, likeminded in most matters.[7] On 29 April 1835 Charles Emerson delivered a lengthy "Lecture on Slavery" in Concord. Why he felt he needed to make a public statement then is not clear. Certainly the issue was becoming heated, and perhaps the attitudes and involvement of Ripley and Aunt Mary had had some effect. Ralph Waldo was certainly aware of this agitation and in some respects approved of it. In a journal entry dated 16 April 1835 (two weeks after Charles Burleigh's visit to Concord) Emerson notes that the slavery question was one on which a man "may exhaust his whole love of truth,—his heart & his mind," and that "this is one of those causes which will make a man" (*JMN* 5:32). Whatever the immediate stimulus for his address, Charles took a strong and unequivocal stand for immediate emancipation (the more radical position among abolitionists) and argued at length for the basic humanity of the slaves. "Nothing, not even slavery, is able to transform man into beast. No, we see in the slaves fellow creatures, defrauded of the privileges of men. We recognize the truth of what the first of Poets said, 'The day that makes a man a slave takes away half his worth' —but we see notwithstanding that the image of God in his human creature is ineffaceable. The slave is still open to the influence of kindness, still capable of religious sentiment, & never wholly loses sight of the distinction betwixt right & wrong."[8]

Charles then quotes knowledgeably from various works dealing with emancipation in the West Indies and refers approvingly to Touissant, the liberating hero of St. Domingo, as a symbol of the worthy spirit of the black race.[9] Those who would advocate "abolition by gradual advances" would find this course "impracticable." The only course to take was that of "immediate emancipation," because "nothing will prepare the slave for freedom, except freedom." It was undoubtedly a stirring performance.

Less outspoken but unquestionably more influential with Ralph Waldo than Ripley, Aunt Mary, or his brother Charles was Emerson's wife, Lidian. Emerson married Lidian and moved into his new home in Concord in September 1835. Lidian held fixed ideas, and the abolition cause was particularly dear to her. A Women's Anti-slavery Society was formed in Concord around 1835, and Lidian Emerson was one of its most active members from the outset; other notables in the group were Mrs. Mary Merrick Brooks and the Thoreau women.[10] Mrs. Brooks, who has been described as "the leading woman abolitionist in Concord," was particularly influential with the Emerson family and often encouraged Ralph Waldo to speak out publicly on social issues, especially slavery.[11] Ellen Emerson points out in her biography of her mother that "her [friendship] with Mrs. Nathan Brooks was always satisfactory" and that "they were equally ardent in the Anti-Slavery cause, and equally interested in politics as far as they related to that." Ellen further suggests that her mother's naturally sensitive personality inspired her sympathy for the slaves. Lidian "read the papers faithfully and their pro-slavery tone made her hate her country. She learned all the horrors of slavery and dwelt upon them, so that it was as if she continually witnessed the whippings and the selling away of little children from their mothers. She joined the Anti-Slavery Society and remained a zealous member till Slavery was abolished."[12]

The environment of Concord in the 1830s and 1840s was quite favorable to the abolition cause, in vivid contrast to nearby Boston. One nineteenth-century commentator noted that "Middlesex County, in 1840, was a stronghold of abolition principles; and Concord, then a more important town politically than now, played a great part in the beginning of the political abolition movement." Also, Concord was well known as a depot of the underground railroad.[13] The local Concord newspapers, the *Yeoman's Gazette* and the *Concord Freeman*, contributed to this generally liberal attitude as they vied with one another in their support of abolitionism. Between 1835 and 1837 the two weeklies published over 125 articles on the slavery question. Such items were included as the minutes of various antislavery association meetings, editorials, reports of the political speeches of John Quincy Adams and Concord's own representative, Samuel Hoar, on the controversial question of slavery in the District of Columbia, and also their fight against the infamous "gag rule." Additionally, there were numerous accounts of antiabolition riots, reports on abolition speakers such as George Thompson and Angelina Grimké, articles refuting accusations of black racial inferiority, and also grim stories of the middle passage.

Well-known abolitionists such as George Thompson and the British novelist and social commentator Harriet Martineau occasionally visited Concord and were generally well received, another sharp contrast to the experience of Boston. Miss Martineau had been touring America in 1835, and before arriving in Boston had stayed for some time in Philadelphia with Emerson's lifelong friend William Henry Furness.[14] During her visit to Boston, late in 1835, Miss Martineau addressed the Female Anti-slavery Society and, when asked, presented her views on the question of abolition. The result is described in a letter from Ellis Gray Loring, a friend of Emerson's since their Boston Latin Grammar days and now an ardent abolitionist, to William Lloyd Garrison.

> You see, I presume the storm of abuse which Miss Martineau has called on herself from the newspapers, for her independent conduct at the ladies' meeting. . . . She says she spoke of her full agreement with the *principles* of the abolitionists, because she knew what they were—but that she did not know enough of their *measures* to venture to pronounce upon them. She feels evidently a very strong interest in the Anti Slavery Society—though she has taken up Dr. Channing's notion (a mistaken one I think) of the superiority of *individual* to *associated* action. On our corner-stone-principles she is clear & strong. She believes in the propriety & duty of creating & exerting a moral influence against Slavery, in the free States.[15]

These sentiments, expressed in Boston, caused a furor, and it was Charles and Waldo Emerson who came to Miss Martineau's rescue; Concord would serve as a refuge from the hostility of Boston. Miss Martineau later recalled the episode.

> At the time of the hubbub against me in Boston, Charles Emerson stood alone in a large company and declared that he would rather see Boston in ashes than that I or anybody should be debarred in any way from perfectly free speech. His brother Waldo invited me to be his guest in the midst of my unpopularity, and during my visit told me his course about this matter of slavery. He did not see that there was any particular thing for him to do in it then; but when, in coaches or steamboats or anywhere else, he saw people of color ill treated, or heard bad doctrine or sentiment propounded, he did what he could and said what he thought.[16]

Later, in her *Retrospect of Western Travel* (1838), Martineau praised Emerson extravagantly and looked to him as one who would eventually do much to improve American society. "Great things are expected for him, and great things, it seems, he cannot but do if he have life and health to prosecute his course." Martineau also took note of Emerson's reserve regarding issues of public debate. Undoubtedly she saw this as merely a prelude to his emergence onto the scene as a doer as well as a thinker. She points out that "he is a thinker and a scholar," and that he has at the moment "modestly and silently withdrawn himself from the perturbations and conflicts of the crowd of men." [17]

The quiet Emerson was embarrassed by such notice, and Lidian explained in a letter to her sister at the time that he was "sorry to see such a thing" because "he does not wish to be brought in this manner out of an incognito which he values and wishes to preserve" (*LL* 78). Similarly, Emerson himself wrote to Carlyle that Martineau's comment "does me a great annoyance–to take away from me my privacy & thrust me before my time (if ever there be a time) into the arena of the gladiators, to be stared at" (*CEC* 185). However, with the Divinity School controversy about to explode around him, Emerson would soon have an opportunity to test his gladiatorial skills, whether he wanted to or not.

Another famous spokeswoman for the abolition movement, Angelina Grimké, was also drawn to Concord, and one of her visits occurred in September 1837. The *Yeoman's Gazette* (9 September) reported that "she was listened to by a crowded audience and we are happy to think that she has awakened an increasing interest in this solemn and important subject among our citizens. We believe that she will be the means, under Providence, of doing great good for she brings to the aid of the holy cause she has espoused, eloquence of no common order, fortified by heartfelt and untiring zeal. God speed her on her errand of mercy and humanity." Indeed, so many abolition speakers appeared in Concord in the 1830s that Emerson was moved to remark in his journal that in Concord "every third man lectures on Slavery" (*JMN* 5:505).

Concord was especially well informed about the slavery issue not only by virtue of the number of lecturers who visited the place and the large number of articles published by the Concord newspapers but also because the library committee, of which Ralph Waldo Emerson was frequently a member, ensured that relevant works were on hand. The Standing Committee for the Concord Social Library for the year 1836 reported the acquisition of several new books, among them *Channing on Slavery*, *Andrews on Slavery*, and *Madden's West Indies*. The committee's report, which appeared in the *Yeoman's Gazette* (7 January 1837), was submitted by R. Waldo Emerson and Nehemiah Bell. For those desiring to go beyond the resources of the library, works on abolition were offered for sale at the printing office of the *Concord Freeman*. Among those listed in February 1837, for example, were the *Anti-slavery Almanac*, *Grimké's Appeal*, and *Right and Wrong*. The last work was a record of abolition efforts in Boston written by Maria Chapman. Emerson was known to have a copy in his library.[18]

Despite the many activities and concerns of friends and family, Emerson managed to remain largely disengaged from the antislavery agitation until November 1837, even though his journals show that from November 1822 on he was almost constantly aware of the issue. Indeed, one of Emerson's earliest references to slavery appears in his 1821 student essay "The Present State of Ethical Philosophy," where he notes that "the plague spot of slavery must be purged thoroughly out" of American society.[19] The reference is only a passing one, but it does suggest that the problem of slavery was on Emerson's mind, and even in his dreams, while a Harvard undergraduate. One of his most extensive early considerations of the slavery question appears at the very beginning of his 1822 "Wide World" journal. "In my dreams, I departed to distant climes and to many different periods and my fancy presented before me many extraordinary societies, and many old and curious institutions" (*JMN* 2:41). He then describes "the brilliant spectacle of an African morning" and the observation of a "band of families . . . naked men, women, and children" who sing "a hymn to the sun and [come] merrily down to the river with nets in their hands to fish." The tranquil and pleasant scene soon changes, however, when "many men dressed in foreign garb" descend upon the group, bind them with cords, and carry them away in boats while "they that were bound, gnashed their teeth and uttered so piteous a howl" that it seemed it would be "a mercy if the river had swallowed them" (*JMN* 2:42). Emerson goes on, "In my dream, I launched my skiff to follow the boats and redeem the captives," but his rescue attempt failed and "in the nations to which they were brought [the slaves] were sold for a price and compelled to labor all the day long and scourged with whips until they fell dead in the fields, and found rest in the grave."

After thus describing his dream, the young Emerson then sets about to pursue to its logical conclusion the question "Why Providence suffers the land of its richest productions to be thus defiled?" (*JMN* 2:42). What follows is an academic exercise in moral philosophy that first examines "all that is offered *in behalf* of slavery," followed immediately by an "attempt to knock down the hydra" (*JMN* 2:49). In stating the case *for* slavery Emerson postulates that "Nature has plainly assigned different degrees of intellect" to the various races, and "the barriers between are insurmountable." Consequently, "this inequality is an indication of the design of Providence that some should lead, and some should serve" (*JMN* 2:43). In furthering this aspect of the argument, Emerson also notes that the same circumstances that result in man's dominion over the beasts might imply a justification for the enslaving of blacks, "viz. their want of reason; their adaptation to our wants; and their own advantage." The last point obviously assumes a benevolent master, as many Unitarians and others at the time did.[20] In considering further whether the presence of "reason" distinguishes the slave from the animal kingdom, Emerson observes that "it can hardly be true . . . that the difference lies in the attribute of Reason; I saw ten, twenty, a hundred large lipped, lowbrowed black men in the streets who, except in the mere matter of language, did not exceed the sagacity of the elephant" (*JMN* 2:48).

Turning then to the other side of the question, Emerson's preference for moral sentiment, even at age nineteen, becomes very clear. In terms that resemble strikingly his condemnation of Daniel Webster's constitutional defense of slavery almost thirty years later, Emerson asserts, "To establish by whatever specious argumentation the perfect expediency of the worst institution on earth is *prima facie* an assault upon Reason and Common sense. No ingenious sophistry can ever reconcile the unperverted mind to the pardon of *Slavery*; nothing but tremendous familiarity, and the bias of private *interest*." Every man deserves to be free because "it offends the attributes of God to have him otherwise" (*JMN* 2:57–58). Although Emerson would from time to time in the future wrestle again with the question of Negro equality, it is accurate to say that he never deviated from the moral position stated here. Thus, twelve years later, for example, after his transcendental conversion, Emerson would argue for human equality on a spiritual, if not a material, level. In a journal entry where he uses the term "Reason" in its new transcendental sense, that is, as descriptive of the soul or spirit of man rather than mere rationality, Emerson attacks the institution of slavery because it denies the basic divinity of man. "Democracy/Freedom has its root in the Sacred truth that every man hath in him the divine Reason." That is "the equality & the only equality of all men," and "because every man has within him somewhat really divine therefore is slavery the unpardonable outrage it is" (*JMN* 4:357).

On several occasions in this early period Emerson raised the moral question of slavery publicly. For example, in his very first sermon, "Pray Without Ceasing" (1826), he makes the point that men should not think "lightly of all other things in comparison with riches" and should not ignore "the poor man's virtue or the slave's misery as they cross his path in life."[21] Obviously, in the 1820s the paths of slaves were seldom crossed by Emerson or anyone else in Massachusetts, but the following year young Ralph Waldo did come face to face with the miseries of the institution. The occasion was a slave auction at St. Augustine, Florida, where Emerson had been vacationing for his health. His journal account of the incident emphasizes the irony of the juxtaposition of Christianity with slavery, an irony of which abolitionists would later remind him.

> A fortnight since I attended a meeting of the Bible Society. The Treasurer of this institution is Marshall of the district & by a somewhat unfortunate arrangement had appointed a special meeting of the Society & a Slave Auction at the same time & place, one being in the Government house & the other in the adjoining yard. One ear therefore heard the glad tidings of great joy whilst the other was regaled with "Going gentlemen, Going!" And almost without changing our position we might aid in sending the scriptures into Africa or bid for "four children without the mother who had been kidnapped therefrom" (*JMN* 3:117).

In the years following this incident Emerson made several statements in his journals regarding the moral implications of the institution of slavery. In almost all these instances, however, his consideration remained on the level of moral abstraction. In fact, in these early years he often referred to slavery in his sermons, as Rusk points out, "when he needed examples of man's inhumanity to man."[22]

As his journals show, Emerson continued to give considerable thought to the slavery question and the condition of blacks generally. In November 1837, for example, while considering the apparent inequality of blacks in their material capabilities, Emerson was nevertheless encouraged by recent positive developments in the black colony of Liberia.

> I think it cannot be maintained by any candid person that the African race have ever occupied or do promise ever to occupy a very high place in the human family. Their present condition is the strongest proof that they cannot. The Irish cannot; the American Indian cannot; the Chinese cannot. Before the energy of the Caucasian race all the other races have quailed and done obeisance.
>
> Yet the Colony at Liberia is somewhat. The black merchants are so fond of their lucrative occupations that it is with difficulty any of them can be prevailed upon to take office in the Colony. They dislike the trouble of it. Civilized arts are found to be as attractive to the wild negro as they are disagreeable to the wild Indian.[23]

Given, then, the "unpardonable outrage" of slavery and the newly demonstrated capacity of blacks to improve when freed from such a dehumanizing institution (Emerson called slavery "an institution for converting men into monkeys" [*JMN* 5:295]), a question remained for Emerson at this time: What are the obligations of the moral man when faced with this outrage? Several contending inclinations led to the ambiguity that Emerson felt. One of the cornerstones of Emerson's transcendental philosophy was the importance of individuality, especially individual moral responsibility. For Emerson, all social problems were really manifestations of individual moral deficiencies, and only individual moral reform could ameliorate social problems. In 1833 he noted in his journal that "a man contains all that is needed to his government within himself. He is made a law unto himself. . . . He only can do himself any good or any harm" (*JMN* 4:84). If, on a moral level, a man, even a slave, is "a law unto himself," and if "all real good or evil . . . must be from himself," then it must follow that both slaves and slave owners are responsible for the unpardonable outrage of slavery, and only they themselves, as individuals, can correct the situation. Reformers, Emerson felt, must rely upon moral suasion rather than agitation in order to precipitate the desired result. Social reformation that comes as a result of the forceful imposition of change upon individuals or institutions from without is not true reformation because it deals with symptoms and not causes, sins but not sinners. As will be shown, this attitude was largely the result of Emerson's Unitarian background and training. It would continue to exercise a strong influence on his thinking regarding social reform generally for some time to come.

Despite the widespread support for the antislavery cause in Concord and in the Emerson family, and despite the entrance into the controversy of such distinguished and respected men as William Ellery Channing, Emerson's highly respected former teacher, Emerson himself continued to avoid making any public statement on the issue, preferring instead, as he told Harriet Martineau, to speak his opinions individually and privately when the opportunity arose. Also, Emerson continued to share in the common dislike for active abolitionists. Without making a purely social distinction, Emerson once referred to abolitionists as "an altogether odious set of people, whom one would be sure to shun as the worst of bores & canters" (*JMN* 9:120). He therefore wished to avoid them and to concentrate instead on developing through his lectures and writings a broad-based respect for "self-culture" among individuals. This, he felt, would have a reforming effect throughout the society.

However, the period from 1834 to 1837 was a trying one for those moralists like Emerson and Channing who relied primarily upon some form of moral suasion and self-culture to redress the evils of society. In 1834, 1835, and 1836 a great deal of mob violence was directed against abolitionists in the northern states.[24] In October 1835 William Lloyd Garrison was seized by a mob and paraded through the streets of Boston in ropes. Also in 1835, the governor of South Carolina announced to his legislature that northern abolitionist literature ought not to be tolerated in the state. On 29 July a boatload of abolitionist tracts from New York was impounded by the Charlestown postmaster, seized by a mob, and then publicly burned. This event had national repercussions. President Andrew Jackson, arguing that such information was "incendiary" and therefore harmful to the general peace, recommended that a law be passed to prohibit the circulation of antislavery information through the federal system. The House of Representatives in 1836 adopted a rule providing that all antislavery petitions be tabled. This "gag rule" was vigorously opposed by John Quincy Adams and Concord's Samuel Hoar, and their struggle was given broad coverage in the press. A front-page story in the *Yeoman's Gazette* (21 January 1837) reported one of the many tumultuous confrontations that took place over this issue. "Mr. Adams was as angry as a trained bear. Speak he would and speak he did, first by proclaiming in a voice louder than the Stentorian lungs around him, that the petition was worthy to be read; that it contained the sentiments of Liberty, and came from freemen, and that to oppose it and him was an attack upon the liberty of speech."

Despite such vigorous opposition, however, the gag rule was not rescinded until 1845. William Ellery Channing and others like him who relied upon moral suasion as the primary instrument of social reform were greatly upset by these developments. Obviously, if moral reformers were effectively prevented from making their position known and from exhorting others to follow the example of righteousness, then the cause was all but lost. Free speech was the sine qua non of their approach. Channing was so deeply distressed by these developments that he issued a public letter, which appeared in the *Yeoman's Gazette* on 7 January 1837. Channing's letter states that "in regard to the methods adopted by the abolitionists of promoting emancipation, I might find much to censure; but when I regard their firm, fearless assertion of the rights of free discussion, of speech and the press, I look on them with unmixed respect." He goes on to condemn "the violences against abolitionists" and asserts his "earnest desire and hope, that the abolitionists will maintain the liberty of speech and the press, not only by asserting it firmly, but by using it wisely, deliberately, generously, and under the control of the severest moral principle." A commentary on this letter that appeared in the same issue of the *Gazette* agreed emphatically with Channing's position and noted that "the North has been criminally silent and negligent on this subject."

These events also had a profound effect on Emerson, and the crisis year 1837 marked the culmination for him of a sixteen-year struggle with the thorny problem of slavery. Although in August the transcendental reformer had told the young men of Harvard, in his famous "American Scholar Address," that "action is with the Scholar subordinate, but it is essential" (*CW* 1:59), in March of that year Emerson was still firm in his belief that only moral self-reliance could bring about true reform. Thus, in a lecture entitled "The Individual" he was led to remark that "all philosophy, all theory, all hope are defeated when applied to society. There is in it an inconvertible brute force and it is not for the society of any actual present moment that is now or ever shall be, that we can hope or augur well. Progress is not for society. Progress belongs to the Individual."[25]

Emerson's environment was alive with opposing opinions on the most vexed social question of the day: Lidian, Mrs. Brooks, and the Thoreau women were actively involved in the Women's Anti-slavery Society; Dr. Ripley was attending the meetings of the Middlesex County Anti-slavery Society; Aunt Mary Moody Emerson was enthusiastic about the cause; and Charles had publicly declared himself an abolitionist two years earlier and called for immediate emancipation. But it was probably the dramatic murder of Elijah P. Lovejoy, a little-known abolitionist publisher, at the hands of an angry mob in Alton, Illinois, on 7 November 1837 that ultimately precipitated Emerson's somewhat reluctant entry into the conflict. This startling event was seen by many, including Channing, as yet another assault upon the principles of free speech, without which no reform was possible. The repercussions from the event were equally disturbing. For example, when Channing and others petitioned the Board of Aldermen of the city of Boston "for the use of Fanueil [*sic*] Hall, in order that there might be an expression of public sentiment in regard to the late ferocious assault on the liberty of the press at Alton," the petition was denied, even though, as Channing insisted, his "intention was, to exclude all reference to parties; all topics about which there could be division among the friends of liberty."[26]

A journal entry dated 24 November, indicates Emerson's increasing uneasiness: "When a zealot comes to me & represents the importance of this Temperance Reform my hands drop—I have no excuse—I honor him with shame at my own inaction. Then a friend of the slave shows me the horrors of Southern slavery—I cry guilty guilty" (*JMN* 5:437). But Emerson "rejoices" over those who have made active sacrifices for the improvement of the human condition; foremost among them is Lovejoy. "It seems to me that Circumstances of man are historically somewhat better here & now than ever. That more freedom exists for Culture. It will not now run against an axe at the first step. In other places it is not so: the brave Lovejoy has given his breast to the bullet for his part and has died when it was better not to live. . . . I sternly rejoice, that one was found to die for humanity & the rights of free speech & opinion (*JMN* 5:437). Emerson was so moved by the event in Alton that in his lecture "Heroism," delivered in January 1838, and again in his 1841 essay of the same title, he heralded Lovejoy as an authentic hero.[27]

Clearly, the time had come for Emerson to speak out on the slavery issue. Circumstances demanded a statement. There was much that pushed him forward, but there was also much that held him back. The concept of external social reform brought about by the agitation of groups ran counter to his commitment to individuality and self-redemption; many of the abolitionists themselves (Thompson, for example) he perceived to be shallow and self-aggrandizing; he had a great distaste for public debate and the rhetoric of "causes"; and finally, there was still the question of racial inferiority. Could blacks redeem themselves from slavery, or was it their inevitable condition? Despite these reservations, however, Emerson clearly recognized that slavery was a moral abomination and a blight upon the American character, and that freedom of speech was essential to any reform. Not surprisingly, therefore, one discovers in the outline of the speech, which he delivered sometime in late November in Concord, more emphasis upon the need to allow and encourage a free discussion of the question than upon the problem of slavery itself. "Our great duty on this matter is to open our halls to the discussion of this question steadily day after day, year after year until no man dare wag his finger at us" (*JMN* 12:152). He also suggests that "the professed aim of the abolitionist is to awaken the conscience of the Northern States in the hope thereby to awaken the conscience of the Southern states; a hope just & sublime" (*JMN* 12:153).

This "awakening" would presumably result in peaceful and individual reforms that would eventually be reflected in laws. "Our duty in the matter is to Settle the right & wrong so that whenever we are called to vote in the matter, we may not dodge the question; we may not trifle with it" (*JMN* 12:154). At the end of his original draft outline Emerson makes it clear that his obligations to the cause were limited. "Beyond this I do not feel a call to act[;] Nearer duties" (*JMN* 12:152).

The only extant account of the actual speech, which appears in Cabot's *Memoir*, indicates that its major thrust concerned the question of freedom of speech, as the outline suggests. Speaking in the Second Church in Concord, Emerson opened with the statement, "I regret to hear that all the churches but one, and almost all the public halls in Boston, are closed against the discussion of this question. Even the platform of the lyceum, hitherto the freest of all organs, is so bandaged and muffled that it threatens to be silent." Emerson stresses the idea of individual moral judgment regarding the question of slavery and the obligation to express one's opinions individually rather than in an organized movement where individuality is lost. "But, when we have distinctly settled for ourselves the right and wrong of this question, and have covenanted with ourselves to keep the channels of opinion open, each man for himself, I think that we have done all that is incumbent on most of us to do." Finally, emphasizing again the impossibility of imposing moral reform upon others, Emerson urges his audience to look to their own moral well-being and accept that sinfulness in others brings its own punishment. "Let our own evils check the bitterness of our condemnation of our brother, and whilst we insist on calling things by their right names, let us not reproach the planter, but own that his misfortune is at least as great as his sin."[28]

It was an impossible performance for the time, pleasing neither to the abolitionists nor to Emerson. Tepid and philosophical to a fault, the speech was a reflection of the contrary forces that had been at work both within him and in the world around him. The times demanded collective and definitive action to remedy the evil of slavery, but Emerson's philosophy at this time ran counter to those means and measures, despite the fact that his moral sense was outraged at the most egregious

evil of the time. Regarding the speech, Cabot notes: "To the abolitionists this tone appeared rather cool and philosophical, and some of his
friends tried to rouse him to a fuller sense of the occasion. He was in-
sufficiently alive, they told him, to the interests of humanity, and apt to
allow his disgust at the methods or the manners of the philanthropists
to blind him to the substantial importance of their work." [29]

Emerson's time had not yet come. The evil was well defined, but the
proper method of addressing it was not yet determined. His preference
was still for individual self-redemption brought about through moral
suasion rather than for what he saw as public rabble-rousing. With this
speech, as with his letter to President Martin Van Buren five months
later regarding the Cherokees, Emerson felt uncomfortable. "This stirring in the philanthropic mud, gives me no peace. I will let the republic alone until the republic comes to me" (*JMN* 5:479). Eventually
it would.

Chapter Three

The Silent Years: 1838–1844

Following his 1837 address Emerson would not speak again publicly on the subject of slavery until August 1844. During this seven-year period he would experience a growing awareness that the pernicious influence of the institution was spreading ominously throughout the fabric of American society, and that it would be necessary for him and all other Americans capable of rational thought and moral purpose to vigorously oppose this moral contagion. The problem for Emerson throughout this period, however, would be in determining exactly what role he should play in the crusade against slavery.

As suggested earlier, Emerson's attitude toward reform in general was very much a product of his early Unitarian experience. Although there was a great diversity of opinion within the Unitarian church regarding the problem of slavery and the church's responsibilities in promoting social reform, the theological principles were quite clear. As Daniel Walker Howe points out in *The Unitarian Conscience*, Unitarians traditionally emphasized the idea "that spiritual advancement was dependent upon men's own efforts," and that social improvement would be "a by-product of the salvation of individuals."[1] Regarding a social problem such as slavery, therefore, Unitarians would hold that any reform movement that sought to impose a solution through coercive legislation or some other outside force was doomed to failure because such action would do nothing to change the hearts of the individuals most affected, in this case the slaves and the slaveholders, and thus would limit itself to dealing with mere symptoms rather than the causes of the evil. This emphasis upon moral self-reliance would also cause Unitarians generally to eschew organizations that tended to subvert individual moral judgment in preference for a mandated collective view. As Howe points out, "The Harvard Liberals, like their Transcendental offspring, distrusted the moral effects of collective action," and he quotes William Ellery Channing. "Our danger is that we shall substitute the consciences of others for our own, that we shall paralyze our faculties through dependence on foreign guides."[2]

Unitarians were less than consistent in applying these principles to the volatile issue of slavery because of the various social and economic implications of the controversy, especially in Boston, where strong commercial ties existed between wealthy Unitarian businessmen and the cotton growers of the South. Proponents of abolition were well aware of this inconsistency, and Maria Chapman, one of Boston's leading abolitionists, noted in the *Eleventh Annual Report of the Boston Female Antislavery Society*, 9 October 1844 (Boston), that "as respects our cause, they [Unitarians] are a mingled and confused throng—no two of them at the same stage of advance—some, it is to be feared, on the retreat—. . . . Their clergy-men, generally, exhibit the pitiable spectacle of men trying to be well with the slaveholder and the slave, the pro-slavery merchant and politician, and the Abolitionist."[3] Howe notes the severity of this internal conflict when he points out that "like many other American religious groups in the middle of the nineteenth century, the Unitarian moralists shattered themselves upon the rock of slavery."[4]

Not all Unitarians, however, were intimidated by the hostility of the powerful and prominent commercial class. Among the most famous of those who dared to speak out was the Reverend William Ellery Channing. Channing was Emerson's best-known Harvard professor and a man he greatly admired. He first expressed his views on the slavery question comprehensively in 1835 in a work entitled *Slavery*.[5] In this work Channing maintains that only slaves and slaveholders can work directly to remove the evil of slavery, and "none of us are anxious to take the office from their hands." Further, he insists that slavery would soon disappear "were the obligation to remove it thoroughly understood and deeply felt!" The obligation of the moral man in this matter is to offer "prayers and persuasions" to bring this about.[6] Channing also felt that moral persons had a further obligation to avoid opposition to those who actively sought to abolish such abominations as slavery. Thus in an 1836 essay entitled "The Abolitionists" he states: "Then, in the commercial class, there are unworthy opposers of Abolitionism. There are those, whose interests rouse them to withstand every movement, which may offend the South. They have profitable connections with the slave-holder, which must not be endangered by expressions of sympathy with the slave. Gain is their god, and they sacrifice on this altar without compunction the rights and happiness of their fellow-creatures."[7]

The expression of these views caused a furor in Boston. Samuel May, reflecting on this matter a few years later, noted in a letter to the Reverend George Armstrong, a British abolitionist and fellow Unitarian, that "when Dr. Channing first made it known by a timely & vigorous act, that he was not of the number who thought Slavery was to come to an end by letting it alone, that moment did the zealous admiration for him become cold. . . . Dr. C. was censured privately & publicly . . . [and] . . . deep regrets were felt & expressed by Unitarians extensively for what he did in the Anti-Slavery Cause."[8] Howe notes that "his [Channing's] own parishioners and colleagues in Boston shunned him. Though none ventured to offer violence to his person, the gentle minister was deeply wounded by this blow to his status in the community."[9] Not surprisingly, Harvard, the bastion of Unitarianism, maintained a conservative attitude toward the slavery question for social as well as theological reasons. Thus an alumnus recalled that "during his three years there (1830–1833), the faculty-student Philanthropic Society discussed prison reform, temperance, peace, and the improvement of sailors' conditions and other causes—but never slavery."[10]

Despite the hostility of the genteel class, Channing continued to speak his mind, and in the mid-1830s he could rightly be considered one of the most outspoken of the Unitarian clergy on the matter of slavery. In a later work, "Emancipation" (1840), Channing again reiterated his faith in a conservative form of moral suasion, stating that the duty of individuals regarding the problem of slavery is "to speak their minds freely and fully, and thus to contribute what they may to the moral power of public opinion," which, he felt, would eventually have its effect. It is by "such a broad, generous improvement of society . . . embracing all the interests of the country" that the final solution will come, and not through a narrow reform movement that "confines itself to a single point."[11] This last issue was an important one for Channing, as it would be for Emerson. It would remain for some time a major source of friction between abolitionists and transcendental reformers. As Larry Gara notes, Channing "deplored the 'extremism' of the Garrisonians" because, in Channing's words, "they have fallen into the common error of the enthusiasts . . . that of exaggerating their object, of feeling as if no evil existed but that which they opposed."[12] The Garrisonians found Channing's position on associations equally deplorable.

Regarding the duties of the "Free States," Channing offered two injunctions: the first, "to abstain as rigidly from the use of political power against slavery in the States where it is established as from exercising it against slavery in foreign communities"; the second, "to free ourselves from all obligation to use the power of the National or State governments in any manner whatever for the support of slavery."[13] In subsequent works such as "Emancipation in the British West-Indies" (1842) Channing would consistently maintain the necessity of speaking out against slavery whenever the occasion required, but he would also continue to oppose associated action and political enterprises that "dictate . . . [a] mode of conferring freedom." His confidence was in the power of principle to lead men to self-redemption. "We ask only a settled purpose to bring slavery to an end; and we are sure this will devise a safe and happy way of exercising justice and love."[14]

Although Channing's position may appear somewhat vague and naïvely idealistic, it should be pointed out that many abolitionists themselves were uncertain as to just how the abolition of slavery would be brought about. Most eschewed formal association with established political parties as a matter of principle, as Channing did, but would cooperate with them when it was beneficial to the cause. Thus, Merton Dillon points out in *The Abolitionists* that Garrison "thought politics useful as a means of agitating the issue in public forums and thus of spreading antislavery views," and yet "he favored the ending of slavery through a change of heart rather than by the compulsion that must be the ultimate recourse of political power."[15] Emerson's friend W. H. Furness expressed a similar view as late as 1854 in a letter to Wendell Phillips: "Yes, these *are* times, & not the least remarkable thing in them is the hearing that our good old orthodox Abolitionism got in N.Y. last week. That is all, I take it, that Mr. Garrison wants, the ear of the country. Everything else that should follow, will follow. Whether slavery is to be abolished—how & when, God only knows. But one thing is plain, it is a blessed work to be engaged in."[16]

Channing's position was generally irritating to most abolitionists. Garrison once referred to Channing's attacks on slavery as "moral plagiarisms from the writings of abolitionists."[17] While they appreciated his outspoken condemnation of the moral outrage of slavery and regularly listed his works along with other abolitionist tracts in the *Liberator*, his opposition to organized abolition activity cut at the very heart of the movement. This concern is reflected in the *Eighth Annual Report of the Boston Female Anti-slavery Society* (1841), which points out defensively that "our experience confutes the assertion of Dr. Channing, that organization weakens individual energy, cramps the freedom of the individual mind, and confines it to the contemplation of one idea, till its judgment of the relative importance of things is impaired." Channing's emphasis upon the absolute need for each individual to deal with the overall moral status of the entire society on his own terms and in his own way tended to diminish the singular focus that abolitionists wished to maintain on the problem of slavery. They felt that this attitude encouraged many potential abolitionist crusaders to lose themselves in diverse and personal enterprises for moral reform. Thus James S. Gibbons complains in a letter to Caroline Weston, written two weeks after Channing's address "Emancipation in the British West-Indies," that "there are thousands to whom light would come, were it not that Dr. Channing, & such as he, intercept it." And later he adds, "I read your remarks about Dr. Channing to Mrs. Child. Her esteem for the Dr. is very great, yet I think she has grown latterly, somewhat more dissatisfied with his course. What claim he has to consideration as a *reformer* I cannot conceive." [18]

Maria Chapman, reflecting some years later on the influence of Channing in the cause of abolition, was even less kind. "He blamed us for forming and uniting as societies: He blamed us for admitting colored men to our associations. He blamed us for sending copies of our publications in the mails. He blamed us for rousing the community to the condemnation of the subject. He blamed us for awakening the youth to the question. And he made our lives unsafe, & exposed us to the fury of street mobs & the invasion of, & the setting fire to our houses." [19]

Emerson, on the other hand, found Channing's position very congenial, not only because his own transcendental values reflected the vestigial influence of this Unitarian emphasis upon moral self-reliance and the power of commitment to principle but also because it probably relieved him of an obligation he sometimes felt to speak more directly to specific and controversial social issues, which, as we have seen, he was temperamentally and philosophically loath to do. Emerson was personally delighted with Channing's *Slavery* and in his journal refers to it as one of the "perfectly genuine works of the times," along with the "marine Railway, the U.S. Bank, [and] the Bunker Hill Monument" (*JMN* 5:150). Undoubtedly he felt that much of his own thinking was expressed in the piece.

There can be little doubt that Emerson took substantial note of the uproar in the Unitarian community and elsewhere caused by Channing's statements on abolition and slavery. It is also clear that Channing's philosophy of reform had a significant influence in the development of Emerson's thinking on such matters. Emerson was an early admirer of Channing, as is reflected in an 1827 letter to his brother William where he points out that he is "glad [that] when God touches with fire such minds as Channing I feel the swift contagion that issues from such as he & stimulates the young to purposes of great & awful effort" (*L* 1:174). Although Emerson's attitude toward slavery and his thoughts on the best way of eradicating the institution would go through a substantial process of development, in the period before 1844 his thinking on such matters resembled Channings's in many important respects. Douglas Stange, in his study of antislavery and Unitarianism, describes Channing as a "philosophical abolitionist" who "dealt with slavery in abstract terms, worshiped individualism, ignored emotional appeals, inculcated moderation, deplored unnecessarily disturbing the social order, favored a gradual emancipation scheme usually with compensation, [was] somewhat naïve politically, and displayed a prejudiced paternalism toward black people." Prior to 1844, most of these characteristics applied to Emerson as well, but even in the early period there were differences.[20]

Regarding the similarities, both Channing and Emerson stressed the need for *individual* efforts at reform and were generally opposed to associations. They objected to the apparent myopia of abolitionists who concentrated on the "single idea" of slavery and consequently failed to see the need for a general reformation of individuals. Both also agreed on the importance of "moral suasion" and the promotion of self-culture as appropriate means for effecting that reform. Also, Channing and Emerson were both uncomfortable with the abusive personalities and unruly conduct of many abolitionists. Stange reports, for example, that "Theodore Parker and Wendell Phillips were specialists in vulgarity" and that abolitionists' attacks on conservative clergy were "a heavy cross to bear" because of this.[21] Undoubtedly Emerson's perception of the "odiousness" of many abolitionists was stimulated in part by such attacks. Finally, both Channing and Emerson found in the mercantile class many unworthy opponents of abolition whose "moral outrage" at the movement was really a thin disguise for their own self-interest.

Even in the early years, however, there were substantial differences between Emerson and his teacher on matters of reform. Probably the most significant relates to their views on politics. While Channing was, as Stange points out, "adamantly firm in his opposition to political action," and remained so throughout his lifetime, Emerson very early appreciated the power of the vote in at least mitigating the evils of society. He therefore not only voted regularly himself but encouraged others to do the same. This appreciation for the political process, despite his early recognition of the pitfalls of American politics, would eventually culminate in his stump campaign for John Gorham Palfrey in the congressional elections in the spring of 1851, and his outspoken support of Senator Charles Sumner throughout the 1850s and later.

Another important area of early disagreement between Channing and Emerson relates to the use of force to achieve moral ends. Channing deplored violence and was shocked and dismayed at the conduct of Elijah Lovejoy during the Alton riot. In the lengthy "Letter to the Abolitionists," which was published in the *Liberator* (22 December 1837) following the incident, Channing notes his longstanding objection to the "organization and union of numerous and wide-spread societies for the subversion of slavery." However, he had been satisfied that "the many and dangerous tendencies of such an association would be obliterated by [their] adoption of what is called 'the peace principle,' in other words, by [their] unwillingness to use physical force for self-defense." Unfortunately, that principle apparently had now been abrogated by virtue of "the tragedy of Alton, where one of [their] respected brethren fell with arms in his hands." The result for Channing was that a cloud had now gathered over the society, and "a dangerous precedent [had] been given in the cause of humanity." Obviously, Emerson felt very differently about the matter and applauded Lovejoy's heroism. Later, he would provide funds to purchase Sharpe's rifles to aid John Brown and his followers in the Kansas land wars in the 1850s, and, eventually, he would welcome the Civil War as a "cleansing" therapy to cure America's moral malaise.

Despite these differences, which would become more prominent with the passage of time, the striking similarity between Channing's Unitarianism and Emerson's transcendentalism in regard to social reform was not lost on the abolitionists. Thus the *Eleventh Annual Report of the Boston Female Anti-slavery Society* notes: "There has been, from old time, a school of philosophy which ascribes to loneliness and quiet, and individualism, not only their own great and characteristic powers, but which would also endow them with those of society, activity, and cooperation. The ideas of this school have been brought to bear upon our association by those who wished to disband it, from the commencement of our enterprise. . . . Dr. Channing and the transcendental school borrowed the idea from old philosophers, and applied it unsuccessfully to prevent men from associating as Abolitionists."

That the abolitionists had Emerson and "his" transcendentalists clearly in mind in such instances is suggested by Edmund Quincy's comment in a letter to a friend in 1841 regarding Theodore Parker's recent conversion to active abolitionism. "I do not know whether you have heard that Theodore Parker came out on Sunday before last with an Anti-Slavery sermon. . . . He has now recognized the A[nti]. S[lavery]. & N[on]. R[esistance]. movements as the Chief, if not the only, manifestations of Christianity in the present age, *without any Emersonian or Channingian qualifications* [emphasis mine].[22]

In an earlier letter that describes the appearance of a group of the transcendental Brook Farmers (with whom Emerson was at times associated) at an abolition picnic, Quincy notes that none of them spoke at the affair and concludes, "I do not think we have anything to hope from them."[23] Last, the association between Emerson and Channing, and their pernicious effect on the abolition movement, are described clearly in a draft article on Emerson that Maria Chapman prepared as late as 1844. "His [Emerson's] character being rather contemplative than active, at least according to popular acceptation of those words, he has been a philosophical speculator rather than a reformer. His wisdom has therefore made fools of some, & his naturalness [has] been the occasion of affectation in others. Hundreds of young persons have made him their excuse for avoiding the Anti Slavery battle & talking about the clear light; just as thousands have refused their aid to the cause because Dr. Channing wrote essays against associations."[24]

The entire question of the relationship of the transcendental and abolition movements is complex and resistant to generalizations, although many scholars have tried to discern it.[25] John Humphrey Noyes maintains that Brook Farm, the most famous experiment in living according to transcendental principles, "was the child of New England Unitarianism" and was suggested by Dr. Channing. He quotes Emerson as his source for this. Not surprisingly, because of the Unitarian/transcendental concern for universal rather than specific moral reform, the emphasis of abolitionism was seen by this group as myopic and undesirable.[26] While there were some abolitionists among the transcendentalists in the 1830s and early 1840s, the two were generally on divergent paths during this time, and there was often friction between them. Thus Lindsay Swift points out that when Frederick Cabot joined the transcendental community at Brook Farm in 1844 after being a member of the Massachusetts Antislavery Society, he was criticized for it by old abolitionist friends like Caroline Weston. His defensive response was that "while he loves the slave no less he loves humanity more."[27]

For some this friction would prove enduring. One of the better-known Brook Farmers, George Curtis, in a letter to a friend written some seven years after that famous experiment ended, refers to "the remembrance of Brook Farm & the thousand memories that consecrate that place." The tranquil tone of his letter soon changes, however, when the subject turns to "stiffnecked" reformers who fail to realize "that the landscape stretches backward as well as forward & that because they are doing one thing they are not fulfilling all." Specifically, Curtis relates that the day before, he had "read an AntiSlavery resolution denouncing as damned, all churches & ministers that do not entirely & openly condemn Southern bondage." Curtis was outraged at this blanket condemnation and sadly observes that "these facts of AntiSlavery—& Slavery . . . cross the land, seeking whom they may devour, & their prey is the majority of men." For the former Brook Farmer, Americans in general and abolitionists in particular seemed to have forgotten, if they ever knew, that "the sum of wisdom is the knowledge that things have two sides."[28]

By the mid-1840s, however, such objections would become less common as major transcendentalists such as Emerson, Parker, Thoreau, Alcott, Furness, Margaret Fuller, and others became more active in the abolition crusade and more closely associated with abolitionists such as William Lloyd Garrison, Wendell Phillips, Ellis Gray Loring, Lucretia Mott, Edmund Quincy, and others. This association would become most prominent with the frenetic activity of the 1850s following the passage of the Fugitive Slave Law. However, some transcendentalists like Curtis, George Ripley, Frederic Henry Hedge, Orestes Brownson, and others would continue to object to the abolitionists on a variety of grounds. Ultimately, any discussion of the relationship of transcendentalism to abolitionism necessarily requires a careful consideration of which transcendentalist and time period one is discussing.

An element of transcendental passivism was sometimes perceived by Emerson's critics in the lectures he delivered in the late 1830s, especially those dealing with the times. Thus in a lecture entitled "Being and Seeming," which was addressed to a Cambridge audience in March 1838, Emerson states: "The young man relying on his instincts who has only a good intention is apt to feel ashamed of his inaction and the slightness of his virtue when in the presence of the active and zealous leaders of the philanthropic enterprizes, of Universal Temperance, Peace, and Freedom. He only loves like Cordelia after his duty. Trust it nevertheless. A man's income is not sufficient for all things. If he spend here he must save there."[29] This emphasis on a potentially passive individuality was upsetting to those who felt the need for active and organized abolition. After hearing this lecture, Ellis Gray Loring, a Boston lawyer and ardent abolitionist, sent Emerson the following commentary:

> I fancy sometimes that you suggest or imply the impossibility of the same man's performing adequately, both public & private duties. Is it a fact that the great & active philanthropists to whom you sometimes allude—such men as Clarkson [the famous British abolitionist] . . . —do less than their quieter neighbors for the true & free development of their nature? I would not say that all men can be Clarksons, but is any man the worse, in any respect, for trying in an honest and good heart to do like him— . . . You are sometimes *thought* to teach, that, in the great struggles between right and wrong going on in society, we may safely & innocently stand neuter, altogether;—gratifying mere tastes, so they be elegant, intellectual tastes, —This is surely a misconstruction of your words.[30]

Loring's statement here reflects a basic and common misunderstanding of Emerson's philosophy of reform as it had evolved up to this point. As noted earlier, this misunderstanding was shared by many abolitionists who saw him as a "contemplative" intellectual and presumably unconcerned with active social reform. Their sensitivity regarding Emerson's assumed antipathy toward their cause would persist until his landmark 1 August 1844 address, "Emancipation in the British West Indies." For some, it would continue for a much longer time.

To clarify this issue it should be pointed out that Emerson did not object to the noble services and activism of focused antislavery crusaders like Thomas Clarkson, whom he would memorialize in his 1844 address. And he genuinely admired and publicly praised the overt heroism and sacrifice of Elijah Lovejoy, whom he saw as a martyr to the cause. However, he was greatly concerned, as was Channing, with the myopia and hypocrisy evinced by some reformers such as Francis Thompson. More important, he resisted the efforts of many, including members of his own household, to push him into a particular social role that he felt he had no vocation or inclination to play at the time. His basic philosophy was that every individual must discover for himself the best way to serve God and his fellow man. The role he had envisioned for himself in the early 1830s was that of "scholar," and later, "scholar/poet."[31] It was through his efforts in this role that he felt he could best contribute to the ideal development of American society. However, this does not mean that he disparaged others who followed a different vocation, like Garrison, Lovejoy, or Clarkson.

The concept of "vocation" is critically important in understanding Emerson's attitude toward the abolition movement and his role in the antislavery crusade of the 1840s. Unfortunately, some scholarly discussions of the idea have served to reinforce the same type of misunderstanding suggested by Loring's letter. For example, Henry Nash Smith was correct in pointing out in his seminal 1939 essay "Emerson's Problem of Vocation" that after leaving the Unitarian ministry Ralph Waldo Emerson sought to determine precisely what his proper vocation should be.[32] It was always Emerson's belief, as noted in his journal in 1834, that the "blessed God has given to each his calling in his ruling love. . . . God has adapted the brain and the body of men to the work that is to be done in the world" (*JMN* 4:372). Smith is also correct in noting that Emerson's final opinion in the matter was that the lecture platform was the "new pulpit of the age," and that it would be as scholar that he could best serve his fellow man. However, he sets up a false distinction when he goes on to suggest that, as a scholar, Emerson sought to remain aloof from the social reforms of his day in order to cultivate "the highly individualistic and passive cult of self-reliance." In order to justify his position he points to Emerson's rejection of George Ripley's invitation to join the transcendental Brook Farm enterprise in 1840. Emerson's journal remarks regarding the Brook Farm invitation, however, indicate that his intent in rejecting it was related more to preserving his freedom to act rather than an effort at isolation, as Smith concludes. An entry dated 17 October 1840 states, "Yesterday George and Sophia Ripley, & Margaret Fuller & Alcott discussed here the new social plans [about Brook Farm]." In contemplating their attempts to encourage him to join their community, Emerson notes pointedly, "I do not wish to remove from my present prison to a prison a little larger. I wish to break all prisons. I have not yet conquered my own house." Emerson remained interested in reform and the improvement of society, but felt that these ends would not be best served by joining a community such as Brook Farm. His reason was simple and well established by this time: "to join this body would be to traverse all my long trumpeted theory, and the instinct which spoke from it, that one man is a counterpoise to a city, —that a man is stronger than a city, that his solitude is more prevalent & beneficent than the concert of crowds" (*JMN* 7:407–8). Obviously Emerson's emphasis here, like Channing's, is on an individual approach to reform. Eventually, however, Emerson would forgo even this commitment as developments in the mid-1840s and early 1850s would suggest the value of organized resistance to the threat of slavery.

Also, despite Smith's claims for Emerson's scholarly aloofness, as early as 1837 and the "American Scholar Address" he presented a very clear statement on the importance of action to the scholar. In fact, the "American Scholar Address" itself is, among other things, a clarion call for students to descend from the ivory towers of the academy and reconnect themselves to society, there to play their proper and important role as "man thinking." He clearly opposes aloofness and rejects outright the "notion that the scholar should be a recluse, a valetudinarian,—as unfit for any handiwork or public labor, as a penknife for an axe." Indeed, Emerson goes on to insist, as was noted in chapter 2, that "action is with the scholar subordinate, but it is essential. Without it, he is not yet a man" (*CW* 1:159). He is also very clear in this address regarding the kind of action appropriate to the scholar in the struggle for man's improvement. For Emerson, the scholar is "the world's eye. He is the world's heart. He is to resist the vulgar prosperity that retrogrades ever to barbarism, by preserving and communicating heroic sentiments, noble biographies, melodious verse, and the conclusions of history. Whatsoever oracles the human heart in all emergencies, in all solemn hours has uttered as its commentary on the world of actions,—these he shall receive and impart. And whatsoever new verdict Reason from her inviolable seat pronounces on the passing events of to-day,—this he shall hear and promulgate" (CW 1:62–63).

While at first blush this exhortation may have seemed philosophically vague to social reformers in 1837 who had a highly specific reform issue in mind, the responsibility Emerson here places upon the shoulders of the scholar is a weighty one indeed. Clearly, the scholar is to be both the repository and the living incarnation of the essence of civilization. It was Emerson's firm belief at this time that the progress of mankind would be determined by the influence of the enlightenment and poetic spirit at work in society at any given moment. The difference between an enlightened, just, and progressive society and a benighted, cruel, and primitive one could be measured by the relative influence of "culture" in either. This cultural influence, according to Emerson, must be "domestic," that is, wrought through the education of individuals. The results of this influence could be truly revolutionary. As Emerson points out later in his address, the revolution he envisions "is to be wrought by the gradual domestication of the idea of Culture. The main enterprise of the world for splendor, for extent, is the upbuilding of a man. Here are the materials strown along the ground. The private life of one man shall be a more illustrious monarchy,—more formidable to its enemy, more sweet and serene in its influence to its friend, than any kingdom in history" (CW 1:66).[33] Emerson's disagreement with the abolition activists in the 1830s and early 1840s, then, was mainly with their unwillingness to recognize that the problem of slavery was only one of myriad deficiencies bred by the vulgar and barbaric prosperity of American society. Also, he insisted more than they on the need for *individual* reform as a prelude to a general reform of society. Unfortunately, his unwillingness to participate in the various reform activities undertaken

by the abolitionists at this time and his insistence upon individual reform were often construed as a rejection of abolitionism itself. Also,
in some measure Emerson was the victim of society's tendency, then
and now, to see speculative or philosophical persons as recluses, despite
the rather ironic fact that he made his living as a public lecturer. As
indicated above, Emerson was not unaware of society's narrow view of
scholars. He also recorded in his 1836 journal that "the Scholar works
with invisible tools to invisible ends. So passes for an idler or worse;
brain sick; defenceless to idle carpenters, masons, & merchants, that
having done nothing most laboriously all day pounce on him for fresh
spoil at night" (*JMN* 5:116).

Emerson was nevertheless determined to hold his ground in the matter of reform, and many of his concerns about his own "self-reliance"
and social reform would find expression in his famous 1841 essay by
that name. In this essay Emerson offers some rather specific and harsh
criticism of certain abolitionists who attempt to reform the world without reforming themselves first. "If an angry bigot assumes this bountiful
cause of Abolition, and comes to me with his last news from Barbadoes,
why should I not say to him, 'Go love thy infant; love thy woodchopper:
be good-natured and modest: have that grace; and never varnish your
hard uncharitable ambition with this incredible tenderness for black
folk a thousand miles off. Thy love afar is spite at home.' Rough and
graceless would be such greeting, but truth is handsomer than the affectation of love. Your goodness must have some edge to it—else it is none"
(*CW* 2:30).

Such comments were undoubtedly disturbing to Boston's abolitionists and probably explain in part the antipathy evident in some of their
statements noted earlier. However, it must be pointed out that Emerson here does not condemn *all* abolitionists, or the movement itself, but
only those who use the cause for self-aggrandizement. Also, Emerson
goes on in this famous essay to make comments that seem to be directed
at those around him who might have attempted to move him into a
more specific involvement in abolition. "The doctrine of hatred must be
preached as the counteraction of the doctrine of love when that pules
and whines. I shun father and mother and wife and brother, when my

genius calls me. I would write on the lintels of the door-post, *Whim*. I hope it is somewhat better than whim at last, but we cannot spend the day in explanation" (*CW* 2:30).

In this passage Emerson combines three separate biblical allusions in order to make his point. The first is to Luke 14:26: "If any man come to me, and hate not his father, and mother, and wife, and children and brethren, and sisters, yea, and his own life also, he cannot be my disciple." The second refers to Matthew 10:36–37: "And a man's foes shall be they of his own household. He that loveth father or mother more than me is not worthy of me: and he that loveth son or daughter more than me is not worthy of me." Both passages develop a similar theme. The command of Christ to his followers is that they commit themselves, above all other things, including family, to the fulfillment of their spiritual obligations, even when this will bring them into conflict with those they love. As Emerson stated in the journal passage noted earlier, God visits the responsibilities of "vocation" or "calling" upon every man, each in his own way. It is interesting that Emerson here emphasizes the need to put aside family pressures when they run counter to the call of one's genius. Given the strong interests in active abolitionism in Emerson's immediate family, this is possibly a covert apologia intended in particular for domestic consumption, and it may explain further his earlier journal comment that "I have not yet conquered my own house." Indeed, while the principles Emerson articulates here apply to the entire spectrum of his intellectual growth and development, especially following the Divinity School controversy, the application of these principles to the question of antislavery and other reform enterprises of the day, like Brook Farm, is obvious. As if to clarify his position in the matter yet further, Emerson goes on in his essay to note: "What I must do, is all that concerns me, not what the people think. This rule, equally arduous in actual and in intellectual life, may serve for the whole distinction between greatness and meanness. It is the harder, because you will always find those who think they know what is your duty better than you know it. It is easy in the world to live after the world's opinion; it is easy in solitude to live after your own; but the great man is he who in the midst of the crowd keeps with perfect sweetness the independence of solitude" (*CW* 2:31).

The final biblical allusion in Emerson's brief passage suggests his willingness, as ever, to accept the possibly negative consequences of his decision to act in his own way. The reference is to Exodus 12:21–26, where Moses orders the men of Israel to mark the lintels of their doorways with blood, "for the Lord will pass through to smite the Egyptians; and when he seeth the blood upon the lintel and the two side posts, the Lord will pass over the door, and will not suffer the destroyer to come into your houses to smite you." If Emerson is prepared to write "Whim" on the lintels as an expression of his willingness to act on impulse or the promptings of the voice within, then he is also willing to accept whatever ruination may result from his gesture. But, as he says, "I hope it is somewhat better than whim at last, but we cannot spend the day in explanation."

Throughout his lengthy career Emerson would remain true to his role as scholar and poet. The problems he would incur would inevitably revolve around his efforts to determine the extent to which a scholar might directly speak to critical social issues without compromising his commitment to the more general principles of self-culture. Occasionally in the late 1830s, despite his strong reservations, Emerson would allow himself to be persuaded to assume the role of a specific social reformer, but his feelings about these efforts were ambiguous, to say the least. One of these was his antislavery address in the fall of 1837, and another was his open letter to Martin Van Buren, president of the United States, on the Cherokee question (*W* 11:90–96). In the spring of 1838 the Cherokee Indians were being removed from Georgia to west of the Mississippi River in accordance with a treaty considered by many to be a fraud. A protest meeting was held in Concord, and Emerson spoke at it, although very unwillingly. As Lidian noted later in a letter to Lucy Jackson Brown, he preferred "individual action" (*LL* 74–75).[34] In his brief letter Emerson makes many points regarding the plight of the Cherokees that he would later reiterate when speaking of the plight of the Negro slaves. He states that in Massachusetts there is a real interest in the situation of the Cherokees. "We have learned with joy their improvement in the social arts. We have read their newspapers. We have seen some of them in our schools and colleges. In common with the great body of the American people, we have witnessed with sympathy the painful labors of these red men to redeem their own race from the doom of eternal inferiority, and to borrow and domesticate in the tribe the arts and customs of the Caucasian race" (W 11:90).

After establishing the inherent humanity of the Cherokees, something that he realized many Americans would doubt, Emerson went on to express his concern that the conduct of the United States government toward them constituted the greatest perfidy. "Such a dereliction of all faith and virtue, such a denial of justice, and such deafness to screams for mercy were never heard of in times of peace and in the dealings of a nation with its own allies and wards, since earth was made" (W 11:92). As would be the case in many antislavery speeches in the next decade, Emerson ends his brief appeal by pointing out his own faith in the ultimate triumph of goodness in society and the "futility of opposition to the moral sentiment." For Emerson at this time, the law of compensation would inevitably play its part. "However feeble the sufferer and however great the oppressor, it is in the nature of things that the blow should recoil upon the aggressor. For God is in the sentiment, and it cannot be withstood. The potentate and the people perish before it; but with it, and as its executor, they are omnipotent" (W 11:96).

The statement was made, and, in a move that was highly unusual for him, Emerson provided for the publication of the letter in several newspapers, including the *Daily National Intelligencer* [Washington, D.C.] (14 May 1838), the *Yeoman's Gazette* (19 May 1838), and the *Liberator* (22 June 1838). However, he was no more satisfied with this effort than he was with his speech in November. Later, he would note in his journal: "Yesterday went the letter to V[an]. B[uren]. a letter hated of me. A deliverance that does not deliver the soul. . . . [T]his stirring in the philanthropic mud, gives me no peace. . . . I fully sympathise, be sure, with the sentiment I write, but I accept it rather from my friends than dictate it. It is not my impulse to say it & therefore my genius deserts me, no muse befriends, no music of thought or of word accompanies. Bah!" (*JMN* 5:479).

Despite Emerson's natural and deep-seated aversion to public controversy, in a matter of four short months he would be thrust into what was perhaps the most significant public controversy of his entire career. The "Divinity School Address," delivered on 15 July 1838, would serve to propel him into the dusty lists of life to a degree that he had never imagined and would, indirectly, establish the groundwork for a closer association with the abolitionists whom he had studiously avoided.

There is every reason to believe that Emerson was taken by surprise by the uproar resulting from his speech at the Divinity School. He had expressed the same views on earlier occasions without causing a row, and, as Eleanor Tilton points out, "It can scarcely be said that Harvard was unprepared for the Divinity College Address."[35] But surprised it apparently was. Three weeks after the event Emerson wrote to Carlyle that two addresses, one at Cambridge and the other at Dartmouth, "are now in the press," and added in a quiet understatement, "The first, I hear is very offensive" (*CEC* 191). By October the situation had become so bad that Emerson was led to suggest that Carlyle postpone his planned trip to America because "the publication of my 'Address to the Divinity College' . . . has been the occasion of an outcry in all our leading local newspapers against my 'infidelity,' 'pantheism,' & 'atheism.' The writers warn all & sundry against me, & against whatever is supposed to be related to my connection of opinion &c; against Transcendentalism, Goethe, and *Carlyle*" (*CEC* 196). Gay Wilson Allen notes that the outcry was so great that "Emerson began to fear it might affect his ability to supplement his income with more public lectures."[36] (This concern was also possibly a factor in Emerson's initial desire to avoid, as much as possible, the abolition controversy.) At the same time Emerson recorded in his journal his disgust with "the great army of cowards who bellow & bully from their bed chamber windows" and "the feminine vehemence with which the A[ndrews]. N[orton]. of the Daily Advertiser beseeches the dear people to whip that naughty heretic" (*JMN* 7:110).

The effects of this episode were many. For one, it tended to radicalize Emerson to a larger extent than before. It established him in the public eye, for better or worse, as a spokesman for unorthodox reform ideas, and it led to the development on his part of a greater personal self-reliance when confronting head-on the displeasure of society. The Divinity School controversy was Emerson's baptism of fire into the realm of public controversy. Not surprisingly, the event served to associate him in the minds of many with those "other" radicals and social outcasts, the abolitionists. Additionally, it raised, at least momentarily, the hopes of some that Emerson would soon become, if not one of them, at least more publicly sympathetic to their cause. Thus Maria Chapman, in the month after the address, notes the following in a letter to William Lloyd Garrison:

> I send you Emerson's oration. It is rousing the wrath of the Cambridge "powers that be" in an astonishing manner. How cowardly are Unitarians generally! They take alarm at sentiments which differ only in shading from their own, (in matters of doctrine I mean). The commencement exercises at Cambridge have been strangely tinged this year with both abolition & anti-abolition. I did not attend, but Caroline, who was there, speaks highly of an oration by Mr. Shackford of Portsmouth, whose forth-right manner of declaring his sentiments on the subject of prejudice against colour shocked some of the audience as much as it delighted others.[37]

This tendency to speak of Emerson's new radicalism and the hopes of the abolition movement in the same breath is repeated in the correspondence of some of the best-known abolitionists of the time. Harriet Martineau, in a letter to William Ware (the brother of Henry Ware, Jr., one of Emerson's more benign Unitarian critics), confirms her high opinion of Emerson despite his "heresy" and goes on to note that all American abolitionists are held in high esteem by the British. "I am very sorry you think of Emerson as you do. We think here that his last oration is even more beautiful than the former,—all pervaded with truth & beauty. . . . Every known abolitionist is taken to the heart of our people at once, while the feeling against your country grows, on account of that matter & some others, stronger every day."[38] Martineau had been impressed with Emerson since meeting him in Boston in 1835 and taking refuge in his home at the time of the antiabolition outcry against her. That she expected him to eventually exercise a strong influence in reforming American society is clear from her previously noted comment that "great things are expected from him; and great things, it seems, he cannot but do, if he have life and health to prosecute his course."[39]

Emerson's "Divinity School Address" brought him the same kind of vitriolic response from conservative Boston as William Ellery Channing experienced following his 1835 pronouncements on slavery. Convers Francis's journal of September 1838 indicates that Boston conservatives had come "to abhor and abominate R. W. Emerson as a sort of mad dog."[40] Despite such vile attacks, and the stern condemnation of Emerson by Andrews Norton and other Boston notables, the bard did not withdraw from this public controversy but instead chose to quietly but persistently weather the storm. And he continued to speak out and to express his views even on unpopular issues. Arrangements were made to publish his address, and it would appear in August. In June 1838 he joined with Dr. Channing, Ellis Gray Loring, and 164 others in signing a petition demanding the release of the radical Abner Kneeland, who at the time was serving a sixty-day sentence in the Suffolk County Jail in Boston for blasphemy. Kneeland has the dubious honor of being the last citizen of the Commonwealth to be convicted of that crime.[41]

Perhaps as a result of this show of support, as well as the controversy generated by his own Harvard Divinity School address, as Robert Burkholder notes, "Emerson became one of Kneeland's causes, joining Free Inquiry, utopian socialism, birth control, and Jacksonian democracy" as an issue to be defended in the pages of Kneeland's radical journal, the *Investigator*.[42] Emerson may not have been especially comfortable with his newfound defender, because the association thus formed served only to draw him further into the kind of public controversy and agitation he had always preferred to avoid. Also, ironically, Emerson had said of Kneeland, who was the leader of Boston's First Society of Free Inquirers and an atheist, just three years earlier, "I know nothing of the source of my being but I will not soil my nest. . . . God himself contradicts through me & all his creatures the miserable babble of Kneeland & his crew" (*JMN* 5:71). Apparently adversity could make strange bedfellows even for Emerson. This radical association also undoubtedly contributed somewhat to the "odium & aversion" Emerson experienced in August at Harvard, where he had attended the Phi Beta Kappa exercises (*JMN* 7:60). Despite this discomfort and some additional worries about the possibly negative effects of the controversy on his lecturing revenue, which he expressed in a letter to his brother William (*L* 2:162), Emerson never rejected Kneeland's support. Two years later the radical reformer would leave Boston for the West with visions of establishing a Utopian community.

Overall, the events of 1838 undoubtedly encouraged abolitionists to anticipate a more active involvement by Emerson in their cause, and they were not without evidence to support their hope that he would eventually enter the fray on their side. As a young Unitarian minister Emerson did not entirely avoid the question of slavery (as many of his colleagues did). As noted earlier, he actually referred to it as a matter for concern in his first sermon, and he mentioned the issue with some frequency thereafter. Additionally, there were two occasions in the early 1830s when he allowed abolitionists to deliver antislavery sermons in his church.[43] It should also be noted that the general tendency of Emerson's transcendental concern for the universal improvement of mankind did inspire many reformers who would point to the "American Scholar Address" in 1837 as their own declaration of independence. Finally, Emerson's speech on abolition in November 1837 and his letter to President Van Buren concerning the Cherokees, both so untypical, seemed to signal his imminent entry onto the field. The *Liberator*, which printed Emerson's Cherokee letter on 22 June 1838, prefaced it with the following statement: "The bold, energetic, and independent tone of the following letter is worthy of the highest admiration. It ought to be printed in every newspaper, and sent to every family in the United States. Can it be possible that the mind and heart which gave it birth are unaffected by the woes of the slaves! We hope not."

Other factors would also serve to encourage Emerson's increasingly active involvement in the movement. In the late 1830s and early 1840s a number of respectable citizens, including some prominent Unitarians, were declaring their allegiance to the organized efforts of abolition.

Prior to this important development, virtually all of Boston's organized abolitionists were people derived from the lower classes, and hence they were often looked down upon by the socially elite as mere rabble-rousers. Octavius Frothingham once pointed out that "enough account is not generally made of the purely social element in the opposition of the Unitarian ministers, as a rule, to the Abolitionists. They were gentlemen; they occupied a high position in the community; they belonged to a privileged order." The abolitionists, on the other hand, were generally "poor, humble, despised people, of no influence; men one could not ask to dine."[44] To a certain extent Emerson shared this aversion. His dislike of the famous British abolitionist George Thompson was noted earlier, and on one occasion in his journal, as we saw, he referred to abolitionists in general as "an altogether odious set of people, whom one would be sure to shun as the worst of bores & canters" (*JMN* 5:91; *JMN* 9:120).

Gradually, however, from the late 1830s onward, a number of individuals from society's upper levels were drawn into the abolition movement. One of the most prominent was Theodore Parker. Parker was a well-known Unitarian intellectual who possessed one of the finest private libraries in America and whose parish at one point was said to be the largest in Boston, some claimed the largest in America.[45] Parker was also associated with the transcendentalists and was an early defender of Emerson and the "New School" in the controversy that followed the "Divinity School Address."[46] Undoubtedly this early orientation toward radicalism encouraged abolitionists to think of Parker as potentially one of their own, and at times they seemed impatient in awaiting his conversion. Thus, in a letter referred to earlier describing the events at an abolition picnic in 1840, Edmund Quincy notes almost plaintively, "You ask 'why Parker was not there?' There he was—but refused to speak. Alas! how long & difficult is the route by which a *Unitarian Minister* is transformed into a Man!"[47] Parker's "transformation" did, of course, finally come, almost exactly one year later, and he was welcomed into the cause with open arms. He would serve long and well in the abolition ranks until his death in 1860.

Somewhat more distant from Emerson geographically than Parker, but certainly much closer in temperament, was William Henry Furness.

Furness, who has been described as Emerson's "lifelong (and possibly his only really intimate) friend," became actively involved in the abolition movement in 1839 when he delivered his first antislavery sermon in his Philadelphia church.[48] In the early 1830s Furness had resisted any direct involvement in the abolition movement even more strenuously than Emerson. For, while Emerson had allowed Samuel May to preach an antislavery sermon to his Boston congregation as early as 1832, Furness was shocked when May requested the same opportunity from him a year later. In speaking of this event years later in a letter to Wendell Phillips, Furness recalled that "twenty years ago when S. J. May was here helping to form this A[merican]. A[ntislavery]. Society, which now has so grand a history, he preached for me one day. 'I believe,' said he to me before we went into church, 'I must bring *this subject* before your people.' 'For mercy's sake, don't!' I exclaimed, & we went to church, & he preached a couple of good old Unitarian Sermons, & you would not have imagined there was a slave on earth."[49]

Undoubtedly the proximity of his parish to the slaveholding South was somewhat inhibiting to Furness, but eventually his moral outrage at the abomination of slavery and the encouragement of individuals like Lucretia Mott and Harriet Martineau precipitated his entry into the ranks. Like Emerson, Furness wished to maintain his independence from formal antislavery associations but regularly preached antislavery sermons in his church and refrained from criticizing those who did join abolition organizations. Perhaps because of this independence, and his transcendental credentials, some abolitionists had reservations about the nature of Furness's commitment and wondered if he would become another Channing. Thus James Gibbons, in a letter to Caroline Weston, says, "I had thought about saying something to you about Furness, whose words indeed are fine and who has to some extent identified himself with persecuted antislavery. I hope he is an abolitionist more than 10 out of the 52 Sundays in the year, but he wears his head in a pro slavery community & church—a patriot, & escapes the guillotine!" Gibbons underscores his reservations by noting, "I don't feel ready to endorse 'abolition' in very big letters across Furness' shoulders."[50]

Samuel May showed a similar concern about the Unitarian clergy in general in the letter to the Reverend George Armstrong mentioned earlier. "It is true that there are but few of our ministers who do not, occasionally, once or twice a year it may be, bring the matter of Slavery before their people, so far as to call it a great evil, to avow themselves its enemies, & to express the hope that it may be made to cease; but as a general rule . . . this language has been accompanied as an offset with a sharp rebuke of the Abolitionists for their vehemence, their intolerance, and their ultraism, for in that word, I believe their sins may be summed up."[51] As it turned out, Gibbons's concerns about Furness, at least, were unfounded. The Philadelphia preacher went on to become one of the most active abolitionist clergymen of the time.

Despite the increasing momentum of the movement toward active and organized abolition efforts within Emerson's society and, to a surprising extent, within his own family, Emerson continued to resist efforts to draw him more directly into the fray. Regardless of his reluctance, however, his journals and other sources indicate that the problem was never far from his thoughts. Several entries from the period present virtual echoes of Channing's statements concerning the perils of myopic associationism where all other concerns are subordinated to one principal cause. Thus, using words that later he reiterated in "Self-Reliance," Emerson states in July 1839: "Perception is not whimsical but fatal. If I see a trait my children will see it after me & all men & all women for my perception is as much a fact as is the sun. Abolitionist. You have not voted for Mr B because you have made so much of the slave question. You have ceased to be a man that you may be an abolitionist" (*JMN* 7:223). Earlier, Emerson advises that "you must treat the men of one idea & women of one idea, the Abolitionist, the Phrenologist, the Swedenborgian, as insane persons with a continual tenderness & special reference in every remark & action to their known state, which reference presently becomes embarrassing & tedious" (*JMN* 7:30). And again, in 1842, he states in a passage that later appeared in his lecture "New England Reformers" (1844): "When we see an Abolitionist or a special Reformer, we feel like asking him What right have you Sir to your one virtue? Is virtue piecemeal? This is like a costly scarf or a jewel on the rags of a beggar" (*JMN* 8:162; *W* 3:263). Indeed, many passages such as these are recorded in the journals of the period.[52]

Perhaps the greatest obstacle to Emerson's more active participation in the abolition movement at this time, however, was his belief in the basic inferiority of the Negro. This belief, while it was not uncommon even among the most ardent abolitionists of the age, was especially problematical to Emerson because of his strong commitment to self-reliance on all levels, a commitment that was reinforced by his experience in the Divinity School controversy.[53] Like Channing, Emerson felt that all social reformation begins with the individual. The necessary corollary to this belief was the assumption that the slaves had an obligation to participate in their own salvation, which would come about only when, and if, they earned it, which in 1840 was questionable to Emerson. Thus, in one journal entry that seems to preempt both Darwin and Herbert Spencer, Emerson says, "Strange history this of *abolition*. The negro must be very old & belongs, one would say, to the fossil formations. What right has he to be intruding into the late & civil daylight of this dynasty of the Caucasians & Saxons? It is plain that so inferior a race must perish shortly like the poor Indians." Emerson then goes on to note "S[arah]. C[larke]. said, 'the Indians perish because there is no place for them.' That is the very fact of their inferiority. There is always place for the superior" (*JMN* 7:393).

However, despite his strong reservations about the value of associated efforts at social reform, and despite his concern about the possible inferiority of the Negro, a fact that could nullify any effort to save them, Emerson nevertheless maintained a strong and active interest in the development of the abolition movement in the late 1830s and early 1840s. During this period he sometimes attended abolition meetings in Concord and elsewhere, and on these occasions he was generally pleased with what he heard.[54] Emerson also eventually was able to meet some of the leading abolitionists of the age, including Lucretia Mott, Wendell Phillips, and William Lloyd Garrison. He felt that Mott was "a noble woman," and that Phillips was one of the best speakers of the age.[55] His earliest comments on Garrison (1839) describe him as "a man of great ability in conversation, of a certain longsightedness in debate which is a great excellence . . . and an eloquence of illustration which contents the ear & the mind" (*JMN* 7:281). As their relationship developed over the next few years, Emerson's respect for Garrison's personal integrity and dedication grew, and his estimation of the association Garrison had founded improved. At times Emerson was moved to downright sympathy for Garrison, Phillips, and others who were frequently attacked because they dared to speak out against slavery. The northerner, Emerson felt, "is surrounded with churches & Sunday schools & is hypocritical. How gladly, . . . if he dared, he would seal the lips of these poor men & poor women who speak for him [the slave]." Emerson's final estimation of Garrison is probably best summed up in the simple statement, "I cannot speak of that gentleman without respect" (*JMN* 9:132–34). Although there is no evidence that Emerson spoke at any of the abolition gatherings he attended during this time, the expectation that he eventually would was growing, and on at least one occasion he provided a statement to be read at a Concord abolition gathering that he was not able to attend.[56]

Emerson's growing interest in the abolition movement and his long-standing commitment to the principle of free speech led him into one of the few slavery-issue controversies to upset the normal tranquility of Concord. Although the village was from the earliest times generally sympathetic toward the abolition movement and its proponents, the fiery oratory of inspired abolitionists like Wendell Phillips occasionally offended the sensibilities of some conservatives. Thus an antislavery speech Phillips delivered before the Concord Lyceum in December 1842 was later described by a local critic as "vile, pernicious, and abominable."[57] At a subsequent meeting of the lyceum Phillips was attacked vigorously. Nevertheless, when the proposal was made to invite an antislavery speaker for the following year, Emerson, who was a curator at the time, consented, "provided Mr. Phillips [could] be obtained."[58] At this point Emerson was obviously not afraid to ruffle the feathers of at least some of his Concord neighbors.

Another area of Emerson's life that was touched by his growing concern for abolition at this time was that famous experiment in transcendental publication, the *Dial*. In July 1840 Emerson had high hopes for this new vehicle of thought and expression and felt that it might serve as a means for improving society. Not surprisingly, abolition was a concern with which he hoped the *Dial* might effectively deal. Thus he notes in his journal: "I think that our Dial ought not to be a mere literary journal but that the times demand of us all a more earnest aim. It ought to contain the best advice on topics of Government, Temperance, Abolition, Trade, & Domestic Life" (*JMN* 7:388). As a means toward this end, Emerson, after reluctantly assuming full editorial responsibilities for the *Dial* in 1842, included such items as an article by B. P. Hunt, an American businessman in Haiti, entitled "Saturday and Sunday Among the Creoles: A Letter from the West Indies." This piece compares black children with white in West Indian Sunday schools and finds the blacks fully equal in intelligence, ability, and manners.[59] Emerson was undoubtedly pleased with this report because it probably eased some of his reservations about the equality of the Negro, and the article also contributed to a growing body of works on the subject. In addition to such items, Emerson also personally reviewed John Pierpont's *Antislavery Poems* and William Lloyd Garrison's *Sonnets and Other Poems* in the July 1843 issue. In the former review Emerson expressed his surprise at "how little poetry this old outrage of negro slavery has produced" and applauded Pierpont's efforts. Regarding Garrison's somewhat hobbled attempts at verse, Emerson's innate sense of kindness led him to remark that Garrison "is far more likely to be the subject than the author of good poems."[60]

Despite these gentle personal efforts to promote the principle of abolition, national events in the early 1840s contributed to a growing unease, which Emerson surely felt, regarding both the entrenchment and the threatened expansion of slavery. He was painfully aware of the conspicuous failure of individual moral suasion in ameliorating the problem. The greatest immediate threat came with the movement to annex Texas. A strong, and apparently proslavery, effort had been made to accomplish this goal in the 1830s, and the issue was hotly debated throughout the period of the early 1840s. Abolitionists considered resistance to the movement to be resistance to the slave powers' continued dominance of the Union, and as such it was a matter of utmost importance.[61] Emerson also felt the moral significance of the struggle, and an 1844 journal entry states that "we should . . . resist the annexation [of Texas] with tooth & nail" (*JMN* 9:74). Of course, the most viable and effective resistance on the issue was that offered by organized abolitionists.

Emerson was generally disappointed with what he saw as the failure of elected officials and leaders of the nation to address the problem of slavery from a principled perspective, and their tendency to emphasize mere pragmatic expediency instead. Chief among these was the man who had once been something of a hero to him, Daniel Webster. Although Emerson would eventually castigate Webster publicly in the strongest possible terms because of his support of the Fugitive Slave Law of 1850, as early as 1844 his journals show a growing concern about Webster's lack of principle and his willingness to sidestep such problems as abolition. Webster showed "no respect for an affection to a principle," and if he had "given himself to the cause of Abolition of Slavery in Congress, he would have been the darling of this continent, of all the youth, all the genius, all the virtue in America" (*JMN* 9:90–91).

Undoubtedly adding to Emerson's sense of frustration at this time was the fact that Channing, whose articulate views on the abolition question most resembled Emerson's own, died in 1842. Appropriately enough, Channing's last public address was "Emancipation in the British West-Indies," which he was impelled to give, he said, because he found that "no other voice would be raised."[62] Clearly the time had now come for Emerson himself to speak out specifically and publicly against the moral outrage of slavery. In 1840 he had delivered his lecture "Reforms" in his course "The Present Age," and in the following year he spoke favorably of "Man the Reformer" before the Boston Mercantile Library Association. As late as March 1844 he had delivered his "New England Reformers" lecture in Armory Hall, Boston. However, his emphasis in all of these addresses was, as Channing's had been, on the need for total reform of individuals rather than trying to "make a sally against evil by some single improvement, without supporting it by a total regeneration" (*W* 3:261). In another clear echo of Channing's philosophy, Emerson also applauded the "steady tendency of the thoughtful and virtuous to a deeper belief and reliance on spiritual facts" rather than, for example, political power per se (W 3:255).[63] Clearly it was not in keeping with Emerson's philosophy, his temperament, or his perceived vocation as "scholar" to speak to a single moral and social problem. But the inexorable press of events over the preceding seven years would finally have its effect. His experience in the Divinity School controversy had taught him that he could face the wrath of society and not wilt in the process. His increasing contact with a growing number of active abolitionists, some of whom were among his closest friends, served to raise considerably his opinion of the movement itself, and the pressures from within his own family must also have played a part. But probably most compelling was the clear realization that the power of slavery in the nation was growing ominously. The annexation of Texas was all but inevitable, and the further possibilities for expansion after this were virtually unlimited. The great Webster had faltered, and only a few lesser lights stood ready to shoulder the burden of maintaining government based on principle. In a very real sense Emerson undoubtedly felt that the government he had left alone for the past seven years had finally come to him. Consequently, when the ladies of Concord invited him to speak at their annual August first celebration of emancipation in the British West Indies, he accepted.

Like the scholar he always was and would continue to be, Emerson prepared for his presentation by researching his subject thoroughly. The result of this research itself would be rather remarkable. It served to alter forever Emerson's view of slavery, and it provided him, for the first time, with a vivid and compelling image of the true horror of the institution. Although Emerson had referred to the institution of slavery on many occasions in both sermons and lectures in the 1820s, 1830s, and early 1840s, in all of these instances he saw slavery as a moral abstraction and little more. A brief review of Emerson's previous references to the institution of slavery provides a telling contrast to his 1844 address.

As noted earlier, Emerson's first public reference to the institution of slavery came in his first sermon as a Unitarian minister, which he delivered in 1826. In this sermon, titled "Pray Without Ceasing," the young minister refers to slavery as an example of human suffering that demands a sympathetic Christian response. He tells his listeners that they should avoid being one "who thinks little of the poor man's suffering, or the slave's misery as they cross his path in life."[64] However, despite this early antislavery sentiment, the fact of slavery would remain largely an abstraction for Emerson, something literally remote from his everyday life and the lives of his fold. Additionally, the evil of slavery seemed to be well contained within its borders as a result of the Missouri Compromise of 1820, and he was at this time generally confident that it would eventually succumb to the positive influences of culture and Christian civilization. Thus, in a later sermon entitled "Religion and Society" (1833) Emerson pointed to the existence of abolition societies as evidence that the positive influence of Christianity was being brought to bear on the evils of the world. "Liberal humane Christian associations are correcting the manners and relieving the sufferings of vast masses of men. Bible societies, Temperance societies, Sunday Schools, Peace societies, Seamen's societies, Associations for the correction of Prison Discipline, for the Diffusion of Useful knowledge, for the abolition of slavery, and every other benevolent enterprize,—are they not all the fruit of the life and teaching of that lowly Nazarene?"[65]

Such fragmentary and abstract allusions to slavery and abolition occur frequently in Emerson's early sermons. After leaving the Unitarian church in 1832, he substituted the lecture platform for the pulpit. In the early part of his career as a lecturer he often referred to slavery, but now his references took on a more philosophical cast. For Emerson, the abomination of slavery was simply one more aspect of the general material corruption of American society. Thus, in a lecture entitled "Tragedy," which he delivered in 1839, he points out: "We read King Lear and hate the unkind daughters. But meantime our fathers and mothers find us hard and forgetful as the civility of the times will allow. We swell the cry of horror at the slaveholder and we treat our laborer or farmer or debtor as a thing; women, children, the poor; and so [we] do hold slaves. In the base hour we become slaveholders. We use persons as things."[66]

As with his sermons, Emerson's emphasis here is clearly on the immediate circumstances and experiences of his listeners, and not on the actual fact of slavery, which remains a distant abstraction. One of the reasons for this may well be that Emerson's knowledge of slavery at this time was generally metaphorical; that is, to him it was *like* something else rather than being something in itself. And, as in the case of the example above, the comparisons were often inaccurate. The limitations of Emerson's actual knowledge of slavery are suggested strikingly in a later statement in this same lecture, where he says: "A tender American girl doubts of Divine Providence whilst she reads the horrors of the middle passage. And they are bad enough. But to such as she these crucifixions do not come. They come to the obtuse and barbarous to whom they are not horrid, but only a little worse than the old sufferings. They exchange a cannibal war for the stench of the hold. They have gratifications which would be none to the civilized girl. The market man never damned the lady because she had not paid her bill, but the good Irish woman has that to suffer once a month. She in return never feels weakness in her back because of the slave trade."[67]

Only occasionally would Emerson demonstrate any specific knowledge of the actual conditions suffered by slaves. For example, in "Man the Reformer," a lecture he delivered in January 1841, he points out that "the abolitionist has shown us our dreadful debt to the Southern negro. In the island of Cuba, in addition to the ordinary abominations of slavery, it appears only men are bought for the plantations, and one dies in ten every year, of these miserable bachelors, to yield us sugar" (*CW* 1:147). However, despite such knowledge of conditions, Emerson would continue to suggest that the actual sufferings of the slaves were less significant than might be imagined. In "Lecture on the Times," which he delivered later in the same year, Emerson states: "Then again, how trivial seem the contests of the abolitionist, whilst he aims merely at the circumstance of the slave. Give that slave the least elevation of religious sentiment, and he is no slave; you are the slave; he not only in his humility feels his superiority, feels that much deplored condition of his to be a fading trifle, but he makes you feel it too. He is the master. The exaggeration which our young people make of his wrongs, characterizes themselves. What are no trifles to them, they naturally think are no trifles to Pompey" (*CW* 1:178).

Emerson's transcendental point here, and throughout his lecture, is that true reform cannot come about by merely changing individual circumstances. True reform can come about only as the result of interior changes that reflect "new infusions of the spirit." However, by minimizing the actual horror of the slaves' conditions, Emerson tends to diminish the enthusiasm for reform that would be necessary to move the abolition cause forward effectively. Again, it is the abstract evil of slavery that is foremost in his mind.

In addition to his lack of knowledge regarding the actual conditions of slavery, Emerson apparently had even less knowledge of the nature of Negro slaves themselves. As his earlier comments on the middle passage suggest, he seemed initially to assume that the Negro slaves were generally barbarous and uncivilized, and that for them the hardships of slavery would be only slightly worse than their earlier African existence. Where development does occur, it tends to appear as a natural and uncivilized phenomenon. Thus, in a lecture entitled "Prospects," which Emerson delivered early in 1842, he asserts:

> Nature pours her energy into human beings as she does into particular regions of the world, feeding this from a thousand springs and elements and starving that other. The travellers in some parts of the southwestern country of the United States say that the planter or the factor of the planter becomes a little better than a cottongin; he has no conversation, no thoughts but cotton,—qualities of cotton, long staple and short staple, and its advance or fall a penny or a farthing. They say therefore that the negro is more a man in some districts than the white; alive to more human interests, much the best companion of the two; and how should he not be, since, though low in his organization he is yet no wooden machine but a wild cedar swamp rich with all vegetation of grass and moss and ferns and flags whither come in turn rains and sunshine, mist and moonlight, birds and insects, filling its wilderness with life and promise?[68]

Here Emerson seems to equate the Negro slave with an underdeveloped life form, primitive but full of promise. The statement is positive in this respect but negative in that it seems to deny a full share of intelligence and sensitivity to the slave. Perhaps for this reason more than any other, the problem of slavery would remain a moral and philosophical abstraction for Emerson until August 1844.

The two most important sources for Emerson's emancipation address were, first, *The History of the Rise, Progress, and Accomplishment of the Abolition of the African Slave Trade by the British Parliament*, written by one of Britain's greatest abolitionists, Thomas Clarkson.[69] The work was first published in 1808 and had appeared in a new edition with "remarks on the subsequent abolition of slavery" by Lord Brougham in 1839. Of this work a modern commentator has said, this "large 615-page volume, crammed with facts, depositions, charts, tables, and paraphrases of parliamentary debates . . . is at once history and autobiography. Even today it transmits movingly the simple, powerful personality of its author and his terrible, triumphant testimony. . . . There is a Smolett-like verisimilitude in Clarkson's account of how he interrogated sailors and slavers in the waterfront saloons of Liverpool, and even in his dogged parliamentary reporting one feels what Conrad called the fascination of the abomination. For a reader of 1844 it must have meant what the records of the Nuremberg Trials meant a hundred years later."[70] This commentator continues, "Emerson found in Clarkson's book all he needed to know about the abomination and about the early history of the abolitionist movement."

The second of Emerson's major sources was a work entitled *Emancipation in the West Indies: A Six Month's Tour in Antigua, Barbadoes, and Jamaica, in the Year 1837*, written by James A. Thome and J. Horace Kimball and published in 1838. From this work Emerson learned more about the horrors of slavery, including the dungeons that were attached to every plantation house, the pregnant women forced to work and punished on the treadmill, and a twelve-year-old boy who was made to strip and beat his mother. "As the boy was small, the mother was obliged to get down upon her hands and knees so that the child could inflict the blows on her naked person with a rod. This was done on the public highway, before the mistress's door."[71]

In addition to such distressing revelations, however, Thome and Kimball also found that the experiment in emancipation in the West Indies had been a tremendous success. They reported that the freemen were grateful, happy, industrious, pious, and courteous. Promiscuity and drunkenness had almost vanished, and a multitude of other improvements had occurred, to the point that the white men of the islands, planters and preachers alike, regretted that emancipation had not come sooner. The effect of this reading and other research on Emerson's understanding of the actual character of slavery, and the general nature of the Negro slave, was dramatic. His August 1844 address "Emancipation in the British West Indies" is alive with the emotions of sympathy, outrage, and hope.

The day itself was an auspicious one. Although there were many active abolitionists in Concord in the early 1840s, especially among the women, the movement was not universally appreciated by the more conservative element in the town. Consequently, when the Women's Anti-slavery Association attempted to locate a place for their gathering, they were turned down by all the local churches and had to settle for the courthouse. Henry Thoreau, whose mother was one of the influential women who persuaded Emerson to speak on the subject, was delighted with the prospect and went from door to door to urge his fellow Concordians to attend the meeting. However, the sexton of the First Parish Church refused to ring the town bell in the church steeple to announce the meeting, and the selectmen refused to order him to do so. Never one to be discouraged by such passive resistance in others, Thoreau rushed to the church and rang the bell himself. When he finished, one account indicates, "the key [was] speedily removed, lest the trespass be repeated" (*Liberator*, 23 August 1844). Later, Thoreau would arrange for the publication of the speech in pamphlet form.[72]

Emerson's address begins with the statement that August first has been set aside to celebrate a day in history "which gave the immense fortification of a fact . . . to ethical abstraction," a statement that might be said to describe his own experience as well as the British emancipation to which he actually refers (*W* 11:99). Unlike his earlier statements on slavery in his sermons and lectures, which were characterized by moral and philosophical coolness, Emerson's statements here are fired with an emotional as well as an intellectual appreciation of his subject. He states, for example: "I am heart-sick when I read how they came there, and how they are kept there. Their case was left out of the mind and out of the heart of their brothers. The prizes of society, the trumpet of fame, the privileges of learning, of culture, of religion, the decencies

and joys of marriage, honor, obedience, personal authority and a perpetual melioration into a finer civility,—these were for all, but not for
them" (W 11:102). He goes on to detail specifically the actual sufferings
associated with the slave's condition.

> For the negro, was the slave-ship to begin with, in whose filthy hold he sat
> in irons, unable to lie down; bad food, and insufficiency of that; disfran-
> chisement; no property in the rags that covered him; no marriage, no right
> in the poor black woman that cherished him in her bosom, no right to the
> children of his body; no security from the humors, none from the crimes,
> none from the appetites of his master; toil, famine, insult, and flogging;
> and, when he sank in the furrow, no wind of good fame blew over him,
> no priest of salvation visited him with glad tidings; but he went down to
> death with dusky dreams of African shadow-catchers and Obeahs hunting
> him. (W 11:102–3)

Much of Emerson's factual material was obviously drawn directly
from Thomas Clarkson's vivid account. "But if we saw the whip applied to old men, to tender women; and, undeniably, though I shrink
to say so, to pregnant women set in the treadmill for refusing to work
. . . if we saw men's backs flayed with cowhides, and 'hot rum poured
on, superinduced with brine or pickle, rubbed in with a cornhusk, in
the scorching heat of the sun';—if we saw the runaways hunted with
bloodhounds into swamps and hills; and in cases of passion, a planter
throwing his negro into a copper of boiling cane-juice,—if we saw these
things with eyes, we too should wince" (W 11:104).

Such vivid and gruesome accounts brought home to the gentle Emerson, for the first time, the understanding that the suffering of slavery
was a hard and horrible fact, not an abstraction. The effect on him was
clear and immediate. He says, following the description noted above,
"The blood is moral: the blood is anti-slavery: it runs cold in the veins;
the stomach rises with disgust, and curses slavery" (W 11:104).

In addition to these emotional descriptions of the slave's lot, Emerson
offers a detailed account of his new thinking on the matter of slavery
and abolition. At the outset he makes it clear that he is addressing those
who are "not yet persuaded" (W 11:100) on the slavery question, particularly those who remain indifferent, like the person who "would not

so much as part with his ice cream, to save [the slaves] from rapine and manacles" (*W* 11:101). It is Emerson's intention here to demonstrate to these as well as to the "oldest planters of Jamaica . . . that it is cheaper to pay wages than to own the slave" (*W* 11:101). With this practical as well as moral concern in mind, Emerson offers a lengthy and detailed exposition of the history of black slavery in the British Empire, which includes the moving and emotional accounts of cruelty and exploitation described above. Emerson makes note of the efforts of Granville and William Sharpe in their successful effort in the British courts to emancipate a slave, George Somerset, by emphasizing the spirit as well as the letter of British law in their arguments before Lord Mansfield. Mansfield's decision was monumental and in its effect "established the principle that the 'air of England is too pure for any slave to breathe' " (*W* 11:107), and hence abolished the institution from the mother country. However, the job was not yet complete because "the wrongs in the [British] islands were not thereby touched" (*W* 11:107).

Emerson goes on to present an account of the lengthy but eventually successful efforts of many heroic individuals in England and elsewhere to secure "the relief and liberation of the negro slaves in the West Indies, and for the discouragement of the slave-trade on the coast of Africa" (*W* 11:107). The first victory came on 25 March 1807, when the African trade was abolished. Probably with the American situation in mind, Emerson points out that this significant victory was won when "three hundred thousand persons in Britain pledged themselves to abstain from all articles of island produce," and "the planters were obliged to give way." This development came about despite the opposition of "cold prudence, barefaced selfishness and silent votes," because those who cared insisted on bringing the issue forward until "every horrid fact became known" and "the nation was aroused to enthusiasm" (*W* 11:109), all of which would seem to constitute a fine example of the power of moral suasion. What remained, of course, was the problem of slavery in the West Indies, and this would prove to be a more formidable challenge to the British abolitionists. Horrid details of outrageous abuses of slaves were recounted to the British public, and "these outrages rekindled the flame of British indignation. Petitions poured into Parliament: a million persons signed their names to these," and eventually the British Parliament was persuaded to consider a bill which provided that "all and every person who, on the first August, 1834, shall be holden in slavery within any such British colony as aforesaid, shall upon and from and after the said first August, become and be to all intents and purposes free" (W 11:112). The ministers also wished to provide compensation for the slave owners, and "after much debate, the bill passed by large majorities" (W 11:113).

Emerson goes on to describe briefly the scene of liberation. "The negroes were called together by the missionaries and by the planters, and the news explained to them. On the night of the 31st of July, they met everywhere in their churches, and chapels, and at midnight, when the clock struck twelve, on their knees, the silent, weeping assembly became men; they rose and embraced each other; they cried, they sung, they prayed, they were wild with joy, but there was no riot, [and] no feasting." He had "never read anything in history more touching than the moderation of the negroes," which he refrained from expanding upon because it was generally known and also, "Dr. Channing has given it additional fame" (W 11:115).

The pleasure of freedom was not unmixed for the emancipated slaves in the West Indies, however, because "the habit of oppression was not destroyed by a law and a day of jubilee." Indeed, "it soon appeared in all the islands that the planters were disposed to use their old privileges, and overwork the apprentices; to take from them, under various pretences, their fourth part of time; and to exert the same licentious despotism as before" (W 11:117). This leads Emerson to suggest that while some even now in America, say that "the planter does not want slaves, he only wants the immunities and the luxuries which the slaves yield him," it is his considered opinion that "experience . . . shows the existence, besides the covetousness, of a bitter element [in human nature], the love of power, the voluptuousness of holding a human being in . . . absolute control" (W 11:118).[73] As a result of this unfortunate situation, "Parliament was compelled to pass additional laws for the defense and security of the negro" (W 11:119).

In a summary of the British experience with slavery and abolition,

Emerson notes, first, that England, like America, is a nation primarily interested in commerce, and consequently it possesses "a shopkeeping civility." As a result of this, consciences have often been subordinated to profit, and it was, or it seemed, the dictate of trade to keep the Negro down because "by the aid of a little whipping, we could get their work for nothing" (W 11:123). For some time people seemed satisfied with this arrangement because "the sugar they raised was excellent [and] nobody tasted blood in it." However, says Emerson, this situation could not continue forever, because "man is born with intellect, as well as with a love of sugar; and with a sense of justice, as well as a taste for strong drink" (W 11:124). As a result, as the British example shows, "the repression of the slave recoiled" on the owners, and, "like other robbers, they could not sleep in security" (W 11:125). Along with this fear came the recognition that, economically, freedom is more profitable than slavery because "in every naked negro of those thousands" British merchants "saw a future customer. More than this, the West Indian estate was owned or mortgaged in England, and the owner and the mortgagee had very plain intimations that the feeling of English liberty was gaining every hour new mass and velocity, and the hostility to such as resisted it would be fatal" (W 11:127). Overall, then, Emerson makes it clear that the process of emancipation in the British Empire involved a conjunction of fatalistic forces, including two that most would see as divergent, namely, the development of trade and the instinctive pursuit of justice. Also, the application of moral suasion by British abolitionists, and the consequent willingness of a multitude of average British citizens to make sacrifices in the name of truth and justice, resulted in a great moral victory. As Emerson notes, "On reviewing this history, I think the whole transaction reflects infinite honor on the people and parliament of England" (W 11:127).

Clearly it is Emerson's sublime desire that the same should happen eventually in America. Along these lines he notes, "In the last few days my attention has been occupied with this history, [and] I have not been able to read a page of it without the most painful comparisons. Whilst I have read of England, I have thought of New England" (W 11:129). In America, despite its tradition of freedom and justice, the "patriots and senators" have apparently turned their backs on the slave (W 11:129). The laws of the nation, which presumably protect and defend its citizens, have proved no defense for the black man, whether technically free or not. "Poor black men of obscure employment as mariners, cooks or stewards, in ships, yet citizens of this our Commonwealth of Massachusetts,—freeborn as we," have been arrested under the "slave-laws of the states of South Carolina, Georgia, and Louisiana . . . in vessels in which they visited those ports." Emerson is outraged by this abuse of American manhood and is determined that "this crime will not be hushed up any longer" (W 11:130). In Emerson's view, "the deck of a Massachusetts ship [is] as much the territory of Massachusetts as the floor on which we stand," and he quotes Article 4 of the Constitution of the United States: "The citizens of each State shall be entitled to all privileges and immunities of citizens in the several States." It is clearly Emerson's belief, despite what many have said about his emphasis on self-reliance and his disdain for institutions of all types, that government does have a necessary function, namely, to protect and preserve the freedom that makes self-reliance possible. Hence, he goes on to assert, regarding the illegal arrest and detention of black citizens of Massachusetts in southern ports, "If such a damnable outrage can be committed on the person of a citizen with impunity, let the Governor break the broad seal of the State; he bears the sword in vain." Obviously the power invested in the state has the potential, at least, for constructive use. Laws exist for a purpose, and "the Governor of Massachusetts is a trifler; the State-House in Boston a playhouse; the General Court is a dishonored body, if they make laws which they cannot execute." In such a situation it would seem that "the great-hearted Puritans have left no posterity" to protect the tradition of action based upon principle (W 11:131).

Emerson goes on to suggest that the representatives of the state of Massachusetts should introduce into Congress "extraordinary" legislation, if necessary, to rectify this situation. "The Congress should instruct the President to send to those ports of Charleston, Savannah and New Orleans such orders and such force as should release, forthwith, all such citizens of Massachusetts as were holden in prison without the allegation of any crime" (W 11:132). If the use of force in such a situation should threaten to tear the fabric of the Union, so be it. "The Union already is at an end when the first citizen of Massachusetts is thus outraged."

Emerson reserved his harshest criticism for the elected representatives of the state who failed to address this problem. If, as Emerson believed, every person has a vocation in life through which he serves himself *and* the common good, then these servants of the public have failed miserably. He notes, therefore, that while "loath to say harsh things," he is "at a loss how to characterize the tameness and silence of the two senators and the ten representatives of the State at Washington." To what purpose, wonders Emerson aloud, have we clothed each of these representatives with power, if they "sit dumb at their desks and see their constituents captured and sold." Indeed, it seems to Emerson that at present "there is a disastrous want of *men* from New England" among the representatives in Washington (W 11:133). He sums up his diatribe against these failed politicians by suggesting that "the citizens in their primary capacity take up their cause . . . and say to the government of the State, and of the Union, that government exists to defend the weak and the poor and the injured party; the rich and the strong can better take care of themselves" (W 11:135). Clearly, Emerson was hopeful that the British example of cooperative action between morally concerned citizens and their parliamentary representatives would inform the American scene. Indeed, he ends this portion of his lengthy address with, "As an omen and assurance of success, I point you to the bright example which England set you, on this day, ten years ago." For Emerson, "this event was a moral revolution," and it "was achieved by plain means of plain men, working not under a leader, but under a sentiment. . . . The end was noble and the means were pure" (W 11:135).

In America, as in England, Emerson saw the abolition of slavery as a certainty because the "moral force perpetually reinforces and dignifies the friends of this cause [and] gave that tenacity to their point which has insured ultimate triumph" (W 11:137). This moral force provides strength and inspiration to those who fight on the side of righteousness, with the result that it is "a proverb in Massachusetts, that 'eloquence is dog-cheap at the anti-slavery chapel.'" Perhaps in order to compensate for some of the harsh statements he had made about certain abolitionists in the past, statements that had been mistakenly taken by some as an indictment of the cause itself, Emerson here is nothing less than laudatory. "I will say farther that we are indebted mainly to this movement and to the continuers of it, for the popular discussion of every point of practical ethics, and a reference of every question to the absolute standard." It is the result of the "free and daring discussions of [their] assemblies" that men are now considering the political, religious, and social schemes which will bring an end to slavery. Because of the obvious inertia of the political leadership of the moment, it is necessary to develop strategies that go beyond conventional political means in order to bring about reform. "Virtuous men will not again rely on political agents," because "the seats of power are filled by underlings, ignorant, timid and selfish to a degree to destroy all claim . . . to the society of the just and generous. . . . Up to this day we have allowed to statesmen a paramount social standing, and we bow low to them as to the great" (*W* 11:138). But no more. The political process must be made subordinate to the expressed will of the people because "the stream of human affairs flows its own way, and is very little affected by the activity of legislators." Ultimately, says Emerson, in an almost Jacksonian statement of political philosophy, "what great masses of men wish done, will be done" (*W* 11:139).

The last issue that Emerson deals with in his address is a matter of critical importance in the evolution of his abolitionism, namely, the equality of the Negro. As Emerson makes clear in this presentation, and as he would affirm in several subsequent public presentations over the next three decades, the Negro is indeed a person in every sense of the word. "The First of August marks the entrance of a new element into modern politics, namely, the civilization of the negro. A man is added to the human family." In Emerson's eyes, "not the least affecting part of this history of abolition is the annihilation of the old indecent nonsense about the nature of the negro" (*W* 11:140). Clearly, Emerson's study of the subject has brought him to a new understanding of the depth of black culture, and he relates from his readings how "Mr. Clarkson, early in his career, made a collection of African productions and manufactures, as specimens of the art and culture of the negro; comprising cloths and loom, weapons, polished stones and woods, leather, glass, dyes, ornaments, soap, pipe-bowls and trinkets" (W 11:140). Clarkson's effort was persuasive, and, as Emerson relates, "In 1791, Mr. Wilberforce announced to the House of Commons, 'we have already gained one victory: we have obtained for these poor creatures the recognition of their human nature, which for a time was most shamefully denied them.'" Clearly, for Emerson, the sometimes degraded situation of the Negro is the product of his enslavement and the resulting state of arrested development. "The white has, for ages, done what he could to keep the negro in that hoggish state. His laws have been furies." Fortunately, the situation can be reversed, and it now appears that "the negro race is, more than any other, susceptible of rapid civilization" (W 11:141). In describing the positive developments that followed the British emancipation, Emerson stresses the fact that the blacks "won the pity and respect which they have received, by their powers and native endowments" (W 11:142). For Emerson, this is "a circumstance of the highest import [because] their whole future is in it." The question that had so disturbed him in his earlier speculations regarding the future of the Negro race has now been answered. Because blacks have within them the talents and capacities necessary for survival and progress, their triumph is assured. With this new insight, the concerns of the past, and even the sins of the past, are transcended. "Who cares for oppressing whites, or oppressed blacks, twenty centuries ago, more than for bad dreams." While some have assumed that what has been done always will be done, Emerson disagrees. There is a spirit that animates man and his world, a spirit that both creates and destroys, and "it will only save what is worth saving; and it saves not by compassion, but by power" (W 11:143). In this view of things, "if the black man is feeble and not important to the existing races, not on a parity with the best race, the black man must serve, and be exterminated. But if the black man carries in his bosom an indispensable element of a new and coming civilization; for the sake of that element, no wrong nor strength nor circumstance can hurt him; he will survive and play his part." The well-documented exploits and sacrifices of such representative figures as "Touissant, and the Haytian heroes, or of the leaders of their race in Barbadoes and Jamaica" are compelling; they suggest to Emerson that the American struggle will be crowned with a similar success.[74] "The anti-slavery of the whole world is dust in the balance before this,—is a poor squeamishness and nervousness: the might and the right are here: here is the anti-slave: he is man: and if you have man, black or white is an insignificance" (W 11:144).

Emerson's address concludes on an optimistic and inspiring note that shows his willingness to consider, now, the possibility of a collective rather than an exclusively individualistic development of society. "Seen in masses, it cannot be disputed, there is progress in human society. There is a blessed necessity by which the interest of men is always driving them to the right; and, again, making all crime mean and ugly." The amelioration of social ills is assured by the steady and continuous development of human culture. "The sentiment of Right, once very low and indistinct, but ever more articulate, because it is the voice of the universe, pronounces Freedom," and "the Power that built the fabric of things affirms it in the heart; and in the history of the First of August, has made a sign to the ages, of his will" (W 11:147).[75]

Unlike his faltering effort in 1837, this speech was a huge success with the abolitionists. In the minds of many it aligned Emerson clearly with their cause. Thus, on 23 August, the *Liberator*, which had already reported the speech thoroughly in the 16 August issue, ran an article that had appeared earlier in the *Boston Courier* and that noted pointedly, "Before we saw notice of this celebration, we were not aware that Mr. Emerson had sufficiently identified himself with the abolitionists, as a party, to receive such a distinguished token of their confidence." Now it seems he was.

George Curtis, who was a young Brook Farmer at the time, was present for the address and testified to Emerson's personal exuberance on the occasion in a letter to Isaac Hecker. "On Thursday, August 1, the Abolitionists celebrated the Anniversary of W. I. Emancipation and Mr. Emerson read an address. It was not of that cold, clear, intellectual character that chills so many people, but full of ardent Life. His recent study of Anti Slavery history has infused a fine enthusiasm into his spirit & the address was very eloquent."[76]

The event certainly was a giant step forward for Emerson. The historical developments of the 1840s would draw him deeper into the vortex of active abolitionism and further from the conservative principles of moralists such as Channing. Clearly, in Emerson's view at this time the British experience offered a compelling example of the magnificent results that can be wrought when, through the free expression of truth and the power of moral suasion, action devolves from principle. Unlike Channing, Emerson saw the role that government can and must play in either enforcing laws that ensure the freedom of individuals or removing laws that are an obstacle to that freedom, with the sword if necessary. If elected representatives fail to represent the best sentiments of the people, then they should be removed. In any event, what the masses of men want done will be done, in America as in England. Unfortunately, as events in the latter half of the decade would show, the power of freedom was not necessarily in the ascendancy. Faced with the aggressive expansion of slavery, Emerson would feel increasingly compelled to amplify his own participation in an organized opposition to this growing evil. There can be no doubt that in August 1844 Emerson made the transition from antislavery to abolition, and his association with organized abolitionists would continue to grow from this point forward.

Chapter Four

Confusion
and Commitment:
1844–1849

The remainder of the 1840s was a period of increasing involvement and, at times, depression and confusion for Emerson regarding the growing national debate over abolition, the means by which it might best be effected, and the particular role he would play in the process. On the one hand, he remained committed to his earlier belief in the obligation of the individual to improve his world, an idea he had expressed so eloquently in "The American Scholar." On the other hand, however, he began to think seriously about the concept of inevitable amelioration alluded to in his emancipation address. In the extensive journal notes for that address, for example, he indicates that "the use of geology has been to wont the mind to a new chronology. The little dame school measures by which we had gauged everything, we have learned to disuse, & [we] break up our European & Mosaic & Ptolemaic schemes for the grand style of nature & fact." What Emerson sees now in nature is an "evergoing progression" that leads "onward & onward" (*JMN* 9:123–24). Positive progressive development appeared inevitable to him, and he felt confident that social melioration would certainly occur regardless of individual efforts at reform.[1] The tension between these essentially opposing views of the freedom of the individual and the deterministic nature of his world would remain problematical for Emerson throughout the decade.

Contributing to this tension was the continuing ambiguity that Emerson felt regarding his proper role in a necessary and noble abolition effort. He felt strongly the presence of the evils of the world and held that the correction of these evils was "not a work for society, but for me to do," and that "if I am born to it, I shall see the way" (*JMN* 9:85). However, at the same time he continued to be very uncomfortable with the tactics of public debate and associated action, and for the most part preferred to promote the cultivation of virtue in individuals. Thus, immediately following the journal outline of his 1844 address, he asks, "Does not he do more to abolish Slavery who works all day steadily in his garden, than he who goes to the abolition meeting & makes a speech?" (*JMN* 9:126). Despite this reluctance, however, the dramatic historical events of the decade would repeatedly draw Emerson to the heated agitation of the antislavery platform.

As we have seen, Emerson's August first speech was a milestone in the development of his abolitionism, and it served to bring him closer to many relatives, friends, and associates who had been encouraging him for some time to become more actively involved in the movement. The speech itself was widely noticed and warmly received by abolitionists. Garrison praised it in the *Liberator*, Nathaniel Rogers enthusiastically approved in an article in the *Herald of Freedom*, and the speech was published in pamphlet form in both the United States and Great Britain. One abolitionist recalled years later that Wendell Phillips "was wont for years to keep it on hand for distribution."[2] Emerson received many expressions of thanks and appreciation for his effort from both near and far. Aunt Mary Moody, who had remained an enthusiastic supporter of the abolition cause since her conversion in 1835, wrote a warm letter of praise to her famous nephew on the day of the oration. It was apparently a long-awaited event for Aunt Mary, and she begins, "I am writing to the very orator of this auspicious day, to congratulate his condition." She indicates her concern regarding his seven years of silence and explains, "I ask no pardon for suspicion; for I am so ignorant of any one of the sides of your interior, that *that* given to this day I've heard nothing of since you canonized Lovejoy as a martyr." Despite this concern, Aunt Mary concludes her missive on a positive note and assures her nephew, somewhat prophetically, that if a moment arrives "when the antagonist powers of evil shall prevail for a time over the good, you shall be found among the faithful few, bearing a witness . . . and truth and love will finally cover the whole race of redeemed man and slave."[3]

As might be expected, Concord's most indefatigable abolitionist, Mary Merrick Brooks, was delighted with Emerson's August first performance. In a letter written several weeks after the event she conveyed to him a medal, probably awarded by the American Anti-slavery Society, in recognition of his service to the abolition cause. It was now assumed, noted Mrs. Brooks, that Emerson had reached "the same conclusions" regarding "the necessary disposition of heart for the prosecution of the Cause [of] anti-slavery . . . to which the American Society came when the idea was presented by Garrison."[4] In a similar vein, John Greenleaf Whittier, the outstanding abolitionist poet of the age, wrote to Emerson a short time after his address to request his appearance at an upcoming "Middlesex County Convention of the Friends of Liberty." Whittier states in his letter, "that you join with us in supporting the great *idea* which underlies our machinery of conventions & organizations, I have little doubt after reading thy Address."[5] And last, Maria Chapman, one of Boston's leading female abolitionists, noted in a draft article on Emerson sometime after his speech in 1844 that "the abolitionists have been greatly cheered & strengthened by the words of Emerson."[6]

When preparing "Emancipation in the West Indies" for publication, Emerson went to considerable lengths to gather precise and detailed information on his topic. As with his "Concord Discourse" in 1835 and *English Traits* in 1856, Emerson was determined to master his subject as thoroughly as possible. In this case his research would bring him into further contact with prominent abolitionists. Among them was his friend Ellis Gray Loring, to whom he wrote requesting further information on several specific issues touched upon in his speech. Loring, a prominent abolition lawyer and one of the founders of the New England Anti-slavery Society, was more than happy to comply with Emerson's requests. In his lengthy letter Loring provided specific and detailed information on several matters, including accounts of black citizens of New England who were "imprisoned in New Orleans without the allegation of any crime"; the English Act of Emancipation, a description of which Loring provided in a volume of the *Law Reporter*, which, he indicated, "it is important to have returned soon"; and the Somerset case, where a Negro who was brought by his master from Boston to England in 1772 successfully sued for a writ of habeas corpus when his master attempted to take him back to America. According to Loring, Lord Mansfield allowed the writ on the grounds that "the state of slavery is of such a nature that it is incapable of being introduced [into England] on any reason, moral or political." Mansfield considered the institution "so odious that nothing [could] be suffered to support it but positive Law." The case was described in *Loffts' Reports*, which Loring also forwarded to Emerson, pointing out that "Hargraves' argument" in the case is "justly celebrated." The last specific item Loring refers to in his letter is "Ship Zong," a case where a slave ship captain in 1781 ordered several slaves thrown overboard and was later prosecuted for the crime. Loring states that "the presiding judge *must* have instructed [the jury] that the Captain was justified in throwing over Slaves, if the scarcity of water made it necessary for the safety & health of the crew," and he adds, "the case was never reported till 1831."

At the conclusion of his letter Loring refers to Emerson's recent address, which he was unable to attend. However, he expected "much satisfaction from it judging by W. H. Channing's sketch." Loring was uncomfortable with one aspect of the speech, however, and that was Emerson's statement that if the black man proved feeble and not important to the existing races, he would be made to serve and finally "exterminated." Of course, as noted earlier, Emerson was confident that this would *not* be the case, but Loring did not "like the idea of 'extermination' of the feebler races of men," and while "W. Geo. Ticknor's remedy for Slavery is . . . 'extermination,'" this seems to be "a cool and summary mode of settling the question." Ticknor, a professor of modern languages at Harvard, was an outspoken opponent of abolitionism, and Loring was apparently concerned that Emerson, by mentioning "extermination," may have inadvertently reinforced Ticknor's position. Loring hoped Ticknor and others like him had "more to do than to prove the inferiority of the negro, before [they] can make [extermination] the established doctrine." In Loring's view, "The negro may be inferior, but a man's a man for a' that."[7]

Loring's letter concludes on a positive and personal note by expressing gratitude to Emerson for providing encouragement at a time in the past when he had sorely needed it. Emerson, ever the optimist, had apparently once rebuked Loring for his despondency following "an Anti-Slavery meeting at Faneuil Hall, which proved spiritless." Loring never forgot the incident, and the lesson, "given some years since," was apparently much appreciated. "It is due to you & a satisfaction to me to make this acknowledgement," said Loring, and he signed his letter "truly your friend, Ellis Gray Loring."

Emerson returned the *Law Reporter* volume to Loring within a few days, as requested. In his accompanying letter he expressed his gratitude for Loring's "generous & prompt attention" to his requests, which "must have been very troublesome on a busy day." But "you have answered them so well, that I only believe you delight to oblige." Emerson apparently read carefully the materials Loring had provided, and he agreed with Loring's assessment that "Mr. Hargraves' argument was justly celebrated" and notes that "the matters that went before & followed after it led me far aside from my lesson." The result was that he wished to keep the remaining books "a little longer," and he hoped that he had not already kept them too long. Regarding Loring's concern about his reported statements on the nature and fate of the Negro, Emerson indicates that in revising his manuscript he had not quite reached that which "touches the destiny of the negro race, . . . to see whether any offensive or unauthorized expressions occur." He goes on to note that the comments "shall certainly be considered, when they appear, in the warm light you hold up to me."[8]

Eventually Emerson finished his revisions and apparently made good use of the materials and information provided by Loring. On 9 September 1844 the *Boston Daily Advertiser* announced the publication of "An Address . . . in Concord . . . on 1st August, 1844, on the Anniversary of the Emancipation of the Negroes in the British West Indies" (*L* 3: 259). Before the year was out, John Chapman issued a London edition of the piece, and Emerson pronounced himself "very well contented with the handsome pamphlet" (*L* 3:273). Apparently the printed version of the speech was as pleasing as the original address to the abolitionists, and undoubtedly it allayed any fears that Loring might have had about Emerson's views on "extermination." Whittier, in reviewing it for the 12 September issue of the *Middlesex Standard*, congratulated Emerson for his active commitment to the cause, and undoubtedly he spoke for many abolitionists in noting that "we had previously, we confess, felt half indignant that, while we were struggling against the popular current, mobbed, hunted, denounced, from the legislative forum, cursed from the puplit, sneered at by wealth and fashion and shallow aristocracy, such a man as Ralph Waldo Emerson should be brooding over his pleasant philosophies, writing his quaint and beautiful essays, in his retirement on the banks of the Concord, unconcerned and 'calm as a summer's morning.' "[9] Clearly, he was now perceived in a distinctly different light. In the eyes of many abolitionists Emerson had crossed a major threshold.

Although pleased with the success of his speech, Emerson was not altogether at ease with the role of public crusader that was thus thrust upon him.[10] He was also sensitive to the perception that such presentations were highly relevant and useful for the times, while others of a more philosophical or general nature, by implication at least, were not. This criticism was disturbing to Emerson because he believed that the best contribution that he, or anyone, could make to the cause of freedom and justice would be to follow his own talents and virtuous inclinations, and in his case neither of these would naturally lead to an abolition platform. It is not surprising, then, that in a letter to Carlyle in December 1844 Emerson sounds more than a bit defensive on the subject.

> You Londoners know little of the dignities & duties of country Lyceums But of what you say now & heretofore respecting the remoteness of my writing & thinking from real life, though I hear substantially the same criticism made by my countrymen, I do not know what it means. If I can at any time

express the law & the ideal right, that should satisfy me without measuring the divergence from it of the last act of Congress. And though I sometimes accept a popular call, & preach on Temperance or the Abolition of slavery, as lately on the First of August, I am sure to feel before I have done with it, what an intrusion it is into another sphere & so much loss of virtue in my own (*CEC* 373).

These reservations did not prohibit Emerson from maintaining an active interest in the abolition question, however, and, perhaps with future speeches in mind, he sought throughout the period of the 1840s to improve his knowledge of both the history of abolition and of contemporary events related thereto.[11] Also, despite his reluctance, political and social events during this time would continue to stir in Emerson a rather pronounced interest in the relationship between "the ideal right" and the "last act of Congress."

One of the first of these provocative events occurred in the same month as Emerson's letter to Carlyle. His friend and Concord neighbor, Samuel Hoar, had been sent to South Carolina as an agent of the state of Massachusetts to investigate complaints that black sailors on Massachusetts ships were being seized illegally. This appointment must have been particularly pleasing to Emerson given the specific concern he showed regarding this situation in his emancipation address. Before Hoar could even begin his task, however, both he and his daughter Elizabeth (Charles Emerson's former fiancée) were driven from Charleston by the threats of an angry mob, apparently acting with the implicit approval of the governor and legislature. Emerson was outraged, in part because of his personal nearness to the victims but also because he was concerned that the forces of reason, civilization, and culture had again in this instance, as with the antiabolition mobs of the late 1830s, been defeated by brute force. Emerson considered Hoar's courageous behavior to be clearly admirable and in keeping with the highest ideals of the state. In an apparent response to the criticisms of the younger William Ellery Channing, who was working at Horace Greeley's *Tribune* at the time and who questioned, along with Greeley, the propriety of Hoar's apparently hasty retreat, Emerson related in detail the facts of the case as he heard them from Hoar. In his letter, which was published in the

Tribune on 20 December 1844, he concludes that Mr. Hoar "has done all that a man can do in the circumstances and has put his own state in the best position which truth and honor required. When all the particulars of this little history appear, you may be assured they will reflect the greatest credit on the Commissioner."[12]

Regarding South Carolina, Emerson continued to feel a deep contempt for what he saw as the barbarism of the place.[13] In his journal he prepared appropriate remarks for a public "indignation meeting" that was held in Concord on 22 January 1845 to protest the expulsion of Hoar.[14] Clearly, Emerson was still "stirred up," as one observer put it, by this episode even a month later, and he felt that too many people were simply willing to ignore the issue.[15] In his journal he notes that "the Boston merchants would willingly salve the matter over, but they cannot hereafter receive Southern gentlemen at their tables, without a consciousness of shame" (*JMN* 9:161). As for the state of South Carolina, "it has excluded every gentleman, every man of honour, every man of humanity, every freeman from its territory" and, because of this, it is a place "where a great man cannot live" (*JMN* 9:173–74). He then goes on to contrast the culture of Massachusetts with the barbarism of South Carolina in terms that, for Emerson, are unusually acerbic. "I am far from wishing that Mass. should retaliate if we could bring down the New England culture to the Carolina level, if we were to cartwhip gentlemen, it might be possible to retaliate very effectively, and to the apprehensions of Southerners." Massachusetts citizens might also "shut up Mr Calhoun and Mr Rhett when they come to Boston as hostages for the mulattoes & negroes they have kidnapped from the caboose & the cabin of our ships." However, "the New England culture is not so low. Ours is not a brutal people, but intellectual and mild" (*JMN* 9:174).

Emerson's journal remarks undoubtedly reflect the tone of the meeting. George Curtis, who was present at the affair, later reported to his friend Christopher Pearse Cranch that Concord's Unitarian minister was "vehement" in his presentation and "wrote resolutions so fiery, so fiercely redolent of disunion, independency, and Massachusetts dignity, so sadly blood and thunderous, that the committee, Mr. May, Secretary Palfrey, Mr. Emerson, William White, Mr. Mellen, and himself would not report them." Instead, "more sober and discreet resolves were introduced." Curtis was disappointed with the meeting overall because scarcely a hundred people attended, which led him to ask, somewhat like Emerson, if there is "no feeling in the hearts of the people, about this matter?"[16]

Despite this expression of ire and outrage at the incident, Emerson's journal asserts his faith that in the long run the forces of goodness, expressed in the civilizing influence of "culture," will inevitably prevail over brute force. "New times have come & new policy subtler & nobler & more strong than any before. It is the inevitable effect of culture—it cannot be otherwise—to dissolve the animal ties of brute strength, to insulate, to make a country of men" (*JMN* 9:174).

The question of the annexation of Texas was also discussed at the Concord meeting, and here the growing tension between Emerson's long-held belief in the need for individual moral integrity, especially in dealing with the immediate affairs of the world, and his developing belief in the deterministic long-term progress of human experience becomes apparent. In the latter context a proximate evil may be an ultimate good, and such, apparently, is the way Emerson chose to interpret affairs in Texas. Thus, earlier in his journal Emerson had noted that "it is quite necessary & true to our New England character that we should resist the annexation with tooth & nail" because morality requires it. On the other hand, however, he accepted the fact that "it is very certain that the strong British race which have now overrun so much of this continent, must also overrun that tract, & Mexico & Oregon also, and it will in the course of ages be of small import by what particular occasions & methods it was done" (*JMN* 9:74). At the Concord protest meeting he apparently reiterated this fatalistic view and contended confidently that while "the annexation of Texas looks like one of those events which retard or retrograde the civilization of ages," in the long run ultimate good will come from it because "the World Spirit is a good swimmer, and storms & waves cannot easily drown him" (*JMN* 9:180). Of course, such a philosophy could easily suggest a quiet indifference regarding what might be seen as merely momentary social evils, and Emerson was certainly pulled in that direction at times. However, throughout the 1840s he was consistently concerned with current events and their moral implications. Just a week later Emerson attended the Texas convention in Boston in order to hear the issue debated further. There he hoped to "catch some volcanic sparks of the Typhonic rage," but he was disappointed to hear "only smooth whig speeches on moderation" (*JMN* 9:109–10).

Generally, Emerson attempted during this period to accommodate the apparently contrary demands of his philosophy of inevitable improvement and the active call to social reform by insisting that every individual should do what he felt was naturally virtuous and appropriate to further society's inherent tendency toward melioration. Thus, he notes in his journal that while we accept the idea that "the actual world . . . is the best that could yet be," it nevertheless still possesses recognizable evils that must be remedied. "The remedying is not a work for a society but for me to do. . . . I also feel the evil for I am covetous and I do not prosecute the reform because I have another task nearer." Regardless of such disinclination, however, Emerson maintains that "substantial justice can be done," and indeed in his own attack on society's evils he "is to lose no time in fumbling & striking about in all directions but [should] mind the work that is mine, and accept the facilities & openings which my constitution affords me" (*JMN* 9:85). One of these constitutional opportunities came very soon.

In January 1845 Emerson once again was called upon to defend the right of Wendell Phillips to speak on the subject of slavery in the Concord Lyceum. And again he was joined in his effort by Henry Thoreau. In his journal Emerson explains that he argued for the acceptance of Phillips on two grounds. First, the lyceum was poor and could use the services of "one of the best speakers in the Commonwealth," and, second, because "in the present state of this country the particular subject of Slavery had a commanding right to be heard in all places in New England in season & sometimes out of season." The fact of slavery is so outrageous that "the people must consent to be plagued with it from time to time until something was done & we had appeased the negro blood so" (*JMN* 9:102). When the lyceum eventually voted to invite Phillips, the issue had become controversial enough that two curators resigned in protest, and Emerson, Thoreau, and Samuel Barrett were chosen to replace them. On 11 March 1845 Phillips delivered his speech. The next day Thoreau sent his only known "letter to the editor" celebrating the event, and Garrison gladly printed it in the *Liberator* on 28 March.[17] Emerson was delighted with Phillips's presentation, and in a letter to Samuel Ward noted that he "had not learned a better lesson in many weeks than last night in a couple of hours," and that Phillips was "the best generator of eloquence I have met for many a day."[18] As this episode suggests, the process of social melioration that Emerson envisioned at this time continued to rely a good deal upon the effect and influence of individual moral suasion in fostering the natural tendency of things toward goodness and improvement. What was necessary, according to Emerson, as in the case of Massachusetts and South Carolina in the Hoar affair, was the clear recognition of the moral superiority of one position over the other. Through this means culture and civilization would have their day, and the ultimate victory would be ensured.

Further indication of this thinking is evident in Emerson's support of Nathaniel P. Rogers in a dispute that arose at this time regarding his editorship of the antislavery journal the *Herald of Freedom*. This paper, the official organ of the New Hampshire Anti-slavery Society, was greatly admired by both Emerson, who was a subscriber, and Thoreau, and both appreciated the reasonableness and philosophical broadness of its writing. Under the editorship of Rogers the *Herald* was temperate in its views and avoided narrow, vituperative polemics. Thoreau, in an admiring article published in the *Dial* in April 1844, noted that "such timely, pure, and unpremeditated expressions of public sentiment, such publicity of genuine indignation and humanity, as abound everywhere in this journal, are the most generous gifts which a man can make."[19] Eventually, Rogers, like Emerson, became convinced that all reform must be of an individual nature, and in 1844 he began to call for the dissolution of all antislavery societies because they discouraged such necessary individuality. As a result, in December of that year Rogers was removed from the editorship of the *Herald* by William Lloyd Garrison, and eventually he was replaced by Parker Pillsbury, a Garrison loyalist. The event caused quite a stir in abolition circles and elsewhere, and

Confusion and Commitment

Emerson was moved to note, "What driveling is this, the examination of all the papers written on both sides in this brawl of the Herald of Freedom to see whether Rogers or Pillsbury is right. Rogers of course, & without or against any or all statements" (*JMN* 9:204).

Emerson's response to this conflict indicates that despite his growing association with, and admiration for, Garrison, Phillips, and other abolition activists, he still differed substantially from them. Emerson was yet inclined to maintain his faith that in the long run ultimate good would win out. What was necessary now, in his view, was the exercise of sublime patience in awaiting the beneficial effects of consistent moral suasion and cultural "revolution." Emerson's second major address on slavery, which came one year after the first, on 1 August 1845, reflects, in part, the influence of this philosophical position. Although the manuscript has apparently not been preserved, the speech was thoroughly reported in the *New York Tribune* and the *Liberator*, and fragments of it appear in the journals.[20] The oration was delivered at a large gathering, which was part of an all-day celebration sponsored by the abolitionists of Middlesex and Suffolk counties held at Harrington's grove in Waltham, Massachusetts. Occupying the speaker's platform with Emerson on this occasion were, among others, the Reverend William H. Channing, Emerson's friend and a longtime abolitionist; William I. Bowditch, abolitionist and brother of the prominent physician Henry I. Bowditch; and Henry Wilson, a member of the Massachusetts legislature at this time and later a senator and vice president. Also present was Jonathan Walker, a sea captain who had been branded and forced to serve a year in a southern jail for the crime of transporting escaping slaves to the Bahamas. Emerson later remembered "Walker of the branded hand" in his journal (*JMN* 9:411).

Emerson's speech on this occasion emphasizes the justice of the slaves' cause, pointing out that the primary objection that discouraged the helpful cooperation of well-meaning men in the slaves' struggle for freedom has been "the objection of an inferiority of race," summarized in the word "Niggers." For Emerson, "they who say it and they who hear it, think it the voice of nature and fate pronouncing against the Abolitionist and Philanthropist." As was the case a year earlier, Emerson unleashes some of his strongest language in attacking the waywardness of this view and the apathy it encouraged. He asks of those who are convinced of the Negro's inferiority: "And what is the amount of this conclusion in which the men of New England acquiesce? It is, that the Creator of the Negro has given him up to stand as a victim of a caricature of the white man beside him; to stoop under his pack, and to bleed under his whip." Emerson finds such cosmic injustice unacceptable and goes on to assert, "If that be the doctrine, then, I say, if He has given up his cause, He has also given up mine, who feel his wrong, and who in our hearts must curse the Creator who has undone him." As it turns out, however, such a dire response is not required because it is not God but man who has sinned, and "the Universe is not bankrupt," for "still stands the old heart firm in its seat." It is Emerson's belief that "come what will, the right is and shall be. Justice is for ever and ever." Emerson goes on to note that a "sound argument [is] derived from facts collected in the United States and in the West Indies, in reply to this alleged hopeless inferiority of the colored race." It is unnecessary to present such data, however, because the sheer "sentiment of right" is so much stronger as an argument.

Regarding the planters, Emerson here refers to their "unsafe and unblest condition" and warns that "a revolution is preparing at no distant day to set these disjointed matters right." This revolution will be the fulfillment of an inevitable process of improvement, which is both natural and moral. Thus Emerson notes that "moral power secures the welfare of the black man" and "the hope and the refuge of the weaker individual and the weaker races is here." He warns that "it will not always be reputable to steal and to oppress. It will not always be possible. Every new step taken in the true order of human life takes out something of brutality and infuses something of good will." Such improvement will come naturally and inevitably to both the slave and his master because "precisely as it is the necessity of grass to grow, of the child to be born, of light to shine, of heat to radiate, and of matter to attract, so it is of man's race and every race to rise and refine. All things strive to ascend, and ascend in their striving." Unlike a year earlier, Emerson here emphasizes that this process of amelioration requires the special cooperation of the slave owners, and he says of the slaves, "Their fate now, as far as it depends on circumstances, depends on the rising of their masters." Undoubtedly with the Hoar affair still in mind, Emerson recognizes the stubborn barbarism of the South but suggests, nonetheless, that cultural improvement can occur. "Elevate, enlighten, civilize the semi-barbarous nations of South Carolina, Georgia, Alabama—take away from their debauched society the Bowie-knife, the rum bowl, the dice-box, and the stews—take out the brute and infuse a drop of civility and generosity, and you touch those selfish lords with thought and gentleness."

His oration concludes on an optimistic note, as usual, reminding his abolitionist friends that it is "required of every right-thinking and right-feeling man [to] exercise a . . . sublime patience" and to "listen to what the years and centuries say to the hours and the days." It was Emerson's belief at this time that "those who hope and trust, are always proved right." However, the subtle shift in Emerson's presentation from an emphasis on the slave's responsibility to evolve into the "anti-slave," which he asserted in 1844, to a clear recognition that the slave owners must somehow be removed from their oppressive positions before this can come about, would prove an important matter as Emerson's abolitionism continued to evolve.

Not surprisingly, after breaking the ice regarding abolition oratory, Emerson continued to receive many requests throughout the 1840s to speak before antislavery groups. Some of these he accepted and others he rejected, either because he felt that he had nothing new to say on the topic or because he was simply preoccupied with other matters. In most instances, however, he indicated that he would consider such invitations as "a door left open" in case "anything good & reasonable" should come into his thoughts on the subject of slavery.[21]

Emerson returned to the public forum again in September 1845 to attend the Middlesex Convention in Concord, which was called to oppose the annexation of Texas. He probably spoke on this occasion, and the draft of his presentation goes some way toward explaining the apparent ambiguity of his earlier journal comments on the Texas question. His major concern in his September speech is not that Texas will be annexed but that the people of Massachusetts who see the event and the method as evil, whatever its long-range benefits, have accepted the fact sheepishly. He states at the outset that "the great majority of Massachusetts people are essentially opposed to the annexation, but they have allowed their voice to be muffled by the persuasion that it would be of no use." He goes on to complain of such "timorous and imbecile behavior" in the matter and insists that while "the addition of Texas to the Union is not material" because "the same population will possess her in either event," it is his wish that "the private position of the men of this neighborhood, of this country, of this State, should be erect in this matter." Emerson concludes that if the people of the state of Massachusetts oppose the event on any of a variety of moral grounds, then let the state collectively express this opposition and "utter a cheerful and peremptory No, and not a confused, timid, and despairing one." [22] What is important in the great flow of events is not necessarily the events themselves but the moral force that individuals exert in dealing with them. This affirms a long-held belief, first expressed in the "American Scholar," that "this time, like all times, is a very good one, if we but know what to do with it" (CW 1:67). Emerson insists upon a moral sensibility as a necessary ingredient in furthering the movement toward goodness, and he abhors the moral stupor and skepticism that allow evil to thrive. Thus he notes: "A few foolish & cunning managers ride the conscience of this great country with their Texas or Tariff or Democracy or other mumbo jumbo, & all give in & are verily persuaded that that is great,—all else is trifling. And why? Because there is really no great life; not one demonstration in all the broad land of that which is the heart & soul of every rational American Man. . . . Our virtue runs in a narrow rill: we have never a freshet. We ought to be subject to enthusiasms. One would like to see Boston & Massachusetts agitated like a wave with some generosity, mad for learning, for music, for philosophy, for association, for freedom, for art." Obviously, what Emerson had in mind here is the further domestication of the revolutionary ideal of culture, which brings with it progress and light. However, this was manifestly not the case in 1845, and he concludes that, unfortunately, Massachusetts now "goes like a pedlar with its hand ever on its pocket, cautious, calculating" (JMN 9:186, 207–8).

Confusion and Commitment

The Middlesex Convention, after adjourning in Concord, met again on 21 October in Cambridge. Once again Emerson attended, though he arrived late and "found a handful of people, perhaps all told, twenty" (*L* 3:307). He bore with him a letter from Whittier, which was to be read at the meeting and later printed. The letter, which was nominally addressed to Emerson, expresses sentiments very similar to those he uttered in the September meeting. Among other things, Whittier notes that "amidst the general silence and apathy in which the great mass of the community, seems settling down, while this damning inequity of Texas annexation is reaching its consummation, I welcome your manly voice; and receive it, in good faith, as an honest effort to rally all who really love freedom, for a united stand against the encroachment of her eternal foe." Whittier urges all to take specific political action against the supporters of slavery. He asserts that "the northern freeman who is really opposed to slavery, cannot lack an opportunity for assailing it. Those who have voted for slaveholders can at least vote against them," and he goes on to urge support for the Liberty party and its campaign against annexation.[23] Given Emerson's commitment to the power of the ballot box, a commitment that would reach its fulfillment in his stump campaign for John Gorham Palfrey in the spring of 1851, he no doubt agreed with these sentiments. While he did not have an opportunity to read Whittier's letter to the convention because of his late arrival, Emerson did forward it for publication, in accordance with Whittier's request, and it appeared in the *Emancipator* on 1 October 1845.

One month after the October meeting, in November 1845, Emerson was presented with an opportunity to carry on his more personal crusade against the racial bigotry that served to shore up the slaveholding mentality, the same bigotry he attacked so bluntly in his 1845 emancipation address. The affair began with an invitation to speak at the New Bedford Lyceum. Emerson's relationship with the community at New Bedford had always been congenial and dated back to his experience as a preacher, both before and after his formal departure from the Unitarian church. Holmes records the facts that Emerson "preached there several months, greatly to the satisfaction of those who heard him," and that "the Society would have been glad to settle him there as their minister."[24] Additionally, Cabot notes the friendly relation that Emerson enjoyed there and adds that while "at New Bedford he [Emerson] lived among the Quakers with whose faith he felt much sympathy."[25] Emerson himself once noted in a letter to the lyceum that "it is very pleasant to me to go to New Bedford," and also added on a practical note that "I find the fees of Lectures important to my Economy" (L 3:278). New Bedford, therefore, could be seen as representative of Emerson's ideal American audience at this time. It was the audience he wished to enlighten and improve, using his pulpit-lectern as the vehicle, and also, practically speaking, it was the audience upon which he depended for his income and support. Any issue that could drive a wedge between himself and such a group would have to be dire because it would strike at the very heart of his function and philosophy. Racial prejudice and his growing commitment to the cause of antislavery, as it turned out, provided just such an issue.

Emerson had long felt that the lyceum was the most effective vehicle in American society for promoting the qualities of morality, virtue, and culture that he hoped would bring about the progressive reform of American society, a reform that was sorely needed. As early as 1839, he noted in his journal that he looked upon the lecture room as "the true church of today" (JMN 7:277), and what he did in this church was, in his opinion, his primary contribution to the cause. Also, as indicated in his persistent support of Wendell Phillips's right to speak in Concord, Emerson clearly felt that if the lyceum was to fulfill this expectation, it was imperative that it remain open to all those who wished to speak, and also to all who wished to listen. Generally, the lyceum system itself was founded on these principles.

The New Bedford Lyceum had been established on 18 December 1828. The stated purposes of this institution were to enlighten the general populace and to foster the spirit of community and brotherhood. The main speaker at the first meeting of the New Bedford organization, Thomas Greene, stressed these goals and noted that "from all the divisions, ranks, and classes of society we are to meet . . . to instruct and to be instructed. While we mingle together in these pursuits . . . we shall remove many of the prejudices which ignorance or partial acquaintance with each other fostered."[26] However, this statement became somewhat ironic when this same lyceum voted in October 1845 to exclude blacks from regular membership. Although the wording of the proposal provided only that "no more tickets be sold to persons who are not members of the Lyceum," its actual intent was clear because it came on the heels of two earlier votes that had resulted in the rejection of two qualified black candidates for membership. To further clarify the segregationist intent of their action, the members then voted that "the colored people should be admitted to the lectures of the Lyceum, without expense, provided they would sit in the North Gallery."[27] This action was followed by "an unsuccessful attempt on the part of several members to enter a formal Protest" into the records of the meeting. It was signed by several individuals, including Daniel Ricketson, a wealthy member of the Quaker community in New Bedford (and a man destined to become a devoted admirer and friend of Henry Thoreau),[28] and Thomas Greene, who had delivered the eloquent speech on brotherhood at the first meeting of the lyceum seventeen years earlier.

Emerson heard about the events in New Bedford from at least two separate, and divergent, sources. In his letter to the lyceum dated 17 November 1845, he makes clear his understanding of the apparent segregationist intention of the resolution passed in New Bedford and attributes his knowledge to "an informant." He says: "If I come to New Bedford, I should be ready to fix, say the first Tuesday of March, and the second. But I have to say, that I have indirectly received a report of some proceedings in your Lyceum, which, by excluding others, I think ought to exclude me. My informant said that the application of a colored person for membership by purchase of a ticket in the usual manner had been rejected by a vote of the Lyceum, and this for the first time."[29]

Emerson's first "informant" in the matter was probably Benjamin Rodman of New Bedford, a long-standing friend and correspondent. When Emerson lectured in New Bedford he was most likely to stay in the Rodman household (L 3:266). In a lengthy undated letter to Emerson, Rodman describes the events leading to the vote and suggests that, for the most part, matters were dealt with in good faith. He insists that the Negroes who were brought forth for membership were "hunted up" in order to "test" the lyceum's rules, and that their rejections were legitimate and in keeping with the "written constitution" of the institution. He "questioned the justice of selling more tickets—as even now the floor was filled" and adds "that, I think, suggested the location of new comers whose whole association was so distinct from those who had previous rights by purchase." For his part Rodman "protested against the protest" because "no one had a right to infringe a constitutional act —the remedy was to be found in alteration of the laws under which the society acted." His letter concludes with the assertion that the decision to allow Negroes free entry was made to "obviate the very charge that those most needful of instruction were excluded—and it was done in good faith."[30]

Emerson was provided with another, and apparently more compelling, interpretation of the events in New Bedford by his Concord neighbor Mrs. Mary Merrick Brooks, who in turn was apprised of events there by Miss Caroline Weston, another active abolitionist and a citizen of New Bedford. In a letter to Wendell Phillips dated 2 November 1845, Miss Weston presents a lengthy account of the debate in the lyceum regarding membership and seating for blacks, and she adds, "I have written a full account of the matter to Mrs. Brooks & hope that Mr. Emerson may be disposed to refuse to lecture to the Lyceum under the circumstances." She also indicates that "if he [Emerson] will give his reasons in a letter to Mr. Greene to be laid before the audience that he is expected to address he will do great good." And last, she adds, "It is probable that Charles Sumner will think that this proscription forms any reason why he should decline also."[31]

Mrs. Brooks's response to Miss Weston's missive came some days later in a letter dated 19 November 1845 where she recounts her part in the affair. The letter reveals the extent to which abolitionists like Mrs. Brooks and others sought to precipitate Emerson's active involvement in their cause.

> I suppose it is about time to report to you the result of my mission to Mr. Emerson. I made him acquainted with the facts relating to the New Bedford Lyceum. We expected a revelation of these facts in the Liberator of Friday last, but found nothing. Mr. Rotch of your place wrote to Mr. Emer-

son wishing him to appoint the time he would appear before his Lyceum. Mr. Emerson replied that he had received a statement of the expulsion of the colored people . . . that if this statement were true, he could not lecture before the body, if it were not true, he asked information, that he had seen no printed account of the proceedings but merely been informed of them by friends. Thus the case now stands. I sincerely rejoice that Mr. Emerson has taken this stand and every friend of the coloured man will feel deeply grateful to him. I should not be surprised if they, the enemies of these despised ones, should endeavor to keep Mr. Emerson's refusal a secret. I apprise you of this that you may see that no false statement of the affair goes to Mr. E—, or if it does, keep me informed of the real truths.[32]

On the basis of such information as he had received from Mrs. Brooks, Benjamin Rodman, and possibly others, Emerson made his decision and was, for the first time in his career, prepared to refuse to lecture before a willing audience as a protest against their racial prejudice. In his letter to W. J. Rotch, the secretary of the New Bedford Lyceum, Emerson explained what he had heard of the vote there (noted earlier) and went on to say, "Now, as I think the Lyceum exists for popular education, as I work in it for that, and think that it should bribe and importune the humblest and most ignorant to come in, and exclude nobody or if any body, certainly the most cultivated,—the vote quite embarrasses me, and I should not know how to speak to the company."[33]

The final act in the matter was played some days later when Emerson received a reply to his letter to Mr. Rotch. For the most part this letter simply confirmed what Emerson had heard about events in New Bedford, and hence left him committed to the course of action outlined above. It is interesting to note that at this time Emerson's relationship with Mrs. Brooks had grown to the point that he felt it appropriate to visit her home and to relate to her personally the information he had received from New Bedford, and also to inform her of the decision he had made, and now confirmed, not to lecture there. In a lengthy letter to Caroline Weston, Mary Brooks describes that visit. "Mr. Emerson has just been in and read Mr. Wm. Rotch's letter, in reply to the one I mentioned from Mr. E—, asking for information whether the reports which had reached here were facts—Mr. Rotch stated the matter substantially in the same manner as you did, saying, however, that the affair originated from dissatisfaction on the part of some at the contiguity of the colored people with whites in the Lyceum, and that they did not probably foresee the results."[34]

Mrs. Brooks adds with well-deserved emphasis, "You may say *from me* that Mr. E—will not lecture before the Lyceum." She goes on to recount Emerson's protest against excluding any from the lyceum in substantially the same form as it appeared in his letter to Rotch. She also castigates those who did not take a stand in the matter. "I am still more surprised that those whose hearts were so far penetrated with the wrong as to vote right [that is, to admit the blacks], should not be willing to cut consistently enough with this vote to register the Protest." Apparently Emerson felt the same way, and as if to emphasize the extent to which these critical matters continued to separate him from old friends and move him toward new, Mrs. Brooks states that "Mr. Emerson says his friend Benjamin Rodman should have signed the protest." She concludes joyfully with the affirmation that "the main point of this letter is that Mr. E—will not lecture in your town."

Later this very same day, Mrs. Brooks sent along to Emerson additional information on the "sequel" to the New Bedford affair and thanked him again for his contribution to the cause. "I send you the sequel to the humiliating affair of the New Bedford Lyceum. I wish the simple words I thank you, could be made to convey what I as an individual feel for the part *you* have acted in this matter. Since I can't I shall impart to it a deeper meaning than it ordinarily conveys. As it is God will assuredly bless you, and when he says I thank you, it comes to the soul with an emphasis there is no mistaking."[35]

Needless to say, the "protestors" in New Bedford, especially Daniel Ricketson, were pleased with Emerson's decision. In a letter to Emerson, Ricketson asked permission to print the refusal, adding, "Allow me to assure you that you have our deepest respect for the honourable course you have taken in this matter, and that we deem your letter too valuable to the cause of human rights not to be made public."[36] Emerson responded that he had "no objection" to the publication of the letter (*L* 3:323), and subsequently it appeared in the 16 January 1846 edition of the *Liberator* along with a similar letter from Charles Sumner, who, perhaps because of Emerson's example, also refused to lecture at New Bedford because of their racist policies.[37]

Not all of the responses to Emerson's action were positive. Almost a full year after the events described above, Benjamin Rodman sent Emerson a lengthy letter wherein he broached the subject of Emerson lecturing before the New Bedford Lyceum in the upcoming season. Rodman gently berates the bard for his actions the year before. "But your mistake last year was in listening to the reports of the prejudiced who live on one idea & that exaggerated. Had you given us the lecture, you would have had a fine opportunity to reprove those who were prejudiced." Rodman concludes with an admonition to Emerson to avoid those who are committed to narrow causes and that by doing so he will better "know himself. . . . But now in conclusion I must entreat you to act by no such narrow council again—Bear in mind, the people have to hear from those whom they love to hear—and those who have a voice ought not to be fastidious as to before whom it is uttered—The position you hold does not justify your being influenced as the above individual named [Charles Sumner]—and if you do not know who Waldo Emerson is—I am sorry that my present limits do not allow me some space to enlighten you on that point."[38]

The letter no doubt struck a sensitive chord in Emerson because it clearly reflects his own oft-stated objection to those who fix themselves myopically upon one "cause," especially abolition. However, times were changing, and clearly a more concerted public effort would have to be made if the evils of slavery and racial prejudice were to be successfully confronted. By refusing for the first time to lecture before a group because of their blatant racial prejudice, Emerson, as with the Divinity School episode, took another giant step toward separating himself from the comfortable and decorous society that had heretofore been his most congenial and supportive audience. This decision, in conjunction with his two emancipation addresses and his participation in various protest meetings, associated him more closely than ever before with the ranks of the abolitionists.

Following the affair in New Bedford, Emerson continued to become more outspoken on the question of slavery and the moral obligations of the individual in dealing with such evil. Also, despite his consideration of the inevitable influence of fate in determining the destiny of man and his society, Emerson began to emphasize in his lectures in 1845 and 1846 the importance of "great men" in influencing and even shaping the course of events around them. In lectures such as "The Uses of Great Men," "Plato," "Swedenborg," "Montaigne," and others, Emerson took note of the ability of man to affect his world.[39] It is also clear from the journals at this time that despite some occasional reservations, Emerson came to see William Lloyd Garrison as one of the public men who could lead his age toward a greater righteousness. As early as 1844 he expressed his belief that "if two or three persons should come with a high spiritual aim & with great powers the world would fall in to their hands like a ripe peach" (*JMN* 9:111). And in 1845 he commented that "Garrison is a masculine, virile speaker. . . . He seems to be a man in his place. He brings his whole history with him, wherever he goes, & there is no falsehood or patchwork, but sincerity & unity" (*JMN* 9:267). In 1846 he added, "Have you seen Webster? Calhoun? Have you heard Everett, Garrison, Theodore Parker? Do you know Alcott? Then you may as well die." For Emerson these men were "the five or six personalities that make up . . . our American existence" (*JMN* 9:373). Perhaps Emerson himself was encouraged by such examples as Garrison and Parker, and perhaps he was also concerned that the flow of events around him was not moving consistently or rapidly in the direction of the social melioration that he so persistently hoped for and expected. Whatever the stimulus, it is clear that Emerson continued to move throughout this time toward a more conspicuous and public involvement for himself in the cause of freedom.

On 29 December 1845 Texas formally entered the Union, and the prospect of war with Mexico became more of a certainty. For many abolitionists, as for Emerson, the event was a moral catastrophe even if it was "inevitable," and the echoes of "manifest destiny" threatened a further expansion of slavery. For some it seemed that the time for separation of the moral from the immoral elements of American society was clearly at hand, and the cry of "no Union with slaveholders," which was first expressed by Garrison in 1842, was now spoken with greater conviction in many abolitionist quarters.[40] Undoubtedly with this idea in mind, Mrs. Brooks again approached Emerson, this time with a petition of protest against the annexation and the Union. In a letter to a friend in February 1846 she indicates that she "had been laboring with Mr. Emerson" and "Mr. Hoar," and that the matter "is not yet settled in their minds."[41] In a letter to Lidian Emerson at the same time she implores Mrs. Emerson's support in the matter. "I think if he [Emerson] reads again the petition his difficulty will be removed, for, as you will perceive, it asks men on coming out from the old government, to form one based on the self-evident principles of the declaration of independence and to carry out these principles fully." The letter suggests that the value of such beliefs is the only "treasure" of the antislavery cause, and, "though a diamond is as much a diamond in an old cracking bowl as in a golden vase, yet men can much more easily be made to look for the diamond in the vase. . . . If Mr. Emerson shall see fit to sign the petition, please ask him to put it at the head, it is seldom we get such coin, and when we do I am anxious to make it pay for all it is worth."[42]

In a letter to Emerson himself this forthright woman recounts a recent note to Mr. Hoar where, in asking him to sign the petition, she reminded him that "he has said again & again before the annexation of Texas that in case that event took place, war with all its horrors, or anything that might happen, would be greatly preferable to continuing in a union of robbery, perjury, and extended oppression." Although Hoar declined to sign the petition despite such cajoling, Mrs. Brooks nevertheless was determined to approach Mr. Emerson with her request because he is "a man who has faith in moral principle, who believes that truth will subdue to itself principalities and powers, and moreover [he] has the force and courage, when he sees a thing to be right, to do it." Her appeal concludes with "Now if you, and a few like you, should see what is demanded in this our nation's trial hour, we shall be saved."[43]

Despite this eloquent and personal appeal, and despite a journal entry at the time that echoes the words of his first emancipation address in stating "let us not pretend an union where union is not. Let us not cowardly say that all is right where all is damnable" (*JMN* 9:176), it is unlikely that Emerson signed the petition. His thinking at this time continued to emphasize, although not exclusively, the redeeming influence of culture in solving the problems of society, including slavery. In Emerson's view it was precisely this influence that would be lost if the moral elements of the North chose to isolate themselves from the immoral South. As later events would clearly indicate, Emerson was very much opposed in the 1840s to such apparently negative responses to the problems of American society.[44] Indeed, his inclination at this time was increasingly to confront the evil head-on.

Emerson's insistence upon the value of positive moral suasion encouraged him to be more aggressively outspoken himself in matters of social import, and thereby to promote and exemplify the kind of moral enthusiasm in which he placed his hopes for true social reform. Perhaps it was this very concern, coupled with the influence of Mrs. Brooks and others, that led Emerson to attend the public funeral of Charles Turner Torrey later in the spring of 1846. Torrey was an abolitionist who died in a Maryland state prison while serving a term for aiding escaping slaves. Emerson attended his funeral on 19 May. The ceremony was held in the Tremont Temple in Boston after the directors of the Park Street Church withdrew their earlier permission to allow the funeral there. The Reverend Joseph C. Lovejoy delivered the funeral oration, and the Reverend William Henry Channing also spoke. Although Emerson did not speak on this occasion, his presence at such an affair was undoubtedly considered significant, and even Nathaniel Bowditch remarked when recalling the event years later, "I was delighted at the sight of him, even as looker-on."[45] Emerson's interest in the funeral of Torrey is another reflection of his growing association with the abolitionists. Additionally, Torrey's case was somewhat special by virtue of the fact that almost two years earlier, when Torrey was first jailed, Emerson apparently refused a request from Whittier that he write a letter to be read at an abolition meeting, "touching upon Torrey's case, or some other point involved in our movement [which] would be of great Service to our cause" (L 3:260). Perhaps Emerson's refusal was based upon his reaction to an open letter from Torrey that was published in the *Baltimore Sunday Visitor* at the time of his incarceration. Emerson noted in his response to Whittier at the time regarding this letter, "I wish I liked it better. I do not

get as much of the facts as I want, and too much of another element."
However, he added, "But if he has run a great risque out of love & pity,
everything else shall be forgotten how quickly!" (*L* 3:261).

Whatever the specific cause, Emerson chose to attend Torrey's funeral,
and his reaction to the event demonstrates his continuing discomfort
with the general apathy of the citizens of Massachusetts toward the
sin of slavery. Additionally, his journal comments suggest his growing
admiration for martyrs like Torrey whose sacrifices spoke with an eloquence beyond words. "At the funeral of Torrey, it seems almost too
late to say anything for freedom—the battle is already won. You are a
superserviceable echo." However, an obligation to speak nevertheless remains, because "when you come out [you] see the apathy & incredulity,
the wood & the stone of the people, their supple neck, [and] their appetite for pine apple & ice cream" (*JMN* 9:400). He also avers that "if a
man speak in public one right & eloquent word, like . . . Lovejoy's lately
over Torrey's dead body, I have a feeling of gratitude that would wash
the feet of this benefactor" (*JMN* 9:382). Another interesting and curious aspect of Emerson's response to the event is his obvious irritation
at what he considered to be the false rage of many of the abolitionists
regarding the death of Torrey, as well as the conspicuous inability, or
unwillingness, of the state of Massachusetts to actively and aggressively
protect its citizens.

Regarding the first issue, he states in his journal that "the skeptics
have got hold of Park street Church & will not let the body of the Martyr
Torrey . . . spoil their carpets." He also notes that "the skeptics have got
into the Abolition society, & make believe to be enraged" (*JMN* 9:410).
Such a comment clearly reflects Emerson's increasing concern at this
time with the growing feeling among abolitionists and others that the
only way to preserve the moral integrity of American society would
be to abolish the Union and insulate the virtue of the North from the
contagion of the South. As noted above, this idea became particularly
conspicuous with the annexation of Texas, and "no Union with slaveholders" became a prominent rallying cry for abolitionists as a result of
the declaration of war with Mexico on 11 May, just eight days before
Torrey's funeral. Undoubtedly the idea was expressed by the orators on

that occasion, and one of them, William Henry Channing, on 28 May before the New England Anti-slavery Convention at Faneuil Hall, offered a resolution stating "that the people of Massachusetts do here and now deliberately assert, that there is no longer a Union of these States, a National Constitution, [or] a National Executive." He went on to propose a gathering of "primary assemblies of the People and . . . County, State and General Conventions, for the end of re-establishing this prostrate Republic, of forming a new bond of Union, which shall be a Union of Freemen, and of Freemen only."[46]

Up to this time Emerson's attitude toward abolitionists had been growing more positive as he gradually came to know men like Garrison and Phillips and the cause they represented. Also, as noted earlier, he admired them as spokespersons for moral sentiment and freedom in an increasingly immoral age. Even in the matter of this group's "monomania," a significant flaw for Emerson, some improvement had occurred. Thus, while he berated the abolitionists in 1844 for using sugar, tobacco, and cotton while claiming to be foes of slavery (*JMN* 9:127), by 1845 he stated, "I have charged the Abolitionist sometimes with stopping short of the essential act of abstaining from all products of slave-labour. The apology for their use is not comfort & self-indulgence, but, I doubt not, the same feeling which I & others insist on, that we will not be headlong & abandoned to this one mania" (*JMN* 9:195). But despite these changes, Emerson's concern in 1846 was that the separatist attitude of the abolitionists, which was now gaining popularity, represented the ultimate repudiation of faith in the ability of man to develop a better world. It was also an obvious denial of his own belief that things would inevitably meliorate and that the progress of mankind is divinely assured. His accusation that skepticism had invaded the ranks of the abolitionists, as well as the conservative Park Street Church, is particularly damning because, as he would point out later in his essay "Worship," "skepticism is the distrust of human virtue," and for Emerson human virtue was the sine qua non of effective reform (*W* 6:210). Thus the abolitionists' "rage" at slavery, in Emerson's opinion, must be "make believe" because if they were really upset by its existence, they would not turn their backs on the problem through disunion. Emerson's agitation in this matter also suggests the extent to which he had come to rely upon the abolitionists to act as a moral force in furthering the tendency of American society toward melioration.

This same concern is evident in the second issue Emerson raised in his journal at this time—the failure of New England to actively oppose such immoral enterprises as the war with Mexico, and also the abuse of its citizens. In his opinion, "New England is subservient. The President proclaims war, & those senators who dissent are not those who know better, but those who can afford to" (*JMN* 9:412). Regarding the protection of citizens, he states, "If I were a member of the Massachusetts legislature, I should propose to exempt all coloured citizens from taxation because of the inability of the government to protect them," and he also suggests that "the executive [of Massachusetts] wear no sword, and the office of general be abolished & the whole militia disbanded . . . [because] . . . Mr. Hoar of Concord, Walker of the branded hand, [and] Torrey the Martyr, knew that the sword of Massachusetts is a sword of lath, or a turkey feather." Emerson concludes, "It gives me no pleasure to see the governor attended by military men in plumes; I am amazed that they do not feel the ridicule of their position" (*JMN* 9:411–12). It is undoubtedly an index of Emerson's frustration with the evil of this time that he would prefer, as he had suggested in 1844, to reinforce the thrust of moral suasion with the power of the Massachusetts militia.

The war with Mexico was disturbing to Emerson on other grounds, also. It not only pointed up the pusillanimous nature of New England in its failure to effectively oppose the war on moral principle (*JMN* 9:422), but also it suggested the negative rather than positive tendency of developments in American society in general. Further, it seemed to point up the erroneousness of his hope that enlightened culture and general prosperity would meliorate social evil. Thus, while in 1843–44 Emerson was prepared to consider "trade" to be "the principle of liberty . . . [which] . . . settled America, & destroyed feudalism, and made peace & keeps peace," and which, finally, "will abolish slavery" (*JMN* 9:61–62), three years later he would reluctantly conclude, in the face of mounting evidence, that the pursuit of trade was in fact a major element in the growth of barbarism in American society. The purveyors of this "vulgar prosperity" would, he felt, undoubtedly take some comfort in the fact that "the Mexican War is already paid for in the enhanced value of cotton & breadstuffs now to be sold by our people" (*JMN* 9:389).

Emerson's artistic response to this disturbing situation is expressed in one of his most intriguing, and at times difficult, poems, the "Ode Inscribed to W. H. Channing." A brief analysis of the poem in its historical context offers unique insights into the work and also into Emerson's thinking at this time regarding the persistently vexing question of his proper role in social reform. The manuscript of the poem indicates the date of composition as June 1846.[47] While Edward Emerson states in his notes for the piece that "the circumstance which gave rise to this poem [is] not known" (*W* 9:427), it is clear that the work was occasioned by Torrey's funeral in May. The "evil times' sole patriot" referred to in the first line is obviously W. H. Channing, who was a major speaker at the Torrey funeral and who very probably encouraged Emerson to speak on that occasion also. The opening stanza is Emerson's apologia for not doing so, and he explains that "though loath to grieve the evil times' sole patriot" by his refusal, he cannot leave his "honied thought / For the priest's cant, / Or statesman's rant," undoubtedly references to the funeral speeches of Channing and others on that occasion. He goes on to assert that "the angry Muse / Puts confusion" in his brain when he attempts such public polemics, which is in keeping with similar journal comments on the matter, as noted earlier.

In the third stanza, however, Emerson berates himself for his long-held belief that "the culture of mankind" and the "better arts of life" would eventually meliorate the evils of society. Such faith seems ill placed when one can now "Behold the famous States / Harring Mexico / With Rifle and with knife," as only barbarians might do. Emerson berates himself further for having placed his faith in the innate nobility of the New England character only to discover now that "The God who made New Hampshire / Taunted the lofty land / With little men—" and New England has obviously failed the test of moral nobility. In his journal he had noted earlier, in regard to New Hampshire's Democratic and therefore proslavery vote in the presidential election of 1845, that "New Hampshire is treacherous to the honor, honesty, & interest of New England" (*JMN* 9:180). With the tacit acceptance of the war with Mexico,

Confusion and Commitment

it must have seemed to Emerson that New England had now followed New Hampshire's perfidious lead. In New England at this time, as indicated at the service for Torrey, virtue is a subject for eloquence when the occasion demands, but the words ring false and the rage of the skeptics is shallow. Thus,

> Virtue palters; Right is hence;
> Freedom praised but hid;
> Funeral eloquence
> Rattles the coffin-lid.

Emerson's displeasure with the abolitionists at the time of the funeral and thereafter was occasioned by their willingness to forgo the virtue of a true struggle and continued confrontation with evil, by their preference for disunion. He questions the value of such a position as held by Channing and others, asking,

> What boots thy zeal,
> O glowing friend,
> That would indignant rend
> The northland from the south?
> Wherefore? to what good end?

For Emerson, such a negative action would not improve the moral condition of American society in either resulting sphere, because the deficiency of the age was an inner condition, not merely an outer one, and also, the North was not without its faults. Hence, even with disunion, "Boston Bay and Bunker Hill / Would serve things still." Indeed, the problems of slavery and the Mexican War were largely manifestations of the failure of spirit in the face of the growing materialism of the age.

> 'Tis the day of the chattel,
> Web to weave, and corn to grind;
> Things are in the saddle,
> And ride mankind.

On the whole, Emerson is still committed here to the propriety and basic goodness of the development of "things" in society as they signal a necessary element of progress. Thus,

> 'Tis fit the forest fall,
> The steep be graded,
> The mountain tunnelled,
> The sand shaded.

However, such enterprises should be undertaken for the glory and love of man, which is in itself a redeeming concept.

> Let man serve law for man;
> Live for friendship, live for love,
> For truth's and harmony's behoof.

Such an improvement in individuals would inevitably be reflected in their government and is, in fact, the *only* way to improve government. Hence, "the state may follow how it can."

Emerson goes on to indicate that social improvement will come if right-minded individuals go about their business in a natural and virtuous way, "Everyone to his chosen work," a familiar position Emerson had expressed many times before in his journals. And finally, he again reiterates his now somewhat strained faith that the force of goodness working within man and his world will ultimately ameliorate the evil of the times, and culture will triumph over barbarism.

> The over-god
> Who marries Right to Might,
> Who peoples, unpeoples,—
> He who exterminates
> Races by stronger races,
> Black by white faces,
> Knows to bring honey
> Out of the lion;
> Grafts gentlest scion
> On pirate and Turk.

Emerson's comment here regarding the extermination of "black by white faces" undoubtedly reflects his belief that a new and better race would eventually develop in America, a race that would be a composite of all the races present in the New World. Thus, in a journal entry some months earlier he had noted: "I hate the narrowness of the Native

Confusion and Commitment

American Party. . . . It is precisely opposite to all the dictates of love and magnanimity: & therefore, of course, opposite to true wisdom. . . . Man is the most composite of all creatures . . . [and as] by the melting & intermixture of silver & gold & other metals, a new compound more precious than any, called the Corinthian Brass, was formed so in this Continent,—asylum of all nations, the energy of Irish, Germans, Swedes, Poles & Cossacks, & of all the European tribes,—of the Africans, & of the Polynesians, will construct a new race, a new religion, a new State, a new literature, which will be as vigorous as the new Europe which came out of the smelting pot of the Dark Ages" (*JMN* 9: 299–300).

Emerson concluded his ode on a note of optimism supported by the idea suggested in this passage. His conclusion also presents an apostrophe to himself as artist, which explains, in a way, the very existence and hopefulness of the poem. He notes in referring to the barbarism inherent in current world events that "The Cossack eats Poland, / Like stolen fruit"; and that in the face of such cruel force all seems lost for Poland at the moment, "Her last noble is ruined, / Her last poet mute." But at the darkest hour, when things seem at their worst, "Straight, into double band / The victors divide"; and from the barbaric hordes one finds that "Half for freedom strike and stand," with the result that "The astonished Muse finds thousands at her side."

The analogy to the American situation is clear. In America, too, the plundering forces of barbarism and slavery seemed to dominate as Mexico was invaded and the cruelty of the slave powers extended. However, despite these negative developments, for Emerson, goodness and morality would eventually have their day if virtuous men like Channing and others asserted a positive faith and continued the struggle. The first step in that direction was not to destroy the Union or to exhaust oneself with "cant" but to gather round the helpful muse who sings the song of faith. Also, it is interesting to note in relation to Emerson's subsequent abolition activities that the muse who here finds thousands now at her side awaiting inspiration, if not leadership, could be seen as Emerson's own poetic self.

At this critical time Emerson's journals, like the poem, reflect his growing concern with the skepticism and indifference of American society, especially in the North, regarding such problems as slavery and the Mexican War. Emerson continued to hope that a leader, other than himself, would come forth to rouse the public into virtuous awareness. Thus, in one passage he complains of the moral lethargy of the age and comments: "What a blessed world of snivelling nobodies we live in! There is no benefit like a war or a plague. . . . A good hell-cat, spiegato carattere, would stimulate the imagination & enforce the tardy virtue by reaction" (*JMN* 9:427). So far, neither the war nor the plague had produced the kind of response that Emerson had hoped for, but occasionally he would encounter a "hell-cat" or two among the ranks of the abolitionists. Thus on one occasion he refers in his journal to Parker Pillsbury, who had replaced Nathaniel Rogers as editor of the *Herald of Freedom* and whom he had heard speak the night before. Pillsbury is "that very gift from New Hampshire which we have long expected, a tough oak stick of a man not to be silenced or insulted or intimidated by a mob, because he is more mob than they; he mobs the mob" (*JMN* 9:426). On this occasion Emerson especially appreciated Pillsbury's attacks on editorial excuses for the Mexican War and the churches' indifference toward slavery. Obviously, Emerson was now more appreciative of Pillsbury's aggressiveness than he had been at the time of the *Herald* controversy two years earlier. Also, one of the clear implications of Emerson's journalizing at this time is the gradual realization that, as scholar/poet, he himself must make a more explicit and public effort to further the cause of justice in the world. Perhaps it was this very feeling that prompted him to offer his next formal address on slavery. The occasion was a Fourth of July abolition celebration, which was held for the first time in 1846 and would become an annual event thereafter until the Civil War. As with other antislavery speeches of the 1840s, no manuscript has survived, but the text of Emerson's address was published in the *National Anti-slavery Standard* on 16 July 1846, and substantial fragments of it also appear in the journals for the period.[48]

The event was well attended, and included with Emerson on the list of speakers were William Lloyd Garrison, James Freeman Clarke, and Wendell Phillips. Not surprisingly, Emerson used the occasion to air many of the concerns that were expressed more subtly in the "Ode Inscribed to W. H. Channing" and more privately in the journals. Thus in his opening statement he refers to the "despair which [has] crept over Massachusetts and over New England" in response to the national events of the moment. He then specifically castigates the "inaction and apathy" of citizens who should be embarking upon a moral crusade but have thus far failed to do so, and he points out that despite its patriotic heritage, now "on the occurrence of each new event, New England resolves itself, not into a revolutionary committee, . . . but into a debating society." Also, as in his earlier journal statements and in the "Ode," he declaims particularly against the mercantile attitude of "forcible and well-organized individuals" who do as they please and make the "law of their actions," and thus spread the immoral contagion of the South northward in the process. He goes on to note, with a somewhat uncharacteristically biting humor, that New England men could effectively oppose the growing southern hegemony because "the Northerners have as good blood in their veins, and are very well able to give as good as they get," but they generally fail to do so because "they are old traders, and make it a rule rarely to shoot their customers, and never until the bill is paid." Thus, as a result of their concern with maintaining business relationships, northerners respond to southern barbarism with the self-serving attitude that "we can defend our honor, and are not more than others tender of our skin, but we are very tender of our mortgages." The sad fact is that virtually every acre of the South's plantations, according to Emerson, is "covered by bonds and securities held in New York and Boston."

In addition to this informed self-interest of the business element in society, Emerson points to another factor that contributes to moral abominations like slavery and the invasion of Mexico—the existence of the "war-party." He defines this group as "a ferocious minority, which no civilization has yet caused to disappear in any country; that mob which every nation holds within it of young and violent persons craving strong drink, craving blood, craving coarse animal excitement, at any cost." The problem is made worse when the men of this war party "are stimulated and trumpeted on by that needy band of profligate editors and orators who find their selfish account in encouraging this brutal instinct." These barbaric thugs and the instigators who led them undoubtedly represented a potent counterforce to Emerson's own cultural ideal.

The third element contributing to the desperate equation of the times is the opposite of the last, namely, the lack of animal spirits and moral vigor among those who should be the defenders of virtue and culture. Thus in New England, for the most part, "People are respecters, not of essential, but of external law, decorum, routine, and official forms." Ironically, because of this concern for an effete and cultured propriety, "Governor Briggs and his dignified supporters have just now immolated the integrity of the State" in failing to protest vigorously against the invasion of Mexico.

As was his habit and his philosophy, however, Emerson could not allow his presentation to stand as a mere series of negations, and he himself notes, "I am not here to accuse parties or persons." Therefore, in the balance of the speech he offers his most exuberant praise yet, either public or private, for the positive efforts of the abolitionists, who now offer a gleam of hope for American society because they maintain a basic faith in the efficacy of virtue. "I value as a redeeming trait the growth of the abolition party, the true successors of that austere Church, which made nature and history sacred to us all in our youth." Undoubtedly with Elijah Lovejoy and, more recently, Charles Torrey in mind, Emerson goes on to comment, "What can better supply that outward church they [the youth of America] want than this fervent, self-denying school of love and action, which too, the blood of martyrs has already consecrated?" He praises "these brave men and brave women" who have fought on in a valiant struggle against the evil at hand, and he points out that "with the noblest purpose [despite] the general defection and apathy, the Abolitionists have been faithful to themselves." Clearly Emerson had now come to see the abolitionists as among those few who were actively contributing to the positive flow of things toward melioration and, despite some lingering concerns about their "monomania" he had accepted that their destinies would be properly fulfilled in pursuing this goal. Because of the recent thrust within abolition ranks toward the negativity of nonunionism, Emerson undoubtedly wished to use this opportunity to encourage the abolitionists along a more positive route. Thus he goes on to say of his abolitionist cohorts, "They have seen against all appearances, that the right will conquer, and though it has not with it the people of the world, it has the world itself, and the world's Builder; and they have thrown themselves unhesitatingly on that side."

Last, Emerson encourages his abolitionist listeners to become more circumspect in their view of society's problems, and he says of them, "I think they have yet lessons to learn, and [they] are learning them. I shall esteem them, as they cease to be a party, and come to rely on that which is not a party, nor part, but which is the whole." Thus, placing faith in individuals, in cooperation with fate, and in redeeming mankind, Emerson's oration concludes with the statement that he is looking forward to the rise of "those great men" who "like the west wind, bring the sunshine with them; those conquering natures which make the difference by their presence or absence; where they are there is power." Such wholesome and dynamic leaders would realize that "there are other crimes besides Slavery and the Mexican war," and the "more comprehensive faith" of these special individuals would then "resolve all the parts of duty into a harmonious whole." Interestingly enough, the closest thing that America had yet seen to such a universal reformer was, of course, Emerson himself.

While undoubtedly Emerson felt, as he usually did, that his skirts had been cleared somewhat by this specific contribution to the antislavery crusade, he nevertheless remained deeply concerned about the slavery question and the war with Mexico, and also the fact that in this needful time no great leader of the type referred to in his speech had yet appeared to move the world forward. American government seemed dominated by "the rabble at Washington," who were only comparatively better than their "snivelling opposition." And those who were capable of moral leadership were failing. Unfortunately, Webster, "a man by himself of the great mold . . . also underlies the American blight, & wants the power of the initiative, the affirmative talent, and remains like the literary class, only a commentator" (*JMN* 9:444–45). Worse yet, at the end of July an event occurred that upset Emerson profoundly and contributed significantly to the growing ire, confusion, and anxiety that he felt regarding his own proper role in reforming American society. That event was the one-night incarceration of Henry Thoreau, who had refused to pay his poll tax as a protest against slavery and the Mexican War.

There is every reason to believe that up to this time Thoreau had exercised a significant influence in stimulating Emerson's abolition activities. It is entirely possible that Emerson looked to Thoreau for a clear example of practical and virtuous conduct in dealing individually with the moral evil of the world. As early as 1838 Emerson referred approvingly in his journal to Thoreau's "simplicity & clear perception" in his approach to this "doubledealing quacking world," and he compared his rebelliousness favorably with that of Montaigne (*JMN* 5:453, 460). Later, in 1843, Emerson indicated his high expectations for Thoreau. "Young men like Henry Thoreau owe us a new world & they have not acquitted the debt" (*JMN* 8:375). Certainly, one area where this debt was being paid was in relation to the abolition question. On virtually all of those earlier occasions when Emerson was called forth to speak his mind on the slavery issue, Thoreau was there. Thus, when Emerson made his first major address on emancipation in the British West Indies from the courthouse in Concord in 1844, it was Thoreau who defiantly rang the bell and went from door to door to gather the crowd to hear. Later, it was Thoreau who, acting as agent for the antislavery women of Concord, arranged with James Munroe and Company of Boston to have the address printed in pamphlet form, a copy of which he forwarded to Nathaniel Rogers at the *Herald of Freedom*.[49] Also, before this, it was Thoreau who first publicly praised the *Herald of Freedom* for its justness in dealing with the problem of slavery and saw his views published in Emerson's *Dial*. And it was Thoreau who joined with Emerson on those memorable occasions when it was necessary to fight for the right of Wendell Phillips to speak about slavery in the Concord Lyceum. And finally, it was Thoreau who later broadcast their success in the *Liberator*.

Undoubtedly the subject of abolition and reform came up in conversations between Thoreau and Emerson, and on these occasions Henry would have been a source of information and insights regarding current abolition events and the personalities involved in them. All of the women of the Thoreau household were ardent and active abolitionists, and it has been conjectured that there was scarcely a major abolitionist in New England whom Henry would not have met over the dinner table at his mother's boardinghouse.[50] Therefore, when Thoreau decided to go to jail as a protest against the evil of the time, it was a great shock to Emerson because it seemed, unlike Thoreau's earlier activities, to represent a negative and skeptical capitulation to the forces of evil. Also, this radical act on Thoreau's part probably served to underscore what might have appeared to some to be Emerson's decorous passivity in the matter, something that would remain a tender nerve with him for some time to come. His journal remarks concerning the event are sharp and complex, and they grow in intensity as the implications of Thoreau's act become clear to him.

Emerson's initial response to the action comes in the context of a declamation against Governor Briggs and Daniel Webster for their failure to respond adequately to the declaration of war against Mexico, wherein he indicates that the rabble at Washington calculated rightly in anticipating the lack of response of these two. Emerson then goes on to note: "My friend Mr Thoreau has gone to jail rather than pay his tax. On him they could not calculate. . . . The abolitionists denounce the war & give much time to it, but they pay the tax." For Emerson, however, neither course of action is appropriate for the individuals involved, and neither is acceptable because the negative assumption in both is "that the world is no longer a subject for reform." Such attitudes and actions imply that southern policy cannot be effectively and positively opposed, so why try? (*JMN* 9:445).

Emerson insists that the state itself is not the culprit in the matter, because "the State is a poor good beast who means the best" (*JMN* 9:446), and determined people can still compel the state to conform to moral laws rather than allowing themselves to be locked up by such a poor cow. Also, Emerson felt in Thoreau's case that the issue of the tax itself was not dire enough to justify such an extreme reaction from him. In his journal monologue he advises those who seek reform not to "run amuck against the world" in a dispute over trivia. Rather, they should "have a good case to try the question on. It is the part of a fanatic to fight out a revolution on the shape of a hat or surplice. . . . You can not fight heartily for a fraction. But wait until you have a good difference to join issue upon. . . . You will get one by & by. But now I have no sympathy" (*JMN* 9:446).

Regarding the abolitionists who paid the tax, Emerson suggests that they "ought to resist & go to prison in multitudes on their known & described disagreements from the state." Obviously, such an act for them would be a positive rather than a negative step because of their numbers. The state could hardly ignore the incarceration of "multitudes" as easily as it could one man. Also, Emerson felt that such an act would be more appropriate to one-issue reformers, as the abolitionists generally were. However, the fact that they did not go to jail but instead paid the tax was undoubtedly another indication to Emerson of the "skepticism" that infected their ranks and promoted such negative measures as the "no Union" policy.

Emerson made another important distinction at this time between Thoreau and the associated abolitionists, and that is that Thoreau was properly a "generalizer" rather than a "partialist" in the matter of reform. That is to say, Emerson saw Thoreau like he saw himself, as a scholar/poet whose true goal was the *universal* reform of mankind. As such, his actions, thoughts, artistry, and being would, and should, naturally contribute to the tendency toward goodness and light in man and his world. In order to best achieve this the generalist should avoid the obvious monomania of the "partialists." Emerson's ultimate advice to all such reformers, himself included, was to "reserve yourself for your own work" (*JMN* 9:446). For Emerson, going to jail at this time would certainly not be part of such work.

There was also the consideration that negative action such as Thoreau's was indicative of a final rejection of human nature and the power of virtue in improving what is admittedly an imperfect world. Such an attitude is extremely destructive because it denies the possibility of reform and sets the rare individual of high moral character apart from others who are deemed irreparably immoral. By comparison, the selective and partial nature of the abolitionists' objections to society's immorality was preferable to Emerson because it suggests that man is redeemable, at least in this regard. Thus he goes on to comment that "the Abolitionists should resist because they are literalists; they know exactly what they object to, & there is a government possible which will content them. Remove a few specified grievances & this present commonwealth will suit them." He notes here, as he did in his speech earlier in the month, that by virtue of such faith in the basic goodness of man, the abolitionists "are the new Puritans" of the day and "as easily satisfied." Considering the opposite position, as evinced by Thoreau, he says: "But you, nothing will content. No government short of a monarchy consisting of one king & one subject will appease you. Your objection then to the state of Massachusetts is deceptive. Your true quarrel is with the state of Man" (*JMN* 9:447).

Last, Emerson cautions that "a scholar has too humble an opinion of the population, of their possibilities, of their future, to be entitled to go to war with them as with equals," which suggests that a high-minded idealist like Thoreau should be less demanding of those around him and more patient in his anticipation of reform, because a reform movement that demands of all society a moral norm commensurate with that of the reformer is doomed to end in frustration and defeat. Emerson's final warning, then, is that "this prison is one step to suicide" (*JMN* 9:447).[51] Given this frame of mind, it is less surprising that Emerson later told Bronson Alcott that he thought Thoreau's act was "mean and skulking and in bad taste."[52]

Perhaps as a reaction to what he saw as Thoreau's withdrawal from the proper activity of social reform, a week later Emerson delivered his third speech celebrating the annual anniversary of emancipation in the British West Indies. Unfortunately, no record of this address survives other than a brief notation in the *Liberator* (7 August 1846) that recounts the events of the day and describes the featured speaker. "Then there was the calm philosophical Emerson, closely scrutinizing, nicely adjusting the scales, telling us the need be of all things." As an indication of the growing tensions of the time, even in Concord, it is interesting to note that the report also states that "the number present during the day was quite small; [and] in the morning quite so." The reason the correspondent sardonically assigns to this situation is that "Concord people generally had to stay at home, for in common with the people of Massachusetts at large, they are obliged to abridge themselves of holidays, being busy in providing for the wants of their new sister Texas, and her immediate offspring. They are honest men, doubtless, not meaning to repudiate any of their debts, but are willing to pay the last farthing, if that is found to be a possible thing." It is possible, too, that the anonymous author of these words was aware of Thoreau's recent protest against paying any debts of this sort.

Later in August Emerson attended the Harvard commencement exercises and socialized with members of his own graduating class. The affair was undoubtedly a pleasant social experience for him, a welcome interlude in what he now saw as "this sad lint & rag fair" out of which "the web of lasting life is woven" (*L* 3:340). While at the commencement Emerson had an opportunity to hear the annual Phi Beta Kappa address, which was delivered by Charles Sumner. Sumner had been an acquaintance of Emerson for some time before this, and as early as 1837 Emerson had written a letter introducing the young man, whom he described as "a gentleman much known & valued in our community," to Thomas Carlyle and other European friends (*CEC* 169). Emerson's association with Sumner had grown since then, and undoubtedly their mutual protests against the bigotry of the New Bedford Lyceum in November of the previous year served to identify them as persons of like sympathies, at least in that regard. By August 1846 Sumner had become clearly identified with the abolition movement through his antislavery speeches in Boston on the Fourth of July the year before, and also through his participation in the anti-Texas rally at Faneuil Hall some months earlier. It is possible that Emerson saw in this articulate and aggressive young man a potential leader in the cause of freedom, and Sumner's oration on this occasion would certainly have served to reinforce such a notion. In his speech "The Scholar, the Jurist, the Artist and the Philanthropist" Sumner commemorated John Pickering, Joseph Story, Washington Allston, and William Ellery Channing, all members of Phi Beta Kappa who had recently died. Undoubtedly to the surprise of some Harvard conservatives who wished to avoid the antislavery issue entirely, Sumner in his discussion of Channing noted that Channing's maxim was "Anything but slavery," and that he "urged the duty . . . incumbent on the Northern states to free themselves from all support of slavery. To this conclusion he was driven by the ethical principle that *what is wrong for the individual* is wrong for the state."[53] Emerson was delighted with the performance, and he was probably especially pleased with the invocation of the wisdom of his most highly regarded mentor. His journal notes of the occasion, "At Phi Beta Kappa Sumner's oration was marked with a certain magnificence which I do not well know where to parallel" (*JMN* 9:451).

Despite the momentary glimmers of hope suggested by the efforts of individuals such as Sumner, Emerson remained painfully aware that overall the tendency of the times was much more negative than positive. The forces of corruption and bigotry were clearly in the ascendancy, and in the month following Sumner's address an event occurred which suggested to many that the borders of Massachusetts itself were no longer reliable barriers against the encroachments of the persistent and powerful evil of the South. This event would elicit from Emerson yet another public protest.

Early in September 1846 a runaway slave stowed away on the sailing ship *Ottoman* when it left the port of New Orleans. His hope lay in finding freedom in Boston at the journey's end. Unfortunately, when the ship reached its destination and the stowaway was discovered, it was decided by the owners of the ship to return him to Louisiana because, as the report of a protest committee states, the owners feared "the laws of Louisiana and the loss of a gainful traffic rather than the laws of Massachusetts and the loss of their good name."[54] When the captain's intention became clear to the unfortunate fellow, he made a valiant effort to escape in a small boat, but after a two-mile chase he was recaptured and eventually sent back into slavery. Many virtuous men of Boston were outraged by such crass behavior on the part of the merchants, and a protest meeting was called at Faneuil Hall that was presided over by the now aged John Quincy Adams. Also speaking on this occasion were Charles Sumner, Wendell Phillips, and Theodore Parker. Adams expressed his concern in terms that echo Emerson's after the funeral of Torrey. "It is a question whether your and my native Commonwealth is capable of protecting the men under its laws or not."[55] Later, John Andrew, the secretary of the meeting, offered a series of resolutions, including one that states, "that the abducting of a man in the streets of Boston should be felt as an alarming menace against the personal rights and safety of every citizen; and that every person who aided and abetted in the kidnapping and in carrying this individual into slavery deserved the strongest reprobation." Later, Wendell Phillips brought the crowd to its feet with the assertion that "law or no law, Constitution or no Constitution, humanity shall be paramount."

Theodore Parker, who until this time had been reluctant to commit himself fully to the abolition movement, although he had some years before declared his respect for their efforts, took this opportunity to align himself clearly with the cause. In his speech he stressed the importance of the "higher law" and castigated politicians who embraced expediency and forgot principles.[56] The following summer Parker joined Emerson and others in founding the *Massachusetts Quarterly Review*, almost every number of which would carry an article on some phase of the slavery question.[57]

Emerson had been invited to address the meeting at Faneuil Hall by Samuel Howe, and at the bottom of the "circular letter" sent to Emerson at the time Howe wrote in his own hand, "P.S. If you cannot be present the committee will be happy to have an expression of your views."[58] Emerson's response, which was published in the committee's pamphlet *Report*, indicates the depth of his feeling in the matter and his clear recognition that, as he had noted in his Fourth of July address, the mercantile prosperity of American society, rather than leading to the successive amelioration of social evils as he had once hoped, was instead leading to moral bankruptcy. He points out that "our state has suffered many disgraces, of late years, to spoil our pride in it, but never any so flagrant as this. . . . If the merchants tolerate this crime . . . it is very certain they will have the ignominy very faithfully put to their lips." He saw the affair as "a good test of the honesty and manliness of our commerce," and "it is high time our bad wealth came to an end." For his part, Emerson says, "I shall very cheerfully take my share of suffering in the ruin of such prosperity" in order to reassert virtue.[59]

Not surprisingly, as his faith in the theory of melioration and inevitable social progress contracted in the face of such disturbing contrary evidence, Emerson came to place a renewed emphasis at this time on the ability of individuals to improve their world through active efforts at reform. Thus, in a journal entry early in 1847, which he later incorporated into *Representative Men* (1850), he states, "Great men are much when you consider that the race goes, with us, on their credit," and that through their efforts "chaos is reduced to order," and hence, "our hope is in the men" (*JMN* 10:14–15).[60] At the same time, in a draft letter to the Englishman John Heraud, he indicated the extent to which his opinion had now improved regarding the abolition movement and its people. Perhaps because the Texas and Mexican War issues further broadened the scope of abolition interests, for Emerson the movement itself now seemed more mature and circumspect in its concerns. His letter states, "The abolition movement which has taken a strong hold on the conscience & mind of our people is educating both the one & the other & already seems to have ripened a few minds to that degree that the abolition of slavery no longer seems to them the only duty for which the white man was created." As a result of this development, Emerson was now prepared to observe that "the influence of this agitation on the politics of this country, long denounced as futile or mischievous, is lately sensible & salutary, and it brings with it a whole connection of related subjects all tending to novelty & expansion."[61]

Despite this confidence in the salutary effects of the abolition movement, however, Emerson was deeply concerned, and even at times depressed, with the current state of affairs in America and the ambiguity of his own position in relation to them. Thus, in a journal entry in March he speaks of the scholar's role in society. "We must have society, provocation, a whip for the top. A Scholar is a candle which the love & desire of men will light. Let it not lie in a dark box." Turning then to himself, he adds, "But here I am with so much already to be revealed to me as to others if only I could be set aglow." While wishing for "the stimulus of a stated task" and "a sense of direction," Emerson pointedly notes that "N. P. Rogers spoke more truly than he knew, perchance, when he recommended an Abolition-Campaign to me. I doubt not, a course of mobs would do me much good" (*JMN* 10:28).[62]

Also, Emerson was particularly saddened at this time by the depressing conditions in the nation's capital, where it seemed that the barbaric forces of the slave powers were now clearly in control. "The name of Washington city in the newspapers is every day of blacker shade. All the news from that quarter being of a sadder type, more malignant. It seems to be settled that no act of honor or benevolence or justice is to be expected from the American Government, but only this, that they will be as wicked as they dare." This led him to assert that "no man now can have any sort of success in politics without a streak of infamy crossing his name" (*JMN* 10:29).

Emerson's journal commentary concludes with a speculation that is uncharacteristically dark and despondent. Speaking of those who now succeed in Washington, "things have another order in these men's eyes. Heavy is light & good is evil. A western man in Congress the other day spoke of the opponents of the Texan & Mexican plunder as 'Every light character in the house,' & our good friend in State street [the business district in Boston] speaks of 'the solid portion of the community' meaning, of course, the sharpers." Faced with such depressing developments, Emerson concludes his rumination with the melancholy observation that "those who succeed in life, in civilized society, are beasts of prey. It has always been so" (*JMN* 10:29). Clearly, the cultural revolution envisioned nine years earlier in the "American Scholar" was a distant prospect and a frail hope at this moment.

With the world thus lying heavily on his soul, Emerson began to sort out his options and to consider the advice of friends. He wanted very much to get away from the turmoil of the present American scene, and noted of those around him, "In this emergency, one advises Europe, & especially England. If I followed my own advices . . . I should sooner go toward Canada. I should withdraw myself for a time from all domestic & accustomed relations & command an absolute leisure with books—for a time" (*JMN* 10:29). As it turned out, the choice was England.

Emerson sailed for England on 5 October 1847 and would remain there, lecturing, visiting with friends like Carlyle, and touring, until his return in July 1848. During his stay in Europe Emerson found some relief from the tensions and crises of American society, but undoubtedly the turmoil in England generated by the Chartist movement, and the various revolutions in the rest of Europe in 1848, caused him to reflect from time to time on the proper role of the scholar/poet in society and the obligations that awaited him in this regard upon his return to America. Also while in England, Emerson began once again to think seriously and pointedly about the uniqueness of individual races and the effect of race upon the destinies of individuals. Eventually these speculations would be formalized into lectures and a full-length work, *English Traits* (1856).

Shortly after his arrival in Liverpool Emerson began to record in his journals generalizations about the English. Thus, he points out, "the Englishman has . . . a necessary talent of letting alone all that does not belong to him. They are physiognomically & constitutionally distinct from the Americans. They incline more to be large-bodied men; they are stocky, & especially the women seem to have that defect to their beauty; no tall slender girls of flowing shape, but stunted & stocky" (*JMN* 10:178). Eventually Emerson came to see such "racial" character-istics as significant factors that affect the individual's functioning in the world. He says later in *English Traits*, "It is race, is it not, that puts the hundred millions of India under the domination of a remote island in the north of Europe?" "Race is a controlling influence in the Jew, who, for two millenniums, under every climate, has preserved the same char-acter and employments." And, he adds, "Race in the negro is of appalling importance" (*W* 5:47–48).

However, important as it may be, race is not the only factor influ-encing the fate of the individual, and Emerson goes on in his essay to point out the "counteracting forces to race." Among these he men-tions civilization, religion, trades and professions, and even "certain circumstances" of life that have unique effects. In England these in-cluded personal liberty, abundance of food, an open market, and good wages for every kind of labor, in addition to other factors. Also, as noted earlier, Emerson continued to believe in the ultimate good to be wrought through the admixture of racial characteristics. Here he points out that the concept of "pure races" even now is largely a "legend," and that "the best nations are those most widely related"; thus, "navigation, as effecting a world-mixture, is the most potent advancer of nations" (*W* 5:49–50).

Such speculations, and perhaps the therapeutic nature of the trip itself, served to restore Emerson's basic faith in the natural and necessary progress of human civilization. Thus, while he took note of the numerous beggars in England as well as the nation's conspicuous wealth, he foresaw an inevitable future adjustment of the scales. "England is the country of the rich," and "the Great Poor man does not yet appear." However, "whenever he comes, England will fall like France" (*JMN* 10: 295). Undoubtedly Emerson's reference here is to the British Chartist movement, which was very active at the time of his visit to England. In a later entry he describes the tension in the country and, somewhat surprisingly, he is now prepared to suggest that the scholar has a role to play even in dramatic and specific attempts at social reform that go beyond general cultural elevation. "I fancied when I heard that the times were anxious & political that there is to be a Chartist revolution on Monday next, and an Irish revolution in the following week, that the right scholar would feel,—now was the hour to test his genius." Continuing with this speculation about the scholar and his social obligations, "His kingdom is at once over & under these perturbed regions. Let him produce its Charter now, & try whether it cannot win a hearing & make felt its infinite superiority today, even today" (*JMN* 10:310–11).

Later, Emerson became even more pointed in his observations regarding the artists of England and the social turmoil there. The applicability of his comments to himself and the American scene seem obvious and compelling. In England "the writers are bold & democratic," but at the time of revolution they do not side with the Chartists because the leaders of the movement are "gross and bloody" and largely uncivilized. The artist joins with the rich, instead, because they seem to represent culture and stability. In Emerson's opinion, such a reaction is a mistake. Instead, the artist should "accept as necessary the position of armed neutrality abhorring the crimes of the Chartist, yet more abhorring the oppression & hopeless selfishness of the rich." Eventually, "the music & the dance of liberty" will prevail and justice will be done. Finally, in words that might just as easily be applied to those, like himself, who initially objected to the abolitionists because of their apparent vulgarity and lack of sophistication, Emerson warns, "Shame to the fop of philosophy who suffers a little vulgarity of speech & of character to hide from him the true current of Tendency, & who abandons his true position of being priest & poet of those impious & unpoetic doers of God's work" (*JMN* 10:325–26).

Emerson returned to America in late July 1848 with a renewed and more optimistic view of American society. And, indeed, even externally there were some signs of hope. Earlier in July the Mexican War had ended through treaty, and it seemed that that tawdry episode in American history had now passed. There was further evidence of material progress for the society in the continued expansion of the railroad and the dramatic and exciting discovery of gold in California. Such developments could certainly be seen as contributing to the wealth and prosperity of the nation, hence furthering, at least potentially, the ameliorative influence of trade and culture. The contemporary excitement of these events is reflected in Emerson's observation that "the railroad is the only sure topic for conversation in these days . . . and now we have one more rival topic, California gold" (*JMN* 10:353).

However, despite these positive developments, Emerson continued to contemplate the deterministic forces that affect the development of races and societies, and also the tragic consequences of repression as it is brought to bear on such a process. This probably led him to the rather startling observation at this time that "it is better to hold the negro race an inch under water than an inch over" (*JMN* 10:357). While some have taken such statements to be indicative of a latent racism on Emerson's part, it seems clear in the context of his thought at this time that the emphasis here is on the pejorative effect of slavery, which artificially holds a race at a primitive point in its development and thus effectively "arrests" a process that otherwise would tend naturally toward amelioration.[63] Thus, while in his journals Emerson indicates that one cannot "doubt the fate of races" when observing the "position of the English, French, & Germans planting themselves . . . on South America, & monopolizing the commerce of that country" (*JMN* 11:23), speaking more generally later he adds, "We must accept a great deal as Fate. [But] we accept it with protest, merely adjourning our experiment [thus] not squander[ing] our strength in upheaving mountains." For Emerson at this point, "Fate," in terms of racial distinction, is substantial though not insurmountable, and that "mountain is conquerable also" (*JMN* 11:52). Obviously, too, there remained the positive example of the emancipated slaves in the British West Indies who flourished in their new freedom, and whom Emerson had celebrated in two of his earlier anniversary addresses (*W* 11:142).

Corresponding to this renewed tendency to speak of the development of human civilization as a function of natural progression and fatalistic force was a decrease in his tendency to speak of the influence of great men in contributing to the process. *Representative Men* would be published in January 1850, but Emerson's lectures and thoughts had been for some time moving into new subject areas such as "England & the English," "Spirit of the Times," and "Natural Aristocracy."[64] Perhaps one reason for this shift in emphasis from the individual to the historical process was Emerson's recognition that the most gifted leaders of the age were not necessarily those who supported the best moral cause. Thus, while still in England he noted of his friend Carlyle, a man whose intellectual strength and general personal vigor he had always admired, that he "is no idealist in opinions, but a protectionist in political economy, aristocrat in politics, epicure in diet, goes for murder, money, punishment by death, slavery & all the pretty abominations, tempering them with epigrams" (*JMN* 10:551). Back at home, Emerson observed that Jefferson and Franklin had been succeeded in American society by "a buffalo-hunting Frémont, or rowdy Andrew Jackson or Benton or Sam Houston" (*JMN* 11:23). And again he noted the increasingly sad case of Webster and pointed out that in American politics "the rules of the game are paramount, & daunt the genius of the best players." Thus, "Webster does not lead, but always plays a reverential second part to some ancestors, or Whig party, or Constitution, or other primary, who is much his inferior, if he had but courage & a calling" (*JMN* 11:40). Finally, Emerson's opinion of the presidential election in November 1848, which saw the Whig candidate, General Zachary Taylor, victorious over his Democratic and Free Soil opponents, was that it was "the most dismal ever known in this country" (*JMN* 11:47).

Despite such depressing observations regarding the manifest limitations of most leaders in American society, and also an occasional self-questioning as to why "melioration is not more" (*JMN* 11:35), Emerson attempted in the late 1840s to reassert his faith that things would get better naturally. His trip to England was helpful in this regard and served as an effective therapy for the depression that preceded his departure. Ellery Channing observes in his journal that "it was after his English visit that he [Emerson] became so much happier and more joyous . . . & also assumed a more public life & habit, as he became more and more a lecturer."[65] It is not surprising, then, that when William Lloyd Garrison wrote to Emerson in July 1849 to invite him to speak once more at an August celebration of emancipation in the British West Indies, the bard accepted.[66]

The West Indian celebration of 1849 was held on August third rather than the traditional August first, as a protest against President Taylor's proclamation declaring August first as a day of national fasting and prayer because of a cholera epidemic in the country. Because abolitionists objected strenuously to the president's views on slavery, his promotion of the war with Mexico, and his cruel treatment of the Seminole Indians, they saw his proclamation as a hypocritical act of false piety designed to win political popularity. Hence the protest.[67]

The gathering Emerson attended was at Worcester rather than Boston, and, although some feared this might result in a small turnout, the affair went off as a smashing success with an estimated five thousand persons in attendance. Emerson's presentation on this occasion was apparently extempore, something very unusual for him. The fact that the *Liberator*'s account of the talk indicates that the speaker was "very hoarse" suggests that Emerson probably did not intend to speak because of the impediment, and perhaps he felt that his presence alone would lend his support to those gathered there. However, as the account indicates, "on being called on, [he] said he felt it his duty to make some sort of response to the call."

Emerson's remarks on this occasion reflect how strongly the concepts of inevitable reform and melioration had again seized him, and his comments are reflected in various journal entries of the time.[68] He began his oration by noting that it is perhaps the vice of his "habit of speculation" that he is "prone rather to consider the history of the race, the genius and energy of any nation, than to insist very much upon individual action." He felt that "the scope left for human exertion, for individual talent . . . [is] very small," and we should congratulate ourselves as rational beings, "that we are under the control of higher laws than any human will." For Emerson, this fact assures improvement, and he suggests that all should "rejoice in the march of events, in the sequence of the centuries, the progress of the great universal human, [and] . . . divine genius, which overpowers all our vices as well as our virtues, and turns our vices to the general benefit. . . . The course of history is everywhere," and "it is a constant progress of amelioration."

Not all individuals are clearly aware of this inevitability, and the result is often an agitated impatience. Thus Emerson points out that it is "the ardor of our virtuous enthusiasm in behalf of the slave, and of our indignation at this oppressor [which] naturally blinds us a little to the fate that is involved alike in our freedom, and in the slaveholding system at the South." Here, as elsewhere, "fate" refers to the given circumstances of existence, and he suggests that these circumstances cannot be overcome overnight but, like the mountain to be quarried, require patience and confidence in goodness. The "progress of amelioration is very slow," and the slaveholders of the South are not exclusively to blame for the wrongdoing because they are "by their climate enervated" and "demoralized by their vicious habits." Thus, to a certain extent they are "as innocent in their slaveholding as we are in our Northern vices." However, eventually their barbarism will be overcome "as a man rises in the scale of civilization, [and] as the ameliorating and expanding principles find effect in him." In the meantime, it should be the obligation of all to contribute to the general movement of things toward this goal. Of course, among those who contributed most significantly to this cause were the abolitionists, and Emerson speaks of these individuals in laudatory terms: "It should be praise enough for our friends who have carried forward this great work, friends to whom it seems to me always, the country is more and more indebted, that it is the glory of these preachers of freedom that they have strengthened the moral sense, that they have anticipated this triumph which I look upon as inevitable, and which it is not in man to retard." And, perhaps now thinking of his own part to play, Emerson states confidently that it is "the order of Providence that we should conspire heartily in this work."

Emerson concluded his impromptu oration with "an old eastern verse" that seems to sum up the apparent paradox of the human condition as he saw it at the moment. On the one hand is the foolishness of all human activity in a world largely beyond human knowledge and control; and on the other hand is the obvious need for reform activity as an assertion of human morality in a world where choices must be made.

> Fool thou must be, though wisest of the wise,
> Then be the fool of virtue, not of vice.

Despite the optimistic tone of this presentation, Emerson's journals indicate that he still felt severe misgivings regarding the state of American affairs. He also felt at times the shallowness of a blind faith in future goodness in the face of present evil. Thus, in a journal entry on "the Times" recorded in January 1850, he says, "There is Fate; Laws of the world; what then? we are thrown back on Rectitude, forever & ever. Only rectitude: to mend one; that is all we can do. But that the world stigmatises as a sterile, chimney-corner philosophy" (*JMN* 11: 214). Times were changing, and with every day that passed Emerson seemed to know intuitively that, reluctant as he might be, a more direct and immediate role in social reform would inevitably be his in the decade ahead. It is possible that this very intuition led him to copy into his journal, but a few pages later, again under the heading "The Times," the following prophetic quotation from Shakespeare's *Hamlet*.

> The times are out of joint, O cursed spite,
> That ever I was born to set them right.
>   (*JMN* 11:217)

Chapter Five

Counterattack: 1850–1852

The feeling of well-being and confident optimism that Emerson experienced on his return from England persisted into the spring of 1850. Dramatic and disturbing national events would gradually erode this confidence, however, and once again Emerson would be forced to confront a reality where the forces of social evil were undeniably in the ascendancy. The first tremor of the impending eruption came on 7 March 1850, when Daniel Webster, now for some time a northern apologist for southern slavery, stated unequivocally his support for the series of resolutions that were introduced into the U.S. Congress to settle differences between the North and the South. These came to be known collectively as the Compromise of 1850. Among other things, the resolutions provided for the organization of New Mexico as a territory without restriction on slavery, the admission of California as a free state, and more effective provisions for the return of fugitive slaves. The Senatè debate on the issues was historic and continued from January to September 1850. In his March seventh speech in support of the compromise Webster insisted that his action was dictated by his concern for the preservation of the Union. Abolitionists, however, were horrified by the compromise, and they indicted Webster for his apparent perfidy in the affair. Lidian Emerson read Mr. Webster's speech with "grief and indignation," and the anniversary of its infamous presentation would be kept every year in the Emerson household.[1]

Support for Webster was strong in mercantile Boston. It is not surprising that the commercial element would be in the forefront applauding the compromise, and with it the preservation of the Union and the economic status quo. Toward the end of March nearly a thousand citizens of Boston (including Oliver Wendell Holmes and Orestes Brownson) published an open letter of support for Webster. Emerson was very critical of this expression of misplaced sympathy, and his journal states, "I think there was never an event half so painful occurred in Boston as the letter with 800 [sic] signatures to Webster." He further notes, somewhat caustically, "Many of the names very properly belong there, —they are the names of idiots, of aged & infirm people, who have outlived everything, but their night cap & their tea & toast." Unfortunately, in addition to these predictables Emerson also observed, much to his chagrin, "some names of men under forty!" (*JMN* 11:249).

One result of these dramatic political developments was that Emerson became even more interested in, and concerned with, the political process in the 1850s. At one point in his journal he observes that "the misfortune of New England is,—that the Southern always beats us in Politics. And for this reason, that it comes at Washington to a game of personalities." In this context the "cold Yankee" was at a disadvantage when confronting the temperament and "terror" of the southerner (something Preston Brooks would demonstrate only too well). Emerson's solution to the problem was to "borrow a hint from the military art . . . [and] let our representative know that if he misrepresents his constituency there is no recovery from social damnation at home" (*JMN* 11: 233). Unfortunately, in 1850 it was the *mis*representatives, like Daniel Webster, who were afforded the applause of the multitudes, while the moral crusaders like William Seward, the senator from New York who opposed the Compromise of 1850 on the basis of its clear opposition to a "higher law," were castigated. Such developments led Emerson to comment in his journal that "the worst symptom I have noticed in our politics lately is the attempt to make a gibe out of Seward's appeal to a higher law than the Constitution, & Webster has taken part in it. I have seen him snubbed as 'Higher Law Seward.' And now followed by Rufus Choate [U.S. senator from Massachusetts] in his phrase, 'the trashy sentimentalism of our lutestring enthusiasts'" (*JMN* 11:248). Emerson was very impressed with Seward's concern for a higher moral principle than conventional political compromise, and within a year he would employ that very concept in his first public attack on the most hateful element of the compromise, the Fugitive Slave Law.

Despite this onslaught of negative developments, Emerson strove to maintain his confidence that the ongoing and irresistible force of amelioration was still at work in American society. In April Emerson told his friend William Fisher that "a vital power in man, identical with that which makes grass grow, & the sweet breeze blow . . . should abolish slavery" (*JMN* 11:292). In the same month in Philadelphia he had high praise for Lucretia Mott, "the flower of Quakerism," who persisted in her outspoken abolitionism despite threats of violence. "No mob could remain a mob where she went," Emerson notes in his journal. "She brings domesticity & common sense, & that propriety which every man loves, directly into this hurly-burly, & makes every bully ashamed. Her courage is no merit, one almost says, where triumph is so sure" (*JMN* 11: 249). Later, Emerson told Lidian that he "dined with Lucretia Mott, who is benignity itself." And, he added, "I think that woman a blessing & an ornament" (*L* 4:194). As an indication of Emerson's growing regard for those practical idealists who pursued social reform directly, it is interesting to note that after he first met Mott in Philadelphia in 1843 he told Elizabeth Hoar, "I like her very well, yet she is not quite enough an abstractionist for me" (*L* 3:131). By 1850 Emerson was obviously becoming somewhat less "abstract" himself.

Unfortunately, at this time not all of the possessors of vital force were at work on the side of abolition and social justice. As abolitionists like Mott, Garrison, Phillips, and Emerson's friend William Henry Furness became more and more persistent in their attacks on slavery, and the compromise in particular, resistance to their efforts became more virulent and obnoxious. While at one time the abolitionists were generally perceived as rabble-rousers and low-minded agitators who were opposed in their devilment by "gentlemen of property and standing," the tables were now turned. One of the most dramatic indicators of this development came on 7 May 1850. On this date Garrison convened the annual meeting of the American Anti-slavery Society in New York City. In order to demonstrate their opposition to this meeting, and abolitionism in general, the merchants of that city organized a Union Safety Committee. The ostensible purposes of this committee were to put down abolitionism and to draw the Union back together with commercial ties.[2] As a means toward this end, the New York group employed Captain Isaiah Rynders to harass and disrupt the meeting. Rynders was a forty-six-year-old Tammany ward heeler and minor politician who was prepared to do his job well. On the evening of the seventh the meeting was called to order with Garrison, Furness, Charles Burleigh, and Frederick Douglass, among others, present. Before the meeting concluded, Rynders and his thugs had succeeded in occupying the stage, shouting down the speakers, and delivering a wild and incoherent harangue that attempted to show, on the basis of physiognomy, that Negroes were not men but animals. Eventually Rynders succeeded in breaking up the meeting entirely.

The effects of this episode and others like it were significant. One commentator noted that at this time opposition to the abolitionists was greater and more vicious than at any time since 1835, and that "it became impossible for [abolitionists] to hold meetings in great cities for some time afterwards."[3] The abolitionists themselves, however, were enhanced by this new and virulent opposition. It seemed that those who opposed abolition were showing their true brutish colors at last. In a letter to his wife Garrison described the disruptive antics of the "mobocrats" with their "yelling, cheering, swearing, etc." but added that he got through his speech, following which "Mr. Furness made a capital speech," and that the entire evening "wound up with electrical effect."[4] Furness would remember the evening until the day he died. An account of his life that appeared in the *Nation* in 1896 notes: "The proudest recollection of his life was of the meeting of the American Anti-Slavery Society in New York in 1850, signalized by the Rynders mob. He saw it all and was part of it as one of the speakers of the day. 'Never before or since,' wrote Dr. Furness, 'have I been so deeply moved as on that occasion. Depths were stirred in me never before reached.' "[5]

Emerson was very distressed by events such as these, as indicated in his later journal comments: "Were the gentlemen of N.Y. entirely satisfied with their manly performance? As far as I am informed they are ruled by some rowdy aldermen who are notorious rogues & blacklegs. They must feel very clean in going down Wall-street, whilst Mr Rhynders cows them. Is their political conscience sweet & serene, as they find themselves represented at Albany & at Washington?" However, despite these perturbations, Emerson remained hopeful that righteousness would prevail. "As for these people, they have miserably failed, & 'tis very fine for them to put on airs. The veriest monk in a college is better than they" (*JMN* 13:36).

As Emerson's comment here suggests, his concern with the evidence of barbarism derived largely from the fact that it represented the tawdry reality that underlay the sham façade of polite civilization in America. It was further evidence of the apparent failure of culture to redeem. In *Representative Men*, which had only recently been published (on 1 January 1850), Emerson presented his belief that a few sturdy and vigorous men could change the world. Such a proposition could obviously lend hope to those who sought reform through leadership, and indeed, Emerson had been lecturing on this topic for a good part of the 1840s. Unfortunately, the actions of the rowdy Rynders and the polite gentlemen he served suggested that the dominant personalities were leading society away from reform. It is especially ironic that Emerson had actually named Rynders in his journal of 1849 as "a good example of personal force" (*JMN* 11:120), and earlier referred to him as "a great deal of a man" whom he classed with Napoleon and Webster (*JMN* 9:388). Emerson was undoubtedly reminded once again of the brutish barbarism inherent in American civilization when, in journeying to St. Louis the following month, he observed among his riverboat traveling companions several planters, "one with his family of slaves," which included "6 blacks." Despite the fact that these were generally "peaceable looking farmerlike men," Emerson observed that "when they stretch themselves in the pauses of conversation [they] disclose the butts of their pistols in their breast pockets" (*L* 4:210–11).

From 26 August to 12 September 1850 the Fugitive Slave Bill was debated in Congress. It finally passed and went into effect on 18 September 1850. Perhaps no other element of the infamous compromise so outraged abolitionists as this. According to this law, all citizens were now required to apprehend fugitive slaves, and severe penalties were imposed on persons who helped slaves to escape. While there had been a federal Fugitive Slave Law dating back to 1793, that law was not generally observed in the northern states.[6] Indeed, even before the passage of the Fugitive Slave Law of 1850 Concord had something of a reputation as a haven for runaway slaves. Thus, for example, a local resident from nearby Lincoln recorded in his diary for 16 March 1849 that he had "been to Concord" that evening and that "there was a meeting there of some fugitive slaves. . . . Concord is a great resort for such people; there are many people there who are active members of the Anti Slavery society and they assist as many as they can from slavery."[7] In order to continue such efforts after the passage of the new Fugitive Slave Act, abolitionists in many northern cities formed vigilance committees to aid runaway slaves and to protect free Negroes from kidnapping.[8] Many in the North were prepared to resist the new law with force if necessary. The Boston committee included several of Emerson's friends and associates such as Dr. Bowditch, Ellis Gray Loring, Samuel May, Wendell Phillips, and Theodore Parker.[9] So confident were the moralists of the North in the effectiveness of their anticipated opposition to the law that Parker advised all fugitive slaves to stay in Boston because, as he noted, "we have not the smallest fear that any one of them will be taken from us and carried off into bondage."[10]

Emerson's initial reaction to the Fugitive Slave Law was somewhat muted, undoubtedly because he shared the assumption of his abolitionist colleagues that the law simply would not, indeed could not, be enforced in New England or anywhere outside the South. An interesting example of Emerson's mood at this time and his still persistent, though now somewhat strained, optimism is seen in his response to a request from Edmund Quincy that he submit something for publication to the antislavery annual, the *Liberty Bell*. Initially, Emerson was reluctant to accede to Quincy's request, reporting that he was "never more at a loss than when asked to send a scrap for an annual."[11] A few weeks later, however, shortly after the passage of the Fugitive Slave Law, Quincy renewed his request, noting, "I think a little wholesome rage is a good thing to set one agoing. If you approve of the treatment, I advise you to read the infernal fugitive slave bill & then the case of the first victim under it as told in last night's (Saturday's) Traveller. It is enough to create a soul under the ribs of death and to put a voice into his mouldering jaws."[12]

The case of the "first victim" to which Quincy refers is undoubtedly that of James Hamlet, a free Negro in New York who was arrested as a fugitive slave belonging to Mary Brown of Baltimore.[13] An account of Hamlet's arrest appeared in the *Liberator* on 4 October 1850 and related the particulars of his hearing before a U.S. commissioner. The *Liberator* account, which was copied from the *New York Tribune*, is prefaced with an editorial comment that states, "It will be noticed that there is very little of 'the law's delay' here; the proceedings were as summary as an Arkansas court audience could desire." As a result of this action, Hamlet was returned to his owner, but money was soon raised for him, and the following month he was restored to his freedom. Thus, the first contest under the law could be seen as a draw. Nevertheless, shortly after Quincy's second request Emerson was moved to send along no fewer than five poems that were subsequently included in the upcoming issue of the *Liberty Bell*. These five poems, all "translations from the Persian," provide an interesting insight into Emerson's understanding at this time of the relationship of art to reform and his own function as a scholar/poet in a time of social crisis.

At this time Emerson still remained confident that culture and the growing prosperity of the nation would have an ameliorative effect on the problem of slavery. Additionally, his reading in Oriental literature and philosophy throughout the 1840s tended to reinforce his basic optimism that all things tend naturally to goodness, and that even an abomination like slavery would finally yield to this "beautiful necessity." Fate was a potent and positive force in the affairs of men, and the obligation of individuals was primarily to cooperate with the fatalistic evolution of goodness and to contribute their energies in ways appropriate to themselves. This optimism and confidence are reflected in virtually all of Emerson's abolition speeches in the 1840s, including his last in August 1849, which concluded with a verse that seems to sum up the apparent paradox of the human condition as he saw it then.

> Fool thou must be, though wisest of the wise,
> Then be the fool of virtue, not of vice.

This provocative quotation is actually drawn from Emerson's favorite Persian poetry. His knowledge of Persian poetry and the Oriental philosophy it reflected developed throughout the same period (mid to late 1840s) as his initial evolution from passive to active abolitionist. The primary sources of his knowledge of Persian poetry were the two volumes of German translations published by Joseph von Hammer Purgstall in the early nineteenth century.[14] Emerson owned copies of these works and translated several selections from the German that would serve as the basis for his 1858 *Atlantic* article "Persian Poetry." They were also the source for the poems he submitted to the *Liberty Bell*.

Emerson was attracted to Persian poetry for many reasons, but the most important here is the fact that he found in it a philosophical rendering of attitudes toward fate and freedom that resembled his own. For example, in his *Atlantic* essay "Persian Poetry," he says in speaking of the Persians: "Religion and poetry are all their civilization. The religion teaches an inexorable Destiny. It distinguishes only two days in each man's history,—his birthday, called *The Day of the Lot*, and the Day of Judgment. Courage and absolute submission to what is appointed him are his virtues" (W 8:238–39). Despite this dominance of fate, however, the Persian poets also assert the intellectual freedom of the individual to act. Thus the "merit of Hafiz is his intellectual liberty, which is a certificate of profound thought. We accept the religions and politics into which we fall, and it is only a few delicate spirits who are sufficient to see that the whole web of convention is the imbecility of those whom it entangles,—that the mind suffers no religion and no empire but its own" (W 8:248). Later he adds, "his complete intellectual emancipation he [Hafiz] communicates to the reader" (W 8:249).

Scholars have noted these attitudes in the past, and Frederic Carpenter points out that "Emerson loved both Hafiz and Saadi because they were joyful. And they were joyful because, trusting in themselves and in the fullness of life, they had escaped from the ambush of fatalism."[15] Some scholars have gone so far as to suggest that Emerson's ideal image of the Persian poets Saadi and Hafiz is really a self-portrait.[16] It is this ideal that he presents in "Persian Poetry" and his preface to the *Gulistan* (1865).[17] Indeed, Emerson's own journal comments seem to confirm this conjecture. After describing the courageous character of Hafiz, Emerson commented in 1847, "Such is the only man I wish to see and to be. The scholar's courage is as distinct as the soldier's and the statesman's, and a man who has it not cannot write for me" (*JMN* 10:165). The Persian poets suggest how man might find unity in a diverse and seemingly contradictory world that is dominated by fatalistic forces and yet demands individual identity and action. The solution exists in their joyful celebration of life in art, which naturally furthers the evolution of fate and goodness, which are life's dominant forces. They are the "fools of virtue." Their poetry is an expression of "culture," and, as Emerson continued to believe, it is culture that pushes man toward improvement and ultimate good and, in the final analysis, makes "all crime mean and ugly."

Emerson found this same Oriental unity in Plato, about whom he lectured throughout the later 1840s and whom he memorialized as "The Philosopher" in *Representative Men* (1850).[18] In Plato, who represents "the unity of Asia and the detail of Europe," Emerson also found justification for his faith that "all things are in a scale; and, begin where we will, ascend and ascend," and "as every pool reflects the image of the sun, so every thought and thing restores us an image and creature of the supreme Good. The universe is perforated by a million channels for his activity. All things mount and mount" (W 4:53, 68, 69). The attractiveness of such a philosophy to Emerson, especially when dealing with the thorny issue of abolition, is suggested by William Torrey Harris in his early essay "Emerson's Orientalism." "It is the problem of evil that continually haunts him [Emerson], and leads him to search its solution in the Oriental unity which is above all dualism of good and evil. It is his love of freedom that leads him to seek in the same source an elevation of thought above the trammels of finitude and complications. Finally, it is his love of beauty, which is the vision of freedom manifested in matter, that leads him to Oriental poetry, which sports with the finite elements of the world as though they were unsubstantial dreams."[19]

It was in this philosophical and historical context, then, that Emerson greeted the news of the passage of the Fugitive Slave Law in September 1850. While his journals show that he was disappointed with this apparent insult to national morality, he was certainly not outraged. Instead, he remained confident that the law would be ignored and, practically speaking, would become a "dead letter" just as the Fugitive Slave Law of 1793 had. Even Quincy's letter pointing to the "first victim" of the "infernal fugitive slave bill" did not upset this philosophical equanimity. In fact, it probably reinforced it. The result of this first instance of arrest under the new law must have encouraged Emerson's belief that civilization and culture, as the agents of benign fatality, were having their blessed effects, and through whatever means the Fugitive Slave Law had yet to permanently return one free man to slavery. Emerson would shortly forgo this position as a result of further national developments, but for the moment it was optimism, not outrage, that characterized his mood and is reflected in the poems he sent to the *Liberty Bell* in the fall of 1850.[20] It is not appropriate to present here a complete exegesis of each poem, but it is possible to suggest briefly the significance of each as it relates to the circumstances of the moment. Also, the poems collectively offer a convenient summary of Emerson's philosophy of reform as it evolved in the middle to late 1840s. Practically speaking, these poems constitute Emerson's last expression of this position.

The first poem, "The Phoenix," suggests initially a kind of world-weariness similar to that Emerson expressed in his journals shortly before his departure for England in 1847. The personified soul, the Phoenix, is "weary of life's hope" as he flies around "this heap of ashes," which is the world as we know it. However, this condition does not last for long. The Phoenix, like his mythological namesake, "flies upward" and perches on a golden bough of the "Tree of Life," where he is restored. He thereafter spreads his wings and provides "soul-refreshing shade" for those below, who are in turn reminded of the universal goodness that pervades all, despite times of momentary darkness and despair. The poem clearly expresses Emerson's optimistic belief in the "beautiful necessity" of man's progress toward ultimate goodness, no matter how bad things may look at any particular moment.

The second selection is entitled "Faith," and as the name suggests, it furthers the image of hope suggested in "The Phoenix" and stresses the need to maintain a hopeful attitude that defies "doubt and care" in a world of vexations. Possibly Emerson intended this work to remind his abolitionist friends that despite the setbacks of the moment, "and though thy fortune and thy form / Be broken, waste, and void," the "life-root" of faith is not destroyed, and final victory is assured.

The third selection, "The Poet," stresses the idea that the true value of the poet lies in his "gift of song / And the true insight." It is difficult to resist the temptation to see this work, like the "Ode Inscribed to W. H. Channing," as yet another reminder from Emerson to his fellow abolitionists that he considered himself primarily a scholar/poet, not a stump orator. This treasure brings him "rich content" and is the true means of his service to mankind and the abolition cause. As he states,

> Courage! Hafiz, though not thine
> Gold wedge and silver ore,
> More worth to thee the gift of song,
> And the clear insight more.

Emerson's contribution of these unique poems to an annual like the *Liberty Bell*, which was almost exclusively dedicated to partisan polemics, would be yet another subtle reminder of this fact.

The fourth selection, "To Himself," could very well be, as the title suggests, Emerson's gentle reminder to himself that rather than contemplating a "course of mobs" in order to satisfy the demands of friends and others that he contribute to the struggle against slavery, he should instead be satisfied that "these verses" are his and constitute an appropriate poetic response to the needs of the times. The poem, in its entirety, states,

> Hafiz, speak not of thy need,
> Are not these verses thine?
> Then, all the poets are agreed,
> Thou canst at nought repine.

The piece is dated "Concord, October, 1850."

The fifth and final selection, "Word and Deed," was taken from the works of the Persian poet Nisami and appeared separate from the others in the issue. It can be seen as Emerson's final apologia regarding his own function in the war against social immorality. In the poem the Nightingale asks the Falcon why he, the Falcon, is rewarded with a privileged position close to the king and the finest of meals, despite the fact that he is "dumb," that is, he does not sing. For his part, the Nightingale, who squanders a "hundred thousand jewels . . . in a single tone" must feed himself with worms and dwell among the thorns. The answer to this apparent anomaly is suggested by the title. The Falcon is a hunter who does his job well, and though he is "experienced in affairs," he does not speak of them but quietly pursues what he does best. This is reminiscent of Emerson's journal statement in 1836 that "the scholar works with invisible tools to invisible ends" (*JMN* 5:116). The Nightingale, however, is a "chatterer . . . whom the people prizes not" because nothing comes of his prattle. It is not difficult to presume that in this poem Emerson sees himself as the Falcon, that is, a performer. He vigorously pursues his own vocation as scholar/poet without concern for those who would prefer that he take a more direct approach in dealing with society's problems. On the other hand, the chattering Nightingale is possibly Emerson's depiction of abolitionists who spent their energies in noisy, myopic, and self-aggrandizing polemics rather than simply living virtuous lives.

The actual submission of these poems undoubtedly served an ideal purpose for Emerson, which reflects his own commitment to the philosophy they contain. On the one hand, the works are a manifestation of culture, artistry, and intellectual freedom that deny the narrow re-

straints of the well-defined goals and organized ambitions of the abolition movement, something Emerson always chafed at, even in his own
abolition speeches. Also, unlike those speeches, these contributions to
the cause are works of art that are more in keeping with the talents and
inclinations of the scholar/poet Emerson always considered himself to
be. On the other hand, these bits of artistry appeared in an abolition annual that served as a vehicle of expression for those who actively sought
the immediate abolition of slavery and agitated in society for this purpose. Thus Emerson's contributions were simultaneously passive and
active, philosophical and immediate, confident of the benevolent forces
of fate, and yet at the same time enhancing that fatalistic process.

A month after Emerson acceded to Quincy's request an attempt was
made to seize two fugitive slaves, Ellen and William Craft, in the streets
of Boston. The vigilance committee was forewarned and, under Parker's
direction, spirited the proposed victims out of town. Following this,
Parker confronted the Georgia slave catchers in their quarters at the
United States Hotel and warned them that they were not safe in Boston. Indeed, they could not show their faces on the streets but a crowd
would gather, shouting "Slave-hunters, slave-hunters, there go the slave-
hunters." Prudently, the gentlemen from Georgia soon left town.[21] It was
just the kind of result Emerson hoped for and expected. Militant morality won the day, and Emerson recorded the event in his "Anti-slavery
Almanac" (*JMN* 14:429), which he began keeping around this time.

Events such as this undoubtedly encouraged Emerson's optimism and
his confidence in the fatalistic power of reform, despite some recent
shocks. Thus in December 1850 he could say in his journal something
he later repeated in his essay "Power" (1860): "At the South, they are
really insensible to the criminality of their laws & customs. They are
still semibarbarous, have got but one step beyond scalping. But I like to
see the growth of material interests here, as power educates its potentate." It doesn't matter what "half orator, half assassin" barbarous states
send to Washington to represent their "wrath & cupidity," because the
necessity of keeping things in order in the nation "will bestow prompt-
ness, address, & reason at last on our buffalo-hunter, & authority &
majesty of manners" (*JMN* 11:314–15; *W* 6:62–63).

Emerson continued to follow current events closely in the press. In a letter to his brother William, also in December, he indicates that "we are all in tolerable health, & in good human hope, & even have not lost our faith in Divine Order." He adds that "we are good patriots, & read the vivacious little Chronotype, eating rebellion with our daily bread" (L 4:238). The paper mentioned here, the *Chronotype*, was established in Boston in 1846 by Elizur Wright. Its purpose was to promote "good nature, good neighborhood, and good government," as well as antislavery and other causes. Significantly for Emerson, the paper was not bound by "the creed or cause of any clique, association, party, sect or set of men." Later, the paper would support the Free Soil party and the political efforts of John Gorham Palfrey, an antislavery candidate for Congress who would be fortunate enough to win Emerson's support.[22]

A journal entry, probably from late December 1850, reveals Emerson's continuing confidence that the force of conscience, feeble as it may seem, will reinforce the world against the evil of the Fugitive Slave Law. "The principle thing that occurs now is the might of the law which makes slavery the single topic of conversation in this Country. A great wrong is attempted to be done & the money power is engaged to do it. But unhappily because it is criminal the feeble force of conscience is found to set the whole world against it. Hallelujah!" (*JMN* 11:323).

The dramatic and disturbing events of the spring of 1851, however, all but destroyed Emerson's optimism regarding the social realities of the moment. They served to elicit the pure outrage one would expect when a high-minded moralist directly confronts the face of evil, and they catapulted him yet further into the rancorous realm of public polemics and party politics.

On 18 February 1851 Fredrich Jenkins (Wilkins), or "Shadrach," a black waiter in a Boston coffeehouse, was arrested as a fugitive slave. Richard Henry Dana appealed to Chief Justice Lemuel Shaw for a writ of habeas corpus but was told that the disposition of a fugitive slave was too insignificant a matter to justify such a writ. In the meantime, Lewis Hayden, a black member of the vigilance committee formed by Parker, gathered together a group of some twenty black men, stormed the courthouse where Shadrach was being held, and spirited the prisoner away.

The first stop was Concord, then the party moved northward through Vermont to Canada.[23] In Concord the fugitive was aided by Mary Merrick Brooks and others. At first, her husband, Nathan, objected to any involvement, insisting that the new law made such actions illegal, but when he saw the pitiful state the escaped slave was in, human sympathy overcame legalistic scruple, and Squire Brooks gave the fugitive his own coat and hat.[24] Such events would remain as common in Concord in the coming years as they had been in the past. Edward Emerson's "Notes on the Underground Railway in Concord" (written in 1892 as a result of an interview with Mrs. Edwin Bigelow, wife of the blacksmith who drove Shadrach out of Concord that fateful night) indicate that "from the day of the passage of the Fugitive Slave Law, the Underground R.R. was organized and active, and nearly every week some fugitive would be forwarded with the utmost secrecy to Concord to be harbored overnight and usually was sped on his way before daylight." Dr. Emerson's notes also allude to an earlier history of Underground Railroad activity in Concord. He points out that "while Henry Thoreau was in the woods the slaves were sometimes brought to him there but obviously there was no possible concealment in his house . . . so he would look after them by day, and at night fall get them to his mother's or some other house of hiding."[25] While the rescue of Shadrach was in many respects similar to that of Ellen and William Craft, it involved the storming of a federal courthouse and was thus a flagrant and widely noted flouting of the law. The event outraged proslavery forces in Washington. To southerners the Fugitive Slave Law was one of the most important elements of the Compromise of 1850, and many southern states insisted that they would stay in the Union only as long as there was strict adherence to it.[26]

In response to the furor raised over the rescue, President Millard Fillmore issued a proclamation calling upon all citizens and officials "in the vicinity of this outrage, to aid and assist in quelling this and all such combinations." The secretaries of war and the navy ordered their subordinate officers to guard against further occurrences. Henry Clay professed horror in the Senate that the rescue had been accomplished by a "band who are not of our people" and, in an obvious reference to the racial composition of the rescue group, expressed concern that "the government of white men [was] to be yielded to a government by blacks." Daniel Webster called the incident "a case of treason."[27] Eventually, one black and five white abolitionists were arrested and tried for the offense, including Elizur Wright, the editor of the *Chronotype*. After a jury trial wherein Richard Henry Dana and John P. Hale, senator from New Hampshire, provided the defense, the men were acquitted. Two years later, Dana learned that the jury was deadlocked at eleven to one for conviction. The lone holdout was Francis Bigelow, the Concord blacksmith who had driven Shadrach out of Concord.[28]

Overall, the event presented a victory for the abolitionists, but at the same time it demonstrated with distressing clarity the determination of the federal government, and its supporters in Boston and elsewhere, to enforce the Fugitive Slave Law with vigor. This development came as something of a shock and a revelation to Emerson, who had assumed, with others, that the overwhelming forces of conscience and culture would simply make the law a "dead letter." Additionally there was the fact that the Massachusetts legislature, in response to petitions arising out of the Latimer case in 1843, had passed laws forbidding state officials from aiding the recapture of fugitive slaves or from using state jails for their incarceration. The penalty for such action was either fine or imprisonment. This Personal Liberty Law was later renewed in 1855.[29] A gradual realization of the seriousness of the problem led Emerson to contribute yet another statement to the growing public debate, this time in the form of an open letter.

On 3 April 1851 the Middlesex Anti-slavery Society held its annual meeting in Concord. The recent turmoil in Boston undoubtedly lent an air of urgency to this gathering. The group was eager to express its outrage at, and defiance of, the Fugitive Slave Law and, in this first annual meeting since its passage, lost no time in passing a resolution introduced by the eloquent Wendell Phillips. "Resolved, that in regard to the recently enacted Fugitive Slave Law, our minds are made up. Let those prove it unconstitutional who choose; constitutional or unconstitutional, we mean to disobey it. Let the knaves who made it repeal it when they can, we shall trample it, now and for ever, utterly under our feet" (*Liberator*, 18 April 1851). The account of the meeting continues,

"To all these contributions of sympathy and encouragement was added a letter of Mr. Emerson to one of our ladies, expressing his regret that he was obliged to be absent from the Liberty Meeting." The lady in question was very probably Mary Merrick Brooks, who was a member of the executive committee (along with Sophia Thoreau) for 1850–51 and, as we have seen, a person who encouraged Emerson's abolitionism on many occasions (*L* 4:245).

Emerson's letter, which was included in its entirety in the *Liberator*'s account of the meeting, is important because it was his first direct public response to the passage of the Fugitive Slave Law. The letter, dated 18 March 1851, clearly indicates Emerson's growing concerns over the implications of recent events in Boston and his realization that elected officials actually did intend to enforce the law fully. It is also Emerson's first public statement encouraging civil disobedience as a response to what he saw as proslavery aggression. He states in part:

Dear Friend:

I had more reasons than one to regret leaving home at this time [he was lecturing in Pittsburgh], and, if my present engagements were not of two seasons' standing, I should have made every effort to relieve myself. For your Liberty meeting, I think it has a certain importance just now; and, really, at this moment, it seems imperative that every lover of human rights should, in every manner, singly or socially, in private and in public, by voice and by pen—and, first of all, by substantial help and hospitality to the slave, and defending him against his hunters,—enter his protest for humanity against the detestable statute of the last congress.

Emerson observes that the question of slavery is now "a subject of conversation on all cars and steamboats," and it divides society into "two classes," those who oppose slavery on moral grounds and those who do not oppose it because of "habitual docility to party leading." While this situation is sometimes discouraging, and at time "it seems we must wait for the Almighty to create a new generation, a little more keenly alive to moral impressions, before any improvement in institutions can be looked for," Emerson still appears hopeful. "The momentary interest carries it today; but, presently, the advocates of the liberal principle are victorious,—and the more entirely because they had persisted unshaken under evil report. And, as justice alone satisfies every body, they are sure to prevail at last." Unfortunately, Emerson's optimism, already under substantial stress, would be dealt a severe blow just one month after he penned this letter.

On 3 April 1851, a Negro boy, Thomas Sims, was seized by authorities in Boston. This time elaborate precautions were taken to ensure that there would be no successful rescue attempt. Sims was held in the courthouse surrounded by guards while a dozen policemen guarded the stairs. Iron chains were strung across the courthouse doors, and Judge Shaw bent low as he passed beneath them. Sims's lawyers—Richard Henry Dana, Samuel Sewall, and Robert Rantoul—presented Judge Shaw with a writ of habeas corpus, but, as in previous cases, he refused to honor it. They also argued the unconstitutionality of the Fugitive Slave Law, the applicability of Massachusetts's Personal Liberty Law, insufficiency of evidence, and every other legal alternative they could think of, but the judge would not be moved. Faced with frustration in their pursuit of legal means for Sims's salvation, the vigilance committee, under the leadership of Thomas Wentworth Higginson, concocted an escape plan that involved having Sims jump from an upper-story window onto a pile of mattresses. However, this scheme was later aborted. With all avenues of escape cut off, all legal arguments exhausted, and even attempts at purchase rebuffed, the abolitionists of Boston could do nothing further except protest through hoots and jeers as Sims was delivered to a coastal vessel on the morning of 13 April 1851. An account of the event appeared in the *Liberator* (18 April 1851). "As he [Sims] descended the steps of the Boston courtroom his sable cheeks were bathed in tears, and although he evinced the deepest grief and sorrow, he marched with a firm and manly step, like a martyr and a hero to his fate. The only demonstration made by the spectators, as the procession passed, were frequent cries of 'Shame!' 'Shame!' and questions of 'Where is Liberty?' 'Is this Massachusetts and Boston?' 'Is that Charlestown and Bunker Hill?'"

Thomas Sims was landed at Savannah and publicly whipped on 19 April, the anniversary of the Battle of Concord and Lexington at the outset of the revolutionary war. The South had its victory at last, and

Emerson and the other New Englanders must have felt the pregnant irony of the date.[30] For Emerson, the outrage of the Sims affair brought home undeniably the fact that the great engines of government and society were moving toward the unconscionable execution of a grotesquely immoral law. The words of his first major abolition address in 1844, "what the masses of men want done, will be done," perhaps returned to him now with an ominous significance. His journal entries and correspondence show movement from a slow boil to an outright eruption as the full significance of current events came home to him. His first consideration was that a great moment was lost "when Judge Shaw declined to affirm the unconstitutionality of the Fugitive Slave Law!" (*JMN* 11: 361). Massachusetts had lost its chance to confront the evil directly. The corrupting influence of the institution of slavery now threatened to pervade the entire body politic. The time for dramatic action was at hand. "Now it is not less imperative that this nation should say, this Slavery shall not be, it poisons & depraves everything it touches. . . . There can never be peace whilst this devilish seed of war is in our soil. Root it out. Burn it up. Pay for the damage & let us have done with it" (*JMN* 11:362).

The substantial impact of the Sims affair is further suggested in the tone of a letter that Emerson penned to a friend on 14 April. "At this moment, in the cruelty and ignominy of the laws, & the shocking degradation of Massachusetts, I have no heart to look at books, or to think of anything else than how to retrieve this crime. All sane persons are startled by the treachery not only of the officials, but of the controlling public of the moment in Boston. It is one suasion more to destroy all national pride, all reliance on others."[31] W. H. Furness raised the same question about the future of the nation in a letter to John Gorham Palfrey. "How can we be Union men if the sole value of the Union to the South is that it secures the Northern people as her slave catchers?"[32]

Emerson found some solace in the efforts of Theodore Parker. Parker sent Emerson a copy of his "Fast Day Sermon" delivered in Boston on 10 April 1851, which was largely an attack on the Fugitive Slave Law. In his response Emerson notes that the speech "stands the foremost consolation to me in the bad times." He also indicates that he has been reading "every word of Mann, Dana, Loring, Rantoul, & Sumner [all involved in one way or another with the Sims case]" and that Parker's "brave harangue" has restored to him "a degree of hope & the promise of returning spirits" (*L* 4:249). As a sign of their growing friendship, which was stimulated to a large extent by their mutual interest in abolition, Parker, in a return letter to Emerson, noted that the "kindliness of your letter . . . touches me exceedingly. . . . I do not deserve all the esteem you entertain for me [and] I beg you to remember how much I have got from yourself—how many times I have walked from West-Roxbury to Boston & back again to *hear you.*" His epistle ends with "It is the 19th of April today—& there hang before the two Trophies of the Battle of Lexington—which belonged to my grandfather—they & your letter help inspire me with courage & strength" (*L* 4:250). As with a similar letter from Ellis Gray Loring in 1844, Emerson was no doubt pleased with the suggestion that some of his transcendental "moonshine" had played a part in the social activism of this staunch Unitarian moralist, and now, social reformer.

It soon became painfully clear to Emerson that he himself would have to take a more vigorous and active part in the public denunciation of the Fugitive Slave Law and its adherents. His journals at this time witness a steady accumulation of vitriolic comments on the law, especially on Daniel Webster, Emerson's long-fallen hero, whom he had now come to see as a chief actor in the tragedy of national affairs. The comments clearly suggest the bitter disappointment Emerson felt in the failure of a presumably civilized culture, upon which he had based so much of his hope and energy, to effectively confront the evil of the time. It is also interesting to note Emerson's outline of a new course of action for himself in dealing with social evils.

In his journal indictment of "the most detestable law that was ever enacted by a civilized state" (*JMN* 11:352), Emerson depicts the Fugitive Slave Law as representative of the general failure of American culture in the face of an educated and wealthy barbarism. It is seen as a compelling example of the "vulgar prosperity that retrogrades ever to barbarism," which he had first described in his "American Scholar Address" fourteen years earlier. In considering the proslavery men of Boston, Emerson notes that they are "full of sneers & derision," and that "their reading of Cicero & Plato & of Tacitus has been drowned under the grossness of feeding and the bad company they have kept." He speculates that "it is the want perhaps of a stern & high religious training, like the iron Calvinism which steeled their fathers seventy-five years ago" that is responsible for the present moral malaise. Indeed, among the "old patriots" of Boston it is "only the present venerable Mr. Quincy who has renewed the hereditary honour of his name by scenting the tyranny in the gale." Emerson also takes note of "the want of loftiness of sentiment in the class of wealth & education in the University [which] too is deplorable" (*JMN* 11:353). The ideal "American Scholar" has obviously failed to appear.

But the chief representative of this cultural perfidy was Daniel Webster. Once admired by the young Emerson, the famous senator had now fallen to the deepest depths. Emerson says of him: "I opened a paper today in which he [Webster] pounds on the old strings in a letter to the Washington Birth Day feasters in N.Y. 'Liberty! liberty!' Pho! Let Mr Webster for decency's sake shut his lips once & forever on this word. The word *liberty* in the mouth of Mr Webster sounds like the word *love* in the mouth of a courtezan" (*JMN* 11:345–46). Emerson adds, "The fame of Webster ends in this nasty law" (*JMN* 11:351).

This apparent failure of culture was particularly distressing to Emerson. He had hoped that the combination of education and prosperous trade and commercialism would act like a "vital force" to make things right in America, just as they had in England during the abolition drive there. It is the final irony then, that it was precisely the educated and prosperous commercial class in Boston, with Webster as spokesperson, who so strongly supported the most egregious outrages against civilized man. Such developments not only denied any hope for social progress but actually represented a retrograde development. Thus, Emerson notes that "it was & is penal here in Massachusetts for any sheriff or town or state officer to lend himself or his jail to the slavehunter, & it is also settled that any slave brought here by his master becomes free [a reference to the Personal Liberty Law mentioned earlier]. All this was well. What Mr. Webster has now done is not only to re-enact the old law [the Fugitive Slave Law of 1793] but *to give it force* which it never had before, or to bring down the free & Christian state of Massachusetts to the cannibal level" (*JMN* 11:355). The full impact of this realization is best summed up in a later journal comment where Emerson expresses his genuine amazement that the Fugitive Slave Law, which he calls a "filthy enactment," could have been "made in the 19th century, by people who could read & write." His ultimate conclusion in the matter is simple and forceful, "I will not obey it, by God" (*JMN* 11:412).

Emerson also had no patience with those who attempted to defend the morality of the law, men like Dr. Devey and Dr. Sharpe who, said Emerson, "deduce kidnapping from their Bible." For Emerson, "If this be Christianity, it is a religion of dead dogs." What America must do is "bring back . . . the age when valour was virtue," because at the present time "what is called morality, means nothing but pudding." Emerson ends this bitter speculation with "Pardon the spleen of a professed hermit" (*JMN* 11:351).

In response to this dire situation, Emerson decided to take a more active role in addressing specifically the social concerns of the moment. His new activism would also involve direct criticism of contemporary political leaders. "I make no secret of my intention to keep them [the people of Massachusetts in particular] informed of the baseness of their accustomed leaders" (*JMN* 11:354). In Emerson's view, the role of moral commentator should naturally fall to contemplative persons such as himself precisely because their vision transcends petty political considerations. "It must always happen that the guiding counsels of ages & nations should come not from statesmen or political leaders, always men of scared consciences, 'half villains,' who, it has been said, are more dangerous than whole ones, . . . but from contemplative men aloof by taste & necessity from these doubtful activities, and really aware of the truth long before the contemporary statesman because more impressionable" (*JMN* 11:359).

Emerson's first opportunity to function in his new role as political commentator and public moralist was not long in coming. On 26 April 1851 his townsmen presented him with a petition, signed by thirty-six leading citizens, which indicated that "the subscribers are very desirous of hearing your opinion upon the Fugitive Slave Law, & upon the aspects of the times; & respectfully invite you to give them at such time as will be most agreeable to you yourself."[33] He accepted this invitation, and on 3 May 1851 Emerson delivered his first Fugitive Slave Law address.

Emerson's 1851 address on the Fugitive Slave Law is by far the most strident and acerbic of his career. Not since 1844 had he been moved to such emotional heights by a social cause. Nothing less than pure rage is evident in the pyrotechnical ferocity of this attack on politicians, crass materialism, and especially the cultivated barbarism of the polite classes who defend a moral outrage on the basis of its constitutionality. Emerson's lengthy oration begins with the recognition that the badness of the times has become so pronounced as to require of all good men a statement as to where they stand. His own personal distress with this painful situation is clear.

> Fellow Citizens: I accepted your invitation to speak to you on the great question of these days, with very little consideration of what I might have to offer; for there seems to be no option. The last year has forced us all into politics, and made it a paramount duty to seek what it is often a duty to shun. We do not breathe well. There is infamy in the air. I have a new experience. I wake in the morning with a painful sensation, which I carry about all day, and which, when traced home, is the odious remembrance of that ignominy which has fallen on Massachusetts, which robs the land-scape of its beauty, and takes the sunshine out of every hour. (W 11:179)

Emerson goes on to note that things are getting worse, and "every hour brings us from distant quarters of the Union the expression of mortification at the late events in Massachusetts, and at the behavior of Boston." This great city, once so proud of its revolutionary defense of freedom, has now stooped low enough to creep under the chains that surround the courthouse where fugitive slaves are tried. "Boston, spoiled by prosperity, must bow its ancient honor in the dust, and make us irretrievably ashamed" (W 11:180).

Following the rescue of Shadrach, there was a rush to see "who should first put his name on the list of volunteers in aid of the marshal" who would pursue. Smooth Episcopal clergymen see "Mr. Webster's treachery" as "the great action of his life." The result of this meek obeisance to evil is that "one cannot open a newspaper without being disgusted by some new records of shame" (W 11:181). The culture and civilization of Massachusetts are only sham, and "a man looks gloomily at his children, and thinks, 'What have I done that you should begin life in dishonor?' Every liberal study is discredited,—literature and science appear effeminate, and the hiding of the head. The college, the churches, the schools, the very shops and factories are discredited; real estate, every kind of wealth, every branch of industry, every avenue to power, suffers injury, and the value of life is reduced" (W 11:182).

One of the major causes of the present sad situation, in Emerson's view, is the growing pernicious influence of the dominant political parties. Because these parties lack moral leadership, they habitually subordinate principle to political expediency, and the most egregious evil flourishes with party support. "Who could have believed it, if foretold that a hundred guns would be fired in Boston on the passage of the Fugitive Slave Bill? Nothing proves the want of all thought, the absence of standard in men's minds, more than the domination of party—Here are humane people who have tears for misery, an open pause for want; who should have been the defenders of the poor man, are found his embittered enemies, rejoicing in his rendition,—merely from party ties." Emphasizing again his own shock at this turn of events, Emerson notes, "I thought none, that was not ready to go on all fours, would back this law," and yet the good citizens of Boston do. The poor escaped slave, a mere seventeen-year-old boy as Thomas Sims was, on arriving at Boston seeking sanctuary and freedom, discovers that "the famous town of Boston is his master's hound." Again, Emerson drives home the fact that the civilization, culture, and wealth of Boston, which he had once seen as among the fatalistic forces that would inevitably redeem men, are perverted into the opposite tendency. Hence the unfortunate fugitive slave soon discovers that "the learning of the universities, the culture of elegant society, the acumen of lawyers, the majesty of the bench, the eloquence of the Christian pulpit, the stoutness of Democracy, the respectability of the Whig party are all combined to kidnap him" (W 11:185).

It is still Emerson's opinion that there are divine laws at work in all this, but these laws now prescribe an inevitable suffering. "It is the law of the world,—as much immorality as there is, so much misery. The greatest prosperity will in vain resist the greatest calamity. You borrow the succour of the devil and he must have his fee." There is a kind of negative compensation at work in the present crisis, which results in the fact that "the most prosperous country in the Universe, has the greatest calamity in the Universe, negro slavery" (W 11:185–86).

Emerson argues strongly against the validity of the law by asserting that it is "contravened" by "the sentiment of duty." "An immoral law makes it a man's duty to break it, at every hazard" (W 11:186). For Emerson, the truest opposition to the measure derives from the fact that it is opposed to a higher law that all men feel instinctively in their hearts, and which represents the very essence of man's spiritual and intellectual superiority among God's creations. "Whilst animals have to do with eating the fruits of the ground, men have to do with rectitude" (W 11:188); or at least they should. To believe otherwise invites corruption. "I thought it was this fair mystery, whose foundations are hidden in eternity, which made the basis of human society, and of law; and that to pretend anything else . . . was to confound all distinctions, to make the world a greasy hotel, and, instead of noble motives and inspirations, and a heaven of companions and angels around and before us, to leave us in a grimacing menagerie of monkeys and idiots" (W 11:189).

Emerson was fully aware, as he noted in his journal, that there were those who "respond[ed] that such a concept of 'Higher Law'" was "a good joke in the courts." In fact, in a recent speech in Albany reported in the *Liberator*, Webster had quipped, "'The case [of the Fugitive Slave Law] did not turn so much on the question of the constitutionality of the law, as the unconstitutionality and illegality, and utter inadmissibility of private men and political bodies setting up their notions above it, on the idea of the higher law that exists somewhere between us and the third heaven, I never knew exactly where.' (Cries of 'Good' and laughter)" (*Liberator*, 20 June 1851). In response to this, Emerson notes that "the great jurists, Cicero, Grotius, Coke, Blackstone, Burlamaqui, Montesquieu, Vattel, Burke, Mackintosh, Jefferson," all affirm that it is a principle in law that 'immoral laws are void'" (*W* 11:190). He quotes briefly from several of these notables to establish this point. Such a concern for abstract principles of morality is the essence of human civilization, and "against a principle like this, all the arguments of Mr. Webster are the spray of a child's squirt against a granite wall" (*W* 11:192).

After noting several other principles of moral conduct, legal tradition, and public sentiment that contradict this "filthy law," Emerson then turns to Webster himself and unleashes a scathing attack. Among other things, he asserts that Webster has "irresistibly" taken "the bit in his mouth and the collar on his neck" and harnessed himself "to the chariot of the planters" (*W* 11:201); he has become "the commercial representative" and "the head of the slavery party in this country." He is a person who "obeys his powerful animal nature;—and his finely developed understanding works truly and with all its force, when it stands for animal good; that is for property" (*W* 11:203–4). So far removed is Webster from the grand heroes of Massachusetts past, that "in Massachusetts, in 1776, he would, beyond all question, have been a refugee." So much less than heroic is he that "all the drops of his blood have eyes that look downward. It is neither praise nor blame to say that he has no moral perception, no moral sentiment, but in that region—to use the phrase of the phrenologists—a hole in the head" (*W* 11:204–5).[34] So much for the "hero" of the compromise.

After thus dispensing with Webster, Emerson moves to a point of concern touched upon by many apologists for the compromise, namely, that it was a necessary expedient to preserve the Union. It is Emerson's opinion that despite the technicality of Union "there are really two nations, the North and the South. It is not slavery that severs them, it's climate and temperament," and "the South does not like the North, slavery or no slavery, and never did. The North likes the South well enough, for it knows its own advantages." Despite these differences, Emerson maintains that he himself is a "Unionist as we all are, or nearly all," and he "strongly shares the hope of mankind in the power, and therefore, in the duties of the Union," which include the "necessity of common sense and justice entering into this law." Because of this, "as soon as the constitution ordains an immoral law, it ordains disunion" (*W* 11:206–7). In order to preserve the Union, all people should be interested in pursuing justice rather than an immoral compromise with evil.

Given the severity and seriousness of the present situation, Emerson now, in a very unusual departure from his established habits, offers some very explicit suggestions. "What shall we do? First, abrogate this law; then, proceed to confine slavery to slave states, and help them effectually to make an end to it" (*W* 11:207). As a means toward this latter end, there should be instant negotiations that will "end this dangerous dispute on some ground of fair compensation on one side, and satisfaction on the other to the conscience of the free states." Using the happy and successful example of the British, which he had celebrated on so many occasions in the 1840s, he suggests that an effort be made "to buy that property of the planters, as the British nation bought the West Indian slaves. I say buy,—never conceding the right of the planters to own, but that we may acknowledge the calamity of his position, and bear a countryman's share in relieving him; and because it is the only practicable course, and is innocent" (*W* 11:208). Such a course may be expensive, but it is by no means impossible. "Let them confront this mountain of poison,—bore, blast, excavate, pulverize, and shovel it once for all, down into the bottomless Pit. A thousand millions were cheap" (*W* 11:210).

Whether or not such a plan might work only time, and God, might tell. As far as the immediate moment is concerned, however, Emerson reverts to his original point. "This law must be made inoperative. It must be abrogated and wiped out of the statute-book; but whilst it stands there, it must be disobeyed" (*W* 11:212). Having apparently experienced the exhaustion of the "sublime patience" he had referred to so often in the 1840s, Emerson is prepared now to adopt a course of civil disobedience quite similar to that for which he had chastized Thoreau in 1846. However, he undoubtedly felt that the Fugitive Slave Law was "a good case to try the question on," and, of course, he was now promoting a collective rather than an individualistic response to the evil at hand.

Emerson concludes his presentation with a reaffirmation of this determined course of action. "Here let there be no confusion in our ideas. Let us not lie, not steal, nor help to steal, and let us not call stealing by any fine name, such as 'Union' or 'Patriotism.' Let us know that not by the public, but by ourselves, our safety must be bought" (W 11:213). Finally, while awaiting the result of such active resistance, Emerson looks to the guardians of justice in Massachusetts—the courts—to take the initiative in declaring the law void. "There is sufficient margin in the statute and the law for the spirit of the Magistrate to show itself, and one, two, three occasions have just now occurred, and past, in either of which, if one man had felt the spirit of Coke or Mansfield or Parsons, and read the law with the eye of freedom, the dishonor of Massachusetts had been prevented, and a limit set to these encroachments forever" (W 11:213–14). Unfortunately, Judge Shaw never did find the courage to defy the federal power.

The law Emerson so vigorously attacked in his speech was obviously not without its supporters, even in New England. Just four days after his presentation the *Boston Post* ran a front-page item insisting that "the fugitive slave law, recently enacted by Congress, is a law necessary and proper for carrying into execution the judicial duty imposed by the Constitution." That duty, as the *Post* somewhat delicately puts it, is to return a "fugitive servant" to the party to whom "he owes such service." The *Post* insists that such a law is *necessary* because the Personal Liberty Law of Massachusetts threatens with "one thousand dollars fine and one year's imprisonment any state magistrate or officer" who performs his "constitutional duty" in returning fugitive slaves. Furthermore, says the *Post*, the "running away of a negro from one place to another" does not affect the "rights and duties of the people of the United States" as regards such fugitives, even though "there are fanatics who would have us believe that it has a miraculous effect, and is more potent for these purposes than even the Constitution" (7 May 1851).

Despite such predictable accusations of fanaticism, Emerson's speech was welcomed by abolitionists everywhere. On the same day that the *Post* article appeared, Charles Sumner wrote to Emerson that he "rejoiced in reading this morning that you had spoken on the great enormity" and asked him to repeat the performance in Mr. Palfrey's district and in Boston. "Your judgment of the Fugitive Slave Bill posterity will adopt, even if the men of our day do not. But you have access to many who, other AntiSlavery speakers cannot reach. Your testimony, therefore, is of peculiar importance."[35]

Despite his earlier outspoken condemnation of the effects of "party," Emerson did agree to repeat the speech on several occasions throughout John Gorham Palfrey's district and to aid him in his pursuit of a congressional seat on the Free Soil ticket. While Emerson did not share the reservations of Garrisonians and other abolitionists regarding the dangers and limitations of political organization and activities, it was highly unusual for him to become so directly involved in a political campaign, especially given his long-standing opposition to all types of organizations and institutions.[36] As he said of politics and the slavery question in 1844: "Virtuous men will not rely on political agents. They have found out the deleterious effects of political association" (W 11:138). His decision to become an active political campaigner therefore stands as a further indication of the depth of his concern with the crisis over slavery, and also his new determination to confront the evil more directly and, as he indicated in his journal earlier, to become a more active and outspoken critic of his times. Obviously, a foolish consistency was not to be a hobgoblin of his mind.

John Gorham Palfrey (1796–1881), whom Emerson describes as "my friend" in a letter written at this time, had a long relationship with the Emerson family.[37] As a young Unitarian minister and pastor of the Brattle Street Church, Palfrey was a pronounced favorite of Lidian Emerson before her marriage to Ralph Waldo.[38] Eventually Palfrey became dean of Harvard's Divinity School, where he said of Emerson's famous address there, "that part of it . . . which was not folly was downright Atheism."[39] For his part, Emerson referred to the "snore of the Muses" in turning the pages of the *North American Review* during Palfrey's editorship from 1835 to 1843. Apparently both forgot, or put aside, these early differences. Palfrey eventually left the ministry, as Emerson had done before him, and pursued a career as historian and politician. He was a "conscience Whig" in 1850, and in 1851 he accepted the compromise policy of Charles Sumner. The Free Soil party had been formed in the summer of 1848 as a mélange of antislavery Democrats,

Liberty party supporters, and conscience Whigs. Generally, the party aimed to separate national government from slavery in order to keep it a state institution and confine it to the limits it then occupied. In Massachusetts, under the influence of Charles Francis Adams, Henry Wilson, and Palfrey, Free Soilers were associated also with equal rights.[40] Obviously, these objectives agreed with Emerson's position at the moment as reflected in his speech. Palfrey might have caught Emerson's eye in his earlier attacks on slavery. In his work *Papers on the Slave Power*, in a chapter entitled "What Can the Free States Do About It," Palfrey suggested repealing the 1793 Fugitive Slave Law and opening the federal courts "to the citizens of the Free States threatened with injury to property, person, liberty or life, by the pseudo-legislation of the slave country." He insisted that "the courts of this Union must be open to the people of the Union," and these would presumably include runaway slaves like Thomas Sims.[41] Emerson obviously concurred with these views in his own presentation. Also, as noted earlier, Emerson had served with Palfrey as chairman of the Middlesex Convention, which had been called to protest the annexation of Texas in 1845.

Whatever the specific motivation, Emerson launched himself full throttle into Palfrey's campaign. In a letter to Theodore Parker on 9 May, Emerson responded to a request that he offer his speech in Boston: "I am not sure that it is worthwhile to read my lecture in Boston. I am to read it in Lexington, in Fitchburg, & it is asked for in Cambridge, & Waltham also,—which, if I do, you see, is stumping for Palfrey's district." He adds, "I then think to print it, and send it to my Boston Class in that form."[42] In a letter to Emily Drury he notes, "I am now for a few days, repeating in many places in my county of Middlesex, a speech on the Slave-Bill, . . . in the hope that Dr. Palfrey, my friend, will be elected at the next canvass."[43] A week after this he told Ainsworth Spofford, whose own pamphlet *Higher Laws* served as something of an inspiration for Emerson's speech, that "the Law is so bad & the servility of the people such, that it is better to say the right thing over & over in twenty places, than to be silent in nineteen."[44]

One of the major reasons why Emerson had hoped to stay out of the public controversy regarding slavery is because it invited the kind of public harassment he loathed. Except for polite notices and occasional commentaries on his lectures, and even now and then a gentle satire of his transcendental style, Emerson rarely attracted the attention of the political pundits of the local press. With his new foray into politics all that, unfortunately, changed.

Emerson's stumping for Palfrey did not escape the notice of the opposition, and an article in the *Boston Semi-weekly Advertiser* on 23 May 1851 castigated him thoroughly for everything from his disunion sentiments to his pantheistic religious views. "Mr. Emerson though 'not mingling' as the editor of the [Worcester] Spy observes, 'in the active business of life,' and never attending political meetings, has nevertheless attended and spoken at the meetings of the Garrison Abolitionists, and may therefore be fairly looked upon as a decided Abolitionist of that school." Readers are warned about the "extremes" to which the Free Soilers have carried their views regarding slavery and how dangerous these views are to the preservation of the Union. "All that was urged against the law by Mr. Emerson in his lecture at Worcester, according to the Spy, would have applied equally well to *any* law providing for the surrender of fugitives." Thus, agitators like Mr. Emerson "are doing their utmost to increase an excitement *ostensibly* against this particular law, but *really* against the provision of the Constitution, on which it was founded."[45] The article goes on to note that "a portion of Mr. Emerson's lecture at Worcester consisted in a virulent attack on Mr. Webster," whom the writer defends, largely on the basis that his efforts were aimed at preserving the Union. The article then returns to the point that "if these men were not beyond the reach of their reason on this subject, we should ask Mr. Emerson himself, whether he does not believe and admit, that if the doctrines of his lecture were sustained and enforced in the Free States, the Union would be infallibly severed."

Having thus concluded the substance of his attack on the constitutional implications of Emerson's views, the author launches a personal attack on Emerson. "We see it announced that Mr. Emerson is taking an active part in the agitation carried on the present week, in the Congressional Districts where elections are to be made on the 26th instant. The citizens of those districts will, we think, be inclined to ask themselves a few questions, as to the qualifications of Mr. Emerson to act as their counsellor in the discharge of the important duty, which will devolve upon them next Monday. We live in times that need prudent and practical men. We have never heard Mr. Emerson ranked in that class." The author suggests that Emerson is not "a reliable authority on questions of morals, or a safe guide in the affairs of life." To reinforce the point he reminds his readers that Emerson's "address at the divinity school at Cambridge drew upon him the public rebuke of one of the truest and best of men, the late Dr. Henry Ware, Jr. if we are not mistaken." He adds, "The most dangerous and objectionable sentiments are embodied in that address."

Regarding Emerson's philosophical views, these, while they are clothed in a "misty jargon," have presented Emerson in "the acknowledged character of a perpetual doubter, or inquirer; that he has been most anxious to lead his hearers to the habit of questioning authority of every description." Finally, returning to his concern with Emerson's implied opinion "that the Union of the States ought to be broken up, and the country plunged into Civil War," the author wonders if the "same habit of speculation" led Emerson to these conclusions as "lead him to the expression of perpetual uncertainty, whether Christianity is anything,—or whether God and Nature be not one."

Not only did Emerson have to contend with such bitter attacks in the press, but in at least one instance in the campaign, probably for the first time in his lecturing career, he was booed and hissed by his audience. The occasion was the presentation of the Fugitive Slave Law speech in Cambridge. The account in the *Liberator* (23 May 1851) indicates that "a considerable body of students from Harvard College did what they could to disturb the audience and insult the speaker, by hisses and groans, interspersed with cheers for Webster, Clay, Fillmore, Everett, and 'Old Harvard!' . . . These *young gentlemen* showed themselves qualified to play the part of *rowdies* as completely as any of the disciples of Captain Isaiah Rynders himself. Mr. Emerson's refinement of character, scholarship, and mild and dignified deportment, could not save him from their noisey, yet feeble, insults." The event undoubtedly made a significant impression on the gentle bard, and on others. Thirty years later, James

Thayer, in a letter to Lidian, would recall that "it was one of his [Emerson's] finest nights that I ever saw, to see with what dignity he waited for them to stop and then went on to the next word of his address."[46]

Despite such disturbing events, Emerson followed through on his commitment to Palfrey's campaign and delivered his address on the "several occasions" noted in his letter to Parker.[47] However, he did not consider it to be the best use of his energy. He was, after all, a poet, not a politician. Let each to his own. Thus, he notes in his journal, "I like that Sumner & Mann & Palfrey should not be scrupulous & stand on their dignity but should go to the stump. They should not be above their business" (*JMN* 11:380–81). A few months later, while at work on Margaret Fuller's *Memoirs*, he reflects: "In my memoirs, I must record that I always find myself doing something less than my best task. In the spring I was writing politics; now am I writing a biography, which not the absolute command, but facility & amiable feeling prompted" (*JMN* 11:434).

Regardless of such reservations, Emerson followed the election closely and dutifully recorded the results in his journal (*JMN* 11:379). The voting took place on 26 May, and Palfrey lost in his bid for office in this special election to Whig candidate Benjamin Thompson by a plurality of 87 votes out of 13,000. In Concord, at least, Palfrey was victorious. There was probably some solace also in the fact that in the preceding month Charles Sumner had successfully gained election to the U.S. Senate through the vote of the state legislature. As an outspoken opponent of slavery, Sumner would now assume the seat once occupied by Daniel Webster, and many people saw more than poetic justice in this. One partisan observer commented, "The victory this day consummated dates from the 7th of March, 1850, when that great man [Webster] stood up in the Senate and repudiated the long-cherished sentiments of Massachusetts."[48] Emerson possibly saw some compensation in the event also, and recorded in his journal his neighbor Hosmer's remark that "Sims came on a good errand; for Sumner is elected" (*JMN* 11:363).

Emerson's unique adventure into politics is perhaps less surprising when one considers that despite his reputation as a radical and self-reliant rebel in the matter of man's relationship to various institutions, especially government, Emerson had always taken voting itself seriously, although he saw it at times as a kind of roulette, as Thoreau did. At this point in time, however, he placed more emphasis on it than ever before. He told one correspondent in November 1851, "I make a point of conscience of casting my vote on all second Mondays of November" (*L* 4:265). After the election in the spring he says in his journal, "I do not forgive any one for not knowing & standing by his own order. Here are clergymen & scholars voting with the world, the flesh, & the devil, against Sumner & freedom" (*JMN* 11:375). Emerson reinforces this sentiment later when he notes, "The Purist who refuses to vote, because the govt does not content him in all points, should refuse to feed a starving beggar, lest he should feed his vices" (*JMN* 13:20).

Not surprisingly, Emerson continued to feel somewhat ambivalent about his effort at political campaigning, a feeling perhaps stimulated by the failure of his candidate. Later in the summer he would tell Carlyle, almost offhandedly, that "in the spring the abomination of our own Fugitive Slave Bill drove me to some writing & speechmaking, without hope of effect, but to clear my own skirts. I am sorry I did not print, whilst it was yet time. I am now told the time will come again, more's the pity" (*CEC* 470).

The abolitionists were generally pleased with Emerson's new activism and encouraged him to make further efforts. In July Wendell Phillips invited Emerson to again celebrate the emancipation in the British West Indies, this time in Worcester.[49] Emerson declined, saying, "I know my poverties and the like reasons too well to go oftener than is necessary."[50] Apparently he felt his recent spate of campaigning was enough, for the time at least. Similarly, in August he declined an invitation to speak before the Salem Female Anti-slavery Society but congratulated that organization for their efforts "in a good cause."[51]

Failing to persuade Emerson to make further speaking engagements, some abolitionists hoped to persuade him to publish his now famous, or infamous, attack on the Fugitive Slave Law. Wendell Phillips suggested to Ann Weston that she might encourage Emerson to publish at least parts of the speech in the *Liberty Bell* the following year. Phillips was especially interested in Emerson's "analysis of Webster, which was very acute & finely wrought."[52] When that strategy failed, Phillips persuaded Thomas Wentworth Higginson to try convincing Emerson to allow the printing of the piece. Higginson's letter in November reads in part, "What right have you *not* to print your Lecture on the Fugitive Slave Law? By reading it you have certainly already conceded that you ought to print it. If it was worth putting into plaster it was worth putting into marble."[53] As it turned out, Emerson did not publish the lecture in his lifetime, which is somewhat curious in the light of his remarks to Carlyle and the obvious desire of many abolitionists to see it in print.[54] It is possible that after the election Emerson felt the moment had passed for the publication of such an occasional piece. On the other hand, as he noted in his letter to Spofford, the content of the speech was quite similar to Spofford's own pamphlet *Higher Laws*, which Emerson had read prior to preparing his speech, and perhaps he feared, as he said to Spofford, "I shall not hide the most unblushing plagiarisms if I print it."[55]

In the North resistance to the law continued to grow, and Emerson may have taken heart that it would yet be rendered inoperative. In October 1851 a group of abolitionists including Samuel J. May and Gerrit Smith, who had gathered in Syracuse, New York, for a convention, succeeded in rescuing a fugitive slave named Jerry from his guards and hustling him off to Canada.[56] Emerson and other abolitionists were delighted with the boldness of the action and looked forward to more of the same. For example, Furness stated in a letter at the time that he had been "thinking until now that the North was getting broken into its office of slave catcher & it was very bitter to think so. But we may hope otherwise now. . . . The Fugitive Slave Law will not work, tho they have covered it with their slime." The letter concludes with a statement of optimism that many must have felt: "I trust in God Syracuse has begun the good work."[57] Emerson undoubtedly shared this hope, and a few days later gave Mrs. Thoreau a donation to help yet another fugitive slave on his way through Concord to freedom.[58] Amid the flurry of political activity and the agitation of American society over the question of slavery and the Fugitive Slave Law, Emerson began contemplating the thorny problem of how best to live in such a world. As 1851 rolled into

1852 he began a series of lectures that addressed the problem directly, which he called, appropriately, "Conduct of Life."

In the spring of 1852 Emerson continued to concern himself with developments on the national scene as they related to the question of slavery. He was also concerned with the part he was playing in the drama. At times he recognized that some type of leadership role was appropriate, and perhaps inevitable. In a letter to Ainsworth Spofford in March he observes, "It seems to me there needs some rally or concentration & strict alliance of freedom & honor throughout the land. If I were younger, I would go on such a mission, & put all the good men in knowledge & relations with each other." He then adds, "We must have a new and better Loyola to found a better fraternity."[59] There is probably more than a little truth in Emerson's comment about his age here. In the spring of 1852 Emerson was forty-nine years old, which would make him far more than middle-aged for that time. His campaign for Palfrey undoubtedly proved taxing both physically and emotionally, and, as one critic has commented, "Nobody can blame him for realizing that he himself just did not have the physical strength he would have needed for an active career as a reformer."[60] However, despite such momentary instances of fatigue and world-weariness, Emerson's reform efforts accelerated throughout the 1850s. Shortly after writing his letter to Spofford, Emerson received an invitation from the Vigilance Committee of Boston to join with them in commemorating the first anniversary of the return of Thomas Sims to slavery. The event was held on 12 April at Tremont Temple, but Emerson's heavy lecture schedule prevented him from attending. (It was necessary for him to be in Montreal on the nineteenth.)

The month of March also saw a literary event that would have grave consequences for the state of the nation. On 20 March 1852 Harriet Beecher Stowe published *Uncle Tom's Cabin* in book form. Within a year over one million copies of the book would be sold. Emerson noted its popularity in his journal: "It is the distinction of 'Uncle Tom's Cabin,' that, it is read equally in the parlor & the kitchen & the nursery of every house. . . . What the lady reads in the drawing-room in a few hours, is retailed to her in her kitchen by the cook & the chambermaid, as, week by week, they master one scene & character after another" (*JMN* 13:121). It is highly likely, given the abolitionist character of the women in his home, that Emerson was here describing his own domestic reality. He was pleased with the work and encouraged the publication of a British commentary on it, which he felt was "not, to be sure, in itself, a piece of much importance but it is an opinion, one man's opinion more, on the calamitous question on which most men are disheartened into silence" (*L* 4:302–3).

In May Emerson found the time to welcome Hungarian freedom fighter Louis Kossuth to Concord. While perhaps thinking of his own evolving concept of the relationship of individuals to their historical times and the interplay of freedom and fate in that relationship, Emerson said of Kossuth, "The man of Freedom, you are also the man of Fate. You do not elect, but you are elected by God and your genius to the task" (*W* 11:399). It is possible that Emerson felt that he was going through something of an election process of his own.

Meanwhile, the national political situation continued to deteriorate under the burden of the slavery controversy. The Democratic National Convention was held in Baltimore on 1 June 1852 and nominated Franklin Pierce for president. The party platform accepted the finality of the Compromise of 1850 and opposed attempts to agitate the slavery question in Congress. The Whig National Convention met in Baltimore on 16 June and nominated General Winfield Scott for president on a platform that also accepted the compromise, condemned the agitation of the slavery question, and affirmed states' rights. The Free Soil convention met in Pittsburgh on 11 August and nominated John P. Hale for president. The Free Soil platform condemned slavery and, not surprisingly, the Compromise of 1850. Emerson considered these developments while contemplating the visage of Washington that hung in his dining room, which, he thought, expressed an "Apalachian strength." It was a "noble aristocratic head, with all kinds of elevation in it, that come out by turns." He imagines "such majestical ironies, as he [Washington] hears the day's politics, at table." These matters include "the letter of General Cass, the letter of Gen. Scott, the letter of Mr. Pierce, [and] the effronteries of Mr Webster." For Emerson, the comparison was appalling. The noble Washington appears "like a god," while the others seem no better than "low conspirators" (*JMN* 13:63). It was about this time that Emerson penned the following couplet on Webster:

> Why did all manly gifts in Webster fail?
> He wrote on Nature's grandest brow, For Sale.
>
> (*JMN* 13:76; W 9:399)

Faced with this continuously distressing situation, Emerson occasionally felt a sense of guilt that he was not doing more himself to promote the cause of justice. His journal at this time states: "I waked at night, & bemoaned myself, because I had not thrown myself into the deplorable question of Slavery, which seems to want nothing so much as a few assured voices. But then, in hours of sanity, I recover myself, & say, God must govern his own world, & knows his way out of this pit, without my desertion of my post which has none to guard it but me. I have quite other slaves to free than those negroes, to wit, imprisoned spirits, imprisoned thoughts, far back in the brain of man,—far retired in the heaven of invention, &, which, important to the republic of Man, have no watchman, or lover, or defender, but I—" (*JMN* 13:80).

In this statement Emerson again articulates his 1840s position, namely, that he could do more to foster reform by pursuing his goals as a scholar/poet than by becoming a stump orator for political hopefuls or other such exploits. His experience with Palfrey's campaign was an immediate reaction to the rendition of Thomas Sims and the dire "badness of the times." Following what must have been the bitter experience of that campaign, the controversy involved in it, the public castigation that it brought down upon him in the press—and finally, the ultimate failure of the effort itself, Emerson probably wondered if his initial philosophy of "each to his own" in the pursuit of social reform might have been correct after all. Perhaps because of this feeling, despite numerous invitations for further abolition activity, Emerson did not speak again publicly on the antislavery issue until 1854, when the rendition of another fugitive slave would raise his ire and cause him to burst forth once again in a wrathful condemnation of the evil of the times.[61]

Despite this disinclination for public debate, however, Emerson continued to be greatly concerned about the issue of slavery. He exercised every opportunity to promote the abolition cause among members of "his set" and to dissuade those who would give encouragement to the enemy, whether directly or indirectly. One of those opportunities came with the beginning of his friendship with the American sculptor Horatio Greenough. Emerson's personal relationship with Greenough began in December 1851 when the sculptor wrote to Emerson asking permission to visit Concord to discuss his theory of structure in architecture. This theory held that "the fundamental law of all structure is the adaptation of forms to their uses and functions." It was a revolutionary concept that had been circulating in Europe for some time but was new to America.[62] Emerson was delighted with the theory and was pleased to invite Greenough to Concord, where he arrived in August 1852. Emerson was very impressed with the man and his ideas, and his journal records the following comment: "Horatio Greenough came here & spent a day:—an extraordinary man—'Forty seven years of joy,' he says, 'he has lived'; and is a man of sense, of virtue, & of great elevation. He makes many of my accustomed stars pale by his clear light. His magnanimity, his idea of a great man, his courage, & cheer, & selfreliance, & depth, & selfderived knowledge, charmed & invigorated me; as none has . . . these many months" (*JMN* 13:85).

Following this, Greenough sent Emerson an unbound copy of his new book, *The Travels, Observations, and Experience of a Yankee Stonecutter*, which he was then apparently preparing for distribution. He asked Emerson for his comments on the work, which contained essays on artistic subjects along with commentary on a variety of social, moral, and political matters. In the latter Greenough addressed the subject of abolition. In the context of that discussion Greenough states: "I am not partial to negroes. I dislike their neighborhood even in a menial capacity. I prefer doing many tiresome, and some very disagreeable things for myself rather than be very near a black man. . . . I avoid a black man as I avoid a dirty, low, white man. I turn my back on him, as all animals spurn their own ordure." Regarding the question of Negro development, Greenough is just as blunt. "The evidence of the senses places a gulph between me and the negro, and I forgo him. I shall not quarrel about superiority." This "gulph" is apparently permanent, because he adds, "Now there is a process, more rapid than geological formation, by which the low, white man can become 'nobility and tranquility.' [But] the black perishes in the process of civilization. The free negroes at the north do not prosper, develop or do good."[63]

Emerson was generally pleased with those parts of Greenough's book that dealt with aesthetics, but he scolded Greenough for his comments on the Negro. In a letter dated 6 September 1852 he says of the work: "So right & high minded as it is, I am only the more sorry that it should confound things on the negro question, & put weapons from a most unexpected quarter into the hands of the base & greedy partisan. . . . That the negro was a preAdamite, I early discovered, but now that he too reads books, the courtesy to present company seems to require that it be a little parliamentarily stated." Emerson then insists that he requires "every reasonable Saxon man not to hold slaves or praise the holding" and concludes with, "When I began this leaf I did not mean to be betrayed into preaching."[64]

Greenough was pleased with Emerson's praise of his aesthetic commentaries. Regarding the criticism of his opinions of the Negro, he states in a return letter: "So far as the negro himself is concerned I fully believe & roundly declare that I believe he *can exist here* only as bondsman— Are we not a little rash in asserting our own freedom? We are parts of an organization—and being such can have no *freedom* as I understand that term but by the dissolution of the system of which we are fractional and functional components."[65]

In his response to this argument Emerson attacks Greenough's position as articulated in his book, which includes the statement that the North should not be so intolerant of the "sin of the south in holding slaves," while it is so "tolerant of the sin of the north in holding prostitutes."[66] Emerson bluntly states: "On the *black* question, I see you are incorrigible—for a time. Why offset prostitution against slavery legislation? I do not find the parallelism. We do not ordain prostitution. We ordain kidnapping. Had we tried to force you to prostitution under penalty of a thousand dollars' fine, & jail, you might allege strict parallelism. Besides, the prostitution is not the act of the wellmeaning & thoughtful classes who are aggrieved by slavery;—No; but precisely of the overfed & animal class, who, at the north, like slavery, &, at the south, are the drivers & breeders." Emerson ends with the statement, "Ah no, Slavery is a poor hoggish thing, with which you & I have nothing to do." [67]

Following this, Greenough again requested an invitation to visit Emerson in Concord, which he received, and he made his visit in late October 1852. After this day of discussion Emerson again wrote to Greenough with comments on his book. Greenough apparently had asked if any portion of the book should be cut before it was in its final form. Emerson's answer was unequivocal. Most of it he liked but "that on abolition, I have told you, is bad,—if you print it, we will roast you." [68]

Greenough thanked Emerson for his suggestions and later requested that he send to him his copy of the work, adding, "If you should still hold Addenda about Slavery I shall beg you to send that with them." [69] It seems that Greenough had been asked to deliver two lectures and intended to use his book for that purpose. Emerson acceded to the request, apparently sending the chapter on slavery separately. In his covering letter Emerson once again expresses his feeling that the entire discussion "is very splendidly wasted powder & all makes only more flagrant this new example of genius spent in a bad cause." [70]

Eventually Greenough delivered his two lectures, on 24 and 29 November in Boston. His topic was "Art as Related to Life," a subject that seems to exclude the topic of abolition. A few days after this he became deranged, and he died suddenly on 18 December 1852 of a condition diagnosed as "brain fever." Emerson bemoaned his loss and commented to Carlyle that "our few fine persons are apt to die" (*CEC* 486). Emerson was prepared to go to great lengths in order to preserve "one of his own" from the sin of proslavery sentiment and influence.

The statement Emerson made in his first letter to Greenough, to the effect that the Negro is "a pre-Adamite," raises a question that deserves consideration at this point. In his 1844 "Emancipation in the British West Indies Address" Emerson seemed quite unequivocally to put aside "the old indecent nonsense about the nature of the negro" (*W* 11:140) and to insist that "it now appears that the negro race is, more than any other, susceptible of rapid civilization" (*W* 11:141). As we have seen, in subsequent speeches in the 1840s he affirmed this positive opinion and attacked those who insisted upon Negro inferiority as an excuse for slavery. Publicly he maintained this position throughout his lifetime. Privately, however, in his journals, he did reveal on occasion, especially in the early and mid-1850s, some doubt about the Negro's equality and ability to compete successfully in the struggle for survival. Sometimes these doubts seemed to be based upon his feeling that the Negro represented a case of "arrested development." That is, because of the deprivations resulting from centuries of slavery, the Negro had been rendered inferior to whites. In other instances the comments seem to suggest a belief in the innate inferiority of blacks.[71] Because of these private comments, some scholars over the years have been led to the conclusion that Emerson saw blacks as racially inferior and resigned himself to their eventual extinction. In his *Emerson on Race and History* Philip Nicoloff notes that while Emerson was not "willing to adopt the rash and arbitrary racial designations of many of his contemporaries . . . he did look upon the plight of the repressed races and the triumphs of the aggressive races with a philosophical resignation."[72] He quotes from Emerson's lecture "The Fortune of the Republic": "nature works in immense time, and spends individuals and races prodigally to prepare new individuals and races. The lower kinds are one after one extinguished" (*W* 11: 525). Nicoloff also maintains that Emerson believed that "races which lacked primitive energies, whose blood was pale and diluted, or whose capacity for 'refinement' was otherwise 'arrested' did not achieve a true national status, and were exterminated rather than civilized. Such had been the fate of the American Indian. Such, apparently would be the fate of the Negro."[73] All of this informs Nicoloff's statement that "his intellectual environment considered, Emerson never became more than a relatively 'mild racist,' if only because of his impatience with the extreme claims which radical racialists were making."[74] This opinion is shared by other scholars. For example, judging from the evidence of the journals, Emerson's most recent editors were led to comment, "Curiously, like many of his contemporaries who found slavery indefensible, Emerson did not find blacks fully human, or even capable of reaching the same intellectual or moral level as whites" (*JMN* 13:xiv).

Certainly these ideas of Negro racial inferiority were very much in the air in Emerson's circle and elsewhere. The episode with Greenough speaks for itself. Several other people in Emerson's environment also held pronounced racist opinions. Lidian, in a letter to Ralph Waldo dated 19 February 1852, describes a gathering at Alcott's house where Mr. Garrison was one of the company. Alcott declared "all black eyed and black haired people to be of a coarse & evil nature" and went on to maintain that while eating animal food was generally "an evil practice it might not be amiss for people of coarse nature, dark complexioned people for instance, to follow it [since] they were only acting out their gross nature and fitting themselves to do the coarse work of the world, which also must be done." Upon saying this, Mr. Alcott suffered "a rather savage attack" from Mr. Garrison who, not surprisingly, found the ideas out of line (*LL* 176–77). In his journal two years after this Emerson records Plato's speculation that "the black man is courageous, but the white men are the children of God," and adds, "It will happen by & by, that the black man will only be destined for museums like the Dodo. . . . Alcott compassionately thought that if necessary to bring them sooner to an end, polygamy might be introduced & these made the eunuchs, polygamy, I suppose, to increase the white births" (*JMN* 13:286).

In 1849 Emerson's friend Carlyle published in *Fraser's Magazine* (December) his famous essay "The Nigger Question," which was reprinted as a separate pamphlet in 1853. In this essay Carlyle attacked the abolitionists of England and their concern for blacks in the West Indies and the empire. In regard to West Indian affairs, it is reported "that the Negroes are all very happy and doing well. A fact very comfortable indeed. West-Indian Whites, it is admitted, are far enough from happy; West-Indian Colonies not unlike sinking wholly into ruin."[75] The reason for this, according to Carlyle, is that the former slaves have reverted to a primitive and unproductive life-style. One finds them now "sitting yonder with their beautiful muzzles up to their ears in pumpkins, imbibing sweet pulps and juices; the grinder and incisor teeth ready for ever new work, and the pumpkins cheap as grass in those rich climates." The result of this atavism is that "the sugar-crops rot round them uncut, because labour cannot be hired, so cheap are the pumpkins;—and at home we are but required to rasp from the breakfast-loaves of our own English labourers some slight 'differential sugar-duties,' and lend a poor half million or a few poor millions now and then, to keep that beautiful state of matters going on."[76] The problem here, as Carlyle sees it, is that the whites are naturally the masters, and if civilization is to prosper, those who are naturally superior must not be reluctant to impose their more productive ways on those who are inferior. Thus he suggests that the royal governors should tell the newly emancipated blacks, "You are not 'slaves' now; nor do I wish, if it can be avoided, to see you slaves again: but decidedly you have to be servants to those that are born *wiser* than you, that are born lords of you; servants to the Whites, if they *are* (as what mortal can doubt they are?) born wiser than you."[77] Emerson was probably not surprised by these statements, knowing his friend as he did. After all, in a journal entry noted earlier, Emerson had said of him, "Carlyle is no idealist in opinion, but a protectionist in political economy, aristocrat in politics, epicure in diet, goes for murder, money, punishment by death, slavery, & all the pretty abominations, tempering them with epigrams" (*JMN* 10:551).

Emerson's greatest friend in the scientific community was undoubtedly Louis Agassiz, a Swiss-American naturalist who was a professor of natural history in the Lawrence Scientific School of Harvard University from 1848 until his death in 1873. He was a member of the Saturday Club and at one time served as schoolmaster to Emerson's daughter Ellen and other children.[78] He also gave a lecture in Concord every year and was, at those times, a guest of the Emersons.[79] Agassiz believed that man had from the beginning been diverted into distinct types. His belief in this theory was reinforced as a result of his observations in the South.[80] In 1854 he published a "Sketch of the Natural Provinces of the Animal World and Their Relation to the Different Types of Man" (*Types of Mankind* lviii–lxxxvi), which articulated his position on this matter. Included in this same volume are other essays by different authors elaborating upon the consequences of such "types," or distinctions, among mankind.[81] In one of them, by J. C. Nott, we find the following statement: "The monuments of Egypt prove, that *Negro* races have not, during 4000 years at least, been able to make one solitary step, in Negro-land, from their savage state; the modern experiences of the United States and the West Indies confirms the teachings of monuments and of history; and our remarks on *Crania*, hereinafter, seem to render fugacious all probability of a brighter future for these organically-inferior types, however sad the thought may be."[82]

Other prominent members of Emerson's social circle held similar beliefs. Oliver Wendell Holmes had no sympathy for blacks or the cause of abolition. When he was dean of Harvard's Medical School in 1851–52, white students petitioned him to rid the class of its black members. After meeting at Holmes's residence, the faculty acceded to the white students' request.[83] Later, Holmes would express his opinion to Theodore Parker that "the white race at the south must always have the upper hand."[84] For his part, Parker, although an ardent abolitionist, believed that there was "no doubt [that] the African race is greatly inferior to the Caucasian in general intellectual power, and also in that instinct for Liberty which is so strong in the Teutonic family.[85] Similarly, James Freeman Clarke, another transcendental abolitionist, believed that the Negro did not have the "sturdy, self-reliance of the Anglo-Saxon" and was "easily depressed by unkindness."[86] Indeed, one historian points out that "a belief in the inferiority of the black pervaded the consciousness of white America: abolitionists themselves did not escape it entirely."[87]

Obviously, Emerson could not help but be affected in some way by these opinions as they were expressed by individuals in his environment both near and far. He was an intellectual and a scholar, and while the dictates of intuition were always of great significance to him, he never relinquished his belief that the intellect must also affirm and find harmony with those intuitions. The ideal was always a balance between the Reason and the Understanding. His heart was always against slavery —as he said in 1844, his very blood was antislavery—but for Emerson that could not be enough in itself. As we have seen, in his preparations for his abolition speeches he researched his subject extensively. His first major address, in 1844, was based on an exhaustive study of the history of abolition in the British Empire and the results of emancipation in the West Indies. His readings in Thome, Kimbal, and others, and the materials supplied him, at his request, by Edmund Quincy, reinforced his faith that the time for liberation had come, and that blacks "could compete with the white man." Later developments in Haiti, however, possibly served to discourage this optimism. Following the peace of 1844 there was a series of bitter internecine struggles for power between the Negroes and the mulattoes, who were descended from Africans and the early French settlers on the island. In 1849 the Negro president, Faustin Elie Soulouque, proclaimed himself Emperor Faustin I. A ten-year period of despotic rule followed. The *Liberator* occasionally reported on these unfortunate developments. On 18 April 1851, for example, the paper carried a story about the "Dethronement Plot in Hayti," which indicated that "an extensive conspiracy has recently been detected, and persons have been apprehended here, and also brought from different towns to the capital for trial." After apprehending the former chief justice of the empire, authorities provided him and four others with "a short trial by Court Martial" and all were condemned to death. Unfortunately, such tragic developments in Haiti were not new. As early as 1845 the *Boston Post* (7 August) carried a story criticizing the emancipation of slaves in the West Indies as too early, and noted: "This terrible evil, withering the country that is obliged to endure it, can only be cured by a slow process. The guardian who would thrust an imbecile ward upon the world, houseless and friendless, would not get much credit for wisdom or philanthropy." The article concludes with a quotation from a report to the British Parliament regarding Haiti, which states "the melancholy truth that they are relapsing into the indolent barbarism of their native wilds."

Such developments must have been upsetting to Emerson and, perhaps, seemed in some ways to justify Carlyle's harsh opinions and those of others regarding the capacity of the blacks to evolve democratic and civilized social institutions, despite promising developments earlier. It is possible that these very developments lie behind some of Emerson's negative journal comments on the fate of at least some free Negroes. The following entry from his 1853 journal is typical of others: "The brute instinct rallies & centres in the black man. He is created on a lower plane than the white, & eats men & kidnaps & tortures, if he can. The Negro is imitative, secondary, in short, reactionary merely in his successes, &

there is no origination with him in mental & moral sphere" (*JMN* 13: 198). Earlier, he commented that "the free negro is the type & exponent of that very animal law; standing as he does in nature below the series of thought, & in the plane of vegetable & animal existence, whose law is to prey on one another, and the strongest has it" (*JMN* 13:35).

While these views appear harsh indeed, it should be borne in mind that they are not conclusions but elements in the evolution of Emerson's understanding of the Negro race. Emerson was always a dialectical thinker, and he attempted to see not only both sides but all sides of an issue before reaching conclusions. In the case of slavery, it is clear that comments such as these represent only half of the dialectic. Indeed, Emerson headed the first statement quoted above with the designation "The sad side of the Negro question" (*JMN* 13:198). Also, even within this framework such observations must be qualified by Emerson's generally growing belief that a process of human evolution was under way, and very little could be said with certainty about man and his civilizations because the process had barely begun. Thus, a few pages later in the same journal he records the observation that "the effect of geology so much studied for the last forty years must be to throw an air of novelty & mushroom speed over history. The oldest Empires, all that we have called venerable antiquity, now that we have true measures of duration, become things of yesterday; and our millenniums & Kelts & Copts become the first experimental pullulations & transitional melioration of the Chimpanzee." Emerson concludes this rumination with, "It is yet all too early to draw sound conclusions" (*JMN* 13:199). In a later journal entry he presents the "affirmative" side of the question of the Negro's real and potential development. In this instance he clearly indicates his belief that barbarism and amelioration are not issues dominated by considerations of race alone, because "Negro & Negro holder are of one class, and, like animal & vegetable, feed on each other. What one eats robs the rest; they are mutually destructive." Despite the distressing nature of this situation, improvement is still possible for victim and criminal alike because "thought & virtue help, and science & genius would serve all" (*JMN* 14:221). Additionally, Emerson's observations on the present state of the Negro generally recognize the pernicious effects of centuries of oppression and do not preclude the beneficial effects of freedom and the advantages of civilization, all of which he pointed to in his earliest abolition speeches in the 1840s.

Also on the positive side, in 1854–55 Emerson observed of the Negro: " 'Tis a gentle joyous race very capable of social virtues & graces. Where manners are such an aristocratic element, why not theirs? They are not in a hurry, they have dignity, grace, repose. They have produced some persons of ability." Emerson goes on to note a common opinion of his time, and his explanation of it. "But now, to be sure, we are told, they are not men but chimpanzees. Montesquieu said, 'It will not do to grant them to be men, lest it appear that the whites are not'" (*JMN* 14:387–88), something Emerson believed and stated in 1844 also. Following this train of thought, Emerson then turns the tables completely on those who degrade blacks and applaud their paternal and "civilized" masters. He points out that the real barbarism of the time belongs to the white slave owners who "have continued down to this day this mild form of cannibalism as the obsolete piece of barbarism has survived in the South the wreck & ruin of the old barbarities: they do not eat men, but only steal them, & steal their earnings" (*JMN* 14:388).

Finally, it should be noted that throughout his long struggle with slavery Emerson considered the institution itself to be a moral outrage against mankind, and not justifiable on any account. As he notes in his journal in 1852, "The argument of the slaveholder is one & simple: he pleads Fate. Here is an inferior race requiring wardship,—it is sentimentality to deny it." For the abolitionists, and for Emerson, the counter-argument is as simple as it is compelling: "It is inhuman to treat a man thus" (*JMN* 13:114). Ultimately, then, it seems clear that while Emerson at times speculated about the possibility of an innate Negro inferiority, especially in the early 1850s, in the final analysis he rejected the position, and his many statements during the Civil War indicate that he looked upon the rapid cultural development of blacks as an inevitable consequence of emancipation that would finally redeem them from the debilitating effects of the institution of slavery. As Emerson indicated in his 1845 emancipation address, it was inconceivable to him that God would create an inferior race of men destined to be either the victims or the burden of others. Such an idea simply flew in the face of his own transcendental sense of cosmic justice and self-reliance.

As 1852 moved inexorably to its close, one of the grand players in the agitated drama of national politics passed away. On 24 October 1852 Daniel Webster died quietly at his home in Marshfield, Massachusetts. Emerson, who was across the bay at Plymouth at the time, later reflected upon the once-great man: "The sea, the rocks, the woods, gave no sign that America & the world had lost the completest man. Nature had not in our days, or, not since Napoleon, cut out such a masterpiece. He brought the strength of a savage into the height of culture" (*JMN* 13:111). His generally laudatory commentary ends with the sadly ironic postscript, "But alas! he was the victim of his ambition; to please the South betrayed the North, and was thrown out by both" (*JMN* 13:112).

Perhaps with Webster's legalistic defense of slavery in mind, Emerson goes on in his journal to articulate his own rather detailed argument against the constitutionality of the Fugitive Slave Law, an argument that he obviously hoped Judge Shaw and others would make. In the context of his discussion he asks pointedly why "all our northern Judges have made a cowardly interpretation of the law, in favor of the crime, & not of the right?" Still, Emerson seemed to have regained some of his former optimism now that the Sims affair was past. His speculation concludes with the statement that "Thoreau remarks that the cause of Freedom advances, for all the able debaters are now freesoilers" (*JMN* 13:114). The next three years would sorely test that faith.

Chapter Six

The Struggle Intensifies: 1853–1855

American commercial expansion continued unabated in the early 1850s, and the spring of 1853 found Emerson speculating about the problem of encouraging moral behavior in an increasingly mercantile society. Perhaps because he was preoccupied with the book that would eventually be known as *English Traits* (1856), his thoughts were led to England. For Emerson, the British experience would always be something of a cultural and social paradigm for America. He observes in one journal entry that "England never stands for the cause of freedom on the continent, but always for her trade." Generally this was also true for America, where "our people will not go for liberty of other people, no, nor for their own, but for annexation of territory, or a tariff, or whatever promises new chances for young men [and] more money to men of business" (*JMN* 13:118). And yet surprisingly, despite their gross materialism, the British "have exceeded the humanity of other governments. Cheap postage they have adopted. Free trade they have adopted. Reform Bill passed;—Emancipation of negroes; [and] abolition of slave trade" (*JMN* 13:153). In considering this apparent paradox, Emerson surmises that the efforts of gifted and committed moral leaders in England tipped the balance in favor of humanistic culture, and that generally "the cause of right can only succeed against all this gravitation or materialism, by means of [such] immense personalities." In America, unfortunately, most of the powerful men, like Calhoun, Webster, Clay, and Benton, "are not found to be philanthropists, but attorneys of great & gross interests" (*JMN* 13:118). Given this situation, perhaps something could be accomplished by more vigorous support of those potentially influential personalities who pursue social reform in the political arena. It might have been with just such an idea in mind that in the spring of 1853 Emerson accepted an invitation to attend a dinner in honor of Senator John Parker Hale of New Hampshire, a leader of the Free Soilers and recent unsuccessful candidate for president.

Emerson's response to the proffered invitation is short and enthusiastic. "I will gladly come & pay my respects to Senator Hale, on the occasion you kindly offer me. For the matter of a speech,—I will say something, if there is need, and shall be gladly be left out, if you have speakers enough" (*L* 4:354). The dinner was held on 5 May 1853 in the hall of the Fitchburg Station in Boston. Among some six hundred people who attended were Charles Sumner, William Lloyd Garrison, and Horace Mann. The account in the *Boston Daily Courier* (6 May 1853) does not indicate that Emerson spoke that evening, but apparently he did prepare remarks for the occasion should he be called upon to speak. His journals contain a "Sketch of an undelivered speech, May 1853." The content of this speech indicates that Emerson had recovered some of his confidence that slavery might still be "a subject of that slow & secular melioration which expels in time every wrong." Again he maintains, perhaps given the example of the British, that trade and the cultural development of society will ensure abolition. "If anything is pure, the riddance of this piece of barbarism cannot long be postponed. . . . In the infancy of society all the institutions are on a war-foundation, & slavery came in. Now all the institutions are all on a commercial foundation, & it must go out." Emerson also remains convinced, as he was in 1844, that "slavery is bad economy" (*JMN* 14:410). However, unlike his addresses in the 1840s, where the emphasis was on a natural process of amelioration, here he stresses the present need for individual leaders like Hale and Sumner to push the process of reform along with vigor. He notes that "the senator has not failed in his part. Justice has been done to his merits. And yet I cannot help adding a word of homage because they are so signal, & because I wish to extend my thanks to the like merits of others besides himself" (*JMN* 14:411). Emerson then adds a comment that seems to be a reflection on his own earlier calls for "sublime patience" in awaiting the slow amelioration of slavery. "Whilst this inconsistency of slavery with the principles on which the world is built, guarantees its downfall, I own that the patience it requires is almost too sublime for mortals, & it seems to demand of us a little more than mere hoping." Significantly he adds, "I think we demand of superior men, that they be superior in this; that the mind & the virtue in the country give their verdict in their day, & accelerate so far the progress of civilization" (*JMN* 14:411). (Emerson later used this statement in his 1854 "Fugitive Slave Law" speech, *W* 11:240–41.) This urging that "superior men" be superior in the matter of abolishing slavery might have been further reinforced by President-elect Pierce's inauguration speech in March, in which he pledged full support to the Compromise of 1850.

Sometime in the autumn of 1853 Emerson returned again to a consideration of how he, as scholar/poet, might make a more specific contribution to the "progress of civilization" in addressing the slavery problem. One result of this speculation is an untitled poem that appears in his journal. Eventually it received the title "Freedom" (*W* 9:198). The poem was actually composed in response to a request from Julia Griffiths in August for a contribution to a projected antislavery volume to benefit the Rochester Anti-slavery Society. It was eventually published in December 1853 in *Autographs for Freedom*.[1] Interestingly enough, the poem, like those submitted three years earlier to the *Liberty Bell*, presents Emerson's apologia for the fact that he could not, at this time at least, bring himself to write propagandistic poetry in support of abolition. The finished poem reads in part,

> Once I wished I might rehearse
> Freedom's paean in my verse,
> That the slave who caught the strain
> Should throb until he snapped his Chain.
> But the Spirit said, "Not so."

The poem goes on to indicate that freedom cannot be simply invoked in this way. It is a "gift too precious to be prayed" and can only be elicited spontaneously from the "deity."

> And, when it lists him, waken can
> Brute or savage into man.

In other words, individuals must discover the gift of freedom through their own lights and means. Where, then, does this leave the individual who wishes to promote the cause of freedom for others?

> Freedom's secret wilt thou know?—
> Counsel not with flesh and blood;
> Loiter not for cloak and food;
> Right thou feelest, rush to do.

The answer seems to be one Emerson had articulated on many occasions before, namely, "rush to do" what you feel right in doing. To Emerson at this time that obviously did not include producing propagandistic poems or, for the moment at least, additional political speeches. Edward Emerson's comment on the work seems to confirm this. He suggests that the poem expresses Emerson's "feeling that no muse would help should he attack in song African Slavery" (*W* 9:467). Indeed, Emerson's muse could not be compelled in this way, and there would remain, for a time, a chasm between politics and poetry.

Occasionally, Emerson defended his approach to reform by pointing out the limitations of those who were more conspicuously active in the cause. While he was prepared to tolerate these totally public lives, he continued to see such an emphasis as extremely limiting to the development of the individual. Thus it is around this time that he notes in his journal, "Of Phillips, Garrison, & others I have always the feeling that they may wake up some morning & find that they have made a capital mistake, & are not the persons they took themselves for. Very dangerous is this thoroughly social & related life, whether antagonistic or *co*-operative. In a lonely world, or a world with half a dozen inhabitants, these would find nothing to do." Regarding Phillips in particular: "The first discovery I made of Phillips was that while I admired his eloquence, I had not the faintest wish to meet the man. He had only a *platform*-existence, & no personality. Mere mouthpieces of a party, take away the party & they shrivel & vanish" (*JMN* 13:281–82). Emerson's attitude toward the dynamic Phillips seems always to have been somewhat ambivalent. In a letter to a friend in 1855 Emerson notes that, like Henry Ward Beecher, Phillips is "essentially public in his nature & mind." Furthermore, "one who likes private people better, is sometimes a little impatient of this" (*L* 4:499). Despite these personal reservations, however, it is clear that Emerson greatly respected Phillips's very public contribution to the cause of abolition. Despite his initial disinterest in meeting the man, a personal friendship eventually did develop between the two, and, as Ellen Emerson later pointed out, "Mr Phillips often came to our house."[2]

The dawn of the new year seemed to promise only more distressing developments in the struggle with slavery. On 23 January 1854 Senator Stephen Douglas introduced a bill for organizing the territories of Kansas and Nebraska. The bill incorporated the principle of "popular sovereignty," which essentially allowed each territory to decide by majority vote for or against slavery. Thus, by implication the bill effectively repealed the Missouri Compromise of 1820, which specifically excluded slavery from the territories of the Louisiana Purchase north of the line 36°30'. In its final form the bill expressly repealed the Missouri Compromise. The bill was approved after three months of bitter debate and became law on 30 May 1854. Northern opposition to the measure was overwhelming. Abolitionists and antisouthern politicians now declared that all the compromises of 1850 were void. Harriet Beecher Stowe donated part of her royalties from *Uncle Tom's Cabin* to organize the opposition, and more than three thousand New England clergymen signed a two-hundred-foot-long petition against the bill, which was presented to Congress by Edward Everett.[3] An "Appeal of the Independent Democrats" published on 24 January 1854 condemned the measure as a "gross violation of a sacred pledge." Among the signers of this widely circulated document was Senator Charles Sumner of Massachusetts.

Emerson was also greatly disturbed at the measure. After the general lull that followed his abortive adventure into the political world, he was once again brought to a degree of ire that would precipitate him into the dusty lists of public agitation. While the bill was still being debated in Congress, Emerson noted in his journal: "There is nobody in Washington who can explain this Nebraska business to the people,—nobody of weight. And nobody of importance on the bad side. It is only done by Douglass [sic] & his accomplices by calculation on the brutal ignorance of the people, upon the wretched masses of Pennsylvania, Indiana, Illinois, Kentucky, & so on, people who can't read or know anything beyond what the village democrat tells them." Clearly, the forces of vulgar corruption and ignorance were on the rise. Culture itself and the best-established laws and arguments were threatened by this regrettable and retrogressive development. Emerson notes, "But what effrontery it required to fly in the face of what was supposed settled law & how it shows that we have no guards whatever, that there is no proposition whatever, that is too audacious to be offered us by the southerner" (*JMN* 13: 283). The end result of this perturbation was Emerson's decision to speak publicly, once again, on the agitated question of the day. The date was appropriate enough, 7 March 1854, the fourth anniversary of Webster's perfidy. Undoubtedly Emerson hoped that his contribution would help in some way in the struggle against the passage of the bill. He titled the speech "The Fugitive Slave Law," and he delivered it at the Tabernacle in New York City.

Emerson began the speech with a personal apologia that he had recorded in his journal some months earlier. "I do not often speak to public questions;—they are odious and hurtful, and it seems like meddling or leaving your work. I have my own spirits in prison;—spirits in deeper prisons, whom no man visits if I do not. . . . The one thing not to be forgiven to intellectual persons is, not to know their own task." His "own habitual view is to the well-being of students or scholars" (*W* 11:217). However, he has come to feel that the thinkers and readers of America in 1854 are really everyone, because "owing to the silent revolution which the newspaper has wrought, this class has come in this country to take in all classes" (*W* 11:218). Hence Emerson is now prepared to lecture, via the press, to all of America, at least on this important subject. He no doubt felt that in this manner he might supply some of the moral leadership that was otherwise lacking at the moment.

Emerson then turns to the subject of his address, the Fugitive Slave Law, which he maintains was brought on the country largely by Mr. Webster. "I say Mr. Webster for though the Bill was not his, it is yet notorious that he was the life and soul of it" (*W* 11:219). This, in turn, leads him to a consideration of Webster himself. Unlike his earlier Fugitive Slave Law speech, Emerson here is more philosophical and less vituperative in his discussion of this now-deceased political paragon. After considering the enormous talents of the man as intellectual and orator, he turns to his glaring defect, a lack of moral sensibility. "It is a law of our nature that great thoughts come from the heart. If his moral sensibility had been proportioned to the force of his understanding, what limits could have been set to his genius and beneficent power?" (*W* 11: 223). Because of this deficiency of the spirit, however, when the crisis of the moment arose, Webster was found lacking. Emerson stresses here the absolute need in a cultured and civilized society for recognition of and belief in the efficacy of the spirit. Without this vital ingredient even an affluent and seemingly prosperous society remains essentially barbarous. "Here was the question, Are you for man and for the good of man; or are you for the hurt and harm of man? It was the question whether man shall be treated as leather? Whether the Negro shall be, as the Indians were in Spanish America, a piece of money? Whether this system, which is a kind of mill or factory for converting men into monkeys, shall be upheld and enlarged? And Mr. Webster and the country went for the quadruped law" (*W* 11:227).

The speech offers an account of Webster's vigorous support of the Fugitive Slave Law and notes his oft-stated opinion that "agitation of the subject of slavery must be suppressed." Nor did Emerson forget Webster's snide indictment of his own insistence, four years earlier, on the importance of a higher law in dealing with such matters. He points out here that Webster "very frankly said, at Albany," that there were those who relied on " 'some higher law. Something existing somewhere between here and the third heaven,—' And if reporters say true, this wretched atheism found some laughter in the company" (*W* 11:228).

Emerson then turns more specifically to the problem of the Fugitive Slave Law. He begins by noting how he himself came to be affected by the law, and his remarks explain clearly why he was not initially upset by its passage in September 1850. Up until the last few years he had never suffered directly from the slave institution: "Slavery in Virginia or Carolina was like Slavery in Africa or the Feejies for me. . . . There was an old fugitive slave law [1793], but it had become, or was fast becoming, a dead letter, and by the genius and laws of Massachusetts, [expressed in the Personal Liberty Law], inoperative." Emerson had assumed that this would be the case with the new law also. However, as he soon discovered, "the new Bill . . . required me to hunt slaves, and it found citizens in Massachusetts willing to act as judges and captors" (W 11:228–29). It was now painfully clear that "slavery was no longer mendicant, but was become aggressive and dangerous" (W 11:229). This evidence compels one to recognize the clear failure of culture and civilization in bringing about the progressive amelioration of social evil, a failure which, as scholar/poet, Emerson felt most acutely. "It showed that the old religion and the sense of the right had faded and gone out; that while we reckoned ourselves a highly cultivated nation, our bellies had run away with our brains, and the principles of culture and progress did not exist" (W 11:229).

Emerson then outlines the present social/political conflict in philosophical terms. "We are all conservatives, half Whig, half Democrat, in our essences; and might as well try to jump out of our skins as to escape from our Whiggery." He renders these qualities in more conventional terms. "There are two forces in Nature, by whose antagonism we exist; the power of Fate, Fortune, the laws of the world, the order of things, or however else we choose to phrase it, the material necessities, on the one hand,—and Will or Duty or Freedom on the other" (W 11:231). Emerson's willingness to equate duty with freedom here indicates clearly his understanding that, despite the obvious limitations the world places on individuals, man has not only the ability but the responsibility to act for the betterment of mankind. Ultimately, Emerson saw the dominant elements of life to be less in opposition to this process than one might first assume. The "musts" of life include not only the physical facts of appetite and the conservative desire for acquisition and protection, but also the instinct for love. Thus he states: "I too think the *musts* are a safe company to follow, and even agreeable. But if we are Whigs, let us be Whigs of nature and science, and so for all the necessities. Let us know that, over and above all the *musts* of poverty and appetite, is the instinct of man to rise, and the instinct to love and help his brother" (*W* 11:232).

Having settled this matter, Emerson goes on to consider the possibilities of acting on this philosophy at the present moment. First of all, he notes that traditional methods of political activity are inadequate. "The events of this month are teaching one thing plain and clear, the worthlessness of good tools to bad workmen; that official papers are of no use; resolutions of public meetings, platforms of conventions, no, nor laws, nor constitutions, any more" (*W* 11:232–33). Emerson's reasons for assuming the failure of such efforts include the clear recognition that they have failed even to *contain* slavery, let alone remove it. The Constitution, which "has not the word *slave* in it," has been ignored when used in arguments against slavery; the Supreme Court has failed to strike down an evil law that injures the humanity of all; the Missouri Compromise is "ridden over;" and "State sovereignty in the Free States" is ignored by the proslavery apologists (*W* 11:233). Indeed, "there is no reliance to be put on any kind of covenant." Instead, "to make good the cause of Freedom, you must draw off from all foolish trust in others. You must be citadels and warriors yourselves, declarations of Independence, the charter, the battle and the victory" (*W* 11:234–35). Unlike his speeches in the 1840s, where he counseled a "sublime patience" and awaited the effects of a "beautiful necessity," Emerson here clearly demands an individual commitment to principle that would either force politicians to respond positively to the moral needs of the moment or compel the general populace to rise above them. He reminds his audience that Cromwell once said, "We can only resist the superior training of the King's soldiers by enlisting godly men," and the same is analogously true now. "No man has a right to hope that the laws of New York will defend him from the contamination of slaves another day until he has made up his mind that he will not owe his protection to the laws of New York, but to his own sense and spirit" (*W* 11:235).

Emerson also considers the arguments against abolition. "The plea in the mouth of a slaveholder that the negro is an inferior race sounds very oddly in my ear. 'The masters of slaves seem generally anxious to prove that they are not of a race superior in any noble quality to the meanest of their bondsmen!' " He then adds a comment that had been noted earlier in his journal, "Indeed when the Southerner points to the anatomy of the negro, and talks of chimpanzee,—I recall Montesquieu's remark, 'It will not do to say that negroes are men, lest it should turn out that whites are not' " (W 11:238). In Emerson's opinion, "Nature is not so helpless but it can rid itself at last of every wrong," but he also adds the ominous suggestion that when the right comes, it will come as an "Avenger" (W 11:238). Recognizing that the patience required to await this happening "is almost too sublime for mortals, and seems to demand of us more than mere hoping," Emerson suggests that people should direct their ire toward the clergy, the bench, and the government itself for their support of slavery (W 11:241). He also points out, perhaps recalling his experience in Cambridge three years earlier, that "the universities are not . . . 'the core of rebellion' no, but the seat of inertness" (W 11:242), and this too is a disappointment.

His conclusion shows Emerson's determination once again to confront the slave powers head-on. He reminds his audience that "Liberty is aggressive, Liberty is the Crusade of all brave and conscientious men, the Epic Poetry, the new religion, the chivalry of all gentlemen." He congratulates the Anti-slavery Society, which he now sees as "the Cassandra that has foretold all that has befallen, fact for fact, years ago" and is confident that the "Anti-Slavery Society will add many members this year." His final statement reinforces his new emphasis on the idea that the abolition of slavery will require a strong and unswerving commitment from every true-spirited person. We cannot simply await the inevitable dissolution of slavery from natural causes, but instead we must remember "that there is a divine Providence in the world, which will not save us but through our own cooperation" (W 11:244).

Abolitionists were pleased with Emerson's powerful contribution to the cause, especially with the Kansas-Nebraska issue so hotly contested. In fact, Samuel May pronounced the entire course of slavery lectures at the Tabernacle "triumphantly successful."[4] As with his previous oration against the Fugitive Slave Law, however, this one also evoked a hostile, at times caustic, response from the proslavery press, especially in Boston. In fact, a strong animosity toward Emerson was one of the few issues on which some northerners and southerners could agree. An editorial in the *Boston Bee* refers to an article on Emerson that had recently appeared in the *New Orleans Picayune*, castigating him for his attack on Webster. "Mr. Emerson is not, as the *Picayune* declares, crazy, but is guilty of assailing the great who are dead, from the meanest of all causes —a sordid envy." The editorial then launches into a bitter ad hominum attack on Emerson and his circle, stating that Emerson "has long been the center of a system, composed of a few hundred ridiculous fools and lazy fellows, who deserve, each, a sound scourging for their impudence in daring to stay in a world where they are just so many nuisances, and of no earthly use whatever,—a parcel of selfish flunkies." Emerson is attacked personally on the basis of his presumed wealth. "Emerson has been made the idol of this collection of human vermin because he is the most ridiculous and the wealthiest of the entire gang . . . Emerson has houses, stocks, and others of those things that are desired by the carnalminded." The editorial contends that this wealth results from the fact that "Emerson's lectures are highly paid for," then closes with further references to Emerson's jealousy of Webster.[5]

An earlier article in the *Boston Transcript* was less caustic and gave a more mixed account of Emerson and his talk. It begins by referring to Emerson as "the great dreamer" who, "like Fine-Ear in the fairy tale, lies upon the greensward and listens to the motion of each blade of grass, to the blossoming of flowers, hears the green leaves opening to the sunshine and the whole harmony of Nature's song, and then tells us—but not often in a language which all men comprehend—what he has heard the grass, and flowers and green leaves say." Despite the satirical tone of the comment, and others like it, the article presents a fairly accurate synopsis of Emerson's speech. Indicative of the tone of the presentation, the commentator notes at one point that "Mr. Emerson discoursed for a time, upon the Fugitive Slave Law, in a manner which would have made a Southerner's hair to stand on end with indignation." The conclusion of the article, surprisingly enough, is positively complimentary.

"So the speech ended; and those who had entered the hall, thinking that the speaker could find no new form in which to exhibit his hackneyed subject, no felicity of illustration that had not been pressed into service, found that, in the hands of the master, the old theme wears a new beauty when clothed with the graces of his thought."[6]

Emerson himself was somewhat uncomfortable with the address, which was almost always the case for his public polemics. In his journal he comments, "At N.Y. Tabernacle, on the 7 March, I saw the great audience with dismay, & told the bragging secretary, that I was most thankful to those who stayed at home; Every auditor was a new affliction, & if all had stayed away, by rain, or preoccupation, I had been best pleased" (*JMN* 13:47). One of the reasons for Emerson's discomfort with the presentation may be that he felt it was somewhat unfinished and fell short of the mark he had set for himself. Certainly it was no stump oration designed to arouse the masses, as his earlier Fugitive Slave Law speech had been, but instead was more reasoned and philosophical, though emotional also. As he explained in a letter to Furness a week later, "I came home near three weeks ago, with good hope to write a plea for freedom addressed *to my set*; which, of course, like a Divinity collegian's first sermon was to exhaust the subject & moral science generally; but I fared much as those young gentlemen do, got no answers to my passionate queries—nothing but the echo of my own cries, and had to carry to New York a makeshift instead of an oracle." Despite this disappointment, Emerson was yet optimistic that he would eventually find success in his task, and he adds, "Yet I am still so foolish as to believe again that the thing I wished can be done, & I shall not cease to try—after a time."[7]

The same note of optimism is heard in a letter to Carlyle penned just three days earlier. "America is growing furiously, town & state, new Kansas new Nebraskas looming up in these days, vicious politicians seething a wretched destiny for them already at Washington. The politicians shall be sodden, the states escape, please God!" Emerson seems prepared to face the inevitable confrontation foreshadowed at the time. As he tells Carlyle, "The fight of slave & freeman drawing nearer, the question is properly, whether slavery or whether freedom shall be abolished. Come & see" (*CEC* 499).

As his letter to Furness indicates, Emerson was at this time considering a treatment of the question of slavery that would be of a philosophical nature and addressed to *his set*. This had also been his intention with regard to the 1851 Fugitive Slave Law speech. This consideration might have been larger in scope than a single speech. Emerson records in his journal that "young [Charles] Lowell said to me that he thought if we had such a tract written for Liberty now, as Milton wrote for unlicensed printing in 16[44] it would have more than equal effect" (*JMN* 14:402). Whether or not Emerson contemplated writing an *Areopagitica* for his time is uncertain, but it is clear that sometime in 1854 he began keeping a notebook devoted exclusively to material about abolition, slavery, and liberty, which he titled *WO Liberty*. Emerson probably used this notebook, some two hundred and fifty pages, from 1854 to 1857. Into it he gathered materials from other notebooks dating back to 1835, and a few later entries date from the 1860s and 1870s. Much of the material in this journal consists of commentary on principles of law (especially those that relate to his own support of the concept of a higher law); his own commentary on current events involving the slavery issue; somewhat detailed drafts of some seven antislavery speeches, the longest of which is the speech titled "American Slavery," which was delivered in Boston in January 1855 but has never been published except in the form of newspaper accounts; and the journal also contains some twelve pages of verse, including drafts of his 4 July 1857 ode on Liberty. The history of this "lost journal" is an interesting one.[8]

Probably because the original manuscript was missing at the time, no part of the *WO Liberty* notebook appeared in the Emerson-Forbes edition of Emerson's journals published between 1909 and 1914, thus depriving scholars of a valuable source of information and insight into Emerson's abolitionism. It has been speculated that because Emerson collected several of his antislavery speeches into this notebook, he might have been considering the publication of a collection of essays on the topic, or, as noted earlier, a single work on the subject of liberty.[9] If this is the case, it is possible that the publication of John Stuart Mill's *On Liberty* in 1859 may have caused Emerson to lay the project aside. At any rate, the extent to which Emerson's thinking was becoming dominated by the slavery issue is clear. Each new public outrage moved him more and more into the vortex of the growing crisis.

One of the most significant of these events occurred just one day after the final vote in which the House of Representatives approved the Kansas-Nebraska Bill, and less than three months after Emerson's New York antislavery speech. On 23 May 1854 Anthony Burns was arrested in the streets of Boston and eventually charged with being a fugitive slave. At the time of Burns's arrest the Anti-slavery Convention was meeting in Boston, and there was optimism among abolitionists that the Fugitive Slave Law could be successfully opposed. It had been three years since Massachusetts had returned a slave.[10] The abolitionists were determined to agitate the case, and Parker published a notice announcing, "A Man Was Stolen Last Night by the Fugitive Slave Bill Commissioner, He Will Hold His Mock Trial on Saturday, May 27, at 9 O'clock in the Kidnapper's Court." The placard raised the question "Shall Boston Steal Another Man?"[11] The agitators developed a plan involving the storming of the courthouse by a small group of men who would be supported immediately by a mob roused to evangelical fervor by Wendell Phillips at an earlier meeting in Faneuil Hall. The plan might have succeeded had not the men stormed the courthouse while the not-yet-fervent mob was still listening to Phillips. Thus a small group of men was met by fifty marshals, one of whom was killed in the resulting melee. Higginson was wounded and retreated with his men. When the mob finally did arrive, Bronson Alcott emerged from their midst and asked, "Why are we not within?" When told that the attack had failed, he mounted the steps himself, despite whizzing bullets from within, and withdrew only when it became apparent that no one was following.[12] When police reinforcements arrived, the rescuers withdrew.

After a week's deliberation, Commissioner Edward G. Loring decided the case in favor of Burns's owner, Colonel Charles F. Suttle of Alexandria, Virginia, despite the able defense provided by Richard Henry Dana and Charles Ellis. Following this decision, President Pierce wired authorities in Boston to spare no expense in returning Burns. As a result, the federal government incurred expenses of $100,000 to return Anthony Burns, and in the process used twenty-two companies of state militia, four platoons of marines, a battalion of U.S. artillerymen, and Boston's entire police force.[13] In the aftermath of the affair Phillips, Parker, and Higginson were arrested for treason.

Emerson was understandably outraged by this latest evidence of barbarism and brutality. The experience confirmed that the ostensible "gentlemen" of Boston were actually in a "quadruped state" (*JMN* 14: 405). He was, however, glad to see that there were also some "heroes" in Massachusetts (*L* 4:502). Indeed, abolitionists generally found some satisfaction in the fact that the Burns case evoked a "wonderful" change in public opinion regarding the rendition of slaves. Even the *Boston Advertiser* recognized that the repeal of the Missouri Compromise had enraged many citizens and moved them to defy the law. It seemed to many that the Compromise of 1850 was binding on only one side.[14] In response to this event, Emerson set to work on what appears to be an undelivered speech attacking those who defended such abominations through reference to the niceties of constitutional law. He also declaimed against the failed leadership of the body politic in America and noted that "Slavery reads the Constitution with a very shrewd & daring & innovating eye" in order to find its own defense (*JMN* 14:420). By contrast, "Liberty is satisfied with a very literal construction." Those who declaim against moralists like Emerson who indict slavery on the grounds of its opposition to higher law and other such abstractions are reminded that "the Declaration of Independence is an abstraction," and it is only the credence of man that gives it force.

Emerson saves his harshest criticism, however, for the political leaders of the moment whose obligation it is to provide moral leadership, even in opposition to constitutional law. Unfortunately, American society now faces a time "when judges do not judge, when governors do not govern; when Presidents do not preside, but sell themselves to somebody who bargains to make them Presidents again" (*JMN* 14:421). As for Massachusetts in particular: "The Governor is not worth his own cockade. He sits in his chair to see the laws of his Commonwealth broken,

& to sanction the proceeding to see every peaceable citizen endangered, every patriotic citizen insulted & hurled to the wall by the riff raff of the dance cellars & the jails of the metropolis" (*JMN* 14:422). Indeed, even the established laws of the Commonwealth were ignored in order to pay homage to the South and avoid a confrontation with the federal power. This aggressive immorality was very distressing to Emerson, and he states most emphatically, "When the guards of personal liberty, writ of habeas corpus & the like, are not used or not enforced for fear of bringing the state & federal courts into collision . . . when the United States Congress passes a law to stop the march of human civility and virtue, by preestablishing the barbarous institution of Slavery over a vast territory that had been pledged by law to freedom [Kansas-Nebraska], and this is done by the help of Northern men;—I submit that all government . . . itself is treason: you the constituency, are swindled in the face of the world." Despite this conspicuous failure, however, Emerson does not give up on government entirely. Instead, he suggests organizing to put pressure on elected representatives to make them more responsive to the will of the majority rather than the corrupted, wealthy elite. "Nothing remains but to begin at the beginning to call every man in America to counsel, Representatives do not represent, we must take new order & see how to make representatives represent us" (*JMN* 14:423). Until then, civil disobedience and public agitation would remain effective tools.

In June Emerson paid the printers for "Nebraska posters," presumably already used in protest against the new Kansas-Nebraska Act. The following month, on the Fourth of July, amid patriotic celebrations in Concord, Lidian covered the front gate and gateposts with black bunting to demonstrate her feeling that the country was "wholly lost to any sense of righteousness." Although the children were a little mortified, Ellen pointed out that "Mother said it did her heart good to express her feelings, and she thought Father quite approved."[15] On the same day Henry Thoreau delivered his powerful address "Slavery in Massachusetts" at the antislavery celebration at Framingham. This speech is perhaps Thoreau's most strident, and, as Walter Harding has noted, it is "in many respects far more outspoken than 'Civil Disobedience.'" The intense feelings generated at this critical time moved Thoreau away from his generally nonresistant views and toward an activist position. Thus, "when Garrison ceremoniously burned a copy of the United States Constitution at the [Framingham] meeting to symbolize his defiance, Thoreau heartily approved."[16] Undoubtedly Emerson did too.

Emerson's interest in the political process continued to grow during this period despite, or perhaps because of his pronounced disappointment with most elected officials on both the state and federal levels. He continued to feel that it was possible to educate the masses on the issues of the time and that most of the evil afoot in society derived from ignorance. Hence he states in his journal that "the American votes rashly & immorally with his party on the question of slavery, with a feeling that he does not seriously endanger anything. He believes that what he has enacted he can repeal, if he does not like it; & does not entertain the possibility of being seriously caught in meshes of legislation. But he may run a risk once too often" (*JMN* 13:303–4).

He goes on to stress the importance of a serious commitment to the electoral process. "Those who stay away from the election think that one vote will do no good; 'tis but one step more to think that one vote will do no harm." Such a belief can be enormously harmful in a democracy, and Emerson suggests that citizens have a moral obligation to look seriously at the issues of the day before voting; and they must vote because "if they should come to be interested in themselves, in their career, they would no more stay from the election than from honesty or from affection" (*JMN* 13:304).

Emerson's concern with the behavior of the masses in the matter of voting is a reflection of his commitment to the democratic process itself and his general confidence that eventually truth and justice would win out as the dominant shaping forces in the lives of individuals and society as a whole. Sometimes, however, Emerson's opinion of the masses has been interpreted in just the opposite fashion. Such interpretations have usually been based upon brief journal passages or comments in the published *Works*. Thus, for example, in his journal notes for the essay "Considerations by the Way," which appeared in *Conduct of Life* (1860), Emerson expressed the idea that the country must never be judged by the majority of its citizens, because "the mass are animal, in pupilage,

& nearer chimpanzee. . . . We are used as brute atoms until we think" (*JMN* 13:440; W 6:248–49), and, hence society should always be judged by its thinking minority. Commenting on this passage in his biography of Emerson, Oliver Wendell Holmes associated this "saving remnant" doctrine with that of Matthew Arnold. "After reading what Emerson says about 'the Masses' one is tempted to ask whether a philosopher can ever have 'a constituency' and be elected to congress. Certainly the essay . . . would not make a very promising campaign document." [17] Indeed, such statements taken out of context would seem to enforce the idea of Emerson's "aloofness" from common life, a failing that many critics and biographers since Holmes have asserted. However, taken in context the remarks clearly suggest just the opposite. Emerson believed great good could be accomplished by the masses, even in the simple matter of voting, if they would take upon themselves the responsibility of moral self-judgment, something he hoped to persuade them to do. Edward Emerson's comment on the passage is enlightening in this respect. "The bad politics of the day, and the stooping of public men to court the multitude which they should enlighten and lead, no doubt gave heat to the utterance. None the less he [Emerson] had faith in the Republic and in true democracy reconceived with 'natural aristocracy.' To give man his true dignity and scope he must be taken out of the herd that follows the bell-wether. His own life work was to teach man his worth and possibilities" (W 6:403). Emerson's optimism in the matter is suggested in the journal comment that follows his observations on the masses. "Nature turns all malfeasance to good. [Thus] California gets peopled & subdued by the general gaol-delivery that pours into it."

Emerson's growing interest in the political scene at this time is also evinced by his desire to offer support and encouragement to Charles Sumner, who as senator from Massachusetts was fighting a heated battle against the proslavery forces that dominated politics in Washington. To many, Sumner was a bright light in a world characterized by political darkness, and he was consistently supported in his efforts by many of the transcendental moralists of New England. [18] In a letter dated 9 June (?) 1854 Emerson thanks Sumner heartily for his "brave temperate & sound Speeches" offered in opposition to the Kansas-Nebraska Act. He also encourages him to carry on the struggle and assures him that, despite the bitterness of the opposition, the good would come forward because "water & intelligence *work down*" from the highest to the lowest, "so that, however slowly, the best opinion is always becoming known as such" (*L* 4:444). Sumner was apparently surprised and pleased by this unexpected letter from one he had so long admired.[19] In his response he states that he has often "felt strong in the sympathy of true hearts, beating . . . in tune with mine. Yours I have often felt, though I had no written word from you till now." Sumner pledged to maintain the struggle and asked for the continuing support of men like Emerson (*L* 4:445). Emerson's response, dated 17 June 1854, shows him still optimistic with the reaction of people to the Burns affair. When recently in Boston, he had observed that many people there were "stung" by the affair and felt "cheated & insulted by the riffraff of the streets," and he was confident that "if every other visitor fell in with half a dozen as good converts" as he did, Sumner would "have Massachusetts sure." He adds, "I came home with more confidence in the future of Massachusetts than I have felt for many a day." Indeed, even the colleges were at last awakening to the crisis of the moment: "At Cambridge, too, I saw good men, & there are heroes at the Divinity College" (*L* 4:448). In this last matter, Emerson may indeed have taken heart at the criticism that rained down on Commissioner Loring. After his decision in the Burns case, students refused to attend his classes at Harvard, where he was a lecturer in the Law School, and the Board of Overseers declined to reappoint him. Following this, a petition that eventually garnered twelve thousand signatures was drawn up to demand his removal from office, something that finally occurred in 1858.[20] Emerson also notes in his letter to Sumner that "Higginson of Worcester means to plead guilty to the charges of attempt to rescue, &c. & to say why judgment should not be pronounced against him." To Emerson this seemed "the simple & decisive way" to handle the matter. He concludes with the statement, "We shall not cease to prize you dearly" (*L* 4:448–49). In his response to this letter five days later, Sumner made it known that he was encouraged that people such as Emerson "believe that the good cause will yet be accepted by the world," an encouragement he obviously needed because he adds, "For

many weeks my life seemed like a bivouac on a field of battle." Sumner
closes with "I often think of you in your quiet retreat, favored by letters
& friendship."[21] Obviously, Emerson's "retreat" was not nearly as quiet
as the senator imagined.

As a means toward the end of promoting a greater public awareness
of the critical issue of the moment, Emerson wrote to Theodore Parker
in July inviting him to address the citizens of Concord. He asked him
to repeat his Fourth of July oration, "A Sermon of the Dangers Which
Threaten the Rights of Man in America," which had been given in Boston earlier. Emerson explained that it was the "design of the inviters . . .
to draw the town to hold weekly meetings on Sunday evening for liberty
& they wish to open the meeting with eclat" (L 4:452). The following
month he wrote to a friend who was traveling to Europe, "Indeed, it
is well that you are already abroad for it seems nothing can excuse an
American for leaving his disgraced & menaced home until better times.
. . . Every vote, every protest, even silent, is wanted; every disgust
even." For Emerson, all this sentiment and agitation should find proper
expression at the polls, and "the sergeant-at-arms must see to it there
is a quorum in November" (L 4:461–62). He must also have taken heart
with the formation of the Republican party in July. Partly as a reaction
to the passage of the Kansas-Nebraska Act, a coalition of Whigs, Free
Soilers, and antislavery Democrats held a meeting in Ripon, Wisconsin,
and formed the Republican party to oppose the extension of slavery into
the territories. By the end of the year the organization was spreading
throughout the North. Among its most prominent leaders was Senator
Charles Sumner.

In addition to encouraging others to a greater participation in the
struggle for justice, Emerson was also prepared at this time to use his
lecture platform to a greater extent than ever before as a vehicle for
addressing the slavery question directly.[22] In September he wrote to
Thomas Wentworth Higginson regarding a major abolition address on
which he was then at work. He told Higginson that he would "like very
well to read the Discourse that shall be written at Worcester on any
night that suits you after it is read in Boston." No doubt with Higginson's
heroic attempt at rescuing Burns in mind, Emerson added, "We hold

your name in so high regard here, that I am happy in having a note from you."[23] The date for Boston was finally set for 25 January, and Emerson appeared in Worcester the following evening.[24] Additionally, Emerson was invited to speak again in New York before an antislavery audience.[25] He was less enthusiastic about the New York affair and told Oliver Johnson, "I am not very ready to come to N.Y. this winter on the errand you offer me, but not so set against it, as to insist on a refusal. I am enjoined on the 30 January, but if 6 February will serve you, you may hold me."[26] Johnson did. Before the year was out, Emerson also agreed to lecture before the Bangor, Maine, Anti-slavery Society on 28 December.[27]

Despite the extensive commitments Emerson made at this time to lecture on the topic of slavery, he still felt that such deliberate efforts at setting the world aright were like Hamlet's task. A letter to his brother William in January 1855 states, "I am trying hard in these days to see some light in the dark Slavery question to which I am to speak next week in Boston. But to me as to many 'tis like Hamlet's task imposed on so unfit an agent as Hamlet." The task was formidable indeed to one who relied on the spirit to persuade the mind, and Emerson notes that "the mountains of cotton & sugar seem unpersuadable by any words as Sebastopol to a herald's oration. Howbeit, if we only drum, we must drum well" (L 4:484–85).

Emerson delivered his "American Slavery Address" as promised, on 25 January 1855 at the Tremont Temple in Boston. Although the speech has never been published, the manuscript has been preserved, and a very complete account of the speech was published the next day in the *Boston Evening Traveller*. Also, several pages of notes for the speech appear in the *WO Liberty* notebook. Unlike his last antislavery speech in the Boston area, this one was well received. The *Traveller* account indicates that Emerson was "listened to throughout with breathless interest and frequently applauded."[28] Emerson's notes for the presentation suggest that he had intended to begin with his usual apologia for entering a field where "I have not found in myself the right qualifications to serve." He also considered noting that he had "neither the taste or the talent that is needed for the disposition of political questions."[29] However, perhaps bearing in mind the tendency of some Boston papers to discount his testimony on this very basis, he apparently decided to forgo such apologetics and go directly to the subject.

Emerson's "American Slavery Address" is a powerful oration. It is somewhat unique among his presentations upon the subject in that, to a larger extent than any other, it presents simultaneously philosophical and practical views that depict the corruption of slavery as but one aspect of a larger malaise afflicting the spirit of man in America. The presentation turns to politics, business, religion, and education to examine how the skepticism (i.e., the spiritual faithlessness of the age) has fostered and abetted the aggressive outrages of the slave power. It is quintessentially Emersonian in its philosophy but is rendered in unusually immediate and practical terms.

At the beginning of his presentation Emerson outlines the major problem of the moment, namely, the expansion of the slave powers. "We sit here, the third generation in the humiliation of our forefathers, when they made an evil contract with the slaveholders at the formation of the government. We have added to that the new stringencies of the fugitive law of 1850. The last year has added the ponderous Nebraska and Kansas legislation." Because of these developments, "the code of slavery in this country . . . is at this hour more malignant, in present and in prospect, than ever before." This contagion is obviously spreading and should be a cause of concern to every American because "a high state of general health cannot long co-exist with a mortal disease in any part." Slavery "will yield at last, and go with cannibalism, sea-kings, duellism, [and] burking." However, the crisis of the moment demands more than patience. We cannot be content "to go to the Southern planter, and say, 'you are you and I am I, and God send you an early conversion.'" The evil of slavery is now so great and the institution so extensive that "it staggers our faith in human progress."

Emerson next turns to a consideration of how this sad state of affairs came about, and submits that it is "an accident of a larger calamity. It rests on scepticism, which is not local, but universal," and, as Emerson had noted before and would note again in *Conduct of Life*, skepticism is "distrust in human virtue" (W 6:210). People no longer believe in the noble possibilities of man, and hence they accept what they see as the best that can be. "I find this scepticism very widespread. Young men want object, want foundation, want ideal object." Because they lack this essential faith, these young men "slip into some niche or crevice of society, some counting-house or railroad" and there abide while the corruption of the world goes onward. This ennui seems, in Emerson's view, to dominate the youth of the nation, especially in the upper reaches of society, from whence, one would assume, the future leaders of the nation might derive. "Go into the festooned and tempered brilliancy of the drawing-rooms, and see the fortunate youth, of both sexes, the flower of our society, for whom every favor, every accomplishment, every faculty has been secured—will you find genius and courage expanding those fair forms? Or is their beauty only a mask for cunning? Have they grown worldly-wise?" There are no dreams for these people; they will live flat lives characterized by "settled practices."

The problem here is one that Emerson addressed frequently throughout his career. The people he describes have lost the capacity to feel as well as think, to dream as well as plan, to look within as well as without for guidance in life. Emerson reminds his audience that "God still instructs through the imagination," and he assures them, lest there be any doubt in these skeptical times, that "God is there still, sitting in his sphere." Because of this lack of thoughtful imagination and faith, "the law, religion and education of the land" suffer. "We send our boys to Universities, but do these institutions inspire the hope and gratitude which at great moments have filled them with enthusiastic crowds?" The answer now, as in 1837, is clearly no.

This want of faith makes men weak in the face of adversity and drains from them the courage and commitment necessary to attack the evils of the world. Thus "the party of property and education, the Whig party" has never "addressed themselves to the solemn purpose of relieving this country of this monumental calamity of slavery." Indeed, it is a sad fact that generally "our politics have run very low, and gentlemen of character will not longer go into them. It is fast becoming, if it has not already become, discreditable work." Politicians generally find themselves representing "the property of their constituency," and "the men of commerce I am afraid do not believe in anything but their trade." Because of this diminished faith in heroic principles and higher laws, based ultimately on faith in God, men are left more and more only with the presumed certainty of *things*, which results ultimately in a vulgar and pernicious materialism. "What happens after periods of extraordinary prosperity has happened now. Men could not see beyond their eyes. The cause being out of sight, is out of mind. They see meat and wine, steam and machinery in the career of wealth."

What seems to be even more disturbing to Emerson is the fact that some people have rejected even the shallow principles of wealth in directing the lives of men, and instead assert the dominance of a blind, indifferent chance. "I saw a man in a calico printing mill who fancied that there was no reason why this pattern should please, and that not —they were all jumbles of color, of which one had the luck to take, and that was all." This simple opinion apparently startled Emerson, and he asked the man "if he had that blue jelly called his eye by chance?" "Everything rests on foundations," the popularity of certain calico prints as well as the "reputation of Parthenon, or the Elgin marbles." To doubt this is to doubt the necessity of the "reputation of Jesus . . . or the reputation of any of the great lawgivers, Socrates, the Stoics, Luther, [or] Washington." Principles, sacred principles, are at work in the lives and activities of all, not "accident or caprice." There are times when human beings are willing to doubt the correctness of this belief in principles. Emerson describes them as "periods of occultation when the light of the mind seems to be partially withdrawn from nations as well as from individuals." For Emerson, "that devastation reached its crisis in the acquiescence in slavery in this country. . . . In 1850 men in Republican America passed a statute which made Justice and Mercy subject to fine and imprisonment, and multitudes were found to declare that there existed no higher law in the universe than their Constitution and this paper statute which uprooted the foundations of rectitude."

"The idea of abstract right exists in the human mind," and one of the most important of these rights is liberty. The Founding Fathers were aware of this and made an unfortunate blunder when they accepted the three-fifths compromise in 1787 in exchange for the "magnificent prosperity of America from 1787 downward," which was "the excuse pleaded for their crime." For Emerson, "they should have refused it at the risk of making no Union." He describes an interesting historical scenario where the North, in 1776, would have formed its own Union, and the South a "separate alliance with England," as a result of which "the [American] slave would have been emancipated at the same time as those in the West Indies, and then the colonies [of the South] would have been annexed to us." Thus, slavery would have been abolished as the result of the insistence upon the principle of liberty over a period of time, but it was not to be.

Emerson then returns to the importance of, and the historical justification for, the idea of a higher law. He cites as authorities Menu, Lycurgus, Moses, Confucius, Jesus, Cicero, Selden, and the "chief Justices of England," all of whom maintain that "you cannot enact a false thing to be true and a wrong thing to be right." Unfortunately, this important principle is not being observed, and despite the fact that "there was law enough . . . in the State of Massachusetts to resist a dishonor and crime . . . no judge had heart to invoke it—no governor was found to execute it. The governor was not worth his own cockade; and the Judge was afraid of the collision of the United States court with the local court." This tragedy happened because "the judges were sceptics. They showed the sickness of the time." However, despite this general corruption in society, there are those who yet stand forward. Emerson undoubtedly had his abolitionist friends in mind when he said, "Men of reason, of truth, private men, have great hearts. This is the compensation of bad governments,—the theatre they afford to illustrious men, and we have all of us a great debt to the brave and conscientious men, who, in the very hour and place of the evil acts, made their protests for themselves and country—men by word and by deed."

Also, to correct any erroneous impressions that may have grown out of his earlier teachings regarding the importance of the individual, Emerson says, "Whilst I insist on the doctrine of the independence and the inspiration of the individual . . . I do not cripple but exalt the social action." The most immediate social action that all Americans should take is the pursuit of liberty for themselves and others. "No citizen will go wrong who upon any question leans to the side of general liberty."

Emerson further suggests the importance of the present crusade and reminds his audience that "Hope is. Love is. Despair is none. . . . It is delicious to act with great masses to great aims," and the abolition of slavery is one of them.

Emerson states once again his suggestion that the slaves be purchased and emancipated as the British did in the West Indies, whatever the cost. His address closes on an optimistic note, reminding the audience that victory is inevitable. "There is longevity in the cause of freedom. It can well afford to wait, if God pleases, for ages. It is the order that chemistry, nature, the stars of Heaven, the thoughts of the mind, are all to be the emancipators of the slave!"

Convers Francis remarked in his journal two days after this presentation that despite his opinion that the speech was "not well adapted on the whole for popular impression," is was "admirable in parts; wise and true in all." The bard's demeanor during his talk apparently compensated considerably for any deficiency of content, and Francis noted further the "deep power" that welled out from Emerson's face during his presentation.[30] Charles Sumner was also pleased with Emerson's latest contribution to the cause and states in a letter written three days after the event, "I have read the report of your late address on slavery with delight & gratitude. I cannot forbear saying so. These words must be felt." The address left Sumner with the hope that "perhaps out of our present chaos, Kosmos may come."[31]

Emerson was pleased enough with the speech to agree to repeat it on at least seven occasions, including Worcester, Massachusetts, on the following day, New York on 6 February, and Philadelphia on 8 February.[32] This speech, more than any of Emerson's earlier addresses on the subject, clearly represents an effort to place the slavery question within the larger context of his most seminal ideas and concerns. The experiment left him only partially satisfied, however, and his reservations about becoming too specific in the matter of reform continued. In his journal he records that "Philip Randolf was surprised to find me speaking to the politics of Antislavery, in Philadelphia. I suppose, because he thought me a believer in general laws, and that it was a kind of distrust of my own general teachings to appear in active sympathy with these temporary heats" (*JMN* 13:405). This statement echoes a similar one made to Carlyle in 1844, and the concern is obviously still with Emerson. Randolf "is right so far as that it is becoming in the scholar to insist on central soundness, rather than on superficial applications." In considering his particular obligation in the matter of slavery, Emerson concludes, "I am to give a wise & just ballot, though no man else in the republic doth. I am not to compromise or mix or accommodate. I am to demand the absolute right, affirm that, & do that." These personal matters are certain and sure. As far as a more public role is concerned, Emerson insists that it is not his duty to "push Boston into a false, showy, & theatrical attitude, endeavoring to persuade her she is more virtuous than she is. Thereby I am robbing myself, more than I am enriching the public" (*JMN* 13:405).

Such Hamlet talk may have been stimulated in part by Emerson's experience in Philadelphia, where, he says in a letter to brother William, the night went "not so well" (*L* 4:491). Additionally, there is the possibility that Emerson was not sure that the route he and other abolitionists were taking at the moment was the best or most effective. He observes in his journal at the time that "there are two ways of attacking slavery." The first is the "man-way," which consists of "voluntary cooperation by parties, by legislation, by compromise, by treaty, etc." In Emerson's opinion "this way is inefficient" because "party besets party. The more you attack, the more you exasperate defence." Also, "there are certain impediments" which occur. "Hopeful young gentlemen are found to be dead against you," and "expense makes young voters Whigs." Also, with public agitation there is bound to be a "general confusion" because "few people are moralists, few have discernment [and] most are quadrupeds" (*JMN* 14:404). "Judges, Bank Presidents, Railroad men, men of fashion, lawyers universally all take the side of slavery," and "what a poor blind devil are you to break your shins for a bit of moonshine against this goodwill of the whole community." As a moralist opposed to slavery, Emerson must have felt himself sometimes like a voice crying out in the wilderness. "What a fool, when the whole world has lost its wits, to be the only sane man" (*JMN* 14:404-5). Another bothersome matter was the disagreement among abolitionists themselves as to how best to attack the monster. Hence, "the friends of freedom fall out: the Abolitionists are waspish egotistical Ishmaelites, not cunning." For these reasons "the man-way does not prosper" (*JMN* 14:405).

On the other hand, Emerson describes the "Godway" of abolishing slavery. This depends very much on natural forces and the amelioration that he describes as "the friction or judgment of God" to bring about "an unexpected hitch" in the working of slavery, despite the cooperation of the social powers that be. Thus, "California did not behave well, but voted to be free. Texas is not quite to be trusted lest it vote itself free. The census is incendiary, & the tables must be cooked." Other natural developments also served to suggest the gradual undermining of the slave powers. "The escape of fugitives is easier & more frequent every year. The difficulty of executing the Fugitive Slave Law always greater." Also, the internal corruption of society in the slave states would eventually tell. "Not a gentleman, not a hero, not a poet, not a Woman, born in all that immense country! There must be such, for nature avenges herself, but they lie perdus, & make no sign in the reign of terror." It is Emerson's opinion that in the South "in fifty years, since Mr. Jefferson, not a breath of air has come to the intellect or heart" (*JMN* 14: 406). Because of these natural forces, slavery would eventually be defeated. However, despite these relatively quiet moments of reflection in his study, far removed from the hisses and jeers of hostile proslavery agitators, the irresistible events of the time would inevitably intrude to draw Emerson forth again into the fray. As he stated in his notes for "American Slavery," "there is somewhat exceptional in this question which seems to require of every citizen, at one time or another, to show his hand." And this would continue to be the case with him.

Emerson also found time in January to follow developments in the upcoming trial of Theodore Parker. Parker, along with Higginson, Phillips, and others, had been indicted by a grand jury for his participation in the attempt to rescue Anthony Burns in May. On 29 November Parker was arrested. Emerson was kept abreast of developments in the case and said in a letter to a friend in December that "Theodore Parker disdains, Socratically, to employ a lawyer & will defend himself at court in March" (*L* 4:480). The trial date was eventually set for April. In the interim Parker began to prepare his defense, something he took very seriously because he felt, as he told Samuel May, "it is the Freedom of Speech which is assailed through me."[33] Emerson apparently wrote to Parker, probably in January 1855, expressing his support, and Parker responded on 19 January. In a letter marked "Private" Parker states, "It was kind & like you to take so deep an interest in my jury trial. . . . I feel no concern for the result—not the least." Parker's confidence resided in the fact that he did not "look on the jury as *emancipators* or F.S.L. Kidnappers, but as honest citizens of Mass. If I can't persuade *one out of XII* in such a case to set me free—then I misunderstand myself & my Mass[achusetts]." Parker also refers in the letter to his present unpopularity in Boston due to his activism. "No-body has been so much attacked—I mean no man not a politician—& no man less defended."[34] Emerson was undoubtedly moved by the courage of this moral crusader and, having been the victim of public abuse himself on more than one occasion, supported Parker both publicly and privately.[35]

As fate and circumstance would have it, Parker was robbed of his opportunity to present an eloquent defense when the case was thrown out upon a technicality. Not to be denied, however, Parker had his defense printed and sent a copy to Emerson. Emerson offered glowing praise of the work, asserting that he was "glad & grateful that the best soldier fights on our side" (*L* 4:536). Not surprisingly, as the struggle went forward these two transcendental moralists would find themselves increasingly united.

After covering the countryside with his "American Slavery" lecture, Emerson seems to have decided to diminish, for a while, his antislavery lecturing. However, he was still prepared to encourage others to continue. In April he sent an invitation to Charles Sumner to lecture on slavery in Concord. In addition to a $25 fee, Emerson also made a promise: "My wife will with pride of heart make her best cake for you on the occasion. Choose your own earliest time, & come to my house" (*L* 4: 500). Unfortunately, the senator was not able to make the engagement.

In early October Emerson wrote to Furness, who had apparently requested an antislavery address for Philadelphia, that he felt that he made "the worst Antislavery discourses that are made in this country" and that "they are only less bad than Slavery." As a result, "I incline this winter to promise none. And have not dared to accept any new invitation."[36] Perhaps in response to further promptings from his friend, later in October Emerson suggested that he had for the moment written himself out on the topic and that "the pain of Slavery & detestation of our politics only work the wrong way to make me more dumb & sterile." Also, Emerson points out that he is "pinned to a printer probably till 1 December" while preparing *English Traits* for publication. And there was his upcoming lecture tour, which would involve "a long Western journey to the Mississippi back & forth for a month or 6 weeks more."[37] Clearly, Emerson simply could not dedicate all of his time and energy to an antislavery campaign. However, he did promise Furness that in the meantime, if any word should come into him "like a sharp sword as it came aforetime to good men, I shall be as swift as now I am slow to carry it to Philadelphia."[38]

Requests came from other quarters, also. Oliver Johnson had written Emerson late in September requesting an antislavery address for New York. He pointed out that "the present state of the slavery question will not permit any man to be silent who has a heart & a tongue for speech," adding, "I am glad to know that you are still among the number of those who will not cease to utter their testimony as long as the victory remains unachieved."[39] However, Johnson undoubtedly received the same reply as Furness. Eventually Emerson's peaceful interlude would end, and the dramatic events of the spring of 1856 would once again precipitate his return to the front lines.

Chapter Seven

The Battle Lines Are Drawn: 1856–1859

Affairs had been growing worse for the antislavery forces in Kansas throughout 1855. The opening of the territory to settlement under the principle of popular sovereignty led to open warfare between pro- and antislavery forces. As a result of this conflict, by the end of 1855 Kansas had in effect two governments, one proslavery and one antislavery. In a special message to Congress on 24 January 1856 President Pierce condemned the antislavery legislature of Kansas, called the "Topeka government," and in effect recognized the proslavery government. Open warfare broke out in Kansas in the spring of 1856, and battles were fought between the pro- and antislavery factions. The latter were supplied with Sharpe's rifles, newly developed breech loaders known as "Beecher's Bibles," by such northern support groups as the New England Emigrant Aid Society, a chapter of which was located in Concord, Massachusetts.[1] Most notable among the antislavery leaders was John Brown of Osawatomie. "Bleeding Kansas," as it came to be known, certainly deserved the name. It is estimated that the total loss in the struggle there from November 1855 to December 1856 was two hundred men killed and $2 million in property destroyed. New England abolitionists followed the struggle closely and with trepidation. Garrison notes in a letter to Samuel May in the spring of 1856 that "the fate of Kansas is still apparently in suspense but my own conviction remains unshaken, that Kansas will be a slave state and that 'border ruffian' legislation will be enforced, if need be, by all the military power of the General Government." It is Garrison's opinion that "Pres. Pierce's last message, on that question, is a 'settler'—and he is ready to do all that the Slave Power demands at his hands." Garrison is now more certain than ever that "the dissolution of the Union must first precede the abolition of slavery." He also objects to the use of violent force in opposing the proslavery forces in Kansas and is upset that men such as "Gerrit Smith, Ward Beecher, and Theodore Parker are finding in Sharpe's rifles more than in the peaceful gospel of Christ to aid the cause of right and freedom!"[2]

Emerson followed events in Kansas closely, especially in the spring of 1856 when developments there were reaching crisis proportions. At this time he frequently visited the home of his friend George Luther Stearns (one of the Massachusetts State Kansas Committee members) in order to get firsthand details of the latest developments. Stearns's son would later note that his father "found Emerson to be fully alive to the dangers from the disturbances in Kansas," and that it was Emerson's expressed opinion that the situation there was "like setting a fire in the woods . . . no one can tell what will be the end of it. . . . [Emerson] thought it was a critical period in the history of the republic, and that the turning point had come which must decide the nation's destiny for a hundred years."[3] Emerson also had frequent reports on Kansas from his Concord neighbor Franklin Sanborn. As a member of the state committee, Sanborn had traveled to Kansas and was a valuable source of information for Emerson. As young Ellen Emerson states in a letter at the time: "I enjoy hearing Father and Mr. Sanborn talk about it [Kansas]. Mr. Sanborn knows everything about it. He has been there and seen, and has constant information from there of what is going on, and he belongs to the State Committee of Massachusetts which takes care of Kansas, so he knows all that is being done for it, and he tells all to Father so the moment Mr. Sanborn makes his appearance the family is all rejoicing, and expectation, for we are exceedingly interested. But what pleases me most is to

hear from any quarter that the North will be bold and leave the South"
(*EL* 1:118).

It was also at this time that Emerson took it upon himself to ad-
monish yet another member of his set who had offered support to the
enemy in the struggle against slavery. In December the *Boston Advertiser* had reported that Oliver Wendell Holmes, in a speech before the
New England Society of New York on 21 December, had "denounced
the abolitionists of New England in good round terms, as 'traitors to the
Union.'" As noted earlier, Holmes was never sympathetic to the abolitionists, but Emerson felt that this public condemnation of abolition
efforts was unjustified and detrimental to the cause. Also, of course,
Emerson himself had by this time questioned publicly the value of maintaining a union with slaveholders. Holmes's remarks were reported and
criticized in Horace Greeley's *Tribune* and the *New York Herald*.[4] Theodore Parker, Wendell Phillips, and others also openly expressed their
disapproval of Holmes's comments. Emerson's concerns were communicated to Holmes privately through Dr. Charles T. Jackson.[5] Apparently,
Holmes responded to these expressions of concern by suggesting that the
press reports misrepresented him. Consequently, in a letter to Holmes
in March, Emerson stated that he had not seen a "true report" of the
speech, and drew his "sad thoughts about it from the comments of the
journals." He was "relieved to know that they misreported" the story,
and "the more they misreported or the wider you are from their notion of you, the better I shall be pleased." Emerson advised Holmes
that "a scholar need not be cynical to feel that the vast multitude are
almost on all fours; that *wealth* always votes after their fears [and] that
cities, churches, [and] colleges all go for the quadruped interest." But
it is against this coalition that "the pathetically small minority of disengaged or thinking men stand for the ideal right, for man as he should
be, &, for the right of every other as for his own." Clearly, Emerson was
still hopeful that his cultural revolution would eventually turn the tide
against mercantile self-interest, and he was therefore especially concerned about Holmes's public criticism of abolitionists. Holmes, like
Greenough, was presumably a man of poetic sensitivity and cultural sophistication. To have such a person announce himself as a partisan for

the wrong side would be a sad loss indeed. As Emerson stated in his letter, "It would have been a poor compliment to your fame, if every humblest aspirant had not showed sorrow & anger at the first rumor that such a leader were lost" (*L* 5:17–18). It is possibly this missive that Holmes responded to later in March. Holmes attempted to defend himself on the grounds that "ultra-abolitionists" had deliberately attempted to "inflame the evil passions" in this incident. The unfortunate consequence of such efforts is "that growing sectional hostility, the nature of which is the disruption of the government which Mr. Parker thinks is near at hand."[6]

In what appears to be his response, Emerson addresses Holmes's delicate concern with "disruption of the government" and disunion and makes it clear that his own opinions on the matter are much closer to the abolitionists than to Holmes. Despite his opposition to the "no Union with slaveholders" movement in the 1840s, Emerson now states frankly, "And for the Union with Slavery no manly person will suffer a day to go by without discrediting disintegrating & finally exploding it. The 'union' they talk of is dead & rotten, the real union, that is, the will to keep & renew union, is like the will to keep & renew life, & this alone gives any tension to the dead letter." This missive ends with a defense of the abolitionists that must have seemed at least somewhat ironic to Emerson, given his own criticisms of the obnoxiousness of many abolitionists in the 1830s and early 1840s. Nevertheless, he now tells Holmes, "You see I am not giving weight to your disgust at the narrowness & ferocity of their virtue for they know that the side is right & it is leading them out of low estate into manhood & culture" (*L* 5:18).[7]

During this tumultuous time the question of Kansas was hotly debated in Washington. Not surprisingly, Charles Sumner was one of the most outspoken critics of the proslavery activities there. In the context of this ongoing debate, in May 1856 Sumner delivered what came to be known as his "Crime Against Kansas" speech, a bitter denunciation of the "slave oligarchy" and the ravages that were visited upon Kansas. In the speech Sumner attacked the character of several proslavery senators, especially Butler from South Carolina and Mason from Virginia.[8] In retribution, Representative Preston S. Brooks, Senator Butler's nephew, assaulted Sumner while he sat at his Senate desk on 22 May, striking him several heavy blows with a cane. Sumner's wounds were so severe that he was unable to resume his normal Senate duties until December 1859. The North was shocked and outraged by this barbaric act. However, attempts to expel Brooks from the House of Representatives failed. He later resigned his chair but was soon unanimously reelected by his district.

An indignation meeting was called in Concord on 26 May to protest the attack on Sumner. Not surprisingly, the featured speaker at the event was Ralph Waldo Emerson. His speech "The Assault upon Mr. Sumner" is short, direct, and acerbic. He states at the outset, "The events of the last few years and months and days have taught us the lessons of centuries. I do not see how a barbarous community and a civilized community can constitute one state. I think we must get rid of slavery, or we must get rid of freedom" (W 11:247). The assault on Sumner is proof positive that the forces of culture and reason cannot coexist with all that bespeaks their opposite. Charles Sumner had "the whitest soul" Emerson ever knew. As his letters to Sumner indicate, he looked upon him as an apostle of culture and truth to a society on the brink of being swallowed by a godless barbarism. He admired Sumner because in many ways he was an unpolitical politician, a welcome exception to the standard rule, a person capable of independent thinking. Thus, Emerson observes, Sumner "had not taken his degrees in the caucuses and in hack politics. It is notorious that, in the long time when his election was pending, he refused to take a single step to secure it." Once elected, "he did not rush into party position" (W 11:249). It is true that he is "an abolitionist," but at this moment in time "every sane human being" is an abolitionist (W 11:250). As far as the "pair of bullies" responsible for the attack are concerned, Emerson's condemnation is biblical. "The murderer's brand shall stamp their foreheads wherever they may wander in the earth." They are fit representatives of an evil and corrupt institution that is maintained by an evil and corrupt society. "The whole state of South Carolina does not now offer one or any number of persons who are to be weighed for a moment in the scale with such a person as the meanest of them all has now struck down" (W 11:248).

Virtue's Hero

In concluding, Emerson notes the "shudder of terror which ran through all this community on the first tidings of this brutal attack." But nevertheless, the people of this society will stand by their most noble representative, "and if our arms at this distance cannot defend him from assassins, we confide the defence of a life so precious to all honorable men and true patriots, and to the Almighty Maker of men" (*W* 11:251–52). Because of Emerson's consistent and public admiration for Sumner, the senator and the philosopher would eventually become associated in the minds of many. Ellen later reported to her father her delight in finding in Mr. Longfellow's study a picture of Emerson "connected by a long wreath of evergreen with a picture of Mr. Sumner" (*EL* 1:125).

The barbaric attack on Sumner suggested to many, including Emerson, that the nation was moving toward a fatal confrontation. In keeping with his earlier remarks to Oliver Wendell Holmes, Emerson recorded in his journal the following observation regarding relations with the South. "Let us not compromise again, or accept the aid of evil agents . . . suppose we raise soldiers in Massachusetts . . . suppose we propose a Northern Union" (*JMN* 14:93). Also, despite all that has been said about Emerson's naïve blindness to the existence of evil in the world, it is clear that he never for a moment doubted the extent of the malevolence that held slavery in place. He had noted this as early as 1844 in his first emancipation address, and now in his journal he observes that in the developing contest between North and South, he has no "benevolent credulity in the honesty of the other party." He goes on to add the prophetic observation that the only reason the Carolinians "do not plant a cannon before Faneuil Hall, & blow Bunker Hill monument to fragments, as a nuisance, is because they have not the power." He then notes ominously, "They are fast acquiring the power, & if they get it, they will do it" (*JMN* 14:95).

In early June 1856 Emerson wrote to his brother William that the times were critical. "I am looking into the map to see where I shall go with my children when Boston & Massachusetts surrender to the slave-trade." It was Emerson's opinion that if the Free States did not obtain the government in the fall election, something he held little hope for, then there would be nothing left "but to form at once a Northern Union, & break the old" (L 5:23). Emerson's opposition to the "no Union" movement in the 1840s was clearly predicated on his assumption that the South was still capable of being influenced by the powers of moral suasion and cultural progress. Events in the 1850s, culminating with the attack on Sumner, served to convince him that the South was clearly beyond such gentle persuasion. Indeed, the use of force in returning fugitive slaves, the violence in Kansas, and the attack on Sumner must have convinced Emerson, as his journal comments indicate, that southern slavery was now not only hostile but aggressive. In light of this, the dissolution of the Union might indeed be a necessary protective measure for the North.

Later in June a Kansas aid meeting was held in Concord to raise funds for the Free State emigrants in Kansas. Earlier, Franklin Sanborn, in a letter to Theodore Parker, indicated that "Mr. Emerson and Judge Hoar" would speak at the meeting. He also added, "We hope to raise a good sum here as there is considerable desire to do something—it will probably be a great meeting."[9] If the monetary results are any indication, it certainly was. Emerson recorded that "$962 were subscribed on the spot," and that the total would "probably reach 1200 or one percent on the valuation of the town." He also noted on 13 September that an additional $640 had been raised for the cause up to that time (JMN 14:96). Clearly, this was a princely sum for a small community, and an indication of the strength of the emotion that Concordians felt regarding the crises of the moment. Young Ellen Emerson notes in a letter at the time that "Kanzas [sic] is all the interest out of doors now." Even the women and children were making their contributions. "The sewing meetings are very large," and "one hundred shirts started this morning for Kanzas" (EL 1:120). Emerson himself donated $50, an amount in excess of what he would make on most lecture engagements, and Lidian probably donated an additional $25.[10]

Obviously, not all of the money raised in Massachusetts went for flannel shirts. A good deal of it went for arms and munitions to put the force of gun power behind the moral resolution of the Free State government. It is interesting to note that Emerson, unlike Garrison and others who were religious nonresisters, supported the arming of the antislavery farmers in Kansas as a necessary measure. Edward Emerson is very clear on this point when he comments on his father's essay "War" (1838), saying that Ralph Waldo "was by no means committed as a nonresistant [and] he saw that war had been a part of evolution, and that its evils might pave the way for good." To support and illustrate the point Edward points out that "it is evident from his words and course of action during the outrages upon the peaceful settlers of Kansas, and when Sumter was fired upon and Washington threatened, that he recognized that the hour [for a friend of peace] had not yet come. He subscribed lavishly from his limited means for the furnishing [of] Sharp's rifles to the 'Free State men' " (W 11:578–79).

In addition to attending Kansas aid meetings in Concord and elsewhere, Emerson was also one of several Massachusetts citizens, along with Henry and John Thoreau, who signed a letter on the Fourth of July addressed to "His Excellency the Governor of Our Commonwealth." The letter expresses the belief that citizens of Massachusetts have been "illegally seized, robbed, and held as prisoners by citizens of the state of Missouri" and that therefore the governor should "take such immediate action as may seem in your judgment best to protect our fellow citizens and the rights of Massachusetts." Additionally, the signers ask the governor "to call together our Legislature," as soon as possible in order that it might "confer and decide on the important questions of this crisis." [11] It is possible that this letter was never sent, which might explain why, in early September, Theodore Parker sent a request to Emerson to circulate a petition in Concord requesting the governor to hold an extra session of the legislature to address the crisis in Kansas. [12] Given Emerson's oft-expressed concern that the state should protect its citizens against attacks on their rights and freedom, with force if necessary, it is likely that he sympathized greatly with the measure.

Emerson continued to be caught up in the rapidly developing affairs of the moment. On 13 August Samuel May invited him to "celebrate again the rescue of Jerry" in Syracuse. The affair celebrating the rescue of a fugitive slave, will, says May in his letter, give a "more emphatic assurance to the Slaveholding Oligarchy and to the world" that the committed people of the North "will not submit to any more aggression upon Liberty—nay—that we intend to drive them back from the encroachments they have hitherto been allowed to make." May goes on to say that "nothing has been gained from the first by concessions to slave-holders, but grounds for further concessions. I fear we have sinned in this way past redemption, except at the expense of a civil war." Recognizing the implication of his position, May, a nonresistant like Garrison, was ambivalent about the possibility of a war because "bullets often do not hit the worst enemies of God and man."[13] As we have seen, Emerson was himself concerned about the problems that result from making concessions on principles, and undoubtedly May's letter struck a familiar chord. In his response he states, "Certainly I ought to hold myself prearranged to come to Syracuse, when you please to call me. And yet I dare not say I will come on the holiday you so honorably keep; for though it looks fair and gay at this interval, I know by much experience that, when it draws nigh it will find me in the thick of my tasks—which, I know, look like game, to all serious people, but are pre-emptory to me." Regarding May's comment about war, Emerson is not above a bit of humor when he tells his correspondent, "I should like well to hear your Tytraean speeches of that rare quality, that—non resistant as you are—drives men to break heads."[14] He concludes, "On 1 October I will keep the day in mind, & try to write you a letter. Honor evermore to your love of freedom & of man. And with my private thanks, Yours, R W Emerson."

Also in August, Emerson received a letter from the fallen soldier, Charles Sumner, who was now at the beginning of a slow and painful recovery. Sumner told Emerson that he wrote in a library "where every printed word of yours is treasured & under a roof where your name is daily mentioned with admiration & delight." He has been joined by Emerson's friend William Henry Furness, whom he describes as "my family guardian." Emerson's support was obviously very much appreciated by Sumner, and the senator notes, "Often since that most beautiful speech of yours have I thought of your sympathy, —as I lay weak & fettered on my bed—& my eyes have moistened."[15] Emerson no doubt felt that his words had served their purpose well.

Yet another meeting for Kansas relief was held in Cambridge on 10 September 1856, and this time Emerson had the opportunity to prepare and present a more complete response to the tragedies of the past few months. In his speech, delivered at the request of the Middlesex County Committee for Aid to Kansas, he clearly and forcefully threw down the gauntlet to those who would preserve the Union but destroy morality. It is Emerson's most militant antislavery speech to this date and is filled with specific details that obviously were the fruits of his many meetings with Sanborn, Stearns, and others. As usual, Emerson was very careful to speak from a position of knowledge, the more firsthand the better. His "Speech on Affairs in Kansas" begins with what had become by now his usual disclaimer. "I had been wiser to have stayed at home, unskilled as I am to address a political meeting, but it is impossible for the most recluse to extricate himself from the questions of the times." Indeed, the testimony of the day is both compelling and disconcerting. "We hear the screams of hunted wives and children answered by the howl of the butchers." The evidence is clear: "The testimony of the telegraphs from St. Louis and the border confirm the worst details. The printed letters of border ruffians avow the facts" (*W* 11:255). Responding to the assertions of the "hostile press" that the gruesome accounts of the Kansas conflict are an "abolition lie," Emerson goes on to name specifically several citizens of Massachusetts who were murdered or imprisoned there. There can be no doubt that the people of Kansas are suffering calamities daily, and they ask for "bread, clothes, arms, and men, to save them alive, and enable them to stand against these enemies of the human race" (*W* 11:256). In response to this situation, says Emerson, "we are to give largely, lavishly to these men," even if as a result "we must learn to do with less" (*W* 11:257). In addition to this help from private citizens, "we must also have aid from the state." The governor and legislators should "neither slumber nor sleep till they have found out how to send effectual aid and comfort to these poor farmers." If they cannot do this, then they "should resign their seats to those who can." Clearly Emerson had not given up on the possibility of the state taking some worthwhile action. As in his "American Slavery" speech a year earlier, he reminds his audience that while he insists on individual action, he also recognizes the value of collective action. In order of importance in dealing with the affairs of society Emerson places "the private man first," then the "primary assembly," and the government last (*W* 11:258). It is also clear that the government of the United States is very much the source of the problems that Kansas faces, and he asks, "Who doubts that Kansas would have been very well settled, if the United States had let it alone?" For Emerson, the passage of the Kansas-Nebraska Act and the de facto repeal of the Compromise of 1820 set the stage for the tragedy called bleeding Kansas. In its attempt to disguise the heinousness of its actions, the government hides behind the cant of democracy. "*Representative Government* is really misrepresentative; *Union* is a conspiracy against the Northern States . . . *Manifest Destiny, Democracy, Freedom*, fine names for an ugly thing." But Emerson and others cannot be so easily fooled. "They call it otto of rose and lavender. I call it bilge-water" (*W* 11:259).

Emerson insists that because of this situation "there is no Union," and he is "glad to see that the terror at disunion and anarchy is disappearing" (*W* 11:261). Indeed, anarchy seems preferable to an organized state where slavery and kidnapping are not only condoned but commanded. Such a situation cannot long endure; "the hour is coming when the strongest will not be strong enough." There is a "new revolution" on the horizon. "Vast property, gigantic interests, family connection, webs of party, cover the land with a network that immensely multiplies the dangers of war." Faced with this crisis and the imminent failure of the Union, Emerson suggests, much as W. H. Channing had when proposing "nounion" in 1846, that rather than descending to a state of anarchy "the town should hold town meetings, and resolve themselves into Committees of Safety" to prepare a response to the challenge of the time. Those who are away should be told to "come home and stay at home, while there is a country to save." Emerson's final words are tinged with an uncommon sadness. "When [the country] is lost it will be time enough then for any who are luckless enough to remain alive to gather up their clothes and depart to some land where freedom exists" (*W* 11:263).

Emerson's speech was noticed extensively and, once again, showed the world where and with whom he stood. In November Garrison wrote to Emerson that "a magnificent lithographic print, of the size and style of the Champions of Freedom" was being prepared and would include portraits of Theodore Parker, Wendell Phillips, Samuel J. May, Gerrit

Smith, and others. It was now deemed "very desirous" that Emerson's portrait "should be among the number designated."[16] Emerson's response to Garrison's offer was both modest and grateful. "For the proposition you convey to me, & so kindly, I hardly know what to say. My claims to fit with such high company, I feel are none but pure good will, faith without works." He has "no tolerable print or drawing of any kind to send "but will call on the lithographer Mr. Brainerd, when next in Boston," though, he warns, "I am a very bad sitter to the Daguerre artists." Despite these reservations, the print did appear.[17]

The presidential campaign in the fall of 1856 did not fail to arouse excitement and interest in Concord and elsewhere. The American (Know-Nothing) party put forth Millard Fillmore on a nativist platform, and the same candidate was also nominated by the Whig National Convention in September. At the Democratic National Convention in June, James Buchanan was nominated on the seventeenth ballot. Pierce was rejected for renomination, presumably because of the distastefulness of the state of affairs in Kansas. The Democratic platform supported both the Compromise of 1850 and the Kansas-Nebraska Act. The Republicans nominated John Frémont on a platform that upheld congressional authority to control slavery in the territories. As might be expected, "bleeding Kansas" was a significant issue in the campaign. In Concord a Frémont Club was organized and enrolled over 150 members, but, despite the enthusiasm of the northeast, Buchanan won the election, and sectional friction would continue to tear at the fabric of American society.[18]

Wendell Phillips came to Concord to lecture in January 1857. Most of the Emersons attended (except Ralph Waldo, who was away lecturing), and they "came home delighted."[19] Undoubtedly his presentation was topical and fiery. In April Furness would thank Phillips for his "grand Disunion Speech" with the exclamation "what a word of Truth & Power it is!"[20] Probably the biggest event in the spring of 1857 in Concord was the appearance there of the most famous of all the Kansas antislavery partisans, John Brown. Brown's efforts in Kansas had already been substantially aided by the two hundred Sharpe's rifles that the concerned citizens of Massachusetts had provided to him.[21] He was now making the rounds in Massachusetts in search of further support. Brown had written to G. L. Stearns in April 1857 asking for funds to purchase two hundred revolvers so that he might be well armed.[22] In May it was agreed.[23] Franklin Sanborn, secretary of the Massachusetts Free Soil party, who had traveled through the Midwest in the summer of 1856 gathering information on affairs there, was the person responsible for bringing Brown to Concord. Eventually, Sanborn, who was at this time the teacher of Emerson's children, became a disciple of Brown and a member of the Secret Six, a group of close associates who aided Brown's antislavery activities up to and including his raid on Harper's Ferry in 1859. The other members of this group, Theodore Parker, Thomas Wentworth Higginson, Gerrit Smith, Samuel Gridley Howe, and George Luther Stearns, were also friends or associates of Emerson.[24]

Brown visited Concord in February and lunched at the Thoreaus', where he regaled Henry and others with tales of his adventures and skirmishes in Kansas. Later in the afternoon Emerson stopped by and was introduced to Brown. He was immediately taken with this forceful and rugged character and invited him to his own house to spend the second night of his two-day visit to Concord.[25] In the evening at the Concord Town Hall over a hundred people gathered to hear Brown speak. His presentation was dramatic and direct. He spoke in ringing phrases about the dire nature of the conflict in Kansas and said that all those who supported liberty and human rights should back his cause. In the context of his emotional presentation Brown displayed a trace chain that had bound his son as he was dragged off to prison for the crime of opposing slavery. Of his seven sons, one was crazed by the ordeal of the struggle and another was murdered, but he vowed that the fight would go on until the battle was won.[26]

Emerson was most impressed by Brown's oration and noted in his journal that "Captain John Brown of Kansas gave a good account of himself in the Town Hall, last night, to a meeting of Citizens." Obviously in a somewhat militant mood himself, as indicated in his recent Kansas speech, Emerson commented approvingly on Brown's indictment of those who condemn armed resistance to the forces of evil in Kansas. "One of his good points was, the folly of the peace party in

Kansas, who believed, that their strength lay in the greatness of their wrongs, & so discountenanced resistance." Using an obvious parallel, Brown "wished to know if their wrong was greater than the negro's, & what kind of strength that gave to the negro?" (*JMN* 14:125).

In Emerson's view at this time, the forces of oppression must be resisted by both moral and physical counterforces, and he was undoubtedly pleased to note Brown's commitment to the importance of principle, in addition to Sharpe's rifles, as a source of strength. Brown "believes on his own experience that one good, believing, strong-minded man is worth a hundred, nay twenty thousand men without character" (*JMN* 14:125). Despite the importance of this commitment to principle in dealing with the forceful issues of life, the one issue on which Emerson took exception to Brown concerned the quality of the fighting man in the South. As a student of the contemporary scene, Emerson was convinced that the prowess of the South was greater than the North imagined. "But 'tis of no use to tell me, as Brown & others do, that the Southerner is not a better fighter than the Northerner,—when I see, that uniformly a Southern minority prevails, & gives the law." The explanation for this situation was clear to Emerson: "the Southerner is a fighting man & the Northerner is not" (*JMN* 14:127). All too soon this proposition would be tested.

In March the proslavery forces of the nation would achieve another substantial victory in the ongoing national struggle. Dred Scott, a Negro slave and the household servant of a Missouri physician with the unlikely name of John Emerson, sued for his freedom in 1846 on the basis of the fact that he had been taken by his master from Missouri to Rock Island, Illinois, where slavery was forbidden by a 1787 ordinance. Later, he was taken to a fort in the northern part of the Louisiana Purchase where slavery was prohibited by the Missouri Compromise. Scott thus lived on free soil for some four years, and, in his opinion, he had become free as a result of his substantial residence in a free state and a free territory. A lower court's favorable ruling was overturned in 1852 by the Missouri State Supreme Court, and the case was then appealed to the federal district court, and finally to the Supreme Court of the United States. The Court decided against Dred Scott. Chief Justice Roger B.

Taney, in his statement of the majority opinion, held that no person of slave descent or blood could be considered a citizen of the United States, and therefore could not be entitled to sue in its courts. The Court affirmed that Negroes were generally regarded "as so far inferior that they had no rights which the white man was bound to respect." Finally, Judge Taney added that because the Missouri Compromise was unconstitutional masters could take their slaves anywhere in the territories and not lose title to them. Needless to say, the ruling was alarming to the North and must have convinced moralists like Emerson, who wished to believe in the redeeming power of culture, that American society had taken yet another giant step backward.[27]

Emerson's immediate reaction to the decision emphasized what he saw as the fallacious logic of Judge Taney's reasoning. It also provides further insight into Emerson's thinking at this time regarding the ongoing debate over the question of Negro inferiority. For Emerson, Taney's decision was really a Catch 22. Because blacks are considered inferior, they have no rights and are forced into the degradation of slavery. As an institution that "turns men into monkeys," slavery ensures that they will always remain inferior, which, in turn, ensures that they will always remain enslaved. Emerson's comment on this matter is brief but telling. He states in his journal, "Servile races! forsooth, Mr. Justice Taney!" (*JMN* 14:429), and he then refers to another journal entry, which records the following account from Thierry's British history dealing with the Norman conquest of England in the eleventh century. "The Normans bought & sold their English villages & domains, together with their inhabitants, body & goods, carried off horses, sheep, & oxen; & the English men, whom, they seized even in towns, they led them away bound with ropes" (*JMN* 13:169). Emerson's point, though undeveloped in his journal, is clear enough. If Taney's logic had been applied throughout Western history, then the English, who were initially enslaved by the invading Normans, would never possess rights that their conquerors were bound to respect. If this situation had continued on the basis of its de facto justification, then the development of English character would have been effectively "arrested," and they would have continued as slavish inferiors to the present day. Obviously, however, the chain of oppression and enslavement was eventually broken, and the English emerged as the leaders in Western civilization and culture. Servile races indeed, Mr. Taney! Such an insight must have also furthered Emerson's growing conviction that if true amelioration was to occur in American society, the chain of oppression that enslaved and demoralized blacks would have to be struck off, by violence if necessary.

A demanding lecture schedule, which included a journey to Ohio, kept Emerson busy throughout the early months of 1857. He did find time, however, on the Fourth of July to read an ode at the Town Hall in Concord. Despite the fact that the purpose of the gathering was primarily to raise money for the improvement of the new cemetery in Sleepy Hollow, Emerson used the occasion to celebrate America's heritage of freedom and to challenge his listeners to extend the fruits of this heritage to all. The time had come, he said, "to take the statute from the mind / And make of duty fate." Our songs of glory and traditions of liberty sound fine to the ear, but they are empty measures and hypocritical if not acted upon. Emerson advises, "Go put your creed into your deed, / Nor speak with double tongue." We must not "See right for which the one hand fights / By the other cloven down." America's identity shall no longer be split, but freedom will be extended to all, and "henceforth there shall be no chain" but only "several songs of liberty." As in so many of his abolition speeches, Emerson here reminds his audience that this development is irresistible and inevitable.

> For He that worketh high and wise,
> Nor pauses in his plan,
> Will take the sun out of the skys
> Ere freedom out of man.
> (W 9:199–200; JMN 14:153)

It is interesting to recall in passing that when Emerson attempted to engage the muses in the struggle for freedom in his earlier poem by that name (1853), he found that they would not come. Apparently by 1857 he had won their cooperation.

It is also important to note that Emerson here is prepared to deny the force of fate as prohibitive to concerted action and to displace it with an emphasis on "duty" that includes action from principle, or, as he says, putting your creed into your deed. The reasons for this shift seem clear enough. Emerson's faith in inevitable amelioration was based largely upon experience. As we saw earlier, he felt that educational enlightenment, or "culture," combined with the prosperity of trade would bring about inevitable improvement. This seemed to have been the case when England declared emancipation in 1833, which he considered a moral revolution. However, the passage of barbaric legislation like the Fugitive Slave Law of 1850 and the Kansas-Nebraska Act of 1854, "by men who could read and write," and Taney's decision in the Dred Scott case, undoubtedly convinced him that culture was failing, or worse yet, that earlier progress was only an illusion. Also, the consistent and sometimes violent support of these measures by the businessmen of the North, "gentlemen of property and standing," served to indicate that trade in America not only did not abolish slavery but was a major factor in its extension. Therefore, fate, which Emerson defined as "the laws of the world," "the order of things," and "material necessities," was now perceived as "opposed to will and Duty" (*W* 11:231). It would require a new assertion of faith to hold that things were still on the right track. Emerson was prepared to make that assertion, which would bring with it a greater commitment to will and duty in addressing the critical social problems of the time. This represents a substantial evolution in Emerson's thinking on the question of fate from the 1840s, where his emphasis was clearly on the "beautiful necessity" that would bring all things to good. In his journal of 1857 Emerson expresses this new view succinctly. "Tis the best use of Fate to teach us courage like the Turk. Go face the burgler, or the fire at sea, or whatever danger lies in the way of duty, knowing you are guarded by the omnipotence of Destiny. If you believe in Fate to your harm, believe it, at least, for your good. And, one more lesson learn,—to balance the ugly fact of temperament & race, which pulls you down,—this, namely, that by that cunning co-presence of the two elements, which we find throughout nature what ever lames you, or paralyzes you, drags in with it the divinity in some form to repay"

(*JMN* 14:156). Emerson would later express this new view of Fate in the work that is most obviously the product of the experience of the 1850s, *Conduct of Life* (1860) (*W* 6:24, 47–48).

As was the case from time to time in the past, Emerson again expressed in his journal his reservations about the personalities of some abolitionists and their continued fixation on a single aspect of reform. For Emerson slavery, while clearly the most conspicuous evil in American society, must be seen in a wider perspective, such as that described in his "American Slavery Address." Because some abolitionists failed to see this, "they have neither abolished slavery in Carolina, nor in me. . . . If they cannot break one fetter of mine, I cannot hope they will of any negro." Regarding the limitations of what might be called the abolitionist personality, Emerson says again, "They are a bitter sterile people, whom I flee from, to the unpretentious whom they disparage." However, Emerson's final statement here explains his continued and inevitable association with the group. Despite their failings in other regards, the cause itself is justified and necessary, and, as Emerson asserts, "I see them to be logically right" (*JMN* 14:166). Also, Emerson would later observe that while not all the abolitionists were gentlemen "it is impossible to be a gentleman, & not be an abolitionist"; something he also noted in his speech on Sumner (*JMN* 14:198; *W* 11:250). Emerson would continue to associate publicly with his abolitionist friends and to support their efforts, sometimes simply by his presence, which undoubtedly gave hope and encouragement to others. Thus, for example, in late December 1857 Charlotte Forten, a free black woman, attended an antislavery fair in Boston and later recorded in her journal that while there she "saw Sumner, Emerson, [and] Wendell Phillips, all in the Fair at once. It was *glorious* to see such a trio. I feasted my eyes."[28]

One of the reasons for Emerson's enduring relationship with even "odious" abolitionists was the fact that they were aggressive opponents of the corrupt political forces of the day. And while they may have been vulgar in their polemics at times, Emerson recognized that it was probably the most effective tactic to utilize against the entrenched and hidebound political opposition and its thuggish operatives such as Captain Rynders. Abolitionists like Parker Pillsbury, whom Emerson admired, were the "tough oak sticks" required to "mob the mob." Thus, speaking of the politicians who dominated the government at both the state and federal levels, and who constituted in large part the proslavery establishment against which the abolitionists had single-mindedly thrown themselves, Emerson asks, "Is there no check to this class of privileged thieves that infest our politics?" And he adds a bit of untypical humor in noting that "there is a serious objection to hounding them out,—that they are nasty prey, which the noble hunter disdains. A good dog even must not be risked on such. They 'spoil his nose'" (*JMN* 14:170).

Emerson was becoming more adamant and determined in his opposition to the sin of slavery with every day that passed. The cause would continue to elicit from him an unusual feistiness, which in turn moved him yet closer to his abolitionist cohorts. Not long after recording the comments noted above, he says in his journal, now without any apparent misgivings about the association, "Why do we not say, We are Abolitionists of the most absolute abolition, as every man that is a man must be?" And to the scoundrels of the South he says, we shall not "suffer you to carry your Thuggism north, south, east, or west into a single rod of territory which we control." Slavery should be treated like the disease that it is, and "we intend to set & keep a *cordon sanitaire* all around the infected district, & by no means suffer the pestilence to spread" (*JMN* 14:197). Appropriately, Emerson later incorporated these remarks into his lecture on courage, which he delivered in Boston the following year.[29]

Emerson's persistent activity in the cause of freedom would continue to make him the subject of public notices, both good and bad. The year 1858 saw the publication of a short work entitled *A Reviewer Reviewed, A Few Remarks upon 'Four Papers from the Boston Globe' Concerning Theodore Parker, Ralph Waldo Emerson, George William Curtis, and the Abolitionists.*[30] In this work the author attacks an anonymous writer for the *Boston Courier* who "has seen fit to republish in a neat volume, certain of his contributions to that journal under the title of 'Radicalism in Religion, Philosophy and Social Life' wherein Ralph Waldo Emerson is described as 'a very unsafe guide, whose teachings end in delusion.'" But here the bard has apparently found his defender. The author contends that "no other man has been so much service to the cause of American letters as Emerson." Additionally, Emerson was defended and supported by his abolitionist associates, among them Theodore Parker, who praised him in glowing terms in an April lecture. Parker applauded Emerson for awakening the religious spirit in America and depicted him as something of a cultural hero who represented the highest values of society. "His words and life charm earnest men with such natural religion as makes them, of their own accord, to trust the Greatest Soul of all, and refine themselves into noble, normal, individual life."[31] Lydia Child said of the performance in a letter written at the time, "I heard Theodore Parker [on] Sunday, and he said a beautiful tribute to the genius and influence of Emerson. I have never before heard such a torrent of eloquence from human lips. I am sure it would have taken you by storm if you had listened to it."[32]

For his part, Franklin Sanborn continued to cast Emerson in the role of social reformer and genius of the cause, sometimes literally. In what appears to be a closet drama in verse, under the title "Prologue. Spoken at the AntiSlavery Festival, Concord, January 28th 1858," Sanborn sketches a debate between the allegorical forces of Slavery and Manifest Destiny. At the height of the drama Manifest Destiny says to Slavery:

> But join with me by purchase or by War
> To gain from Cuba and Nicaragua.
> Then shall your restless course be checked no more,
> Again the slave ship shall approach our shore,
> Not skulking nameless, with no flag displayed,
> But flaunting stars and stripes at her masthead
> Then Boston traders shall not fear to tell
> How many men a year they steal and sell.
> Then Bunker Hill the hunting ground shall be
> Of slaves, not even *Concord* shall be free!

At this critical juncture Sanborn's manuscript reads, "Enter R. W. E. the 'Genius of America,'" who speaks:

> Be gone, vile creature! Do ye plot your shame,
> Here where my maiden spear first won me fame?
> (Slavery and Manifest Destiny run off).[33]

The Battle Lines Are Drawn

There is no evidence that Emerson acted on this opportunity to make his dramatic debut. However, the piece does indicate the extent of the abolitionists' concerns regarding the apparently unlimited avarice of the slaveholding community and the degree to which Emerson was now associated with "the cause" that opposed it.

The situation in Kansas continued to simmer throughout the year. Congress debated the issues regarding a state constitution for Kansas, which the voters then rejected. The decision to retain territorial status there brought disturbances to an end for a time. Although the Dred Scott decision made slavery legal in Kansas and the other territories, the free soil advocates were able to exclude it in fact. The relative peacefulness of 1858 would eventually be shattered by the violent eruptions of the following year.

Emerson began his lecture schedule in January 1859 with a piece entitled "Success." He must have felt that national affairs were improving somewhat overall, especially with affairs in Kansas settled, for the moment at least. While lecturing in Auburn, New York, he found time to visit with Martha Wright, Lucretia Mott's sister. In a letter to Ellen Garrison, wife of William Lloyd II, she describes the visit as "very pleasant, & free, & social." She also notes that she is awaiting the arrival of another guest, Susan B. Anthony.[34] Other abolitionists were experiencing what would turn out to be a false sense of security. Samuel May wrote to a friend in February that "not a press in Boston reviles or slanders us to-day—the Boston Courier only excepted & I had nearly forgotten that—the papers which used to get subscribers by lying about us & caricaturing our meetings, now find it pays to give a fair & truthful report of what is said and done."[35]

John Brown appeared in Concord again on 8 May 1859 in another effort to raise money in support of his cause. Bronson Alcott's journal records "this evening I hear Captain Brown speak at the Town Hall on Kansas affairs, and the part taken by him in the late troubles there. He tells his story with surpassing simplicity and sense, impressing us all deeply by his courage and religious earnestness. Our best people listen to his words—Emerson, Thoreau, Judge Hoar, my wife; and some of them contribute something in aid of his plans without asking particulars, such confidence does he inspire in his integrity and abilities."[36] Whether the

237

transcendentalists of Concord suspected Brown's plans is unclear. Alcott notes, "The Captain leaves us much in the dark concerning his destination and designs for the coming months." Unfortunately, it would not be long before the world would know the fullness of Captain Brown's plan.

On 11 October Emerson recorded in his account book the receipt of $5 from the Thoreau women "for Capt John Brown."[37] Five days later, Brown and eighteen of his followers (including five blacks) attacked the federal arsenal at Harper's Ferry, Virginia. Brown's plan, he claimed, was to open a center of guerrilla activity in Virginia's mountains that would serve as a conduit for passing fugitive slaves on to the North and, finally, into Canada.[38] Unfortunately, the plan did not materialize. After two days of fighting, the arsenal was captured, and Brown and his followers were arrested and charged with treason. Many people in Concord and elsewhere were shocked by the violence and condemned it.[39] Emerson, Thoreau, and other Brown supporters had different reactions. In a letter to his brother William written five days after the attack, Emerson indicates "we are all very well, in spite of the sad Harpers Ferry business, which interests us all who had Brown for our guest twice." It is Emerson's opinion at the moment that Brown "is a true hero, but he lost his head there" (L 5:178). It is not surprising, given Emerson's new militancy at this time and his own personal regard for Brown, that he does not offer a more thorough indictment of the violence precipitated by Brown's attack. In a letter to another correspondent three days later, Emerson is clearly defensive. "For Captain Brown, he is a hero of romance, & seems to have made this fatal blunder only to bring out his virtues. I must hope for his escape to the last moment" (L 5:179–80).

In his letter to William, Emerson had also noted that "the story of 'bushels of letters' which were captured with Brown, and which showed his extensive relationships with many northern supporters who might even have known of his plans, have naturally alarmed some of his friends in Boston." As it turned out, one of these friends was actually in Concord. Franklin Sanborn, who as one of the Secret Six was among Brown's closest supporters, was aware that his own letters to Brown might implicate him in the matter and thus result in his being "suddenly and secretly arrested and hurried out of the protection of Massachusetts law." [40] Therefore Sanborn decided, rather precipitously, to flee to Canada. Before leaving, he scratched off a brief note to Emerson saying that while his conduct might at first appear to be "inexcusable," he had "done nothing of which I or my friends need be ashamed, and I wish to see the day when I can stand up in Concord and vindicate myself." [41]

In a letter to Theodore Parker, another of the Secret Six, on the same day, Sanborn presents a more detailed account of his actions. He refers to newspaper accounts of the "Harper's Ferry insurrection" and says, "Our old friend struck his blow in such a way—either by his own folly or by the direction of Providence that it has recoiled, and ruined him, and perhaps those who were his friends." Regarding his own precarious situation, Sanborn notes, "His [Brown's] letters have fallen into the hands of Buchanan, and as among them are many of mine, and I am the agent of others, I thought it best, and so did Mr. Phillips and Mr. Andrew that I should disappear for awhile, to prevent giving testimony." [42] He will wait to see how things develop "and then return to Concord or go to England as may seem best." As regards Brown's future, Sanborn's comments are prescient. "The poor old man fought like a hero and will die like one—by the rope it is most likely." Sanborn is equally clear regarding the government's response to the situation. "Most likely they will follow up the matter as closely as possible, and shall have plenty of treason trials and bloody threats, and some bloodshed—All this will weaken the Slave Power, and the good of the tragedy will outweigh the evil."

Finally, Sanborn speculates that his actions are likely "to ruin my worldly prospects for years to come," a sacrifice he is willing to make. His major concern, however, is that he "shall be much blamed for it all, and that by many whose good opinion I value highly." Undoubtedly, one of those persons about whom Sanborn was concerned was Ralph Waldo Emerson. In a letter to Phillips just two days later Emerson says, "Every hour makes it more important for Sanborn to be home. Yet the only message that has come from him is long farewells." To a correspondent on 26 October Emerson writes, "We have been all a good deal uneasy about Mr. Sanborn's absence, just at this time" (L 5:179). Emerson was concerned that Sanborn, who had been so much involved in aiding Brown and his efforts, should now be on hand to help arrange a defense for the fallen hero, and also to arrange for the support of Brown's needy family. Emerson consulted with Sanborn's sister on the day following his flight and, after seeing Phillips and acquainting himself with Mr. Andrew's opinion, was "strongly persuaded" as he told her, that Sanborn could "return with safety" to Massachusetts.[43] After seeing Miss Sanborn, Emerson wrote directly to Sanborn urging him "by all means" to "return at the first hour wheels or steam would permit," adding, "I assure every one that you shall be here Wednesday or Thursday."[44] With this encouragement, Sanborn hastened back to Concord and arrived on 26 October.

Alcott's journal indicates that on the evening of Sanborn's return there was a gathering at Emerson's home that included Ellery Channing as well as Sanborn, Emerson, and himself. The purpose of the meeting was to discuss the situation and what could be done. Alcott defended Brown's action and suggested that things be allowed to run their course because a rescue of Brown "would be difficult, even if he would consent to be taken." He also felt that "the spectacle of a martyrdom such as his must needs be, will be of greater service to the country, and to the coming in of a righteous rule."[45] Emerson probably agreed with this sentiment, although he said little at the meeting. Alcott could see that "it seemed to be a painful subject to him."[46] Emerson's journal points out that the slaveholder makes a mistake when he imputes resistance to slavery to Channing or Garrison, or "to some John Brown whom he has just captured." It is not just these few men who are the prime movers of the opposition to slavery, but liberty is "the air which that man breathed," and the force of that inspiration will go on "no matter how many Brown's he can catch & kill" (*JMN* 14:329–30). A few days later, on 30 October, Thoreau read his "Plea for Captain John Brown" in Concord. Feelings were running high in Concord regarding Brown's actions, and many condemned them as treasonous. Members of the Republican Town Committee and others suggested to Thoreau that he postpone his presentation, but Thoreau replied, "I do not send to you for advice, but to announce that I am to speak."[47] In addition to moral support, it was now necessary to raise funds for Brown and his family rather than for Sharpe's rifles.

The Battle Lines Are Drawn

John Brown was condemend to death on 1 November 1859. A printed letter dated 2 November was circulated in the Boston area. "You are invited and urged to contribute and obtain contributions to aid in the defense of Capt. Brown and his companions on trial for their lives in Virginia. *Every moment* is precious, and whatever is done must be done now. The following gentlemen (with others who may be hereafter announced in the papers) will act as a committee to receive money and to appropriate it to this purpose only." It was signed by S. E. Sewall, Esq., S. G. Howe, M.D., R. W. Emerson, Esq., and Rev. T. W. Higginson. On the copy of the circular that is preserved in the Boston Public Library Higginson added a handwritten note indicating that "an expense of about $1000 is already incurred for Counsel. Mrs. Brown must also be aided to join her husband, & her two widowed daughters-in-law, aged 20 & 16, need help greatly."

A week later Thoreau visited Alcott at his home and suggested that "some one from the North should see Governor Wise, or write concerning Brown's character and motives, to influence the governor in his favor."[48] It was Alcott's opinion that Thoreau or Emerson should write such a letter, and apparently the task fell to Emerson. In his journal Emerson inscribed a draft of his letter to Governor Alexander Wise. He begins by stating, "I write most privately to make a plea for Brown." He goes on to note Brown's "courage & integrity" and the fact that he is quickly becoming a respected and noted individual as a result of his eloquent "speeches to the Court." He points out to Governor Wise that he will be in a "most unlucky position" as far as history is concerned if it turns out that he is the "Governor who signs [Brown's] death warrant. . . . History plays mad pranks with dignitaries," and the governor might find himself dragged "into an immortality not desirable." He reminds Governor Wise that "public opinion [is] changing every day . . . [and] has softened every hour its first harsh judgment" of Brown. Probably recognizing that Wise might not be persuaded by these appeals to the judgments of history and the public opinion of Concord, Emerson then seems to offer the governor a curious alternative to hanging Brown. Why not declare the man insane? Emerson's suggestion is indirect but clear. Near the end of his letter he describes Brown as "the rarest of heroes, a pure idealist with no by-ends of his own. He is therefore precisely what lawyers call crazy, being governed by ideas & not by external circumstance." To make his point even clearer, Emerson goes on to note that Brown "has afforded them [lawyers] the first tract marked in the books as betraying insanity, namely, disproportion between means & ends" (*JMN* 14:334).

Possibly because he shared Alcott's opinions that "there seems little hope or no hope of pleas for mercy," and that "slavery must have its way and Wise must do its bidding on peril of his own safety," Emerson apparently did not send his letter. However, he did incorporate key passages into a lecture on Brown on 18 November. Emerson wasted no time in speaking out publicly in defense of Brown. His earliest opportunity came in the form of a lecture entitled "Courage," which he delivered to the Parker Fraternity at the Music Hall in Boston on 8 November. In his address Emerson spoke of Brown as "that new saint, than who, none purer or more brave was led by love of men into conflict and death,— the new saint awaiting his martyrdom, and who, if he shall suffer, will make the gallows like the cross."[49] Emerson apparently borrowed this phrase from Mattie Griffith, a southern abolitionist who had emancipated her slaves (*JMN* 14:333). The remarks were not included in the published essay (*W* 7:427).[50]

Sanborn and other abolitionists were delighted with the transcendentalists of Concord and their unswerving commitment to this martyr of the cause. In a letter to Theodore Parker on the fourteenth he notes that "the feeling of sympathy with Brown is spreading fast over all the North . . . Phillips, Emerson, and Thoreau have spoken unequivocally in his favor . . . Thoreau at the Fraternity Nov 1st and Emerson Nov 8th— all using *unqualified* praise."[51] Indeed, Emerson's extraordinary praise of Brown showed a heroic courage of its own. Boston wasn't much more receptive to defenders of John Brown than was Virginia. Edward Emerson notes that "conservatism of what was then called the 'Old Hunker' type was so strong among the aristocracy of Beacon Street, the business men of State Street, and the negro-hating and ruffianly element of the Democracy, that open-speaking on behalf of Brown had its dangers" (*W* 7:427).

Ten days after the Parker Fraternity address Emerson again offered ringing phrases in defense of John Brown, this time at a meeting "for the Relief of the Family of John Brown" held at Tremont Temple. John A. Andrew, Sanborn's legal adviser and an abolitionist, presided over the meeting. Emerson was preceded in the presentations by the Reverend J. M. Manning of the Old South Church in Boston. After indicating that it was his opinion that Brown's action at Harper's Ferry was one that he "would by no means have advised him to," and that "it might have been an unlawful act—a fool-hardy one," Manning goes on to state, without a hint of irony, that "in this act of his at Harper's Ferry, perhaps there was a providence of God." He compares the event to the Boston massacre, "except that in the one case a black man—Crispus Atticus—was acting in behalf of whites, and in the other of a white man seeking to aid the blacks." Throughout his speech Manning depicts Brown as a hero of the patriot mold, a noble soldier in God's army whose work has furthered "the destiny and doom of the slave tyrant."[52] Clearly, abolitionists found the logical necessity of condemning, on the one hand, the sheer lawlessness and violence of Brown's act, but on the other hand, of praising his commitment to principle and the goodness of his cause. Undoubtedly many people, Emerson among them, realized by this time that in all likelihood Brown had demonstrated the format through which slavery would finally be eradicated.

Emerson's presentation followed Manning's, and he was introduced "in a highly complimentary and merited manner, with patriotic allusions to his town." Not surprisingly, Emerson's speech continued the theme of his predecessor. He depicts Brown as a patriot and a hero. "This commanding event which has brought us together, eclipses all others which have occurred for a long time in our history, and I am very glad to see this sudden interest in the hero of Harper's Ferry." Emerson presents a thumbnail biography of Brown, possibly based on his own conversations with him in Concord, that traces his subject back to the Mayflower and 1620, and then through the Revolution and the War of 1812 (W 11:267–68). Among other things, Emerson notes Brown's idealism, courage, integrity, and his "perfect Puritan faith." He then notes that John Brown believed in two instruments of life, "the Golden Rule and the Declaration of Independence." He also notes that Brown is a Unionist who believes, like Emerson himself, "that the only obstruction to the Union is Slavery, and for that reason, as a patriot, he works for its abolition." Though manifestly not a scholar, "nothing can resist the sympathy which all elevated minds must feel with Brown, and through them, the whole civilized world." Brown represents a kind of ideal reformer. He is a person of principle *and* action, a man who puts his "creed into his deed," as Emerson had recently suggested we all must eventually do. "John Brown was an idealist. He believed in his ideas to the extent that he existed to put them into action; he said 'he did not believe in moral suasion, he believed in putting the thing through.'"

In contrast to Brown's ideal heroism, Emerson turns with vitriolic anger to the pusillanimous judges of Massachusetts who are willing to do "substantial injustice" because they "fear a collision between their two allegiances." Clearly Emerson had not forgotten Judge Shaw and his cohorts, and the victims Sims, Shadrach, and Anthony Burns. If those judges "cannot find law enough to maintain the sovereignty of the state" and "the life and freedom" of its inhabitants, then "what avails their learning or veneration? At a pinch they are no more use than idiots. After the mischance they wring their hands, but they had better never have been born." Clearly, as with Webster, Emerson felt no greater wrath than that he directed toward those who, even with benefit of education and "culture," failed in their obligation to help mankind.

In the final portion of his speech Emerson considers the precarious status of Brown's supporters in Massachusetts, especially Boston. Emerson realized that federal authorities investigating the Harper's Ferry raid were eager to bring the Secret Six to Virginia for examination and interrogation regarding the parts they and others might have played in the preparation for this raid. Distrusting the agents of the South but realizing the weakness of the state courts in protecting Massachusetts citizens, Emerson recognized that the only true safety for Sanborn and others was in the willingness of the populace to protect them physically from federal marshals. In a letter on 14 November Sanborn had communicated this very idea to Higginson in the form of a warning. After pointing out that a material witness may be arrested and forced to appear in a court proceeding under order from a federal judge, he went on to note that "this leaves no room for a writ of *habeas corpus*," unless the state judges were willing to assert that the statute is unconstitutional, which seemed unlikely given past experience. Sanborn's final opinion was that "if arrested a witness can only be released by a tumult." While he thought this "may do very well in Worcester," where supporters were plentiful, Boston was a question mark.[53]

Probably with this very concern in mind, Emerson concludes his speech with an indirect appeal to his fellow citizens to be prepared to act where the courts have failed. Only a simpleton would believe that "when a United States Court in Virginia, now, in its present reign of terror, sends . . . for a witness, it wants him for a witness. No, it wants him for a party; it wants him for meat to slaughter and eat." In the face of this, even the habeas corpus is not a protection, because it merely "takes away [from the victim] his right reliance on himself, and the natural assistance of his friends and fellow citizens" (*W* 11:272–73). Clearly, the only alternative to this compromising of the legal process for the benefit of the corrupt is civil disobedience. Where the state has failed, the man must stand forth. Very shortly Emerson would have the opportunity to show that now, more than ever before, he was prepared to put his creed into his deed. Following the speakers' presentations it was announced that "Mr. Emerson, in addition to his excellent speech, had contributed the sum of $50 in behalf of the Brown family. The announcement was received with great applause."[54] Ten days later Emerson recorded in his account book the receipt of $10 from H. D. Thoreau for the Brown Relief Fund.[55]

Emerson's speech did not find sympathetic listeners in every corner of Boston. Not long after, the *Boston Post* complained at length that "the men who occupy seats of power in New England, the controlling men in the dominant party here, are bound hand and foot in the fetters prepared and riveted by the anti-slavery fanatics." Clearly, "a majority of the Republican party in Massachusetts do inwardly rejoice at the John Brown raid," and this same majority "do not intend to give prompt, cheerful, cordial obedience to all the requirements of the Constitution." As far as the *Post* was concerned, a crisis was at hand. The time had come for "the police men of New England—farmers, merchants, lawyers, doctors, all of every class and interest" to address the situation "before it is too late." The villains of the piece were easily identified and well-known. "Wendell Phillips, Ralph Waldo Emerson, Rev. Mr. Manning and John A. Andrew must not be permitted to falsely assume to proclaim the sentiments of Boston in relation to recent deplorable events in Virginia!" Indeed, it is imperative that the concerned citizens of Massachusetts open their eyes and "see where these mad speculators of the Wendell Phillips school in public affairs are leading them."[56]

Sanborn, possibly after consultation with Emerson, lost no time in deciding what his personal course of action would be if the contemplated crisis should arise. In a letter to Parker just a week after Emerson's Boston speech, he states, somewhat dramatically, "If summonsed as a witness, I shall refuse to obey and shall tell the officer if he arrests me he does it at his peril for I will certainly shoot him if I can and a dozen men in Concord would do the same. I shall . . . refuse all writ of habeas corpus, and only shall allow myself to be rescued by force." Obviously, Sanborn had great confidence in the moral fiber of his fellow Concordians, and they would soon have the opportunity to justify his faith. Regarding Emerson's most recent pronouncement on present matters, Sanborn adds that the meeting at Tremont Temple for Brown was "great" and "very enthusiastic. . . . Mr. Emerson has a great admiration for Brown—and he has spoken bravely for him."[57]

Following his Boston speech Emerson wrote to Lydia Maria Child expressing his hope that Brown's life might yet be spared. "He is one of those upon whom miracles wait" (L 5:182). However, Mrs. Child held only "a little of the same hope," and looked to Brown's execution as "a magnificent martyrdom." She wrote to Maria Chapman, "Whether he lives or dies, he has struck a blow at slavery, from the effects of which it will never recover."[58]

On the day of Brown's execution, 2 December 1859, demonstrations of sympathy were held in towns all over the northeast, and Concord was no exception. Largely through the efforts of Henry Thoreau, arrangements were made for an appropriate testimonial (L 5:182).[59] Thoreau, Emerson, John Keyes, and Simon Brown, a former lieutenant governor, were on the planning committee.[60] Eventually it was decided that the participants in the ceremony would be Thoreau, Emerson, Alcott, Sanborn, and others. Not everyone in Concord was sympathetic toward Brown, and there was opposition to the proposed memorial service. Thoreau noted in his journal that there were reports of plans for "some counter-demonstration . . . such as firing minute guns" and that apparently "a considerable part of Concord are in the condition of Virginia to-day,—afraid of their own shadows."[61] An anonymous letter to the editor of the *Boston Evening Traveller* the day before Brown's execution also indicates the degree of unrest in the town. The correspondent states that "there is some prospect that the citizens of Old Concord will be permitted to hear the mournful sound of tolling bells on next Friday, a vote to that effect having been made last Monday evening." (The *Liberator* had suggested that there be a tolling of bells for one hour on the day of the execution.) The correspondent goes on to note that "there have been some expressions against such a proceeding" since the meeting, and the matter is now uncertain. He also points out that at the meeting "one speaker thought that the flag ought to be raised upon the Liberty pole, half mast and *Union down*" in order to best represent the present condition of the country, and warns, "There is no question that any attempt to thus treat the flag of our country will be strongly opposed."[62]

It was decided by the committee that the speakers would read selections from other peoples' writings, according to Keyes, in order to avoid the "danger of our giving way to treasonable utterances if we allowed ourselves to speak our own sentiments." Only Thoreau did not abide by the agreement.[63] A later account in the *Boston Atlas* commented that "the services were impressive and solemn" and that "Brown's last words [were] read in a most touching and impressive manner by Ralph Waldo Emerson." Additionally, "church service for the death of a martyr was then read by A. B. Alcott."[64] Because of the disagreement within the community, the church bells were not rung. In his account of the day Stearns says that "Mr. Emerson looked very grave and serious; and his wife, who subscribed to the Antislavery Standard, was more than that. 'Are you not going to have the bells tolled?' she said to her husband on his return from the town; and it was difficult for him to persuade her that it would not be wise to attempt so much."[65] Emerson's caution was prudent. An account in the *Boston Post* the next day indicates that the plan of the Brown sympathizers to toll the bells and fly the flag upside down had "created considerable excitement among the conservative men of all parties, and measures were taken to prevent such proceedings." The opposition had made arrangements, in case the flag was raised, to haul it down and raise it up again, *"Union Up,"* and to keep it that way "at all hazards." It was also arranged that if the bells were rung, "a salute of 100 guns" would be fired to honor the Union.[66] The account also notes that early in the morning of the second, "an effigy, life size, of the 'old man Brown,' was discovered hanging on a large tree in front of the Town Hall." Attached to the body was the "Last Will and Testament of Old John Brown." Among the items in the will were the following: "I bequeath to H. D. Thoreau, Esq., my body and soul, he having eulogized my character and actions at Harper's Ferry above the Saints in Heaven. . . . I bequeath to Ralph Waldo Emerson all my personal property, and my execution cap, which contains nearly all the brains I ever had."[67] Obviously, not everybody in old Concord was an abolitionist.

Following the execution of Brown, Emerson continued to be touched by thoughts of the man. On 4 December he delivered a lecture entitled "Morals" to the Parker Fraternity. Lydia Child later wrote to her husband of it: "Heard Emerson yesterday at the Music Hall. Said capital things, as usual, illuminated by the Drummond Light of Harper's Ferry."[68] Later, she told the wife of Senator Mason that "Emerson, the Plato of America, leaves his scholastic seclusion he loves so well, and disliking noise with all his poetic soul, bravely takes his stand among the trumpets."[69] Later in December, Wendell Phillips wrote to Emerson to invite, indeed to plead with him to speak in New York at a Brown relief meeting that was to raise funds for Brown's family.[70] Emerson was reluctant to go to New York unless the meeting would present an established program of speakers that would include the famous evangelist Henry Ward Beecher, George B. Cheever, a vigorous New York abolitionist and Brown supporter, and Phillips himself. He did not wish to carry the weight of the affair himself (*L* 5:183). When it became apparent that

Beecher would not be able to attend the meeting, Emerson declined to participate, saying in a letter to Phillips that he was presently "overlaid with tasks [and] . . . it would require more force than I could command to give you real aid."[71] He later recanted his decision when he received Phillips's heartfelt plea for the family of Brown, which he described as destitute. Emerson agreed to "smother my dislikes to the big town & go" if proper arrangements could be made.[72] Unfortunately, they could not, and Phillips went off to face the meeting alone, telling Emerson, "how shall I wish I was hiding behind you."[73]

Never to be daunted for long, Phillips wrote again to Emerson late in December inviting him to speak on Brown in Salem in January. He reminded Emerson that his "name will bring us dollars—& fifteen minutes talk we'll consider ample, unless you long to make it thirty," adding, "You I need not tell how grand a thing also it is to strike this crystallized hunkerdom of Salem a good blow in these stirring times."[74] Possibly as an indication of Emerson's continued drift toward a more militant confrontation with the evil of the time, he accepted.

Chapter Eight

Conflict and Victory: 1860–1865

Emerson delivered his third public address on John Brown in Salem, Massachusetts, on 6 January 1860. In this presentation, as in the two previous, he depicts Brown as a conscientious, idealistic man of action. "He grew up a religious and manly person . . . a fair specimen of the best stock of New England" (*W* 11:279). Emerson describes Brown as the ideal transcendental hero, "a romantic character absolutely without any vulgar trait; living to ideal ends, without any mixture of self-indulgence or compromise, such as lowers the value of benevolent and thoughtful men we know." To Emerson, Brown was a virtuous man of action, and "all people, in proportion to their sensibility and self respect, sympathize with him" (*W* 11:280).

In praising the individual heroism of Brown, Emerson suggested in his presentation that the fatalistic forces of goodness continued to have a substantial influence in rectifying the evil of the times by working through such heroic persons. The sheer force of this goodness in its natural antipathy to evil brings forth heroes like Brown, and others inevitably feel the pull. As in his earlier ode, Emerson obviously saw Brown as a dynamic person who had "made of duty fate." He notes accordingly that "nothing is more absurd than to complain of this sympathy, or to complain of a party of men in opposition to slavery. As well complain of gravity, or the ebb of the tide. Who makes the abolitionist?" The answer is "the slave-holder," because the "sentiment of mercy is the natural re-coil which the laws of the universe provide to protect mankind from destruction by strange passions." His short presentation concludes on an optimistic note with the observation that "the arch-abolitionist, older than Brown, and older than the Shenandoah Mountains, is Love, whose other name is Justice, which was before Alfred, before Lycurgus, be-fore slavery, and will be after it" (*W* 11:281). Eventually love and virtue would have their effect.

The repercussions of Brown's raid, and his subsequent trial and exe-cution, continued to be felt throughout the nation in the early days of 1860, and Concord was soon to become something of a minor epicenter of activity. Within weeks of Brown's execution the United State Senate, amid great internal turmoil, passed a motion to open an inquiry into the Harper's Ferry raid. The committee was chaired by Senator James Mason of Virginia and began hearings in mid-December 1859. The hear-ings would continue intermittently for almost six months. Recognizing the strong possibility that he might be called to testify in Washington, Frank Sanborn wrote to Higginson with some trepidation that "there are a thousand better ways of spending a year in warfare against slavery than by lying in a Washington prison" and he added, "I hope you burn all my letters about these things."[1]

Later in January, Sanborn, as expected, received a summons to appear before the committee. He refused to do so, fearing for his personal safety. Instead, Sanborn put his school in the care of Miss Hoar, Miss Elizabeth Ripley, and others, and departed for Montreal. There, on 24 January, he penned a letter to Emerson, who was lecturing in Toronto at the time. The letter states, in part: "You have no doubt heard before this by your letters from home that I was summoned by the Marshall the same day you left Edward. Today I should have been in Washington to answer the summons, but am here instead. I have sent to the Committee declining to comply with their summons from an apprehension of personal dan-ger, but offering to testify in Mass. This was at the suggestion of Messrs. Keyes and Andrew, and I hope will not place me in a false position—for it is not the personal risk that keeps me away—What notice the Senate will take of this paper you may perhaps know before this reaches you" (*L* 5:193). Given Emerson's earlier comments in Boston regarding the weakness of the state in protecting its citizens from the harassment of the slave powers, he no doubt sympathized with Sanborn's situation. In a letter to Ellen from Toronto Emerson mentions Sanborn's missive and comments, " 'Tis a calamity for the present to Concord and to him" (*L* 5:193–94).

After a short time Sanborn returned home, but fearing his sudden arrest, his friends lodged him in their houses, sometimes Colonel Whiting's, sometimes Emerson's, sometimes Mrs. Thoreau's.[2] However, eventually growing confident that he would not be forced to testify, Sanborn resumed normal residence in his own home. He began once again to attend to the pressing business at hand. At the end of February he wrote to Wendell Phillips to inform him that "Anne and Sarah Brown [John Brown's daughters] are now here, at Mr. Emerson's, preparing to go into my school next Monday."[3] The Emerson children were excited by the stirring events that had such an impact on the nation, on their town, and indeed on their very household. Ellen notes in a letter to her cousin that "Mr. Sanborn's doings are at present our chief interest. He disappears, and we say goodbye, supposing that he will be gone for months. In the course of a week or two, he astonishes us by opening the parlour door, and saying 'Good evening,' in the most common tone in the world. . . . Captain Brown's daughters have just come here to school, and they are staying with us at present. They are very willing to talk and it is very interesting to hear them. The eldest, who is sixteen, kept house for her father at Harper's Ferry all summer, and knows all about it" (*EL* 1:210–11).

Emerson was no doubt pleased with this opportunity to lend further immediate material aid to the family of his fallen hero. But his commitment to Brown would not be without its cost. He had been scheduled to lecture in Philadelphia, but now learned from his friend Dr. Furness that the turmoil following Harper's Ferry had caused considerable disorder in the city, and, as he stated in a letter to his brother William, he was informed that "there was no room for me in Philadelphia . . .—no room since John Brown" (*L* 5:206). Furness, now and for some time an established crusader in the abolition cause, was also greatly moved by the execution of John Brown. A later newspaper account reflecting on the events of that time indicates that Furness "took part in the public prayer meeting held in the city on the day of John Brown's execution . . . and afterwards went with several others to the railroad station, when Brown's body was brought from the gallows by General Hector Tyndale and James Miller McKin."[4] Another account indicates further that "the excited state of public opinion at that time made it probable that Dr. Furness and his church might suffer from mob violence and on one occasion many of his parishioners came to the church armed to protect their pastor and church should assassination or destruction of property be attempted."[5] Despite such violent opposition, however, Furness, like Emerson, was determined to see the thing through, and, as he told his friend in a letter shortly after these events, he wanted to precipitate results.

In early March Sanborn again wrote to Emerson, this time to request that he print his Salem speech on Brown, which Sanborn found "so pertinent and good that I should not know what to omit, but were it left to me should print the whole" (L 5:188). Eventually the speech appeared in James Redpath's Echoes of Harper's Ferry (1860), which was dedicated to Emerson, Phillips, Thoreau, and other "Defenders of the Faithful." The speech also appeared in The John Brown Invasion, Authentic History of the Harper's Ferry Tragedy (1860).[6]

A few days later, Wendell Phillips wrote to Emerson inviting him to address the American Antislavery Society "at the May anniversary in New York."[7] Perhaps because he felt that he had done what he could for the moment, Emerson declined the invitation, noting that he had read Phillips's "Plea" at Brooklyn "with the thankfulness I have often felt for your existence." He explained "[I] shall not go to New York in May, [because] I know myself better & what is the service I can & what I cannot render."[8] Very soon, however, Emerson would have the opportunity to render a very unusual type of service for the cause.

After returning from his last flight to Canada, Sanborn gradually became convinced that Senate officials had given up their purpose of bringing him to Washington to testify. However, on the evening of 3 April agents of the Mason Committee presented themselves at his Concord door. What resulted might best be described as a transcendental brawl. Sanborn later described the melee in an article for the *New York Tribune*, written only days after the event.[9] There were four men in the posse that presented itself. When the leader among them, Silas Carlton (a Boston tipstaff), announced that Sanborn was under arrest and began to read to him the order of the Senate for his arrest, his sister rushed down the stairs and out onto the street to alarm the neighbors. In the meantime, recognizing the need for haste, the officers tried unsuccessfully to force Sanborn into their carriage. Failing at this, Sanborn was then pushed into the middle of the street, without his slippers, which had been lost in the scuffle. "Mr. George Whittemore, my assistant teacher, now ran up, and soon other neighbors appeared, both men and women, amongst them Col. Whiting, who is an old gentleman, upward of 70, and Miss Ann Whiting, his daughter. The colonel beat the horses with his cane, and Miss Whiting sprang into the carriage, which she refused to leave, although the driver caught her by the throat and tried to drag her out." Eventually a large crowd gathered, and Sanborn's counsel, John S. Keyes, appeared on the scene and demanded to see the deputies' warrant, and the altercation continued. "About this time appeared my neighbor, the Hon. Nathan Brooks, a white-haired gentleman of more than seventy, Mr. R. W. Emerson, Mr. George Heywood, the town clerk; Mr. E. W. Ball, Chairman of the Selectmen, with other well-known citizens, old and young." Words passed between the crowd and the arresting officers. "Mr. Emerson rushed up to Carlton and said, 'Who are you, sir? By what right do you hold this man?' Carlton muttered something about Sergeant-at-Arms. 'Are you the Sergeant-at-Arms?' said Mr. Emerson. 'No.' 'Is he here?' 'No,' reluctantly answered Carlton, or someone else of the band. Everything now began to look badly for the ruffians. The bells were ringing, the people rushing up faster and faster. . . . Threats of violence were made, and I felt one of my guard tremble violently as he held my arm."

Eventually Sanborn's lawyer managed to awaken Judge Hoar and to secure from him a writ of habeas corpus, which was served instantly and read aloud. The arresting officers could clearly see that the moment had been lost, and they unlocked the handcuffs they had managed to force on the struggling Sanborn and prepared to depart. However, "the crowd, which now numbered two or three hundred, including most of the people of the village, pursued the ruffians as they drove off their shattered carriage toward Lexington, and could hardly be restrained from killing them."

Sanborn spent the rest of the evening in the house of George Prescott, who later served as captain of Concord's Militia Company in the Civil War. Henry Thoreau, meanwhile, held down the fort at Sanborn's house.[10] The events of the evening were the cause of a great deal of excitement in the Emerson household, and the next day Ellen wrote to a friend: "We are having the most exciting times here. Have you ever enjoyed the interest of being waked by alarm-bells and joining a street-fight, as most of the ladies and gentlemen of Concord did last night? It must have been delightful, we were so sorry to miss it, but we could not leave Edward [who was ill]. However, Father and the man brought us news occasionally." Her letter goes on to relate various details of the evening's events and concludes by noting that "the town is in a high state of self-complacency, it flatters itself that this is the spirit of '76. The most delightful part is that Miss Anne Whiting got into the carriage and held the door and put herself in the way, and fought with a cane, and so prevented them from getting Mr. Sanborn in, and gave the people time to collect. Wasn't that good" (*EL* 1:212–13).

After his rescue by the combined citizenry of Concord, Mr. Sanborn was taken the following morning to Boston in the custody of Sheriff Moore. There he appeared before the Massachusetts Supreme Court, where he was represented by John A. Andrew (soon to be governor), Samuel Sewall, and C. L. Woodbury. The courtroom was filled with supporters, including Wendell Phillips and Walt Whitman. In the afternoon Chief Justice Shaw ruled that the arresting officers had no authority in Massachusetts and ordered Sanborn released.[11] That evening, after Sanborn's return, a public meeting was held in Concord to protest the outrage offered to a citizen and to the town. In a letter written to Theodore Parker at the time, Sanborn states, "I went down immediately to the Town Hall where we had a good meeting, addressed by Emerson,

Thoreau, Higginson, Scott, Mr. Reynolds, the minister, etc and which vowed to protect me against any Senate officer. . . . Tomorrow or next day the matter is due to come up in Washington . . . I have sent a memorial which I suppose Sumner will present."[12] The events in Concord were widely reported. On the morning following the protest meeting the *Boston Journal* reported that "the Town Hall was crowded at 8 o'clock to consider the events of the day and last night. Great enthusiasm was manifested at the decision of the Supreme Court in the case of Mr. F. B. Sanborn. Mr. Bowers called the meeting to order, and Dr. Josiah Bartlett was chosen Chairman. After a warm tribute to the two women who saved the town from the disgrace of the kidnaping of Mr. Sanborn, he introduced Mr. Sanborn to the audience, which received him with shouts of applause. . . . Mr. Thoreau next spoke, advocating resistance even to law, when it opposed justice. . . . and Mr. R. W. Emerson spoke briefly and pointedly against centralization, and in favor of the two women who had behaved so heroically."[13]

The attempted capture of Sanborn continued to have repercussions, both in and out of Concord, for some time. It must have seemed to Emerson that the aggressive powers of the slaveholder had now literally arrived in his own backyard. Even Concord was no longer safe from invasion. In response to this, the leading citizens of the community held a special meeting "to talk over the affair" at the town hall on the evening of the fifth. A report published in the *Liberator* (13 April 1860) notes, "This meeting was called to order by Mr. Bowers, and Dr. Josiah Bartlett was chosen to preside. Mr. Sanborn was introduced with his manacles and received immense applause. He said that he had learned from the event increasing hatred to slavery, under whatever guise it appeared, or whoever supported it. The Rev. Mr. Reynolds, Mr. Thoreau, A. G. Fay, Ralph Waldo Emerson, Henry Warren, E. W. Bull, and the Reverend Thomas Wentworth Higginson addressed the meeting at considerable length." It was decided at this time that it would be necessary to establish some organization to "guard against future outrages of the sort." Consequently, "a Committee of seven was appointed to make arrangements for an organization after the style of the Vigilance Committee of San Francisco." The meeting ended with the group, including Emerson, unanimously passing resolutions that stated, among other things, that the "fame of old Concord" was served "by the chivalrous rescue of one of our most honored citizens"; that "the doctrine of the Revolution, that 'resistance to tyrants is obedience to God,' is our doctrine"; and "that the attempt of United States officers, by false pretenses, and under cover of darkness, to rob a man of his freedom, is base, mean and cowardly." The patriotic pride of "old Concord" had certainly been aroused, and Emerson was undoubtedly pleased to see his fellow citizens pronounce their commitment to a "higher law" than constitutional authority in unequivocal and vigorous terms.

Meanwhile, in Washington, Emerson's friend Senator Charles Sumner presented a "memorial of Mr. Sanborn" to the Senate on 10 April. Among other things, Sumner recounted in some detail the experience of Sanborn on the evening of his attempted arrest and described this victim of governmental bullying as a "quiet gentleman of excellent fame as a scholar of pure life." He was outraged at the conduct of the officers, and he reminded his fellow senators that this "attempt was made at Concord, where a seizure was once before attempted which ended in the revolution of the State." He then asked the Senate to disavow such actions in the future and to "wash its hands of this transaction." In defense of his committee's actions, Senator Mason maintained "that this man Sanborn was shown to be in correspondence with the man who was hanged at Harper's Ferry as a traitor, or with his friends." He had therefore been summoned before the committee of the Senate to testify, and "a warrant was issued against him when he refused." The discussion ended in a draw when the memorial to Sanborn was tabled.[14]

In the meantime, Concord continued its militant posture. The day after Sumner's presentation to the Senate, Emerson wrote to John Murray Forbes, a businessman and reformer whose son would eventually marry Emerson's daughter Edith, that "Sanborn seemed quite clear headed, & to be also well advised. Last night, we had an intimation here that the sergeant at arms would reach Boston at midnight, and wd. come with force here this morning. Concord waked early, but Mr. Nair [the sergeant-at-arms of the United States Senate] did not arrive in Boston— Sanborn is in his school all day. . . . He [Sanborn] is technically in custody of the deputy sheriff, and means to have his Habeas Corpus before the Supreme Court, whenever arrested" (*L* 5:216). One of the reasons for Sanborn's "technical custody," which he never mentions in any of his accounts of events, is that he was himself being sued for his assault on the arresting officers. The case had been bound over to the June superior court in Concord. Among his sureties were George Prescott, Nathan Brooks, and R. Waldo Emerson (*Liberator* 13 September 1860). Sanborn, in turn, was countersuing, but apparently both cases were dropped with the advent of the Civil War.[15]

In early May Theodore Parker died in Italy after being ill for some time. In him Emerson lost one of the most formidable moral agitators in the abolition cause. He had been a strong and consistent supporter of Parker's reform efforts, dating back to the trial times in the 1850s and earlier. Parker was a talented reformer who felt at home in the midst of public controversy and debate, something that was always uncongenial for Emerson. The gentle bard of Concord understood the difference well, and in a letter to Moncure Conway declining an invitation to speak at Parker's funeral he notes, "Our differences of method & working [were] such as really required and honored all his catholicism and magnanimity to forgive in me" (*L* 5:221). In his journals Emerson reflects that "Theodore Parker has filled up all his years & days & hours. A son of the energy of New England: restless, eager, manly, brave, early old, contumacious, clever. I can well praise him at a spectator's distance, for our minds & methods were unlike—few people more unlike" (*JMN* 14:352–53). Others, especially fellow reformers, recognized this difference but also saw the similarities between the two. In a memorial to Emerson in 1882 Edwin Mead declared that "[William Ellery] Channing was in so true and large a sense the spiritual father of both Emerson and Parker," and that compared with these two spirited revolutionaries, the clergy of their time were "a pertrified and asphyxiated set of men, as destitute of real blood as the pre-Raphaelite saints."[16] Similarly, at the turn of the century Sanborn would reflect that Parker, "during twenty years of his life, and more, was closely associated with Emerson in thoughts and social movements."[17] Higginson would later note the intellectual influence of Emerson by suggesting that "Parker was not absolutely a leader, but rather followed Emerson and popularized him."[18]

Parker was certainly among the group of public people like Garrison, Phillips, Sumner, and others from whom Emerson differed conspicuously in personality and style, but upon whom he depended to "put the thing through" in carrying on the public debate for abolition and other reforms. Like John Brown, he would be dearly missed. In June Emerson memorialized his friend Parker at a special service held at the Music Hall in Boston. In his presentation, he summed up the characteristics that he found admirable in Parker and noted that while Parker was "the gentlest of companions," he was nevertheless "a man of study, fit for a man of the world; with decided opinions and plenty of power to state them" (W 11:286). Recognizing that such vigor and forthrightness necessarily bring with them the antipathy of the faint-hearted, Emerson states: "It was complained that he was bitter and harsh, that his zeal burned with too hot a flame. It is so difficult, in evil times, to escape this charge! for the faithful preacher most of all." The same charge was leveled against "Luther [and] Knox" and other reformers who felt the need "to speak tart truth, when that was peremptory and when there were few to say it." For Emerson, Parker was a man of faith and morals in action, and beyond this there could be no higher praise. "His commanding merit as a reformer is this, that he insisted beyond all men in pulpits . . . that the essence of Christianity is [its] practical morals; it is there for use, or it is nothing" (W 11:289). In his attack on slavery Parker gave ample evidence of his commitment to this proposition. When Boston's officialdom prepared to return Sims and Burns to slaveholders in the South, "in terrible earnest he denounced the public crime, and meted out to every official, high and low, his due portion. By the incessant power of his statement, he made and held a party. It was his great service to freedom" (W 11:290).

The April confrontation in Concord was a microcosm of the larger conflict that was brewing in the nation throughout that year. The political tug of war between North and South came to a climax with the presidential election in November. The Democratic party split along regional lines. The Northern wing of the party convened in Baltimore in June and nominated Stephen Douglas for president. The new platform was basically a reiteration of the party platform of 1856. It approved congressional nonintervention and supported Supreme Court decisions, and also provided for the acquisition of Cuba. The southern Democrats held their convention in June in Baltimore and nominated John C. Breckinridge of Kentucky for president. The party platform supported the admission of new states into the Union on an equal footing with the rest. It also allowed for slavery in the territories and supported the acquisition of Cuba. The Republicans met in Chicago in May and nominated Abraham Lincoln on a platform that, among other things, reaffirmed the Wilmot Proviso and the right of each state to control its domestic institutions. Additionally, the Republican platform denied the authority of Congress, or even a territorial legislature, to legalize slavery in the territories, and it also denounced attempts to resume the African slave trade. Lincoln carried the election without a single southern electoral vote, and Emerson recorded in his journal that "the news of last Wednesday morning (7th) was sublime, the pronunciation of the masses of America against Slavery" (*JMN* 14:363).

On hearing the news of Lincoln's election, several southern states called state conventions, with South Carolina leading the way. On 20 December the South Carolina convention passed unanimously an ordinance stating that "the Union now subsisting between South Carolina and the other States, under the name of the 'United States of America,' is hereby dissolved." South Carolina was soon followed by the ten other states that eventually formed the Confederate States of America.

December also saw the publication of one of Emerson's most important works, *Conduct of Life*. In this ambitious work Emerson grapples with some of the thorniest issues of the moment, and clearly, his experience in the abolition ranks is a telling influence in his conclusions. As he notes in the lead essay, "Fate," "The question of the times resolved itself into a practical question of the conduct of life." The issue he wishes to deal with in the work is quite simply "How shall I live?" While recognizing the many ambiguities that face mankind as the result of the inevitable confrontation between freedom and fate, Emerson here very clearly insists that, despite obvious limitations, there is much that individuals can do to improve the world nevertheless. His experiences throughout the 1850s undoubtedly suggested to him that there were many who would accept slavery and other moral abominations as inevitable because they were apparently fated. Thus he notes, " 'Tis weak and vicious people who cast the blame on Fate" when things go wrong. "The right use of Fate is to bring up our conduct to the loftiest of nature" (W 6:24). When this happens, great reforms can occur because "though Fate is immense, so is Power, which is the other fact in the dual world, immense" (W 6:22).

Thus, while recognizing here that "the German and Irish millions, like the Negro, have a great deal of guano in their destiny" (W 6:16), Emerson generally rejects the notion that nothing can be done to improve their lot. Indeed, it is his view that every person has an obligation to assist the process. He told the graduates of Harvard in 1837, "This time like all times is a perfectly good one, if we but know what to do with it"; and here at the outset he insists "if we must accept Fate, we are not less compelled to affirm liberty, the significance of the individual, the grandeur of duty, the power of character" (W 6:4). Throughout the work Emerson's emphasis is on the capacity of individuals, *all* individuals, to actively pursue the improvement of society. Very shortly this philosophy would be severely tested.

As war clouds continued to gather on the horizon, there were many who hoped to preserve the Union, and peace, by negotiating yet another compromise with the South. Literally dozens of compromise proposals were introduced into the Congress and debated at length.[19] Virtually all such proposals were opposed by abolitionists, who welcomed secession as a means of at least containing the contagion of slavery. The "no Union with slaveholders movement," as noted earlier, dated back to the 1840s. Lydia Maria Child, an outspoken abolitionist, made her position in the present situation very clear in a letter to Charles Sumner in January. "If all this excitement does not settle down into a miserable mush of concession, leaving the country in a worse state than it found it, we shall owe it less to the steadfastness of Republican leaders, than to the utter impossibility of satisfying the demands of the South, however patiently we may crawl in the dust, of whatsoever quantity of dirt we may consent to eat."[20] At the same time, Garrison insisted in the *Liberator* that secession was a welcomed development because by it "at last the covenant with death is annulled, and the agreement with hell broken. The people of the North should recognize the fact that the Union is dissolved, and act accordingly" (*Liberator*, 14 January 1861).

Emerson undoubtedly felt the same way, given his stated desire in the 1850s to place a *cordon sanitaire* around the morally diseased South. Most abolitionists believed that if the South were isolated in this way, the corrupting influence of the slave institution would turn inward and bring about a long-awaited and inevitable self-destruction.[21] Despite his emphatic rejection of this position in the 1840s, Emerson now readily accepted it. "The furious slaveholder does not see that the one thing he is doing, by night & by day, is, to destroy slavery. They who help & they who hinder are all equally diligent in hastening its downfall. Blessed be the inevitabilities" (*JMN* 15:91).

The abolitionist agitation against compromise with the South created a violent backlash among conservatives in the North who favored reconciliation as a means of both avoiding war and also maintaining the commercial status quo. During the "winter of secession," conservative and Democratic papers attacked the abolitionists and blacks as being largely responsible for the crisis at hand.[22] As a result, there was a tremendous increase of mob violence in the North directed against both Negroes and abolitionists. Boston, in particular, was a seething caldron of activity and had been, for the most part, since Brown's execution.[23] Not since the dark days of the 1830s had the violence and destruction been so severe. On the day of Brown's execution a group of abolitionists held a meeting in Boston's Tremont Temple. The topic of the day was "How Can American Slavery Be Abolished?" As soon as the meeting opened, the hall was invaded by a group of "North end Roughs and Beacon Street Aristocrats" led by lawyers and members of the commercial class who had substantial financial investments in the South. The rowdies succeeded in breaking up the meeting, and the crowd was finally dispersed by the police. Later in the day the same mob attacked and assaulted Negroes who had gathered for a meeting at the Negro

Baptist Church on Joy Street. The rioters then proceeded through the Negro section of the city, smashing windows and destroying property on their way.[24]

Abolitionists were shocked by those actions but were nevertheless determined not to be dissuaded from their cause. Oliver Johnson, at the time editor of the *National Anti-slavery Standard*, wrote to Wendell Phillips on 7 December stating, "I take it mob law is not to be revived in Boston. The pro-slavery 'gentlemen of property and standing' are now too weak to wield that instrument successfully. If they persist in trying the experiment they'll surely find that 1860 is not 1835."[25] Phillips himself was undaunted by the mobs, but he now found the protection of a group of armed bodyguards necessary, and he also took to carrying a revolver for self-protection.[26] In an environment such as this all things were possible, both good and evil. Johnson wrote again to Phillips ten days later with a rhetorical question, "Are we on the way to great victory for freedom, or the beginning of a violent and bloody struggle for freedom of speech? . . . Last evening the report went all over New York that you had been killed. I did not believe it, but the minds of many who love you were fearfully anxious. We were all relieved by the telegraph's report this morning."[27] As in the 1830s, abolitionists now found it increasingly difficult to meet and discuss the slavery issue with the threat of mob violence always present. Also, many of the elected officials in power preferred to see them silent. Lydia Maria Child refers to this regrettable situation in a letter to Charles Sumner: "Alas, what a lamentable deficiency of conscience and courage does the present crisis make manifest! Yancey [an Alabama slaveholder] can be invited to Faneuil Hall to *eulogize* slavery, and men applaud it, on the ground that free speech is sacred; but when those *opposed* to slavery hire a hall to hold an Annual Meeting they have held for more than thirty years, they are mobbed out by rowdies . . . with scarcely an appearance of restraint from the Democratic Mayor."[28]

The situation was becoming more critical every day, but it was imperative that those who sought a timely end to slavery step forward, lest the opportunity be compromised away. Emerson recognized this, and his journal in January notes, "Do the duty of the day. Just now the supreme duty of all thinking men is to assert freedom. Go where it is threatened, & say, 'I am for it, & do not wish to live in the world a moment longer than it exists'" (*JMN* 15:111). Being true to his own words, Emerson accepted when Wendell Phillips invited him to make a presentation at the annual meeting of the Massachusetts Anti-slavery Society at Tremont Temple in Boston on 24 January. There is no doubt that he was well aware of the dangers involved in his decision. Indeed, his son Edward maintains that it was on "hearing of the probable danger" that Mr. Emerson "felt bound to go" (*W* 7:396). And go he did. Sharing the platform with Emerson were James Freeman Clarke, transcendental reformer and former editor of the *Western Messenger*, Wendell Phillips, and others. The meeting proved to be calamitous.

According to the report that appeared later in the *Liberator* (1 February 1861), the only surviving record of Emerson's presentation, the audience, as expected, had been infiltrated by prounion rowdies, and a contingent of police were also present. When Francis Jackson, the president of the American Anti-slavery Society, announced the speakers forthcoming, Ralph Waldo Emerson received three vigorous cheers for the Union from the mob and then a succession of disturbing groans and outcries. Wendell Phillips, who had preceded Emerson in speaking, had so aroused the crowd that the police were called upon to "do their duty in restraining order," but did not respond. Consequently, Emerson had to wait some time before beginning his presentation. He began by expressing his pride that "a Boston boy [Phillips], educated here in our schools, here in our colleges, all his life among you, has learned to find in your hearts an answer to every living word he speaks," and noting that the same could not be said of "the young people who have endeavored to interrupt this meeting." He went on to attack the "moral pestilence" of slavery, which "decomposes mankind." Looking especially at the vicious circumstances of the moment, Emerson notes that "the institution of slavery is based on a crime of that fated character that it decomposes man. The barbarism which has lately appeared whenever that question has been touched, and in the action of the States where it prevails, seems to stupify the moral sense." And for Emerson, "the moral injury of slavery is infinitely greater than its pecuniary and political injury."

Emerson explains to his audience that the failure of culture to eradicate this barbarism turns on the fact that those who have been corrupted by the institution have apparently "lost the moral sense." Thus, "young men from the South have been educated here in our institutions, have been educated in Europe, and when they have gone back, they have suffered from this ophthalmia, this blindness, which hides from them the great path of right and wrong." Because of this, these young men "do not perceive the political, economical, and moral mischief done by the institution." There is little hope of effective "moral suasion" with those who are blind to truth and deaf to the call of virtue. They have remained impervious to the redeeming influence of culture, learning, and grace. The solution to the problem now is simply to contain the contagion and allow the disease to run its course. The corruption must cure itself.

Regarding the Union, Emerson states, "No man of patriotism, no man of natural sentiment, can underrate the sacred Union which we possess; but if it is sundered, it will be because it had already ceased to have a vital tension. The action of to-day is only the ultimatum of what had already occurred. The bonds had ceased to exist, because of this vital defect of slavery at the South actually separating them in sympathy, in thought, in character, from the people of the North." For Emerson, the facts are clear enough. It is obvious that North and South are different countries, and "if the separation had gone thus far, what is the use of a pretended tie?" Like other abolitionists, Emerson was in no mood for compromise; "as to concessions we have none to make. The monstrous concession made at the formation of the Constitution is all that can ever be asked; it has blocked the civilization and humanity of the times up to this day."

At this point the rowdies in the audience responded to Emerson's challenge with hisses, groans, and calls of "put him out," "dry up," "unbutton your coat," etc. Finally, the cacophony became so loud and persistent that Emerson was forced to conclude abruptly, and the entire meeting ended with the police clearing the galleries. When the abolitionists returned in the evening to resume their meeting, they found themselves locked out by order of the mayor. In reporting these developments, a newspaper in Atlanta quoted a northern correspondent, who maintained confidently that "a John Brown meeting cannot be held in Boston now. We have got a most powerful organization here that will be heard from in due time."[29] Indeed it would, but even more powerful forces continued to push the nation toward civil war, and the firing on Fort Sumter would soon make the arguments between abolitionists and antiabolitionists in the North nearly moot.

Emerson's reaction to his brutal experience at Tremont Temple is recorded in his journals, where one finds unqualified praise for Wendell Phillips, who had clearly become for Emerson one of the true heroes of the time. "Phillips has the supreme merit in this time, that he & he alone stands in the gap & breach against the assailants. Hold up his hands. He did me the honor to ask me to come to the meeting at Tremont Temple, &, esteeming such invitation a command, though sorely against my inclination & habit, I went, and, though I had nothing to say, showed myself. If I were dumb, yet I would have gone & mowed & muttered or made signs. The mob roared whenever I attempted to speak, and, after several beginnings, I withdrew" (*JMN* 15:111).

Emerson's experience was undoubtedly a significant one for him; as he often had noted in the 1850s, mob oratory was not his forte. Indeed, as we have seen, he often opened his antislavery speeches with a disclaimer that it was not his habit or inclination to speak to "public questions" because they are "odious and hurtful, and it seems like meddling or leaving your work" (*W* 11:217) to do so. Despite the fact that his powerful social conscience would frequently compel his presence in the public arena, his temperament was such that he always found these circumstances uncomfortable in the extreme, and rarely satisfying. It was not, in his opinion, his proper "vocation." However, he did believe that there were people, like Sumner, Garrison, Phillips, and others, who could, and should, do such things, and who were, indeed, good at it. Thus, probably with his recent Tremont Temple experience in mind, Emerson notes in his journal that "ridicule is the natural offset of terror. A mob can be dispersed by a water-engine, or by a contribution box. How many good expedients I have heard of Beecher & of Phillips which succeeded in stopping the hissing of mobs" (*JMN* 15:126). Just a year after the Tremont Temple fiasco he made the following revealing entry in his journal: "I ought to have preserved the Medical Journal's notice of R. W. E. in Philadelphia, that, of all the persons on the plat-form, Mr. E. was the least remarkable looking, etc.—which I could very often match with experiences in hotels, & in private circles."[30] Regard-ing arguments and public polemics, Emerson notes that he is "not equal to any interview with able practical men. Nay, every boy out-argues, out-states me, insults over me, & leaves me rolling in the dirt. Each thinks that 'tis he who has done it, & I know that every body does or can as much" (*JMN* 15:158). Given these concerns, Emerson's persistent contributions to the public crusade against slavery from the 1840s on-ward are all the more remarkable. They also serve to illuminate his comment in the essay "Courage" to the effect that courage is "the per-fect will, which no terror can shake, which is attracted by powers of threats or hostile armies . . . and is never quite itself until the hazard is extreme; then it is serene and fertile, and all its powers play well" (*W* 7:255).

Events in the spring of 1861 continued to point toward an inevitable national conflict. Emerson indicated to Sumner late in February that he had asked Captain Barrett, leader of Concord's militia regiment, "if he was ready to march to Washington?" The captain responded, "Yes, that the great coats, haversacks, etc. of his company had all been made, & the men had been all ready, if the Governor had ordered them." Emerson comments, "I hope it will not be needed, but the readiness is whole-some" (*L* 5:241). Meanwhile, the public debate regarding concessions and abolition continued. Emerson's Tremont Temple presentation was noticed widely enough to be satirized in a pamphlet entitled *The Bal-lad of the Abolition Blunder-Buss*. The author, Lucius M. Sargent, was a successful Boston businessman, a committed proponent of the cause of temperance, and a virulent antiabolitionist. The satire ridiculed not only Emerson but also Walt Whitman, who had been in Boston the pre-vious spring to arrange for the publishing of *Leaves of Grass*. One of the cartoons in Sargent's satire depicts Emerson sitting atop his steed Pegasus while "Pegasus is indulging in 'Leaves of Grass' by Walt Whit-man." Part of the satire refers directly to Emerson's performance at the meeting.

> And them naughty boys can't laugh in the gallery,
> Nor use "free speech out of season" up there;

> While good Mr. Phillips proclaims from the chair
> That the Union is a compact with hell and the devil;
> And Ralph Waldo Emerson plays the uncivil
> By telling the boys that "their mothers bereaved
> Don't know they are out," or says he is grieved
> That they will be so naughty, and make so much noise,
> And assures them that "he *was* once one of the boys."

The writer could not resist poking fun at Emerson's literary reputation and included the following lines:

> Mr. Sanborn was there, from Concord green,
> And Ralph Waldo Emerson also was seen.
> Author of Brahma who in poetry shines.
> By way of a sample, here are two of his lines:
> "The journeying atoms primordial wholes,
> Firmly draw, firmly drive, by their animate soles."[31]

Despite such scurrilous carping and violent opposition, the struggle continued, and in February the antislavery ladies of Concord held a festival in the town to raise money for the Massachusetts Anti-slavery Society. Sanborn invited Wendell Phillips to address the group. "We cannot promise you a mob, but I think we can guarantee a large and worthy audience who would hear you with especial interest at the time. We shall also write Mr. Clarke (J. F.), Mr. Emerson, Mr. Alcott and Mr. Higginson."[32]

On 4 March Lincoln was inaugurated and in his address declared, "I have no purpose directly or indirectly to interfere with the institution of slavery in the States where it exists." However, secession could not be tolerated because "No state, upon its own mere action, can lawfully get out of the Union." The Confederacy, however, continued to assert its independence and to articulate its principles. On 21 March the vice president of the Confederacy, Alexander Stephens, claimed that the new government of the Confederate States, among other things, "rests upon the great truth that the Negro is not equal to the white man, that slavery, subordination to the superior race, is a natural and normal condition [and that] our new Government, is the first in the history of the world, based upon this great physical, philosophical, and moral truth."[33]

The differences were thus well defined and the confrontation inevitable. At 4:30 A.M. on 12 April 1861 the rebels opened fire on Fort Sumter and the Civil War began. Mobilization followed quickly in the North, and on 19 April the Concord militia departed for active service. Emerson reported in a letter to his daughter Edith: "Our village was all alive yesterday with the departure of our braves. Judge Hoar made a speech to them at the Depot, Mr. Reynolds made a prayer in the ring[,] the cannon which was close by us making musical beats every minute to his prayer" (L 5:246).

The Sixth Massachusetts Regiment marched to Washington and was attacked and stoned by a mob while traveling through Baltimore. Edward Emerson notes, recalling the Revolution, that once again, "as at Concord Bridge, a soldier from Acton was the first victim of the war" (W 7:351). The outbreak of the Civil War relieved Emerson of his concern that concessions might finally be made that would preserve the unholy alliance between North and South. In April he had begun a series of lectures on "Life and Literature" in Boston, and, at the time of the attack on Fort Sumter, he had scheduled a presentation on the "Doctrine of Leasts." He decided to drop this in favor of a hastily revised piece appropriately called "Civilization at a Pinch."[34]

At the outset of this lecture Emerson notes, "I had proposed to offer you some illustration of a law which has great social importance, in literature & in daily life, but the tumult of the times gave an impertinence." At the moment the war seemed more blessing than tragedy to Emerson, and his optimism was based on the early evidence of the effects of mobilization. Thus he refers to "the wholesome union which the war effected in the north, the bulk[?] of generous feeling, the prompt sacrifices [and] the humane industry which brought up in every town of every state the women to sew for the soldiers, & now every girl is knitting her seventh & eighth stocking."[35] In contradiction to the selfish materialism Emerson had so often indicted in the past, he now finds that "the profusion with which money was spent by the rich, & by those who were not rich & by the poor, contradicted every proverb about the American's attachment to his dollar."[36]

Emerson was well aware of the peril at hand and the possibility that the sacrifices necessitated by the war would go beyond the merely monetary. Undoubtedly with the recent mobilization in Concord in mind, Emerson describes a father who clings to his eldest son and says, "I cannot let him go," and a mother who puts her arms around her youngest and says, "I cannot spare him." But necessity was to prevail, and "the youngest went first, & the oldest followed soon."[37] Like others, Emerson was uncertain at this time what the ultimate denouement of the drama thus begun would be. "Who knows the future of the war? . . . Who has not been at fault in his guess, up to this time?" The national division that Emerson and other abolitionists had hoped for might be the best outcome and the most beneficial. "Who knows whether a separation will not be its best issue,—a separation for the time?" Within a year, however, Emerson would come to see the war as an opportunity for effecting something more than a mere separation.

Emerson, like other abolitionists, had not actively sought violent confrontation with the South, but now that the southerners had taken the initiative and opened the attack, the opportunity to crush slavery absolutely was not to be missed. As he later noted in his journal, "For Slavery, extirpation is the only cure" (*JMN* 15:182).[38] It was undoubtedly with this idea in mind that, when visiting the Charlestown Navy Yard and observing the warlike preparations going on there, he was reported to have remarked, "Ah! sometimes gunpowder smells good."[39]

At first glance this attitude may seem decidedly untranscendental. The imposition of social reform through the force of arms seems quite out of place in a philosophical reformer who sought initially to touch men's hearts through the gentle powers of "moral suasion." As we have seen, however, in his earlier consideration of the ways of abolishing slavery in the 1850s, Emerson considered the "*man*-way of voluntary cooperation by parties, by legislation, by compromise, by treaty, &c." to be "inefficient" because "party besets party," and "the more you attack, the more you exasperate defence" (*JMN* 14:404). The "Godway," by comparison, was more subtle and represented the "friction or judgement of God," or the natural antipathy of goodness to evil that manifested itself in the "difficulty of executing the Fugitive Slave law" and the general deterioration of southern society (*JMN* 14:406). Interestingly enough, despite the long prologue of social and political agitation that preceded it, Emerson chose to see the Civil War as more representative of the "Godway" of eradicating slavery than the "man-way." One of the reasons for this lies in the curious fact that regardless of their earlier and oft-articulated intimations that agitation on the slavery question would ultimately end in armed conflict, the actual outbreak of the war was totally unexpected by Emerson and other abolitionists. After the attack on Fort Sumter, Emerson noted that "every one was taken by surprise, and the more he knew probably the greater was his surprise. We had plotted against slavery, compromised, made state laws, colonization societies, underground railroads; and we had not done much; the counter action kept pace with the action; the man-way did not succeed." There was another force at work, in Emerson's view, that did precipitate the desired end, "namely, friction, an unexpected hitch in the working of the thing. With everything for it, it did not get on; California and Kansas would have nothing of it, even Texas was doubtful; and at last the slaveholders, blinded with wrath, destroyed their idol with their own hands. It was God's doing, and is marvellous in our eyes."[40]

Thus, while others might see the developments of the war, and the war itself, as the inevitable historical consequences of the evolving political power struggle between northern and southern states, with abolition as a focal point of controversy, Emerson chose to see the entire process as the working out of an inevitable ameliorative fate. Actually, this resembles closely the attitude reflected in most of his abolition speeches of the 1840s. The unexpected outbreak of the war seemed to confirm his sometimes strained faith in the "inevitabilities." Sublime patience finally, it seemed, would achieve its end. As he stated in his journal in 1863, "This revolution is the work of no man, but the effervescence of nature . . . nothing that has occurred but has been a surprise, and as much to the leaders as to the hindmost. And not an abolitionist, not an idealist, can say without effrontery, I did it" (*JMN* 15:405). The war, at least at this moment, was seen as the work of God, a transcendental cleansing, and as such Emerson welcomed it enthusiastically. Undoubtedly this attitude was based at least in part on the assumptions that the war would be a short-lived affair and that the North would most certainly be victorious. This would provide an immediate, spontaneous, and absolute end to the evil of slavery. Eventually, when it became clear that the war was destined to be a long-term and costly affair, both in lives and in material destruction, Emerson would moderate his position substantially and return, for the most part, to the social philosophy that he developed in his speeches of the 1850s; namely, that the reform of society would be wrought through the persistent and cooperative efforts of heroic individuals working with, and through, the fatalistic forces at hand. Eventually the struggle of the Civil War would give rise to many such transcendental heroes.

Emerson noted in his journal in early May that "the country is cheerful & jocund in the belief that it has a government at last. The men in search of a party, parties in search of a principle, interests & dispositions that could not fuse for want of some base,—all joyfully unite in this great Northern party, on the basis of Freedom. What a healthy tone exists!" (*JMN* 15:137). For Emerson this "healthy tone" derived from the fact that the materialism and general faithlessness of American society could now be redeemed by a selfless commitment to principle. Throughout the 1850s, as we have seen, Emerson complained that widespread opposition to abolition reflected both the materialism and the skepticism of the society at large. America had grown comfortable in its wealth, and young people and others generally lacked the faith necessary to precipitate reform. Now all that was changed dramatically, and, as Emerson noted later in his journal: "War heals a deeper wound than any it makes. It heals skepticism, unbelief, the frivolous mind which is the spoiled child of a great material prosperity" (*JMN* 15:63–64).

Emerson's friend and fellow abolitionist William Henry Furness displayed a similar enthusiasm when writing to Samuel May in the same month: "To me the hour is full of hope on account of its rapid educating influence. The Southern character is being laid bare & stript of everything like honor, honesty, or humanity. . . . The one great work which the abolitionists have been doing with steadily increasing effect from the first is compelling slavery to show itself in its unutterable hideousness."[41] For Furness and others, such exposure virtually guaranteed slavery's demise.

Conflict and Victory

On the home front in Concord Emerson did what he could to help the cause. When it appeared that the local drill club lacked muskets, Emerson took it upon himself to call upon the governor personally with a special request, and very soon thirty muskets arrived from the Cambridge arsenal (*EL* 1:249). In June Emerson assured Aunt Mary Moody that when her time came, he would provide an appropriate resting place for her in Sleepy Hollow Cemetery, where "it does not look probable that the foot of any slave owner or slave-catcher will pollute that ground." Emerson also expressed his faith that the war would have an unexpected but nonetheless welcome cleansing effect, and that "the very South wind will come to us cleaner & purer of that taint, until it is sweet as the air of Maine Mountains. What a relief in the political convulsion, you must feel with us. The shame of living seems taken away, & to mature & old age the love of life will return, as we did not anticipate" (*L* 5:249).[42] Considering Aunt Mary's twenty-five years of abolitionism, no doubt she agreed.

Emerson's early hopefulness, and that of the North generally, was dealt a severe blow in July with the crushing and unexpected defeat of the Union army in the First Battle of Bull Run. In early August Emerson remarked in a letter to James Elliot Cabot that "the war,—though from such despicable beginnings, has assumed such huge proportions that it threatens to engulf us all—no pre-occupation can exclude it, & no hermitage hide us." Despite the anxieties of the moment, Emerson remained confident that all was for the best and that "the war with its defeats & uncertainties is immensely better than what we lately called the integrity of the Republic, as amputation is better than cancer." The future remained uncertain, and "there is no end to the views the crisis suggests, & day by day." One thing at least remained clear to Emerson at the moment—his hope that " 'scholar' & 'hermit' will no longer be exempts, neither by the country's permission nor their own, from the public duty. The functionaries . . . have failed. The statesmen are all at fault. The good heart & mind, out of all private corners, should speak & save" (*L* 5:253). Emerson's final statement is especially noteworthy because on several occasions in the past he had referred to himself as "scholar," and sometimes as "hermit." He would now no longer find it necessary to apologize for speaking directly to the affairs of state. In a time of war the interests of all are properly seduced by the gravity of the struggle.

As time passed, it became increasingly clear to Emerson that while he and other abolitionists saw the war as a holy crusade against slavery and the general moral corruption it had spawned, Lincoln and others saw the war primarily as a struggle to preserve the Union. Slavery was a separate issue. The difficulty of Lincoln's position was underscored by the fact that after the "winter of secession" passed, four slave-holding states remained loyal: Delaware, Maryland, Kentucky, and Missouri. Any effort to abolish slavery could alienate these key states and drive them into the arms of the Confederacy. As it became increasingly apparent that Lincoln would not interfere with the institution of slavery wherever it existed, the abolitionists began to grow impatient with his administration. At the 1 August celebration of West Indian emancipation held in Abington, Massachusetts, Parker Pillsbury, one of Emerson's favorite firebrands, introduced a resolution denouncing the Lincoln administration. Pillsbury stated bluntly, "I have no higher opinion of Abraham Lincoln, and his Cabinet . . . than I have of the President and Cabinet . . . of the Confederate States."[43] The measure was defeated, but by September the impatience of abolitionists was growing stronger. Northerners who had entered the war to fight against slavery sometimes found themselves compelled to return fugitive slaves to their owners. In fact, there was no consistent federal policy on captured or fugitive slaves. Union officer Major General John A. Dix would not allow fugitives within his lines, but Brigadier General James H. Lane of Kansas encouraged slaves to flee to his state and fight with Union troops. On 6 August 1861 Congress passed the Confiscation Act, which declared that any property knowingly used by the owner for purposes of furthering the insurrection was to be confiscated. If the property happened to be slaves, they were to be freed. Accordingly, General Frémont proclaimed from his headquarters in Missouri that all slaves of insurrectionists were to be declared free men. Lincoln, however, requested a modification of this policy, and when Frémont refused he was removed from his command.[44]

Stories began to circulate among abolitionists about northern soldiers who were outraged by the treatment of fugitive slaves. Lydia Child reports in a letter to Whittier a story told by a young man about one day meeting "a rude, rough man, a corporal, crying right out, blubbering like a schoolboy. When asked what was the matter, he replied, 'They've just sent a poor fellow back into slavery. I didn't leave my home to do such work as *this*; and I won't do it. I come here to fight for the country and the flag; not to hunt slaves; and if the Col. orders any more such work, I'm afraid I shall shoot him.' "[45] Reacting to this situation in his journal, Emerson insists on the importance of focusing the war on "the cutting out of our cancerous Slavery. Better that war & defeats continue until we have come to that amputation." In his opinion the true issue would emerge, whatever other political considerations might exist. "If the war goes on, it will be impossible to keep the combatants from the extreme ground on either side. In spite of themselves, one army will stand for slavery pure; & the other for freedom pure" (*JMN* 15:145). However, Emerson was not unsympathetic to Lincoln's predicament regarding the loyal states, and in his lecture "American Nationality," which he delivered on 12 November in Boston, he stated, "The war for the Union is broader than any state policy or sectional interest; but, at last, the Union is not broad enough, because of slavery; and we must come to emancipation, with compensation to loyal states. This is a principle. Everything else is an intrigue."[46]

Other abolitionists continued to agitate vigorously for immediate emancipation. In September a group including William Lloyd Garrison, Wendell Phillips, Frank Sanborn, George Stearns, William Henry Channing, and others met in Boston to form the Emancipation League. The purpose of the league was, according to Lydia Child, to promote the concept of emancipation and "to influence popular opinion, through the press, and help on the turning-tide in the right direction."[47] An active participant in the effort was Moncure Conway, who wrote to Emerson in early December to inform him that he planned to lecture in Concord on "The Death and Resurrection of Captain John Brown."[48] The purpose of Conway's lecture was to raise money to be used to defray the cost of distributing his book, *The Rejected Stone*, to thousands of soldiers in winter camp. Conway's book, which went through three editions by

1861–62, contended that the Founding Fathers had cast aside one essential foundation stone in 1776, and that Americans of 1861 were suffering the consequences of this folly. "That stone is, essentially, *Justice.* The form in which it stands for us is *The African Slave.*"[49] Emerson no doubt found the theme familiar.

In his response to Conway's missive Emerson states, "I should think it courageous in you, & a full audience not to be warranted. But my wife thinks it worth trying & has just named it to several persons." Emerson also invited Conway to his home, noting that Lidian had a "warm interest" in "The 'Rejected Stone,'" which she has carefully examined" (*L* 5:259–60). Edward Emerson points out that Emerson "had been much struck with the excellence and cogency of Mr. Conway's arguments, based on his knowledge of Southern economics and character, and in his lecture ["American Civilization," 1862] made free use of them" (*W* 11: 610). Eventually, Conway delivered his presentation in January. Though Emerson was off lecturing in Washington at the time, Ellen reported to her father on Conway's visit to Concord and to their home. According to Ellen, Lidian, Mr. Sanborn, and Mr. Conway had an interesting conversation, which made her think that Conway "must be one of the most active men in America." Also, despite Emerson's early apprehensions, the lecture was an unqualified success and "the Hall was very full" (*EL* 1:264). Before leaving for Washington later in January, Emerson received a request from Phillips that he "come & finish for us that speech which you ended while not quite finishing last mob time Jan 24th '61—our anniversary comes *next week.*"[50] Undoubtedly because of his Washington trip, Emerson did not accept the offer.

Emerson was invited to Washington, D.C., to lecture at the Smithsonian Institution in late January 1862. While visiting the capital he was able to meet with and evaluate several of the wartime leaders of the nation. His chief guide while in Washington was his friend and fellow journeyman in the abolition cause, Senator Charles Sumner. Sumner was chairman of the Committee on Foreign Affairs at the time, and he introduced Emerson to Salmon P. Chase, the secretary of the treasury; Edward Bates, attorney general; Edwin M. Stanton, secretary of war; Gideon Welles, secretary of the navy; and William Seward, secretary of state. Emerson was also introduced to Richard Pennell, first earl of Lyons, who was the British ambassador to Washington (*JMN* 15:186–87). Of course, the most important person Emerson met on his Washington trip was the president, and he was able to see him twice.

Emerson was positively impressed by Lincoln, whom he describes in his journals as "a frank, sincere, well-meaning man, with a lawyer's habit of mind, good clear statement of his fact, correct enough, not vulgar, as described; but with a sort of boyish cheerfulness, or that kind of sincerity & jolly good meaning that our class meetings on Commencement Days show, in telling our old stories over" (*JMN* 15:187). One of the topics of discussion in this first meeting with Lincoln was "the case of Gordon, the slave-trader" who had been sentenced to hang for the crime of slave trading. An effort was being made to have him pardoned as the last of his tribe. Perhaps it is an index of Emerson's sincere regard for the gravity of the crime that when asked his opinion on the case, he replied, "Considering the condition of the country, he felt that this was not a case in which the supreme penalty of the law should be set aside."[51] Shortly thereafter, on 25 February 1862, Gordon was hanged in New York, the first person to be executed for the crime of slave trading in the United States.

After his first meeting with Lincoln, Sumner took Emerson to meet with Salmon Chase, where the topic of discussion was the Port Royal experiment. Chase, as secretary of the treasury and a leader of the anti-slavery forces in the cabinet, had been put in charge of this experiment in organizing and educating a group of slaves captured at Port Royal, South Carolina. From this first large-scale endeavor, which was just getting under way at the time, grew all of the freedman's aid activities that developed during the war and Reconstruction periods.[52] In his discussion Chase told Emerson that "slavery was not to be destroyed by a stroke, but in detail." He had twelve thousand young men at Port Royal whom he was organizing, paying wages for their work, and teaching to read and to maintain themselves. Chase also noted that he had "no objection to put muskets in their hands by & by," and that he had "two men, Mr. Reynolds and Edward L. Pierce, who are taking the care" (*JMN* 15:191).

Emerson was no doubt delighted with the concept because he had long been convinced of the susceptibility of blacks to the positive influences of civilization once the yoke of slavery was removed. He also recognized the importance of education in the rehabilitation process. It is possible that Emerson knew something of the experiment even before his trip to Washington. In a letter to her sister Edith dated 30 January 1861, Ellen states, "Mother had that letter from E. Pierce, which Cousin Elizabeth gave me, and she read it aloud to the [Antislavery] Society, who voted an immediate meeting which is to be held at our house next week."[53] Four days later she states in a letter to her father that the "letter of Edward Pierce's, which you have heard mentioned, having been widely read, there is to be a mass meeting of sewers here on Thursday to make clothes for the negroes at Port Royal. It seems probable that I shall be wanted at home to take care of this." Ellen also encouraged her father to visit General Frémont, who had been dismissed from his position as commander of Union forces in the West in October because of his refusal to modify his order emancipating the slaves of rebels in his area. She tells her father that "Mr. Conway inflamed our minds by his stories of him—he seems to consider him the best man there is" (*EL* 1:266). Emerson did make an effort to visit General Frémont but discovered on arriving at his home that the general, unhappily, "had stepped out." He later noted in his journal that the general was a man ahead of his time and that "Frémont was superseded in 1861, for what his superseders are achieving in 1863" (*JMN* 15:405).

Later in his visit to Washington Emerson breakfasted with John Sherman, senator from Ohio, and Schuyler Colfax, a representative from Indiana, and emancipation was discussed. In this conversation Mr. Colfax mentioned that "Congress had not yet come up to the point of confiscating slaves of rebel masters, no, but only such as were engaged in military service." Emerson responded, "How is it possible Congress can be so slow?" The representative's reply was to the point, "It is owing to the great social power here in Washington of the Border States. They step into the place of the Southerners here, & wield the same power" (*JMN* 15:198). Later in the same day Sumner would show Emerson "several English letters of much interest which he had just received from

Bright, from the Duke of Argyll, & from the Duchess of Argyll, all relating to our politics, & pressing emancipation" (*JMN* 15:198).

Emerson's primary purpose in going to Washington, of course, was to deliver his lecture at the Smithsonian Institution, and this he did on 31 January. Edward Emerson suggests that the speech was essentially an expanded version of "Civilization at a Pinch," which he had read in Boston at the outbreak of the war, but the Washington lecture was "much expanded to deal with the need of the hour"—the cause of emancipation (*W* 11:607).[54] Emerson began by emphasizing the importance of honest labor in maintaining the health and virtue of any society. We all work for one another, and even "God is God because he is the servant of all," but "now here comes this conspiracy of slavery,—they call it an institution, I call it a destitution,—this stealing of men and setting them to work, stealing their labor, and the thief sitting idle himself; and for two or three ages it has lasted, and has yielded a certain quantity of rice, cotton and sugar" (*W* 11:297). Meanwhile, "all honest men are daily striving to earn their bread by their industry." The result is an invisible clash between these disparate cultures. "We have attempted to hold together two states of civilization: a higher state, where labor and the tenure of land and the right of suffrage are democratical; and a lower state, in which the old military tenure of prisoners of slaves, and of power and land in a few hands, makes an oligarchy: we have attempted to hold these two states of society under one law," and the result has been dismal failure (*W* 11:298–99). Emerson would like to see "the best civilization . . . extended over the whole country, since the disorder of the less-civilized portion menaces the existence of the country" (*W* 11:299). That the best should prevail and dominate is virtually a divinely sanctioned destiny because "we live in a new and exceptional age. America is another word for Opportunity. Our whole history appears like a last effort of the Divine Providence in behalf of the human race" (*W* 11:299).

This development can only take place if virtuous men act directly and decisively, which has yet to happen. "The evil you contend with has taken alarming proportions, and you still content yourself with parrying the blows it aims, but, as if enchanted, abstain from striking at the cause" (*W* 11:300). Not unlike his 1844 West Indies address, Emerson here insists that the time has come for the government to take the action that only it can take: "Government must not be a parish clerk, a justice of the peace. It has, of necessity, in any crisis of the state, the absolute powers of a dictator" (*W* 11:302), and it is absolutely clear to Emerson what should now be dictated: "Emancipation is the demand of civilization" (*W* 11:304).

The speech goes on to state the practical military advantage of emancipation, and Emerson does not fail to note the need of paying compensation "for such slaves as we ought to pay for." Once emancipation is declared, "the slaves near our armies will come to us; those in the interior will know in a week what their rights are, and will, where opportunity offers, prepare to take them." When this happens, Emerson concludes rather optimistically, "The armies that now confront you must run home to protect their estates, and must stay there, and your enemies will disappear" (*W* 11:305). The bottom line for Emerson, as for other abolitionists, is that slavery must be abolished absolutely because it is the root cause of the conflict at hand, and hence "it can never go well with us whilst this mischief of slavery remains in our politics, and that by concert or by might we must put an end to it" (*W* 11:306).

Emerson's fear at the moment is that if the measure is not taken soon, people who are "impatient of defeats, or impatient of taxes" will "go with a rush for peace; and what kind of peace shall at that moment be easiest attained." As a result, "They will make concessions for it,—will give up the slaves, and the whole torment of the past half-century will come back to be endured anew" (*W* 11:306). In Emerson's opinion there is a possibility now, through emancipation, to alter "the atomic social constitution of the Southern people," a measure that would ensure a lasting reform (*W* 11:307). To those who fear that violence and bloodshed might result from emancipation, Emerson responds, "What is so foolish as the terror lest the blacks should be made furious by freedom and wages? It is denying these that is the outrage, and makes the danger from blacks. But justice satisfies everybody—white man, red man, yellow man and black man. All like wages, and the appetite grows by feeding" (W 11:308–9).

Emerson concludes with a warning that "this measure, to be effectual, must come speedily. The weapon is slipping out of our hands." He remains convinced that the fatalistic forces at work will assure victory, and that "it is the maxim of history that victory always falls at last where it ought to fall," and "there is perpetual march and progress to ideas." In either case, however, "no link of the chain can drop out. Nature works through her appointed elements; and ideas must work through the brains and the arms of good and brave men, or they are no better than dreams" (W 11:310). Emerson's point was made, and a local newspaper later reported that "the audience received it . . . with unbounded enthusiasm. It was in many respects a wonderful lecture, and those who have often heard Mr. Emerson said that he seemed inspired through nearly the whole of it, especially the part referring to slavery and the war" (W 11:607–8).

Abolition activity continued unabated in the Emerson household after his return from Washington. In March Ellen wrote to Edward that "in the evening they had the Port Royal meeting," where "Mr. Sanborn made a good speech." She also noted a gathering of "seventeen or eighteen girls" who formed the "MacClellan [sic] sewing circle," which turned out clothing for "negro refugees" (EL 1:267).

Emerson was pleased that Lincoln's proposal for the emancipation of Negroes in Washington, D.C., became law in April (with compensation of not more than $300 awarded for each slave), and that in June the president signed a bill abolishing slavery in the territories. Although his proposal to Congress in March to offer compensation for any loyal state adopting a gradual abolition of slavery (a copy of which Emerson pasted into his journal) was rejected, things seemed to be moving in the right direction, generally.[55]

Indeed, the tone of Emerson's 13 April lecture "Moral Forces," which he delivered in Boston before the Parker Fraternity, reflects his optimism. He notes that "things point in the right way. The nation [is] every day more equal to the crisis. A position is taken by the American Executive. That is much. It has been supported by the legislature." Emerson also notes with satisfaction that Congress "has destroyed servitude in the District of Columbia," and other positive developments are on the horizon. Emerson includes among these the valuable role that escaped slaves were beginning to play in the war. "An army of slaves is already escaped from 'the service to which they were held,' in the lavender phrase of the law." Their service has proven to be "an eye-opener" because it "is showing military men values of slaves which . . . were never set down in any advertisement of the most sanguine auctioneer of that species of property." Indeed, the rise of the slave from his position of oppression is already apparent because "you have begun to instruct them by sending noble intelligent youths to teach them to read & to think." Future prospects are improving constantly, and all will have a role to play. Emerson is confident that "if in the next twenty years the government will be only as active for the destruction of evil as it has been in the last twenty years for its increase we cannot complain."[56]

On 6 May Henry Thoreau died, after living for some months as an invalid in his mother's home. Thoreau's interest in the war had declined with his health, despite his earlier, nearly unbounded activity in the name of reform.[57] In the early spring of 1861 Thoreau was interested enough in national events to take the time to express his views in a letter to his cousin George Thatcher in Bangor, Maine. He was impatient with what he perceived as the slow progress of the new administration. "As to the condition of the country, though Lincoln has been president for nearly a month, I continue to feel as if I lived in an interegnum, & we had no government at all. I have not heard that a single person, north or south, has yet been punished for treason—stealing from the public treasury—or murdering on political accounts." Henry, like Emerson and others in the period immediately following Lincoln's election, anticipated that secession would be accomplished by the southern states, and that the North would be morally better off for it. "If the people of the North thus come to see clearly that there can be no *Union* between freemen and slave-holders, & note & act accordingly, I shall think that we have purchased that progress cheaply by this revolution. A nation of 20 million freemen will be far more respectable & powerful, than if 10 millions of slaves & slave holders were added to them." Thoreau closes, however, with a word of caution. "I am only afraid that they will still remember their miserable party watchwords—that Democrats will be Democrats still, & so by their concessions & want of patriotism, keep us in purgatory a spell longer." [58]

Despite this apparent interest in current events, however, less than two weeks later a different tone is evident in a letter from Thoreau to Parker Pillsbury. "I do not so much regret the present condition of things in this country . . . as I do that I ever heard of it." "As for my prospective reader, I hope that he *ignores* Fort Sumter, old Abe, & all that, for that is just the most fatal and indeed the only fatal weapon you can direct against evil ever." [59] Apparently Henry took his own advice. Given his earlier enthusiasm and even leadership in the crusade against the scourge of slavery and, most recently, his valiant defense of John Brown, Emerson must have been disappointed in Thoreau's apparent withdrawal, especially when such a critical time in the battle had come. It is entirely possible that the sense of disappointment that rings in Emerson's famous eulogy delivered at Thoreau's funeral on 9 May is informed by this fact. In a passage that Edward Emerson appropriately describes as "but the expression of a mood," Emerson states, "Had his genius been only contemplative, he had been fitted to his life, but with his energy and practicability he seemed born for great enterprise and for command; and I so much regret the loss of his rare powers of action that I cannot help counting it a fault in him that he had no ambition. Wanting this, instead of engineering for all of America, he was the Captain of a huckleberry-party. Pounding beans is good to the end of pounding empires one of these days; but if, at the end of years it's still only beans!" (W 10:616, 480). As was noted earlier regarding both Parker and Brown, Emerson came to feel keenly the loss of men of action, enterprise, and practical skill in the struggle for social justice, and it is significant and revealing that he emphasizes these very characteristics in his eulogy for Thoreau. [60]

Emancipation continued to be a general concern around the Emerson household. Edward, who was not yet eighteen years old, and frail of health, wanted to enlist. Lidian was opposed to his enlistment because emancipation had not yet been declared as a goal in the war, and hence, in her eyes, the struggle lacked an important moral sanction. As Ellen states in a letter to Edward in late August, "Mother's decree that you shall not enlist will be a great trial to you. She says when emancipation is proclaimed you may, and she believes she takes the true patriotic ground." Lidian's refusal was part of a strategy that she hoped to generalize. If parents forbade their sons to enlist until emancipation was declared, as Ellen goes on to explain, "All the Governors would write to the president as Gov. Andrew [of Mass.] once did. 'Recruiting drags, the policy of the Govt. is not declared. At first word of Emancipation the avenues to the Capital will throng with loyal men, hastening, etc.' and that Emancipation would surely follow" (*EL* 1:298). Thinking such as this undoubtedly served to justify Lidian's family reputation as a "hot & fiery radical."[61] The need for more troops was a real one, however. Throughout the summer the war seemed to be generally a stalemate, and Emerson noted in a letter to his son in June that "our town is still searched for troops" (*L* 5:279). The following month he complained to his brother William that "the war drags on & drags us all into it, in some sort, by ourselves, our children, or our friends" (*L* 5:280). Emerson wished to see the war prosecuted vigorously. Earlier in the year he stated in his journal, "I do not wish to abdicate so extreme a privilege as the use of the sword or bullet. For the peace of the man who has forsworn the use of the bullet seems to me not quite peace." Later, in obvious exasperation at the lack of movement in the military theater, he asks, "Shall we raise an army of ablebodied men, & employ them to catch flies!" (*JMN* 15:172, 173). He goes on to observe that "the government is paralyzed, the army paralyzed. And we are waiters on Providence." But he does conclude that it is "better for us, perhaps, that we should be ruled by slow heads than by bold ones, whilst insight is withheld" (*JMN* 15:175).

In late August Emerson drew up in his journal a list of "several urgent motives [that] point to the Emancipation," perhaps because he was contemplating further speeches on the topic. He begins, not unexpectedly, with "the eternal right of it." His second point was one he had made in Washington: "The military necessity of creating an army in the rear of the Enemy." But the third point suggests a new concern, "the danger of the adoption by the South of the policy of Emancipation." In this event, Emerson feared, "France & England may peaceably recognize the Southern Confederacy, on the condition of Emancipation. Instantly, we are thrown into falsest position. All Europe will back France & England in the act, because the cause of the South will then be the cause of Freedom, the cause of the North will be that of Slavery" (*JMN* 15:207). For Emerson and other abolitionists who saw the war as primarily a crusade against slavery, the lack of emancipation remained anomalous. In a later journal comment he imagines the difficulty that "foreigners" must have in understanding how, due to our Constitution, one party could be "fighting at the same time *for* slavery in the loyal states, &, in the rebel states, *against* it" (*JMN* 15:209).

Emerson's fear about the possibility of the South declaring unilateral emancipation in order to gain European support may have been suggested by a comment from William Ellery Channing, who two weeks before had told Emerson, "As the rebels burned their cotton & their towns, it would not be strange if they should Emancipate their slaves" as a war measure (*JMN* 15:277). Emerson's earlier discussions with Sumner in Washington regarding the desire of the British to encourage emancipation might have reinforced his fears. At any rate, his rumination concludes with the statement "Emancipation makes all this impossible. European govts. dare not interfere for Slavery, as soon as the Union is pronounced for Liberty" (*JMN* 15:207).

The lull on the battlefront eventually gave way in September with the Battle of Antietam on the seventeenth, one of the bloodiest days of the war. The clash produced over twenty thousand casualties and a technical victory for the North. As a result, the British and the French governments were persuaded to withhold plans for recognizing the Confederacy and possibly intervening to force mediation. Also, the victory allowed Lincoln to issue his Preliminary Emancipation Proclamation on 22 September, which specified that as of 1 January 1863, all slaves living in areas still in rebellion against the United States would be considered free.

Emerson was generally pleased with Lincoln's long-awaited move, but there were reservations. As Ellen points out in a letter written six weeks after the announcement, "Emancipation gives this family great pleasure, though Father and Mother complain that it is slow, and the *January* may just counteract the good of it. Still, Mrs. Emerson rejoices often and aloud, and is surprised that the sky doesn't look different" (*EL* 1: 300). The battle for emancipation was far from over, however. Many abolitionists were disappointed with Lincoln's announcement. Garrison had hoped that the emancipation edict would be immediate and complete, but Lincoln's conservative measure limited emancipation to the rebellious states, allowed them a one-hundred-day grace period, and provided for gradual and compensated emancipation. To Garrison the measure represented "circumlocution and delay."[62]

Additionally, there was a concern among abolitionists regarding Lincoln's ability to withstand the strong conservative backlash that his proclamation elicited. The Democratic press saw the measure as unconstitutional, dictatorial, and ruinous, and made it an issue in the 1862 congressional elections. In Massachusetts, especially, there was a great deal of controversy. Charles Sumner's consistent campaigning for emancipation and other reform measures offended many conservatives in the state, who opposed the war at the outset and resisted the tendency to see it as an antislavery campaign. These tensions were apparent in the Republican state convention, held in Worcester in August. On 28 August, before the Republicans met, several "conservative gentlemen" from the eastern part of the state met privately to "consider the best method of overcoming the radical element in Massachusetts at the polls."[63] Three days after the convention the group issued an address "to the People of Massachusetts" which attacked the divisiveness that characterized the northern war effort (largely because of agitation on the emancipation question) and urged all patriots to close ranks behind the president, and that "no discussions about political, social, or party measures or dogmas . . . should be tolerated." The group, which came to be known as the People's party called for a convention of the people to be held in Faneuil Hall on 7 October. This appeal was endorsed by more than a thousand voters representing some of the oldest and most influential families in Massachusetts.

Conflict and Victory

The People's party movement was a considerable threat to Sumner's reelection efforts. The party attempted to capitalize on anti-Negro feelings in the state and claimed, among other things, that Sumner favored racial amalgamation and, more important, that he was an opponent of the president and had fomented an unhealthy divisiveness at a time of crisis when the North should be united and strong. Fortunately for Sumner, the president's September proclamation proved timely. Sumner accepted the president's action as wholly appropriate and necessary and, at a rally held at Faneuil Hall on the day before the People's party convention, he announced, "For myself, I accept the Proclamation without note or comment. . . . I place myself, with the loyal multitudes of the North, firmly and sincerely by the side of the President, where, indeed, I have ever been."[64] Sumner's maneuver effectively stole the thunder from the People's party convention the following day, and in November he was reelected by a comfortable margin.

Emerson's response to these developments emphasizes his consistent concern with the antislavery principles that Sumner so doggedly upheld. In his journal, under the heading "People's Party," he states: "The Proclamation has defined every man's position. In reading every speech, or any sentence of any speech, but a few words show at once the *animus* of the men, shows them friends of Slavery; shows us that the battleground is fast changing from Richmond to Boston. They unmask themselves, &, though we tried to think them freemen, they are not. Look where they rage at Sumner. They find not Lincoln, for they do not think him really antislavery, but the abolitionist they can find is Sumner, and him they hate. If Sumner were pro-slavery, there would be no chemical analysis & magnifying glass needed to exhibit his foibles." Emerson was determined, however, that the struggle must continue no matter what the cost. Reflecting on the possibilities, he concludes, "It seems to promise an extension of the war. For there can be no durable peace, no sound Constitution, until we have fought the battle & the rights of man are vindicated. It were to patch a peace to cry peace whilst this vital difference exists" (*JMN* 15:292–93).

In the context of this violent controversy, Emerson prepared and delivered a formal address entitled "The Emancipation Proclamation" on

12 October in Boston (*L* 5:290). The speech emphasizes Emerson's concern with promoting the cause of antislavery and also represents, de facto, a strong endorsement of Sumner's bid for reelection. The piece was printed in the *Atlantic* in November. In the speech Emerson hails President Lincoln's proclamation as a major historical development, one of those measures that "provoke no noisy joy, but are received into sympathy so deep as to apprise us that mankind are greater and better than we know" (*W* 11:316). He goes on to praise Lincoln extensively and to assert that, "great as the popularity of the President has been, we are beginning to think that we have underestimated the capacity and virtue which the Divine Providence has made an instrument of benefit so vast. He has been permitted to do more for America than any other American man" (*W* 11:317). Despite the fact that until very recently the "President anticipated the resignation of a large number of officers in the army, and the secession of three states, on the promulgation of this policy," it was done nevertheless, and "against all timorous counsel he had the courage to seize the moment" (*W* 11:318).

Despite the rather limited nature of the president's act, Emerson emphasizes its potential significance in stating, "October, November, December will have passed over beating hearts and plotting brains: then the hour will strike, and all men of African descent who have faculty enough to find their way to our lines are assured of the protection of American law" (*W* 11:319). For Emerson, the true victory here is for principle, no matter what the actual effects are. "It is by no means necessary that this measure should be suddenly marked by any signal results on the negroes or on the rebel masters. The force of the act is that it commits the country to this justice,—that it compels the innumerable officers, civil, military, naval, of the Republic to range themselves on the line of this equity" (*W* 11:319).

In considering the effect of the Emancipation Proclamation on the black slaves themselves, Emerson is realistic and true to his former thinking on the matter. "It does not promise the redemption of the black race; that lies not with us: but it relieves it of our opposition. The President by the act has paroled all the slaves in America; they will no more fight against us: and it relieves our race once for all of its crime and false position. The first condition of success is secured as putting ourselves right" (*W* 11:320). Emerson is also concerned with supporting Lincoln's resolve in the light of strong conservative criticism of the measure. "Of course, we are assuming the firmness of the policy thus declared. It must not be a paper proclamation. We confide that Mr. Lincoln is in earnest, and as he has been slow in making up his mind, has resisted the importunacy of parties and of events to the latest moment, he will be as absolute in his adhesion" (*W* 11:320–21).

For those who continue to resist the measure and counsel compromise in the name of peace, Emerson is adamant. "It is wonderful to see the unseasonable senility of what is called the Peace Party, through all its masks, blinding their eyes to the main feature of the war, namely, its inevitableness. The war existed long before the cannonade of Sumter, and could not be postponed. It might have begun otherwise or elsewhere, but war was in the minds and bones of the combatants, it was written on the iron leaf, and you might as easily dodge gravitation" (*W* 11:322–23).

The South, because of the malignancy of the slave institution, has had a pernicious effect upon the entire nation, and it will continue to work its mischief until stopped. "Our habitual proclivity, through the affection of trade and the traditions of the Democratic party, [was] to follow Southern leading," with predictably destructive results (*W* 11:324). In addition to suffering, the war has brought a great opportunity to rectify this wrong and to surgically remove the cause of the disease. As in his Washington address several months earlier, Emerson insists that "the aim of the war on our part is indicated by the aim of the President's Proclamation, namely, to break up the false combination of Southern society, to destroy the piratic feature in it which makes it our enemy only as it is the enemy of the human race, and so allow its reconstruction on a just and healthful basis" (*W* 11:325).

Emerson's final comment is addressed to the black victims of the institutions of the South, and is very possibly intended to mitigate some of the racism that had served to fuel the drive of the People's party and their ilk. "Meantime that ill-fated, much-injured race which the Proclamation respects will lose somewhat of the dejection sculptured for ages in their bronzed countenance, uttered in the wailing of their plaintive music,—a race naturally benevolent, docile, industrious, and whose very miseries sprang from their great talent for usefulness, which, in a more moral age, will not only defend their independence, but will give them a rank among nations" (W 11:326).

Throughout the fall months Emerson continued to be concerned with the apparent lack of progress in the war, and so too was Lincoln, who removed the conservative McClellan from command of the Army of the Potomac on 7 November. Abolitionists were generally pleased with the development, and Oliver Johnson wrote to Garrison, "The removal of McClellan lights up the whole horizon. From all that I can learn, the President is not contemplating any change of policy, so far as emancipation is concerned. . . . The removal of McClellan tends to show that . . . he is satisfied, at last, that all attempts to conciliate the pro-slavery Democracy are vain."[65] Emerson was also pleased with this development, for military as well as political reasons. Earlier in his journals he had wondered, "strange that some strong-minded president of the Women's Rights Convention should not offer to lead the Army of the Potomac. She could not do worse than General Maclellan [sic]" (JMN 15:207). However, he continued to be concerned about the possibility that Lincoln would waver in his resolve on the emancipation issue. As late as August, Lincoln had sent an open letter to Emerson's friend Horace Greeley, which was published in the Tribune at that time. In this famous letter the president said, "If I could save the Union without freeing any slaves, I would do it—if I could save it by freeing all the slaves, I would do it—and if I could do it by saving some and leaving others alone, I would also do that. What I do about slavery and the colored race, I do because I believe it helps to save this Union, and what I forbear, I forbare because I do not believe it would help to save the Union."[66]

It was possibly this statement that Emerson had in mind when he recorded in his journal in November, "It is said Mr. Lincoln has a policy & adheres to it. He thinks emancipation almost morally wrong, & resorts to it only as a desperate measure, & means never to put radicals into power" (JMN 15:296–97). However, despite some strong fears on the part of many abolitionists that Lincoln might finally renege on his promise for emancipation, on 1 January 1863 the historic proclamation was made, amid great celebration in Boston and elsewhere.

Conflict and Victory

Emerson was afforded a special honor when he was asked by John Sullivan Dwight to provide a prefatory poem for what would be an otherwise largely musical celebration of the event at Boston's Music Hall. Emerson, as usual, found some difficulty in guaranteeing the punctual cooperation of his muse in order to produce the requested verse, and so asked that his name be left off the program lest he fail to meet the necessary deadline. Happily, however, the deadline was met and Emerson read his "Boston Hymn" before the crowd on the appointed day. He was probably especially pleased to participate in this particular celebration because it not only commemorated a significant historical event but, as Dwight himself explained it, "The whole plan and programme of this jubilee was based on the conviction that the great thoughts of Humanity and Freedom, the progressive moral instincts of the age, although to this day spit upon and crucified, are yet in most intimate alliance and sympathy with the loftiest inspirations and utmost refinements of creative genius and Art." [67] Here, certainly, was an opportunity for transcendental instincts to find their expression and have their effect. Here was confirmation that the power of culture can revolutionize and redeem a corrupted society. In Emerson's poem one hears the voice of the Lord speaking to the Pilgrims. The work expresses Emerson's faith that divinity has sanctioned the concept of universal human freedom. This fatalistic instinct toward freedom precipitated the founding of the nation through its first revolution, and extends the principle to all citizens in its present second revolution.

Emerson indicates in the poem that the initial impulse for freedom comes from the Lord. God said,

> I am tired of kings,
> I suffer them no more;
> Up to my ear the morning brings
> The outrage of the poor.

Upon observing the suffering of mankind under tyranny, God instructs his pilgrim,

> My angel,—his name is Freedom,—
> Choose him to be your king.

After offering this injunction, God then uncovers the land that he "hid of old time in the West" [America] and which will become the home of his freedom-loving children. In this new land labor will be sacred, and "none but [those that] Toil shall have." In this land freedom must always rule, and "laying hands on another / To coin his labor and sweat" brings about its own punishment because the perpetrator shall thereby go "in pawn to his victim / For eternal years in debt." The injunction of the moment is clear, the will of God inevitable.

> To-day unbind the captive,
> So only are ye unbound;
> Lift up a people from the dust,
> Trump of their rescue, sound!

Regarding the question of compensation, Emerson, here speaking for the ideal rather than the politically expedient, states,

> Pay ransom to the owner
> And fill the bag to the brim.
> Who is the owner? The slave is owner,
> And ever was. Pay him.

The inevitable shall, as Emerson always maintained, come forward, with justice assured. Here, the voice of God offers appropriate affirmation.

> My will fulfilled shall be,
> For, in daylight or in dark,
> My thunderbolt has eyes to see
> His way home to the mark.
>   (W 9:201–4)

The presentation was well received, and Dwight records that Emerson's poem "was a hymn of Liberty and Justice, wide and strong, and musical" and that the bard's rich tones "spell-bound the great assembly." Later that evening, there was a great celebration at the home of Emerson's abolitionist friend George Luther Stearns, to which "all the prominent abolitionists and Free-soilers were invited." Emerson read his poem again, and later sent a handwritten copy to Mrs. Stearns, with whom he and Alcott "talked philosophy to a late hour" that grand evening.[68]

After the euphoria of the emancipation celebrations passed, abolitionists came to realize that the battle may have been won, but the war was far from over. The military situation continued to be ambiguous, and there was still a multitude of conservatives who were more than willing to seek peace through compromise. Undoubtedly with this concern in mind, George Stearns wrote to Emerson in February to encourage him to return to Washington, with Wendell Phillips, in order to impress upon the president the need to maintain the support of New England in "favor of a vigorous prosecution of the war. . . . This can be done by you and Mr. Phillips better than any other persons. . . . I would suggest that Mr. Phillips should make the political statement, leaving the moral and intellectual impression to be made by you."[69] Emerson apparently did not take Stearns up on his suggestion, but he did continue contributing to the cause in other ways, both directly and indirectly.

In 1862 and 1863 Emerson began outlining a "Proposed Book of Occasional Discourses" in his journal (*JMN* 15:167, 362–63). In proposing the selections for the volume, Emerson chose some of his most strident antislavery speeches, including his 7 March speech on Webster and the Fugitive Slave Law given at the Tabernacle in New York in 1854; his "John Brown" speech from December 1859; "Kansas Affairs" and the "Sumner Outrage," both from 1856; and possibly his January 1855 "American Slavery Address" in Boston. He also anticipated including at least three speeches from the 1860s. These were his memorial speech on Theodore Parker, his "American Civilization Address" at the Smithsonian, and his "Emancipation Proclamation Address." In making these choices Emerson included only one of his antislavery speeches from the 1840s, and that was the famous 1 August 1844 "Emancipation in the British West Indies," which already had been printed and widely circulated.

The volume, eventually entitled *Miscellanies*, would not be published until after Emerson's death, in December 1883, with most of the editing done by James Elliot Cabot and Ellen Emerson. Eventually the book was included as volume 11 of the Centenary edition of Emerson's complete works edited by Edward Emerson, who added seven more pieces to the collection, including the letter to Van Buren on the Cherokees (1838) and the speech on the Fugitive Slave Law that Emerson delivered in Concord in 1851. Contemporary scholars have pointed out that while the editors "had to rely on newspaper accounts for some of the occasional speeches," based on Emerson's own journal listings, "all of the reprinted pieces seem to reflect the will of the author."[70]

Emerson's choice of these particular speeches may have been based upon his perception of the needs of the moment. In 1862 and 1863 the war was far from over, and each year gave rise to its own particular crises. Perhaps as a consequence, Emerson chose speeches from the 1850s that were exhortative in tone, and which also placed a strong emphasis upon the obligations of individuals in bringing the struggle forward. Thus, the speeches that he selected tend to emphasize the sacrifices of such strong leaders as John Brown, Theodore Parker, and Charles Sumner. By comparison, the speeches of the 1840s tended to be more philosophical and to emphasize the inevitability of amelioration in the lengthy epochs of time. They also encouraged a "divine patience" in awaiting this amelioration. Another consideration was undoubtedly the availability of manuscripts. As was noted earlier, most of the manuscripts for the 1840s antislavery addresses have apparently not survived. Whatever the reasons for his choices, there was probably a greater element of fate involved in the process than even Emerson knew. There can be little doubt that most of the people who argued the question of Emerson's involvement or noninvolvement in the abolition movement relied heavily upon the volumes of his published works for the evidence to support their arguments. Since only one antislavery speech from the 1840s was included in *Miscellanies,* and even the Cherokee letter to Van Buren was not added until 1903, the tendency to see Emerson as largely detached from pressing issues of social reform, in the 1840s especially, would be amply reinforced. Even those who wished to promote an understanding of Emerson as a social reformer apparently knew next to nothing of his activities in the mid to late 1840s following the "conversion experience" reflected in the 1 August 1844 address. This apparent gap in Emerson's attention to social causes continues to affect scholarly treatment of this aspect of his career.

Other opportunities for Emerson to serve the Union cause continued to arise after the emancipation celebration. In early March Thomas Russell, a Massachusetts superior court justice, informed him of a plan to equip a Negro regiment, the Massachusetts Fifty-fourth, and asked him if he would care to make a speech at a fund-raising gathering to be held at Chickering Hall in Boston on the twentieth (*L* 5:320). The formation of Negro regiments and the regular use of Negro troops were seen by many abolitionists as important elements in the struggle to establish the equality and integrity of free blacks.[71] After Lincoln's preliminary emancipation announcement in September, radicals in Congress pressed for a change in the official government policy in the use of Negro troops. Up to this time Lincoln had generally refused to employ Negro soldiers. On 17 July 1862 Congress had passed the Militia Act, which authorized the president to utilize Negro troops, but on 6 August Lincoln refused the offer of Negro regiments from Indiana and stated that he "was not prepared to go the length of enlisting Negroes as soldiers. He would employ all colored men as laborers, but would not promise to make soldiers of them."[72] Later in 1862, several Negro regiments were organized to serve as guards and scouts.

Governor John Andrew of Massachusetts was very enthusiastic about the employment of Negro troops. He applied to Secretary Stanton in January 1863 for authorization to organize a Negro regiment in his state, and Stanton granted the authorization with the provision that all the officers be white. Both Lincoln and Stanton feared a white backlash if Negroes were allowed to be officers, as Governor Andrew desired, and felt that the enlistment of Negro privates was in itself a significant accomplishment. Andrew reluctantly agreed but was determined that in all matters of pay, treatment, and related issues the Negro regiment would be treated equally. Because the governor was desirous that the regiment should have for its officers "young men of military experience, [and] firm anti-slavery principles," he invited Robert Gould Shaw, son of his abolitionist friend from New York, Francis Shaw, to become its colonel. Robert, a Harvard graduate, combat veteran, and a captain in the second Massachusetts Infantry, eventually accepted command of the Fifty-fourth Massachusetts Volunteers.[73] Emerson may have been prompted to accept the invitation to help raise funds for the regiment not only because he believed in the cause itself but also because Governor Andrew had called upon his friend, George Stearns, to form a

committee of "prominent citizens" to aid in recruiting men for the out-
fit. Also, its newly appointed colonel was a young man whom he knew
and admired. Ellen noted in a letter written in February that she had
recently visited with Pauline Shaw, and, "it so happened that Bob Shaw
arrived that day from the 2nd Regiment. You know he is to be colonel of
our black Regiment, the 54th. We saw and heard a great deal of him and
like him very much. Father was also in town . . . and when he came
home it was to tell of Bob Shaw" (*EL* 1:308).

Black enlistments in the Fifty-fourth proceeded slowly at first, undoubtedly because of skepticism among the blacks regarding how the
regiment would be employed, the practice of paying Negro soldiers less
than whites, and also because blacks undoubtedly resented the fact that
they were not eligible to become officers.[74] According to a report of this
fund-raiser that appeared in the *Boston Traveller* on 21 March, and in the
Liberator on 27 March, Emerson addressed the question of racial prejudice. He pointed out in his presentation that "the hostility of races is an
uniform fact, and the only way of reconciling it is by a closer acquaintance between the opponents. . . . We have kept the black man down
until his name has become a synonym of all that is low and degraded."
An opportunity is now at hand to remove the barriers of oppression because "finally the Government has decided to organize negro regiments,
and Massachusetts is endeavoring to do a part, and elevate this hitherto
oppressed race to a position where they might strike for their rights."
This brief report of Emerson's presentation concludes with the observation that "the speaker thought there was no doubt that the black man
would make a good soldier."

In what appears to be a draft of the speech in his journal, Emerson
also exhorts blacks to accept the challenge and the opportunity afforded
them at the moment and to enlist. He notes that the southern cause
has planted itself on the foundation of slavery, with black inferiority
as the cornerstone, and he goes on to state, "If war means liberty to
you[,] you should enlist. It does mean liberty to you in the opinion of
Jeff Davis for the South says, we fight to plant slavery as our foundation.
And of course we who resist the South, are forced to make liberty of the
negro our foundation." He continues his exhortation with a further call

to arms and words that recall his "rise of the anti-slave" thinking from the 1840s. "If you will not fight for your liberty, who will? If you will not, why then take men as they are and the Universe of men will say you are not worth fighting for. Go & be slaves forever & you shall have our aid to make you such. You had rather be slaves than freemen. Go to your own place" (*JMN* 15:210–11).

Also, possibly with the recent efforts of the Peace party and others to promote reconciliation in mind, Emerson makes perfectly clear here his opinion that the war has come about as a response to the abomination of slavery, and it will not be over until slavery has been dealt a death blow. The sacrifices have been almost too great already; "The best blood of our educated counties, objects of the most romantic hope & love" has been spilt, and have we made those sacrifices, asks Emerson, in order "to bring back into the Capitol of Washington the reckless politicians who had reeled out of it with threats to destroy it, or come back into it to rule again? Never. Better put gunpowder under its foundations & plough up the ground where its streets stand than they die for the disgraceful dynasty which had brought our freedom to be a lie & our civilization & wealth to dishonor as a partnership of thieves" (*JMN* 15:211).

Regarding the war effort overall, Emerson remained convinced that it could not be pursued with the utmost vigor and conviction until the slavery issue was resolved universally, once and for all. He was no doubt especially sensitive at this time to the new wave of conservatism that was making its influence felt in the Copperhead movement, which reached its peak in the spring of 1863 after major Union defeats at Fredricksburg in December 1862 and the later defeat at Chancellorsville in May 1863.[75] His response to this conservative rumbling is clear and unequivocal. "The Governor of the Commonwealth nobly spoke the sense of his people when he said we will enlist if you send us out for freedom & not if you send us out to return slaves," and this is the case "whatever mean carpers & the owls & jackals who squeak and gibber to the contrary will say" (*JMN* 15:212).

In the balance of his draft Emerson records a few random comments about blacks and observes, "Negroes good soldiers they love music, dress, order, parade, they have a couth temperament & *abandon* &

Gen H's opinion of their desperate courage." He also includes a single verse from what may have been contemplated as an occasional poem to accompany his address.

> I am not black in my mind
> But born to make black fair
> On the battlefield my master find,—
> His white corpse taints the air

Overall, the *Boston Traveller* reported, the fund-raiser "was a great success, both socially and financially, and will have a good influence in favor of the regiment." Because of the efforts of Emerson, Stearns, Frederick Douglass, Wendell Phillips, and others, by the end of April black recruits were coming in at the rate of thirty to forty per day. In fact, enough men enlisted to form a second regiment, the Fifty-fifth Massachusetts, and when they drilled, thousands of spectators from Boston went out to their camp to watch.[76]

The southern reaction to the increased use of black soldiers in the Union army was predictable. As early as 1862 captured Negroes were hanged or made to work in leg irons. The Confederate War Department outlawed Union generals who armed Negroes and ordered them to be executed if captured. In general, the southerners viewed Negro soldiers as rebellious slaves and treated them as such.[77] Such behavior only served to confirm Emerson's view of the barbarism of southern society. His reaction to it would continue to be characterized by outrage. It is said that on one occasion he appeared at a support meeting for Massachusetts black regiments, "his face on fire with indignation." He announced to his audience that "he had just learned that South Carolina had given out the threat that colored soldiers, if captured, should not be treated as prisoners, but be put to death." "What answer does Massachusetts send back to South Carolina?" he asked. "Two for one," came the answer. "Is that the answer that Massachusetts sends?" he asked, and the audience answered with its applause. Emerson then left the platform, and one observer noted that he "seemed . . . a little appalled at the spirit he had raised" (W 9:470).

In June Emerson visited the U.S. Military Academy at West Point as a member of a "committee of visitation," and he liked what he found there. "West Point Academy makes a very agreeable impression on me," he notes in his journal. "The innocence of the cadets, the air of probity, of veracity, & of loyalty to each other struck me, & the anecdotes told us confirmed this impression. I think it excellent that such tender youths should be made so manly & masterly in rough exercises of horse & gun & cannon & mortar. So accurate in French, in Mathematics, geology, and engineering, should learn to draw, to dance, & to swim" (*JMN* 15: 215). Perhaps it seemed to Emerson that in some ways these young men represented, somewhat literally, the cutting edge of culture and civilization thrown up against the aristocratic barbarism of the South. Emerson saw West Point as a "true aristocracy, or 'the power of the Best,' best scholars, best soldiers, best engineers, best commanders, best men,— and they will be indispensable to their government & their country . . . they will be the shop of power, the source of instruction, the organization of Victory" (*JMN* 15:215). In Emerson's opinion, these young cadets were not merely military scientists but broadly educated representatives of an aggressively virtuous American culture.

As Emerson was learning, the rigors of the war would frequently require the sacrifice of the best and brightest. In the month following his visit to West Point, on 18 July, despite poor rations, a forced march the day before, and extensive fatigue detail, the Massachusetts Fifty-fourth Colored Infantry led an ill-planned assault on Fort Wagner at Morris Island, South Carolina. The island was taken, but the unit suffered about 42 percent casualties.[78] Colonel Robert Gould Shaw was one of them. The news of Colonel Shaw's death was a shock to his family and friends, especially in Concord. The heroism and courage his colored regiment displayed in battle seemed to demonstrate dramatically the worth of Negro soldiers. The *Anti-slavery Standard* declared that Fort Wagner was "a holy sepulchre" to the Negro race. The *New York Tribune* observed that the battle "made Fort Wagner such a name to the colored race as Bunker Hill had been for ninety years to the white Yankees"; and the *Atlantic Monthly* said that "through the cannon smoke of that black night, the manhood of the colored race shines before many eyes that would not see."[79]

Emerson was personally saddened by the deaths of Robert Shaw and so many of his heroic black soldiers. In the case of the former, his sorrow derived at least in part from his personal knowledge of the man and his family. In the case of the latter, Emerson no doubt recalled his own recent stirring words calling these young black volunteers to fight for their freedom and dignity.[80] Their combined sacrifices led Emerson to compose another of his rare occasional poems, "Voluntaries" (W 9:205–9).

The poem opens to a "low and mournful . . . strain" and describes a cell "where a captive sits in chains." With neither fault nor crime this victim has been

> Dragged from his mother's arms and breast,
> Displaced, disfurnished here,
> His wistful toil to do his best
> Chilled by a ribald jeer.

Despite the overwhelming and undeserved suffering of the slaves, however, "great men in the Senate sate" and "forbore to break the chain,"

> Which bound the dusky tribe,
> Checked by the owners' fierce disdain,
> Lured by "Union" as the bribe.

However, as in his "Boston Hymn," Emerson here describes the inevitable influence of the spirit of "Freedom," who "loves a poor and virtuous race" and assures their ultimate victory over oppression. As the recent sacrifices at Fort Wagner so amply showed of the Negro,

> If once the generous chief arrive
> To lead him willing to be led,
> For freedom he will strike and strive,
> And drain his heart till he be dead.

When the hour demands it, men of virtue and courage will come forward, even though the times seem to present "an age of fops and toys, / Wanting wisdom, void of right."

> So near is God to man,
> When Duty whispers low, *Thou must,*
> The youth replies, *I can.*

Conflict and Victory

Once committed and inspired, the leader and the led can face all challenges.

> Peril around, all else appalling,
> Cannon in front and leaden rain
> Him duty through the clarion calling
> To the van called not in vain.

Sacrifices will undoubtedly be made, and momentary defeats bring death, but ultimately, "justice conquers evermore,"

> And he who battles on her side,
> God, though he were ten times slain,
> Crowns him victor glorified,
> Victor over death and pain.

Emerson ends his poem with a paean to "Eternal Rights," which are always "Victors over daily wrongs." And his confidence remains unshaken that, because of the courageous sacrifices of men like Colonel Shaw and his black troops, victory, no matter how long it may take, is assured. Emerson sent a copy of his poem to Colonel Shaw's parents and received their thanks for "your note & for your copy of the 'Lines' which express your feeling towards our son & his comrades" (L 5:336). The poem was published in the *Atlantic Monthly* in October 1863.

Meanwhile, the war continued. The North took some comfort in the capture of Vicksburg and the victory at Gettysburg in July, but still, decisive victory seemed elusive, and there continued to be talk of a compromised peace. There was a continual need for more troops, and a meeting was held in Concord in November to determine how to respond to the call.[81] Emerson was present but apparently spoke little, for in his journal he records the "speech I should have made on Nov. 22." In this draft it is clear that Emerson remained convinced that the war should go on until the victory was assured. "In the swarming population, the drain of the Army, and all the loss by war, is a drop of the bucket. But the country wants them, wants every body." There are those who should not go because of infirmity, age, or other compelling reason, "but for the multitude of young able men, there is not this necessity to stay. . . . Every kind of man is wanted; every talent, every virtue; the artillerist, the horseman, sharpshooter, engineer, secret-service man, carpenter, teamster, clerk; the Good, to be the soul & religion of the camp; the bad, because to fight & die for one's country not covers, but atones for a multitude of sins." To those who might object that "you send them to die," Emerson answers bluntly, "Yes, when I consider what they have sealed & saved, freedom for the world, yes a thousand times yes. . . . The War an exceptional struggle, in which the first combatants are met, —the highest principles against the worst" (*JMN* 15:333–34).

Also at this time Emerson was becoming increasingly concerned about relations with Great Britain. From the outset the British had not been particularly positive in their attitude toward, and relations with, the Union. As early as July 1861 Emerson's British friend and correspondent Arthur Clough wrote to him, "This cruel war makes itself felt, it seems, even in Concord—you too in Concord send out your young men to the fields & the possible pestilence—people here are brutally ignorant & unfeeling about the matter—so far at least as they express their mind by the newspapers."[82] Although by 1863 there was little likelihood that either France or England would intervene in the war on behalf of the Confederacy, there was a possibility that the Union might drift into a war with England over the issue of British shipbuilding for the Confederate navy.[83] Additionally, as Clough had noted earlier, British intellectuals continued to be generally nonsupportive of the Union cause. Carlyle, for example, who privately favored the South in the war for a variety of reasons, had for the most part, as Joseph Slater notes, "in public utterance . . . preserved a decent neutrality" (*CEC* 46). However, in the August issue of *Macmillan's Magazine* Carlyle published his "Ilias (Americana) in Nuce" (the American Iliad in a Nutshell), a brief satirical comment where Paul and Peter (i.e., the South and the North) attempt to beat each other's brains out because one "hires servants for life" (i.e., southern slaves), and the other hires servants "by the month or the day" (i.e., northern laborers). While the snippet may have appeared to Carlyle to be a mild rebuke to both parties, for some American readers it was an unpardonable insult. Accordingly, Cyrus Bartol, a Harvard Divinity School graduate and an abolition advocate, wrote to Emerson to suggest that something should be done to address the perfidy of British intellectuals in their failure to vigorously support the Union cause. "The unfriendliness of English scholarship to our cause, —is it now worth seriously considering & noticing? Martineau & even Tennyson are against us—Carlyle makes himself a public shame—. . . . Ought there not to be an address of the literary men of this country to their Order across the sea, on the ground which learning, philosophy & poetry should take in the premises which touch them as well as legislation & politics?" Bartol goes on to ask Emerson to "draw up a paper" on the topic, or "Might it not appear to you a duty to put into the press a truly friendly letter to Carlyle?" An alternative to this would be a published statement in the *Atlantic*. Bartol concludes, "I hold it critical *you* should draw it up; whether it be an article simply, or a manifesto signed by yourself, Bryant, Whittier, Lowell, Whipple, Holmes, etc.— by literary & no sort of professional men."[84]

Apparently Emerson took Bartol's suggestion to heart. However, he chose not to resort to the pages of the *Atlantic*, perhaps because his long poem "Voluntaries" was already scheduled to appear in the October issue. He may also have been aware that David Wasson, a liberal Unitarian clergyman and poet, had prepared a lengthy remonstrance entitled "A Letter to Thomas Carlyle," which would also appear in the October number. Emerson thought highly of Wasson, as both a poet and a preacher, and was undoubtedly pleased and satisfied that such a qualified representative of America's cultural class had come forward.[85] Wasson would also be very satisfactory in meeting Bartol's specification of a "literary" spokesperson.

With the written rebuttal thus well provided for, it was to the lecture platform that Emerson turned to unleash a bitter attack on the British in general and Carlyle in particular. Despite the fact that Emerson was obviously well aware of Carlyle's blindness on the subject of slavery, given his earlier journal comments, he was apparently stung by the *Macmillan's* piece and the perfidy and narrowness of the British generally in their failure to appreciate what he saw as the moral imperative represented in the Union cause. The lengthy manuscript of the unpublished lecture, "Fortune of the Republic," gives ample evidence of Emerson's strong feelings at the time.[86] "English nationality is babyish, like the self-esteem of villages, like the nationality of Carolina, . . . or of Hull, or the conceit & insolence of the shabby little kings on the Gambia river, who strut up to the traveller [and ask] What do they say of me in America?" As a people, the British have become "insular, & narrow. They have no higher worship than Fate," and while they are excellent craftsmen and laborers, "their morals do not reach beyond their frontiers." Indeed, the British have become so materialistic and possess such a "passion for plunder" that "never a lofty sentiment, never a duty to civilization, never a generosity, a moral self-restraint, is suffered to stand in the way of a commercial advantage. In sight of a commodity, her religion, her morals are forgotten." In Emerson's view such a situation bespeaks a lack of moral leadership in the society as a whole, and it is Britain's artists and intellectuals who must bear the brunt of the criticism for this failing. Rather than leading the people to loftier sentiment and deeper insights, they have merely played the role of cheerleaders to the nation's baser impulses. "Even Carlyle, England's ablest living writer, . . . is politically a fatalist. In his youth he announced himself as a 'theoretical sansculotte fast threatening to become a practical one.' Now he is practically in the English system, a Venetian aristocracy, with only a private stipulation in favor of men of genius." Emerson's criticism does not stop with the man, however, but extends to his works, also. "In 'The Life History of Frederic [sic] the Great,' the reader is treated as if he were a Prussian adjutant, solely occupied with the army & the campaign. He is ever in the dreamy circle of camp & courts. But of the people you have no glimpse, no hint of their domestic life. Were there no families, no farms, no thoughtful citizens, no beautiful & generous women, no genial youth with beating hearts then alive in all the broad territories of that kingdom?" Emerson also criticizes the common quality of this "pedantic way of writing history," and states that he "would not bring this criticism of another writer. But from Carlyle, who has taught us to make it, we had a right to expect an account of a nation & not of a campaign."[87] Such a failure is especially unfortunate because scholars such as Carlyle should be providing moral leadership and enlightenment for the masses, and "if the leaders of thought take this false direction, what can you expect from those who do not think, but are absorbed in maintaining their class privileges, their luxury, or their trade?"

Undoubtedly Emerson's audiences were pleased that America's honor and the North's moral stand had been vindicated by such a prestigious spokesperson, and also the man who had introduced Carlyle to America. The reading public was not unaware of this association. An article in the *Boston Advertiser* at this time drew attention to both Emerson's poem "Voluntaries" and Carlyle's "Ilias Americana" as the latest productions of the two men who respectively "stand at the head" of "American and English Literature." "It will be noticed that both relate to the same subject—Slavery in America." In comparing the two, the author notes that Carlyle has obviously lost the youthful idealism expressed in *Sartor Resartus*, and "it is hard to believe that this false scoffing 'Ilias Americana' flowed from the same pen and the same heart" that inspired the former. On the other hand, Emerson's poem clearly indicates that "the American scholar at least, has not forgotten the dreams of his youth," and the article closes with the statement, "would to God that the British scholar had allowed the hearts that honor him, to echo the same proud praise."[88]

By the winter of 1863 Emerson began to feel reasonably confident that the end of the war was in sight. At one point he notes in his journal that "the rebels in the effrontery with which, in their failing fortunes, they adhere to their audacious terms of peace, have well instructed us; and I rejoice to see we are likely to plant ourselves with rigor on the condition of absolute emancipation as the first point with which each rebel state must comply" (*JMN* 15:406). In January 1864 the Union armies continued to grind toward ultimate victory, but the cost of this progress was very high. Emerson could take some comfort from the fact that his words continued to inspire those in the field. On 7 January Thomas Wentworth Higginson, who had gone on from the abolitionists' ranks to become a leader of Negro troops, reported in a letter to Emerson that his surgeon, Doctor Rogers, had recently read the bard's "Boston Hymn" to his black soldiers, and that "they understood every word of it. . . .

I recall vividly the thrill that went through me as he read the grand verse beginning 'Pay ransom to the owner,' & thought that these were the owners before us."[89]

In February Emerson spoke at a fair in Concord that was held to raise funds for Negro orphans. The *Boston Transcript* reported that the Concord fair "cleared $500 for the colored orphans," and "most of the distinguished people of Concord were present all day. Mr. Emerson spoke for a short time, to explain the object of the Fair, and the claims of the colored people to education, enforcing his statement with an account of the young colored man who took the *double-first* at the Toronto University" (*L* 5:354). Emerson would consistently stress the importance and benefit of a liberal education for freed blacks, and in a lecture on 25 December in Boston entitled "Books," he stated, "There is much in the calamities which we have suffered which is disinfecting. We have learned to forget foreign nations. We have grown internally— have begun to feel the strength of our strength. While European genius is symbolized by some majestic Corinne crowned in the capitol of Rome, American genius finds its true type—if I dare tell you—in the poor negro soldier lying in the trenches by the Potomac with his spelling book in one hand and his musket in the other."[90]

Emerson wrote to George Stearns in May that he would attend a meeting of the Emancipation League to which he had been invited and that he "hoped for its success" (*L* 5:375). As noted earlier, the league had been established by Stearns, Sanborn, Garrison, and others in the fall of 1861 to promote the cause of general emancipation.[91] At the May meeting Wendell Phillips spoke, stressing his view that the Lincoln administration, in spite of the Emancipation Proclamation, considered slavery the only sacred thing in the country (*L* 5:375). The battle was obviously still not won, and there were several fronts to be considered.

Also in May, Emerson's Concord neighbor and acquaintance Nathaniel Hawthorne passed away. The degree to which politics and national affairs had come to dominate Emerson's thinking at this time is reflected in his comment on Hawthorne's death. He had hoped that one day Hawthorne would eventually come forth from his late seclusion, and "that I could well wait his time,—his unwillingness & caprice,—

and might one day conquer a friendship." However, that was not to be, because lately he "had removed himself the more by the indignation his perverse politics & unfortunate friendship for that paltry Franklin Pierce awaked,—though it rather moved pity for Hawthorne, & the assured belief that he would outlive it, & come right at last" (*JMN* 15:60).

In June the political parties held their national conventions. In Baltimore the Republicans nominated Lincoln, with Andrew Johnson of Tennessee as his running mate. The Democrats met in Chicago in late August and nominated General McClellan for president and George H. Pendleton of Ohio for vice president. The Democratic platform, under the influence of the Copperheads, called for immediate cessation of hostilities and the restoration of peace "on the basis of the Federal Union of the States." Emerson recorded his observation that "our Democratic party shows itself very badly in these days, simply destructive, and would tear down God from Heaven if they could" (*JMN* 15:429). In September he wrote Wendell Phillips, introducing him to "a young English gentleman, Hon. Lyulf Stanley, who has lately taken his degrees at Baliol College, Oxford, and is, if you will permit me to say so, on *our* side in politics, has a strong desire to see you & has taken some pains to that end, in vain" (*L* 5:382). Emerson invited the young man to dine with him on Wednesday next, and extended the same invitation to Phillips. In his return letter three days later, Phillips accepted, adding, "Thank you for phrasing it 'our side'—I am always glad to sail in your fleet."[92]

Emerson was undoubtedly pleased to meet a young British gentleman who supported the Union cause. In general the British continued to show little sympathy for the Union position in the war, and tension between the two countries remained high. Perhaps it was due to this concern that on 26 September Emerson penned a lengthy letter to Carlyle, his first in two years.[93] The length, detail, and tone of the letter all suggest that Emerson may have intended to publish the piece, as Bartol had suggested he do a year earlier. "I have in these last years lamented that you had not made the visit to America, which in earlier years you projected or favored. It would have made it impossible that your name should be cited for one moment on the side of the enemies of mankind. Ten days residence in this country would have made you the organ of sanity of England & of Europe to us & to them, & have shown you the necessity and aspirations which struggle up in our Free States, which, as yet, have no organ to others, & are ill & unsteadily articulated here." Emerson then goes on to discuss the current state of politics in America. "In our today's division of Republican & Democrat, it is certain that the American nationality lies in the Republican party (mixed & multifarious though that party be;) & I hold it not less certain, that, viewing all the nationalities of the world the battle posthumously is, at this hour, in America." Regarding those in the Union who resist the war and its purposes, "A man intelligent and virtuous, is not to be found on that side." Given this situation, Emerson is not averse to calling Carlyle to the cause. "Ah! how gladly I would enlist you with your thunderbolt, on our part! How gladly enlist the wise, thoughtful, efficient pens & movers of England! We want England & Europe to hold our people staunch to their best tendency. Are English of the day incapable of great sentiment? Can they not leave cavilling at petty failures, & bad manners, & at the dunce part, (always the largest part in human affairs,) and leap to the suggestion & fingerpointing of the gods, which, above the understanding, feed the hopes & guide the wills of men?"

The letter also addresses certain concerns and fears that seemed to retard some in the struggle for emancipation. For Emerson, the war remains a God-given solution to the problem of slavery; all ancillary matters would be satisfied by the natural working out of the "inevitabilities" involved in the process. Thus, he notes, "This war has been conducted over the heads of all the actors in it: and the foolish terrors—'what shall we do with the negro?' 'The entire black population is coming forth to be fed,' etc. have strangely ended in the fact, that the black refuses to leave his climate; gets his living *and* the living of his employer there, as he has always done; is the natural ally & soldier of the Republic, in that climate; now takes the place of 200 000 white soldiers; & will be, as the conquest of the country proceeds, its garrison, till peace, without slavery returns."

Emerson makes it clear that his purpose in writing Carlyle is to correct erroneous impressions regarding the war that have apparently circulated for some time among the British. "Slaveholders in London have filled English ears with their wishes, & perhaps beliefs; and our people, generals & politicians, have carried the like, at first, to the war, until connected by irresistible experience." For Emerson, the war as a political force has brought about the possibility of enormous positive change. "I shall always respect war hereafter. The cost of life, the dreary havoc of comfort & time are overpaid by Vistas it opens up of Eternal Life, Eternal Law, reconstructing & uplifting Society,—breaks up the old horizon, & we see through the rifts unveiled." Emerson closes his missive with an apology for "writing a newspaper," but " 'tis wonderful what sublime lessons I have once & again read on the Bulletin-boards in the streets" (*CEC* 541–42).

Moncure Conway, who claims to have been present when Carlyle read this letter from Emerson, reports that Carlyle was "filled with astonishment" at it. His response goes some way in explaining conservative British attitudes at the time. Carlyle reportedly stated, "That the cleanest mind now living—for I don't know Emerson's equal on earth for perception—should write so is quasi miraculous. I have tried to look into the middle of things in America, and I have seen nothing but a people cutting throats indefinitely to put the negro into a position for which all experience shows him unfit." According to Conway, Carlyle went on to note: "You must be patient with me when I say how it all appears to me. I cannot help admiring the Northern people for their determination to maintain this Union," but though "the Americans are powerful . . . they can not make two men equal when the universe has determined that they are not and shall be unequal."[94] Obviously, Carlyle's opinions had not evolved much since "The Nigger Question."[95]

About this same time Emerson began to draft in his journal what appears to be a lecture on the perfidy of British intellectuals and artists in their failure to support the Union cause; it is similar to his indictment of the British in his "Fortune of the Republic" lecture noted earlier. Here he states: "It is mortifying that all events must be seen by wise men even, through the diminishing lens of a petty interest. Could we have believed that England should have disappointed us thus? that no man in all that civil, reading, brave, cosmopolitan country, should have looked at our revolution as a student of history, as philanthropist, eager to see what new possibilities for humanity were to begin,—what the inspirations were: what new move on the Board the Genius of the world was preparing." This failure of intellectuals in England was particularly disturbing to Emerson because, unlike the South, where the disease of slavery and its habitual accommodation served to blind men's eyes and harden their hearts, England seemed to possess all the advantages of a developed and advanced culture, as Emerson had so recently noted in *English Traits* (1856). But instead of flocking to a true cause, "every one squinted; Lords, Ladies, statesmen, scholars, poets, all squinted—. . . . Edinburg, Quarterly, Saturday Review, Gladstone, Russell, Palmerston, Brougham, nay Tennyson; Carlyle, I blush to say it; Arnold. Every one forgot his history, his poetry, his religion, & looked only at his shoptill, whether his salary, whether his small investment in the funds, would not be less." This unfortunate preference for material wealth and comfort over the dictates of culture and virtue, which Emerson saw as the overriding cause for American slavery, had a similarly enervating effect on the British. As a result, when the need arose, "No Milton, no Baron, no Berkeley, no Montesquieu, no Adam Smith was there to hail a new dawn of hope & culture for men." Instead of striking out against slavery, "this filthy pest which dishonored human Nature . . . every poet, every scholar, every great man, as well as the rich, thought only of his pocket book, & to our astonishment cried, *Slavery forever! Down with the North! Why does not England join with France to protect the slaveholder?*"

Emerson ends this somewhat vitriolic commentary with the assertion, "We shall destroy slavery, but by no help of others." His final statement on the British sounds like the litany of indictments in the Declaration of Independence. "They cherished our enemies, they exulted at the factions which crippled us at home; whenever the allies of the rebels obstructed the great will & action of the government, they danced for joy. . . . They ought to have remembered that great actions have mean beginnings" (*JMN* 15:433–34).

In November Emerson addressed a teachers' convention in West Chester, Pennsylvania. He had recently been elected once again to the Concord School Committee, and even here the spirit of the war was being felt. Emerson was no doubt aware that two years earlier, when there was great concern that emancipation would never become a fact, Mary Rice, a normal school teacher, walked from district to district to collect 350 signatures of school children on a petition to free all slave children. Charles Sumner hand carried the petition to the president, who responded with a personal letter to the children's teacher in which he requested that she tell the children, "While I have not the power to grant all they ask, I trust that they will remember that God has, and that, as it seems, He will do it."[96] Emerson might have had this in mind when, in reflecting on the schools in his journal, he notes, "What an education in the public spirit of Massachusetts has been the war songs, speeches & readings of the Schools! Every district school has been an antislavery convention for two or three years last past" (*JMN* 15:36).

Later in November Emerson addressed the Parker Fraternity in Boston. The lecture, "Public and Private Education," was attended by William Lloyd Garrison II, Wendell Phillips, Cyrus Bartol, E. P. Whipple, the Quincys, and "a group of lesser lights whose faces are always to be found in a transcendental assembly," as one contemporary put it.[97] Perhaps on this occasion Emerson was already thinking of what would be necessary to reconstruct America on a more ideal plane once the war had ended. "I think the genius of the country has marked out her true policy. Opportunity—doors wide open—every sort open; if I could have it, free trade with all the world, without toll or custom-house; invitation as we now make to every nation, to every race and skin—white man, red man, yellow man, and black man; hospitality, a fair field, and equal laws to all. Let them compete, and success to the strongest, who are always, at last, the wisest and the best. The land is wide enough, the soil has bread enough, for all."[98] In July Lincoln had pocket vetoed the Wade-Davis Bill, a measure for the radical reconstruction of the South. It remained to be seen now what form reconstruction would finally take.

Emerson's latest lecture series was the subject of a lengthy article at this time in the *Boston Semi-weekly Advertiser* (30 November). In addition to reporting on the content of the presentations, however, the author also took special note of Emerson's contributions to the war

effort and his longtime crusade against slavery. He saw these as fulfillment of Emerson's idealism, as represented particularly in the "American Scholar," which Emerson had delivered at Harvard nearly thirty
years earlier. Emerson, "better than any American, verifies his own
definition of the Scholar who 'is to resist the vulgar prosperity that
retrogrades ever to barbarism, by preserving and communicating heroic
sentiments, noble biographies, melodious verse, and the conclusions of
history.'" Indeed, Emerson "has done much more than this" throughout
his career, and "it should be the pride of Boston that she gave this wise
poet a birthdate." Obviously Boston had not always been positively disposed toward her now-famous son, and "when, in 1837, [Emerson] gave
his tribute to the brave blood of Lovejoy, of which Boston made herself guilty, through her editors and attorneys, a cold chill ran through
his audience, for only a few were then abolitionists, like himself." The
article goes on to recall the negative reaction to Emerson's undaunted
support for John Brown after Harper's Ferry, and his controversial remark that the execution of Brown "would make the gallows glorious
as the cross." All of that has obviously changed, however, for presently
"the *Advertiser* and the *Post* vie in their reports of his lectures, and the
voice of censure seems to be hushed at last."[99] Emerson was no doubt
pleased that the great world had finally come round, at least on the
matter of slavery, and that his earlier philosophizing, once disparaged
as "moonshine" by some, was now seen to be as relevant to the life of
America as he had always assumed it to be.

Emerson continued to meet with George Luther Stearns and others to
discuss the political situation that fall, especially Reconstruction. Regarding a meeting held in October: "The conversation [was] political
altogether, & though no very salient points, yet useful to me as clearing the air, & bringing to view the simplicity of the practical problem
before us. Right-minded men would very easily bring order out of our
American chaos, if working with courage, & without by-ends." Present
at this particular meeting was Joseph Smith Fowler, a Tennessee educa-
tor who was opposed to slavery though sympathetic to the South in the
war. Emerson notes agreeably that "these Tennessee slaveholders in the
land of Midian are far in advance of our New-England politicians" in

understanding what Reconstruction will require in order to be successful. There are two points of utmost importance. The first is "absolute
Emancipation,—establishing the fact that the United States hencefor-
ward knows no color, no race, in its law, but legislates for all alike,—one
law for all men." The second point is to "make the confiscation of rebel
property final, as you did with the tories in the Revolution." If both
of these points were acted upon, the best improvement in the republic
might become a reality. The measures would seem to "open the whole
South to the enterprise & genius of new men of all nations" and to "redeem your wicked Indian policy, & leave no murderous complications
to sow the sure seed of future wars" (*JMN* 15:445).

Emerson lectured again in Boston in December and, probably with
Reconstruction politics in mind, in his presentation ("Books") he lashed
out against the original corruption of the Constitution, which resulted
directly from the compromise with slavery, and he praised the Declaration of Independence as "the greatest achievement of American literature" for its unflinching and brilliant articulation of noble principles.
In referring to the Preamble of the Declaration, with its assertion of
basic and unalienable rights, Emerson notes, "These words, little heeded
at the time, deemed oratorical, lampooned by flippant rhetoricians in
our day as 'glittering generalities,' have turned out to be . . . immor-
tal words, the fresh, the matin song of the universe [which] will burn
forever and forever." By comparison, "the builders of the Constitution
put in some granite" but also "some rotten-stone. They tucked in rub-
bish and a lie, and they will crumble." Such compromises with principle
are always, ultimately, self-defeating and destructive. Indeed, "through
their cracks and crevice[s] have leaped the armed men that now shake
the continent."[100] Soon, however, the armed conflict would end, while
the struggle for freedom, equality, and human rights would continue.
And the bard of Concord, now recognized by many as America's leading
poet, philosopher, and intellectual, would continue his bivouac on the
field of battle.

Chapter Nine

Reconstruction and Other Struggles: 1865 and After

A series of Union victories through the winter and spring of 1865 brought about the inevitable, and on 9 April Lee surrendered to Grant at Appomattox Courthouse. In Concord people celebrated with salutes and bells and promenaded through the town with little flags (*EL* 1:340). In his journal Emerson expresses satisfaction that "the rebels have been pounded instead of negotiated into peace. They must remember it, & their inveterate bray will be humbled, if not cured." He was nevertheless concerned that "General Grant's terms certainly look a little too easy, as foreclosing any action hereafter to convict Lee of treason." His fear was that "the high tragic historic justice which the nation with severest consideration should execute, will be softened & dissipated & toasted away at dinner-tables." Obviously Emerson still had in mind the "atomic restructuring" of southern society that he had described three years earlier in his address at the Smithsonian. His fear now was that "if we let the southern States in to congress, the Northern democrats will join them in thwarting the will of the government." Emerson felt that in order to prevent this effort to return to a morally repugnant status quo, "the obvious remedy is to give the negro his vote" and to require the ability to read as a qualification. Perhaps remembering those stories of the Negro pickets and their spelling books, Emerson notes further that "the negro will learn to write & read . . . before the white will" (*JMN* 15:459).

Even before Lee's surrender and the general capitulation in May, dramatic changes foreshadowing a substantial restructuring of southern society began to appear. On 31 January the House of Representatives passed the Thirteenth Amendment to the Constitution, officially abolishing slavery in the United States. The Senate had previously approved the measure, and it went into effect on 18 December, following ratification by twenty-seven states. There was a great deal of celebrating in the Emerson home following the passage of this act. Lidian, especially, was ecstatic. Ellen states that "Mother didn't see Mrs. Brooks till evening but when she came home she was so exalted that she couldn't understand any other subject and when I went into her room this morning she was looking at the Liberator picture and thinking how little she expected it would come true in her day!"[1] Lidian's enthusiasm carried over to the next day when she insisted on "showing Rosy the Frontpiece of the Liberator, and explaining it all to her, from the Slave Auction to the Emancipation Triumph, and ever since has eaten her rice and sugar, and regarded her sheets with exclamation that these would no longer be due to slave labour" (*EL* 1:331).

Unfortunately, the euphoric feeling that followed the Union's victory was to be abruptly curtailed. Lincoln's assassination on 14 April 1865 shocked the nation, and the difficult course of Reconstruction became an even murkier proposition. Emerson's immediate journal response to the event shows that his mind was still very much on the problem of reforming a thoroughly corrupted southern society. He notes simply, "The assassin Booth is a type of man of a large class of the Southern people. By the destruction of Slavery, we destroy the stove in which the cockatrice eggs are hatched" (*JMN* 15:460). Later, he listed other outrages that must have appeared to him as yet further evidence of the depth of the corruption and barbarism still to be dealt with. "I charge the Southerner with starving prisoners of war; with massacring surrendered men; with the St. Alban's raid; with the plundering [of] railroad passenger trains in peaceful districts; with plots of burning cities; with advertising a price for the life of Lincoln, Butler, Garrison, & others; with assassination of the President; & of Seward; with attempts to import the yellow fever into New York; with the cutting up of the bones of our soldiers to make ornaments & drinking cups of their skulls" (*JMN* 15:471–72).

On 19 April 1865 a memorial funeral service was held in Concord in honor of the fallen president. It was a moving affair, and Ellen noted later, "Today we have kept the funeral of our dear, our good President, with more real grief than would have seemed possible for a people to feel at a President's loss" (*EL* 1:342). Among those speaking at the Unitarian church that day was Ralph Waldo Emerson. It is clear that Emerson, despite his earlier reservations, had come to admire Lincoln unreservedly. "The President stood before us as a man of the people" and "was the most active and hopeful of men" (*W* 11:330). Perhaps recalling his own meetings with the president in 1862, Emerson notes that Lincoln "had a vast good nature, which made him tolerant and accessible to all; fair-minded, leaning to the claim of the petitioner; affable, and not sensible to the affliction which the innumerable visits paid to him when President would have brought to any one else" (*W* 11:332). His service to his country in time of war was an outstanding example of fortitude and virtue. "There, by his courage, his justice, his even temper, his fertile counsel, his humanity, he stood a heroic figure in the centre of a heroic epic. He is the true history of the American people in his time" (*W* 11: 335). Of course, for Emerson, the most important aspect of this American epoch was the abolition of slavery, and this was Lincoln's crowning achievement. For those who felt that Lincoln's untimely death deprived him of the opportunity to see the fulfillment of his labors, Emerson asks rhetorically, "Had he not lived long enough to keep the greatest promise that ever man made to his fellow men,—the practical abolition of slavery? He had seen Tennessee, Missouri and Maryland emancipate their slaves. He had seen Savannah, Charleston and Richmond surrendered; had seen the main army of the rebellion lay down its arms. He had conquered the public opinion of Canada, England and France. Only Washington can compare with him in fortune" (*W* 11:336).

Emerson suggests that perhaps Lincoln's purpose had been served fully in the time allotted him, and that what was now required was a new statesman with a stronger hand and a willingness to subordinate sentiment to justice. "And what if it should turn out, in the unfolding of the web, that he had reached the term; that this heroic deliverer could no longer serve us; that the rebellion had touched its natural conclusion, and what remained to be done required new and uncommitted hands, —a new spirit born out of the ashes of the war; and that Heaven, wishing to show the world a completed benefactor, shall make him serve his country even more by his death, than by his life?" (W 11:336).[2]

Emerson defines briefly the kind of leader now required, and this description places him squarely among the Radical Republicans who would seek a thorough and "atomic" restructuring of southern society as the means and method of Reconstruction. "Nations, like kings, are not good by facility and complaisance. 'The kindness of kings consists in justice and strength.' Easy good nature has been the dangerous foible of the Republic, and it was necessary that its enemies should outrage it, and drive us to unwonted firmness, to secure the salvation of this country in the next ages" (W 11:336–37). It had been the opinion of the Radical Republicans, led by Charles Sumner, that Lincoln was too cautious and too deferential to the border states in the early years of the war, and in the postwar period the radicals would clash repeatedly with Andrew Johnson on Reconstruction policy.[3] Emerson would be the consistent supporter of Sumner throughout this contest.

F. B. Sanborn, who, like many abolitionists, would continue the struggle for Negro rights after the war, was most pleased with Emerson's address on Lincoln and wrote to Wendell Phillips the next day. "I wish you had heard Emerson yesterday on Lincoln. It was one of his best speeches. . . . You must write to him to print it; which he hesitates about doing."[4] Apparently Phillips was successful; Emerson's address was published the following year in *The Lincoln Memorial: A Record of the Life, Assassination, and Obsequies of the Martyred President*.[5]

In late July Emerson was afforded another opportunity to address the issues of war and peace when he was asked to speak at the Harvard commemoration ceremonies that were held to welcome back the alumni of Harvard who had served in the war and to memorialize those who had fallen. The speakers for the day included Charles Loring, Governor Andrew, and General Meade. Emerson was called upon to represent "the poets and scholars whose thoughts had been an inspiration to Harvard's sons in the field" (W 11:615). In his brief presentation Emerson chose to emphasize the fatalistic and benevolent force that was at work in the war, and which promised so much good in its wake. "Revolutions carry their own points, sometimes to the ruin of those who set them on foot. The proof that war also is within the highest right, is a marked benefactor in the hands of the Divine Providence, is its *morale*. The war gave back integrity to this erring and immoral nation" (W 11:342).

This war had not been won without sacrifices, as Emerson was well aware, and with the death of Robert Gould Shaw in mind, he recalls: "One mother said, when her son was offered the command of the first negro regiment, 'If he accepts it, I shall be as proud as if I had heard that he was shot'" (W 11:344). But the lasting good is worth the price, steep as it is. These young Harvard men, educated in the best traditions of humanity, and those others who served simply from a sense of duty, have shown themselves to be "Liberty's and Humanity's bodyguard! We shall not again disparage America, now that we have seen what its men will bear" (W 11:344–45).

Unfortunately, the optimism that characterizes this presentation would be short-lived for Emerson. In the waning days of 1865 it was becoming increasingly clear that Andrew Johnson's policies on Reconstruction differed dramatically from those of the Radical Republicans. In May the president issued an amnesty proclamation that was perceived as very liberal in dealing with the secessionists. It granted amnesty to Confederates who took the oath of allegiance, with the exception of civil and diplomatic officers of the Confederacy, high-ranking military officers, Confederates who left U.S. judicial posts, persons with taxable property valued over $20,000, and some others. These, however, could petition the president for special pardon, and by mid-1866 very few rebels would remain unpardoned.[6] In response to these liberal policies the Radicals in Congress set up the Joint Committee of Fifteen (six senators and nine congressmen) to examine the questions of suffrage and southern representation in Congress. The committee was dominated by Thaddeus Stevens, a Pennsylvania representative and a leader of the Radicals. Stevens saw the Confederate states as "conquered provinces" and joined with Charles Sumner in insisting that Congress alone could restore southern state governments and impose conditions for readmission as necessary.

Johnson, for his part, insisted that Reconstruction policy was the responsibility of the president, and he recognized the loyal state governments of Arkansas, Louisiana, Tennessee, and Virginia. Also, between May and July he appointed governors in North Carolina, Mississippi, Georgia, Texas, Alabama, South Carolina, and Florida. By the end of 1865 these governors had called state conventions, elected by whites only. Eventually the Confederate states elected congressmen to the Thirty-ninth Congress. Among these, elected solely by white electorates, were Alexander Stephens, former vice president of the Confederacy, four former Confederate generals, five colonels, six cabinet officers, and fifty-eight former congressmen. Additionally, individual southern states now began to pass Black Codes, regulations written into the state constitutions to control Negro life. The codes were generally harsh and highly restrictive. In Tennessee Negroes were banned from juries, suffered greater punishments than whites for similar crimes, and were subjected to sale into temporary bondage for vagrancy. Courts were given the power to bind out black children to white men as apprentices. Reports of whippings, shootings, and lynchings began to be heard in the North.[7] Abolitionists were irate on hearing such tales, and Wendell Phillips asserted that "the reconstruction of rebel states without Negro suffrage is a practical surrender to the Confederacy."[8] In response to this situation, in February Congress passed the New Freedmen's Bureau Bill, which sought to enlarge the scope of the Freedmen's Bureau (which had been established in March 1865) to protect the rights of freed slaves. It also sought to empower the bureau to use military commissions to try those people accused of depriving freedmen of their civil rights. Johnson vetoed the bill.

The Radical Republicans, led by Stevens and Sumner, continued to militate for reform; they advocated the disenfranchisement of southern whites and the creation of a new South based on universal Negro suffrage. Congress declared that no representatives or senators from any southern state could be seated until both houses of Congress declared that state entitled to such representation. In June the Fourteenth Amendment was formulated by the Joint Committee of Fifteen. It passed Congress on 13 June and was submitted to the states for ratification. With former slaves obviously in mind, this amendment for the first time defined national citizenship to include "all persons born or naturalized in the United States," and threw the protection of the federal government around rights that might be invaded by the states. Ratification of this amendment was made a condition for readmission of rebel states to the Union. President Johnson denounced the Fourteenth Amendment and urged the southern states not to ratify it (only Tennessee did), but the amendment was declared ratified on 28 July 1868. Earlier, Johnson had also opposed the Civil Rights Act, which had passed both houses of Congress and was designed to nullify the Black Codes. Johnson vetoed the act, but it was later passed over his veto, and the substance of the legislation was incorporated into the first section of the Fourteenth Amendment to ensure its constitutionality.

Open warfare between the president and the Radicals and abolitionists was now all but declared. As early as November 1865 William Lloyd Garrison II wrote to his mother that he had recently been reading "a small monthy [sic] magazine called 'The Radical'" and that this month's issue contained "Mr. Emerson's famous Divinity College address which cost him his standing as a Unitarian Minister and confirmed him as a heretic. It was the first time the Divinity students were ever startled by plain truths & the address made a sensation in its day." In speaking of more contemporary radical affairs, he notes, "It will take a different course of action on the President's part to inspire much trust in his administration. I don't yet think him a knave or that he means any betrayal of the colored man into his enemies' hands." However, "native prejudices make him purblind and he is trying a dangerous experiment which the people will check." Young Garrison felt that abolition meant more than "a removal of the element of Chattelism," and while some might choose to "belittle a great work," he preferred to "believe that the nation means absolute justice which *no* Tennessee president, though backed by diabolism can thwart."[9]

Wendell Phillips's most frequently repeated lecture in the fall of 1865 was "The South Victorious," where he insisted that while the South was beaten on the field of battle it had a good prospect of winning through political stratagems on the Reconstruction front. In December he wrote to Mrs. Brooks in Concord for her continued support for the Anti-slavery Standard Subscription Anniversary. She graciously agreed to contribute, and in her reply noted that the work of abolitionism "is not done, and will not be," until all "God given rights" are assured. "May it [the *Anti-slavery Standard*] be continued for the coming year, and as long as is proper to accomplish this great object. . . . I could ask Mrs. Emerson if you wish, for her name also to place with these. I think she will be willing."[10]

Charles Sumner continued his efforts to move Johnson toward the radical line, but without success. By December 1865 the abolitionists had divided into four groups, ranging from the conservatives, like George Luther Stearns, who hoped that Johnson might yet do the right thing in Reconstruction and wished to cooperate in the effort, to the extreme radicals like Wendell Phillips, who saw Johnson as an obstacle to be overcome on the road to achieving equal justice.[11] Emerson would certainly be included among the latter.

In January 1866 Emerson wrote a lengthy letter to Carlyle that both defended and criticized recent developments in the American body politic. "My countrymen do not content me, but they are susceptible of inspirations. In the war, it was humanity that showed itself to advantage—the leaders were prompted & corrected by the intuitions of the people—they still demanding the more generous & decisive measure, & giving their sons & their estates, as we had no example before." It was a time of great actions inspired by high moral principles, and "we were proud of the people & believed they would not go down from this height." Unfortunately, when peace came, the former materialistic self-interest returned with it, and now, it seemed, citizens could hardly be won to patriotism anymore, "even to the point of chasing away the thieves that are stealing not only the public gold, but the newly won rights of the slave, & the new measures we had contrived to keep the planter from sucking his blood" (*CEC* 548). In this matter Emerson must have been reminded of the similar situation that had followed the British emancipation in the West Indies and which he had noted in his first address on that topic twenty-two years earlier.

In the following month Phillips lectured in Concord, and undoubtedly the subject was radical politics and Reconstruction. Mrs. Brooks told him later that his lecture "was received into good and honest hearts and was considered by almost the whole of the audience as just the right and true thing to be fought for and longed for through thick and thin. . . . Mr. Emerson considered it a finished piece of oratory"; she was hopeful that he would "say many good things" on the topic himself.[12] Emerson was prepared to be impressed. Earlier in the month he had written to his brother William from Michigan, where he was lecturing. "In all this swarming country I have hardly seen anybody I ever saw before, but they treat me very kindly, and they are as anxious for the success of radical politics as the Concord people" (*L* 5:455). Meanwhile, Emerson openly continued to support his radical abolitionist friends. In April he subscribed to a "National Testimonial to William Lloyd Garrison" and saw his name included with many others, like Charles Sumner, who provided a written statement indicating that he hoped "no effort will be spared to carry out the idea of securing an honorable token of the grateful sentiments which his [Garrison's] name must always inspire among the friends of Human Rights."[13]

After the rather extraordinary events in the spring of 1866, Emerson became increasingly suspicious of President Johnson's ultimate intention. The reelection of several rebel congressmen, the passage of the repressive Black Codes, and the efforts of the president to veto radical Reconstruction measures must have suggested to Emerson that American society was fast returning to the degenerate status quo of the antebellum period. By July he was convinced of the president's perfidy in supporting this trend but still confident that the "inevitabilities" of the situation would prevent such a development. His journal notes the "exhilarating news of the landing of the Atlantic telegraph cable," which suggested that the forces of progress were already making themselves felt in this technological miracle. "Our political condition is better, &, though dashed by the treachery of our American President, can hardly go backward to slavery & civil war." Emerson hoped that the laying of the cable, "an event so exceptional & astounding in the history of human arts," would presage a period of "new sensibility to the opinion of mankind," which would in turn "restrain folly & meanness" (*JMN* 16:25). Later in his journal he expresses again his basic optimism that things will work out for the best, in time. "If we had the longevity of a redwood tree, or of a stone, we should not despond under bad politics. We have made a disastrous mistake in the election of a rebel as President. But the blunder is only noxious for the time, & discloses so soon the natural checks & cures, that it would cause no anxiety in a patriot who should live to the age of the antediluvians" (*JMN* 16:27).

In August Johnson attempted unsuccessfully to join all moderates in a new party at a National Union Convention meeting in Philadelphia in preparation for the fall congressional elections. This move convinced many northerners that Johnson's supporters were mainly ex-rebels and Copperheads. That same month the *Atlantic Monthly* published a scathing article on the president, noting of the National Union party that "its great strength is in its Southern supporters, and, if it comes into power, it must obey a Rebel direction." Regarding Johnson himself, "The President of the United States has so singular a combination of defects for the office of a constitutional magistrate, that he could have obtained the opportunity to misrule the nation only by a visitation of Providence." The president is "insincere as well as stubborn, cunning as well as unreasonable, vain as well as ill-tempered, greedy of popularity as well as arbitrary in disposition, veering in his mind as well as fixed in his will, he united in his character the seemingly opposite qualities of demagogue and autocrat, and converts the Presidential chair into a stamp or a throne, according as the impulse seizes him to cajole or to command." [14]

As usual, Emerson saw the ballot box as a way of mitigating the evil at hand, and in September, in a letter to an old Harvard friend, he says, "I hope you will see to it that your neighbors in New-Hampshire are put up to their weighty political duties & go to the polls, to put a check on our mad President" (*L* 5:477). Throughout the struggle, of course, one of the president's main adversaries was Emerson's friend and political hero Charles Sumner. Sumner, as a leader among the Radicals, was a consistent critic of Andrew Johnson's lenient Reconstruction policies. Pressing for a more radical reform, Sumner insisted on the need for universal manhood suffrage, a position Emerson favored. He frequently read on the Senate floor reports that he had received from various correspondents in the South indicating that Negroes were often the victims of "terrorism and extortion," and that in that region the spirit of rebellion was *"fiercer and more intolerant than it was in the middle of 1861."* [15] Sumner tended at times to look upon events fatalistically, as Emerson frequently did, and when one southern state after another rejected the Fourteenth Amendment, he was jubilant because he felt the rebels, unintentionally, were becoming "instruments of Providence for the establishment of human rights." [16] Sumner's style was often haughty and abrasive, and the measures he and other Radicals fought for served to bring down upon them the unrelenting ire of conservatives who supported the president. Emerson, however, stood by his political champion with unwavering faith. "It characterizes a man for me that he hates Charles Sumner: for it shows that he cannot discriminate between a foible and a vice. Sumner's moral instinct & character are so exceptionally pure that he must have perpetual magnetism for honest men; his ability & working energy such, that every good friend of the Republic must stand by him" (*JMN* 15:478).

In April 1867 another of Emerson's crusading activist friends, George Luther Stearns, died. Emerson himself would soon be sixty-four years old, and his powers were beginning to fail rapidly. For the first time in Ellen's memory, his eyes began to fail him, and on occasion he could hardly read.[17] Nevertheless, he continued to lecture and to speak to the issues of the moment. In his memorial for Stearns Emerson recounts his friend's public career as an advocate of human rights and "an early labourer in the resistance to slavery." Undoubtedly drawing upon his own personal knowledge of the man, dating back to his frequent visits with him and others to discuss current affairs in the turbulent 1850s,

Emerson alludes to Stearns's early work in 1855 with the Emigrant Aid Society and the Massachusetts State Kansas Committee, his support of John Brown with both "money and arms," and his testimony before the Mason Committee investigating the Harper's Ferry raid. This latter was "a shining example of the manner in which a truth speaker baffles all statecraft, and extorts at last a reluctant homage from the bitterest adversaries" (W 10:502, 504). For Emerson, Stearns was obviously one of those much-admired reforming activists who, armed with a vision of truth and practical organizational skills, was able to put the thing through. "I look upon him as a type of the American republican. A man of the people, in strictly private life, girt with family ties; an active and intelligent manufacturer and merchant, enlightened enough to see a citizen's interest in the public affairs, and virtuous enough to obey to the uttermost the truth he saw,—he became, in the most natural manner, an indispensable power in the state" (W 10:504–5).

Because of an overall decline in his creative energies and general physical vigor, Emerson came to write less and less in his journals in 1867 and later. Correspondingly, his comments on current events are fewer and less telling. His interest in public matters, however, was still substantial. One of his most significant performances for the year came on 19 April when he was asked to speak at the dedication of the Soldiers' Monument in Concord. His lengthy address once again emphasizes Emerson's understanding that the Civil War was a moral crusade, aimed at eradicating the abomination of slavery. The seeds of the Civil War were planted, according to Emerson, at the time of the Revolution, when "in the necessities of the hour," the Founding Fathers "overlooked the moral law, and winked at a practical exception to the Bill of Rights they had drawn up. They winked at the exception, believing it insignificant. But the moral law, the nature of things, did not wink at it, but kept its eye wide open" (W 11:352). The monument now being dedicated "is built to mark the arrival of the nation at the new principle,—say, rather, at its new acknowledgment, for the principle is as old as Heaven, —that only that state can live, in which injury to the least member is recognized as damage to the whole" (W 11:352).

In Emerson's opinion, the war had been fought to establish that very principle, "but first the North had to be reconstructed. Its own theory and practice of liberty had got sadly out of gear, and must be corrected" (W 11:352–53). After this was done, "the armies mustered in the North [became] as much missionaries to the mind of the country as they were carriers of material force, and had the vast advantage of carrying whither they marched a higher civilization" (W 11:355).

This "civilization," however, was backed by gunpowder, and the process by which these "missionaries" were converted to their task seems an altogether natural, though harsh one. "It is an interesting part of the history, the manner in which this incongruous militia were made soldiers. That was done again on the Kansas plan. Our farmers went to Kansas as peaceable, God-fearing men as the members of our school committee here. But when the Border raids were let loose on their villages, these people, who turned pale at home if called to dress a cut finger, on witnessing the butchery done by the Missouri riders on women and babes, were so beside themselves with rage, that they became on the instant the bravest soldiers and the most determined avengers." Such lessons are learned quickly, "and the first events of the war of the Rebellion gave the like training to the new recruits" (W 11:356). These apostles of culture were obviously dramatically different from those Emerson had envisioned in the 1840s.

Emerson goes on in his address to note, in considerable detail, the sufferings and sacrifices of Concord's volunteers in the battles of Bull Run, Gettysburg, the Campaign in the Wilderness, and McClellan's "retreat in the Peninsula in July, 1862." His details were supplied by the letters sent home by Concord's soldiers. These epistles were apparently circulated through the Emerson household and elsewhere, and he notes that "the letters of the captain are the dearest treasures of this town" (W 11:361). Emerson was fully aware that a commitment to principle had its cost. He notes, for example, that "the Campaign in the Wilderness surpassed all their [Concord's volunteers] worst experiences hitherto of the soldier's life. On the third of May, they crossed the Rapidan for the fifth time. On the twelfth, at Laurel Hill, the regiment had twenty-one killed and seventy-five wounded, including five officers" (W 11:371). Even now, "there are people who can hardly read the names on yonder bronze tablet, the mist so gathers in their eyes. Three of the names are the sons of one family" (W 11:375). His presentation ends in an up-beat fashion, however, because the victory has been won, and a new and better order will arise. "A duty so severe has been discharged, and with such immense results of good, lifting private sacrifice to the sub-lime, that, though the cannon volleys have a sound of funeral echoes, they can yet hear through them the benedictions of their country and mankind" (W 11:376).

This upbeat attitude also characterizes Emerson's "Progress of Cul-ture" address, which he delivered before the Phi Beta Kappa Society at Harvard in July. In this presentation Emerson stressed the enormous potential that Americans now possessed for bringing into the world the finest development of human society, unfettered by the blight of slavery. "Was ever such coincidence of advantages in time and place as in America today?—The fusion of races and religions; the hungry cry for men which goes up from the wide continent; the answering facility of imagination, permitting every wanderer to choose his climate and gov-ernment" (W 8:207). Freedom has gained in all sectors, and "the new claim of woman to a political status is itself an honorable testimony to the civilization which has given her a civil status new in history." Additionally, "the war gave us the abolition of slavery, the success of the Sanitary Commission and of the Freedman's Bureau," and many other moral and social improvements (W 8:208). The "spirit" that has animated the process of change in America contrasts sharply with the moral lethargy Emerson described in his "American Slavery Address" before the war. "A silent revolution has impelled, step by step, all this activity. A great many full-blown conceits have burst. The cox-comb goes to the wall. To his astonishment he has found that this country and this age belong to the most liberal persuasion; and that the day of ruling by scorn and sneers is past; that good sense is now in power, and *that* resting on a past constituency of intelligent labor, and, better yet, on perceptions less and less dim of laws the most sublime" (W 8:209).

This positive development can be seen in all areas of human endeavor, and "a controlling influence of the times has been the wide and success-ful study of Natural Science" (W 8:211). The force of culture, which has destroyed the slave oligarchy of the South, will continue to reshape the American scene, and Emerson reminds his audience that "culture implies all which give the mind possession of its own powers; as, languages to the critic, telescope to the astronomer. Culture alters the political status of an individual" (W 8:217). In Emerson's view, culture also shapes and forms the contours of reality to comport, finally, with divine law; "the foundation of culture, as of character, is at last the moral sentiment. This is the fountain of power, preserves its eternal newness, draws its own rent out of every novelty in science" (W 8:228). Even the newest developments discover the oldest law because "that was older, and awaited expectant these larger insights" (W 8:228).

Emerson, now in the twilight of his career, offers to these ambitious young men of Harvard a new "American Scholar," which includes now not only an exhortation to be active in the world as scholars but also to aggressively address the problems of society and government. "The Divine Nature comes on its administration by good men. Here you all set down, scholars and idealists, as in a barbarous age; amidst insanity, to calm and guide it; amidst fools and blind to see right done; among violent proprietors, to check self-interest, stone-blind and stone-deaf, by considerations of humanity to the workman and to his child." There are political obligations to be faced, also, in the most specific and forceful ways. "Amongst angry politicians swelling with self-esteem, pledged to parties, pledged to clients, you are to make valid the large considerations of equity and good sense; under bad governments to force on them, by your persistence, good laws" (W 8:230).

Emerson's oration ends with a ringing tribute to the young men before him, an entire generation of whom had so recently marched off to fight in the name of principle. "When I look around me and consider the sound material of which the cultivated class here is made up . . . I cannot distrust the great knighthood of virtue, or doubt that the interests of science, of letters, of politics and humanity, are safe. I think their hands are strong enough to hold up the Republic. I read the promise of better times and of greater men" (W 8:234).

Emerson's presentation was well received in Cambridge and elsewhere. A local commentator noted later that "the buoyancy and hopefulness pervading these sentences are to be found to a great extent in all contemporaneous American writing. This is especially true of what has been said and sung since the war." The reason for this, according to the writer, is that slavery was such an onerous evil, and so "particularly odious to a proud and sensitive people, because of the world-wide infamy as well as the inherent meanness of it," that once it was "unexpectedly lifted" from the country, its citizens came to "almost feel as if all evil had disappeared from the earth." He goes on to describe a scene that was all too familiar to Emerson and others who struggled against slavery. "By the cruel wrongs of the negro, who sometimes rushed with his rags and his scars through the streets of peaceful Northern villages, by the corruption of some of their greatest men to servility to it, by the bar it raised against all peaceful studies and pursuits, slavery had become to the more educated American, literally what Wesley called it, rhetorically, 'the sum of all villanies.' . . . Mr. Emerson, who sees in the political changes which have passed upon America the advance of a new earth in response to a new heaven of ideas, represents the particular epoch as well as the general character of its people." [18]

Despite this general optimism, however, the situation in Washington continued to deteriorate in the following year as friction between the Radicals and President Johnson grew more intense, largely on the issue of Reconstruction. In January the thirty-fourth National Anti-slavery Subscription Anniversary was held to raise funds in order to support the continued publication of the *National Anti-slavery Standard*. The advertisement for this event notes that the continual vigilance of the abolitionists is a necessity because "we see the President of the United States planting himself on the old idea of a white man's government, an idea which the nation has fought five years to crush. He upholds the policy of recognizing races and regulating our laws according to the supposed qualities of each—thus ignoring the cardinal principle of the civilization of which he is the official head. . . . Believing that the whole duty of the abolitionists will not be done; nor the pledges of the Anti-Slavery movement redeemed, until the idea of race is eliminated from our civil life, until color is no proscription anywhere under the flag —and seeing with what a slender tie the dominant party is bound to this idea; and how ready the leaders are to loose it, we feel that every word we can utter, and every effort we can make is needed *now*, before the great choice of next year, to secure all that can yet be saved of the harvest for which our husbands, sons and brothers gave their lives." The statement is signed by Mrs. George L. Stearns, Mary M. Brooks, Lidian Emerson, and others.[19] The struggle in Washington reached its climax on 24 February 1868 when the House voted to impeach Johnson on eleven charges. Emerson, who continued to follow political developments, though with much less intensity than before, recorded in his journal in March that Andrew Johnson was one of the "obstructives of the present day" (*JMN* 16:91). On 26 May, after a trial in the Senate, Johnson was acquitted by a vote of thirty-five to nineteen, just one vote short of the two-thirds majority needed to convict.

In the following month a congressional committee on lawlessness and violence issued a report that 373 freedmen had been killed by whites between 1866 and 1868, and 10 whites had been killed by freedmen. For Emerson, this must have been yet another reminder of the old times of violence and oppression. He recopied in his current journal a statement recorded originally in 1846. "The negro should say to the government, your principle is, no tax without representation; but as long as you do not protect me at home & abroad, you do not give me the value for which I have paid" (*JMN* 16:115). Emerson felt that the retrogression to violence and barbarism must be resisted by the militant forms of culture and civilization. The guns of war had played their part, but guns alone were clearly not enough. Hearts must eventually be won to goodness, and the new forces of the world put in their proper light. Hence, Emerson notes, "I wish the American Poet should let old times go & write on Tariff, Universal suffrage; Woman's suffrage; Science shall not be abused to make guns. The poet shall bring out the blazing truth, that he who kills his brother commits suicide" (*JMN* 16:88). Clearly there was much to be done yet in bringing the South, and the rest of the nation, forward into the realm of light, reason, and progress. Freedom, enfranchisement, and opportunity were seen by Emerson to be the keys to this ongoing evolution of American culture. To the critics of this concept Emerson responds, "You complain that the negroes are a base class. Who makes

& keeps the jew or the negro base, who but you, who exclude them from the rights which others enjoy?" (*JMN* 16:55).

In the fall of 1868 the Republicans nominated and then elected Ulysses S. Grant to the presidency on a platform that endorsed Radical Reconstruction. Emerson, withdrawing more and more from the public scene, did not take note of the election in his journal. However, he was undoubtedly pleased with the man, as well as the principle. Earlier he had listed General Grant among "the few stout & sincere persons . . . [who] recommend the country and the planet to us" (*JMN* 16:142). In February 1869 Congress proposed the Fifteenth Amendment, forbidding any state from depriving a citizen of his vote because of race, color, or previous condition of servitude. The amendment was proclaimed on 30 March 1870.

With Grant's presidential victory and the apparent triumph of Radical Reconstruction principles, it must have seemed to Emerson that things were indeed on the right track. As James McPherson has noted: "The abolitionists could look back with considerable satisfaction in 1870 upon the achievements of the past decade. Most of the measures they had originally advocated had been adopted: the immediate and universal abolition of slavery, the enlistment of Negro soldiers, government assistance for the education of freedmen, the creation of a Freedman's Bureau, and the incorporation of the Negro's civil and political equality into the law of the land. Abolitionists themselves had been transformed by the crucible of war from troublesome fanatics to prophets honored in their own country."[20] The following decade would witness the erosion of many of these gains, but at the moment a clear victory certainly seemed won. Throughout the 1870s Emerson, faced with the declining energies of old age, withdrew more and more from the controversies of public life and the cause of social reform. The younger generation of abolitionists would continue the struggle for civil rights and social equality. Emerson had articulated the philosophy and demonstrated a capacity and a willingness to "put his creed into his deed." It was now up to others to carry on.

Throughout the 1870s, and up to the time of his death in the spring of 1882, Emerson received occasional reminders of the role he had played and the services he had rendered in the struggle against slavery. Lidian, ever active in the cause, would maintain an interest in such matters until her death in 1892. Wendell Phillips, who was making the transition from the antislavery crusade to civil rights and the cause of labor, would continue to appeal on occasion for support from his friends in Concord. In June 1870 he wrote to Emerson seeking his help in securing a position for a young lady at the Boston Public Library. The fact that she was one-quarter black had prevented employment in many places, and Phillips was now calling upon Emerson and others for help in "stamping out this race prejudice." He asks, "Will you join me, Whittier & Higginson in saying one word to the trustees that you'd like to have her employed?" and assures Emerson that his name "will mow down whole ranks of opposition" because it is rumored that the head librarian 'worships R. W. E.' "[21] Despite whatever efforts Emerson might have made, Miss Forten, who was an early admirer of Emerson, did not get this post, but she did eventually find employment at the Treasury Department in Washington, D.C.[22] Not all the communications from Phillips concerned distressing matters. In November he sent along to Emerson a box of grapes that had been raised by John Brown, Jr., in Ohio and were now offered "in token of his grateful regard."[23]

In January 1872 Emerson visited Washington, D.C., once again, and as he noted in a letter to Lidian, he had the opportunity to visit "General Howard's Freedmen's Institute, an important college for the colored men," and there he gave an extempore talk (L 6:195). The institute, which later became Howard University, had been established in 1867 by the Freedman's Bureau, along with several other such institutions.[24] Emerson was no doubt pleased with the fact that such schools existed, because education played a prominent part in his vision of the socialization and cultural development of blacks. A local paper reported that Emerson spoke on the topic of "What Books to Read" in his impromptu address. Before making his suggestions, however, he told these young black scholars, "I am very glad this morning to see this institution, and to see so many of its scholars. I have been very happy in hearing the many details of the design of the actual direction and management of the institution. It certainly is making a movement of great promise in the country. It is one from which great good may be expected. I can easily see that it is only in its beginning, and that these results are only the seed-corn."[25]

In March 1874 Emerson's longtime friend and fellow abolition warrior, Senator Charles Sumner, died in Washington, D.C. One of those present at his bedside was Judge Ebenezer Rockwood Hoar, Emerson's friend and neighbor. When the senator opened his eyes and recognized Hoar, he said, "Tell Emerson how much I love and revere him."[26] One of the senator's last major legislative efforts was his Civil Rights Bill, which he had originally proposed in 1870. The year after his death, the measure, which guaranteed Negroes equal rights in conveyances, theaters, inns, and juries, and which went beyond the rights granted by Congress in the Reconstruction amendments, was passed by Congress.

The death of Sumner was a sad blow to the entire Emerson family. In a letter to her sister three days later, Ellen records that "Judge Hoar came to see Father yesterday and while he told his story both wept much. In vain at dinner Father tried to tell us—a second and third time he gave it up—but by degrees he did repeat the best the judge had told him— of the coming home and the concourse that watched the train all the way, whole cities coming to meet it—and in a solitary place one black family drawn up to see it pass and take off their hats." The ceremony in Boston was "beautiful—Bible, prayer, hymns, text, sermon and all, ending with the Governor's message and God save the Commonwealth of Massachusetts." Ellen ends with the notation, "I think everyone is surprised to find out how much they cry about it" (*EL* 2:126). Emerson and Whittier served as pallbearers for their comrade.[27]

Emerson made occasional contacts with other abolitionist cohorts during this time. On 19 April 1875 there was a great celebration in Concord on the one hundredth anniversary of the Battle of Concord and the beginning of the Revolution. The Minute Man monument was dedicated and Emerson made a short address. Also, "President Grant & Cabinet & ladies and bands of music came" to celebrate the event.[28] William Lloyd Garrison was also there, and Emerson apparently attended a meeting with him one evening.[29] The year before, he and Garrison attended the New England Women's Club poetical picnic, where they each read original poems.[30] Garrison continued to be admired and respected in the Emerson household. The following year, when he wrote to request a photo of Emerson, Lidian replied graciously. "Permit me to say that your letter I shall keep as a possession valuable—and increasing in value as the years—and ages—go by. I shall bear it to my children as the autograph of a man without whose heroic labors and sacrifices we could not now rejoice in 'A Nation saved, a Race delivered.'" She signed her note "ever gratefully yours, Lidian Emerson" and added in a postscript, "Mr. Emerson . . . bids me send you his kind regards."[31]

Lidian also stayed in touch with Wendell Phillips, who continued to visit with the Emersons when he was in Concord. Occasionally she would send him information about pressing social problems and, after hearing distressing news about the treatment of Indians in the West, insisted in one letter in 1870 that the "Anti Slavery Standard surely cannot be dispensed with while such crimes as these exist."[32] Six years later she exchanged information with Phillips about General Sherman's suggestion to Grant that "extermination" was a possible solution to the Indian problem in the American West.[33] Emerson himself apparently wrote to Phillips on this issue and received a response in September in which Phillips told of his campaign to help "these friendless victims" who had been threatened with extinction by "Sheridan and Sherman."[34]

Occasionally, Emerson received letters from abolitionists he had never met, testifying to the inspiration they had received from his teachings and example. These must have been especially pleasing to him because he always felt that his true role in matters of social reform was that of the scholar/poet; to inspire and to offer a guiding light to those who mount the stump or bear the rifle. One of these was Alexander Milton Ross, a "red-hot abolitionist" from Canada who had aided many fugitive slaves in locating there.[35] In 1875 Ross wrote to Emerson to thank him for the bard's expression of gratitude for his labors in the field, and he recalled a recent joyous New Year's celebration with former slaves whose escape he had aided.[36] Three years later, he hoped to visit Concord on his way to Europe, and noted in a letter then that he looked forward to meeting one "whose writings have been my guide to a better and higher life."[37] A week later he sent Emerson "a photograph of the very last lines written by my noble friend Capt. John Brown. The original lives on in my possession—they were written just before he was led from prison to martyrdom. Are they not wonderfully prophetic?"[38]

Emerson responded with an invitation for a weekend visit and promised to treat his Canadian guest to an evening with the Saturday Club.[39] Ross was able to keep the date and notes in his *Memoirs* that his visit "was on Friday, and the evening was spent in [Emerson's] library, where we . . . talked until midnight, when I was shown to my bedroom, the same, I understood, as occupied by John Brown, Mrs. Stowe, William Lloyd Garrison, Thoreau, and many other kindred spirits."[40] Ross was undoubtedly pleased with his visit, and in his last letter, in March 1879, he again confirmed the influence of the bard upon him, noting, "I have longed for years to meet you for to your writings I am indebted for the impulse to cast my lot with the workers for a higher law."[41]

Emerson gave very few public presentations in the 1870s, and his son Edward indicates 1872 as the year "Mr. Emerson had withdrawn from literary work" (W 11:642). In 1875 *Letters and Social Aims* was published, but this was largely a confection of early lectures and addresses compiled by James Elliot Cabot, who would eventually be named Emerson's literary executor.[42] On 6 February 1878 he made one of his last public presentations, "The Fortune of the Republic," appropriately at the Concord Lyceum. Emerson chose for his lecture a subject and title that dated back to the dark days of the Civil War. Although the content of the two speeches is substantially different, both are upbeat and optimistic, and undoubtedly both express his final optimism regarding the future of the republic that had so recently struggled so hard to place reason and justice in the ascendancy.[43]

There were rumblings throughout the South that the promises of Reconstruction were not being fulfilled. Occasionally these reached as far as Concord. In March 1879 boatloads of black migrants began to flee from the lower Mississippi Valley to Kansas. In the next two years the "exodus" would swell to thousands. The main cause of migration was economic, but abolitionists also saw the denial of civil and political rights as a factor.[44] Lidian was moved to send "ten dollars in answer to Garrison's appeal for help for the Negro exodus."[45] In general, however, little occurred to disturb the serenity of Emerson's twilight years, and he undoubtedly enjoyed at last the tranquility of his retirement from what was obviously a full, and sometimes frantic, public life. He died peacefully in the spring of 1882 with his family at his bedside.[46] "Hamlet's task" was at last done.

Chapter Ten

Conclusion

Ralph Waldo Emerson was a committed social reformer all of his life. He was deeply concerned with and involved in the major social reform movement of his time, antislavery. Throughout his lifetime Emerson never wavered in his commitment to clearly defined principles of human liberty, equality, and equal rights. The only serious doubts he ever felt in the matter concerned how *he* might best make his contribution to the cause. He did not wish to waste his energies in unproductive enterprises for which he was not fit. Also, he was always convinced, radical that he was, that American society could only be reformed by striking at the *roots* of social evil rather than simply pruning an occasional branch. For Emerson, the major cause of America's moral malaise was its gross materialism—the general tendency to place the value of things above people—and slavery was the epitome of this corrupt philosophy. Against this formidable brick-and-stone opponent Emerson fired the artillery of sympathy, emotion, and idealism, in the hope of precipitating a cultural revolution that would have the effect of elevating the civilization of America to a higher moral plane. He was quintessentially American in his reform efforts. Like the Founding Fathers whom he admired and the Declaration of Independence, which he once described as the "greatest achievement of American literature," he recognized that ideas can be powerful in shaping the course of things. He always believed, as he told the graduates of Harvard in 1837, that "this time, like all times,

337

is a very good one, if we but know what to do with it." And, for the most part, Emerson usually did.

It was as a scholar, an American scholar, that Emerson believed his best contribution could be made in the effort to reform and redeem American society. But he also recognized that while a scholar can enlighten the minds and move the hearts of others, a more specific instrumentality would be necessary to effect specific changes—to make the law of the heart the law of the land also. For Emerson, this instrumentality was the political process. While often critical of politicians for their numerous failures, especially the tendency to compromise principles in the name of expediency, Emerson never eschewed the political process itself. Whatever its shortcomings, the system established by the Founding Fathers had contributed enormously to the evolution of American greatness, and would continue to do so if leaders could be made to lead properly. Government, he felt, had the capacity to relieve social ills. As he noted in 1844, "Government exists to defend the weak and the poor and the injured party." However, he also realized that an effort was often required to compel the government to use its power wisely. He was well aware, as he pointed out in 1854, of the "worthlessness of good tools to bad workmen." He believed that citizens must imbue themselves with the best spirit of American democracy, must thereby become "citadels and warriors . . . declarations of Independence, the charter, the battle and the victory," and must demand that elected representatives follow this example themselves. Emerson always recognized that in America, "what great masses of men wish done, will be done" if the people themselves insist upon it. Change, and for Emerson, evolutionary progress, was always possible in America because "a Congress is a standing insurrection," and no matter how firmly entrenched a given political position, party, or policy is, it can be uprooted, overthrown, and abolished. As a means toward this end Emerson generally favored the ballot box. He always voted and always encouraged others to do so. An enlightened mind and sensitive heart could do much to improve society by the casting of a conscientious vote. Also, he was not above participating directly in a political campaign when it seemed appropriate for him to do so.

Conclusion

Emerson recognized that the casting of votes was not always in itself enough. At times, opposition to the social and moral reform of America appeared in a more violent guise than that of political party. Sometimes, as in Boston in 1835 and 1860, and Alton, Illinois, in 1837, the face of opposition appeared as a violent mob. Opposition to this form of evil often required a violence of its own, at times accompanied by self-sacrifice and even the sacrifice of others. Emerson applauded the heroic action of Elijah Lovejoy, as other abolitionists did, and Lovejoy would be but the first of many heroes who, for Emerson, "put their creed into their deed" and were willing to make the ultimate sacrifice for the moral values they held dear. There would be others, including the Free Soil farmers of Kansas, for whom Emerson would provide Sharpe's rifles; the noble Charles Sumner, struck down on the floor of the Senate; John Brown, executed in 1859; President Lincoln, the victim of an assassin's bullet; and finally, the entire generation of brave young men who willingly gave their lives in the Civil War. To Emerson, all of these were ultimately transcendental heroes, individuals who were prepared to sacrifice all in the name of principle.

Emerson also recognized in the 1850s that government itself may not at all times be susceptible to change through traditional political means. With the shocking passage of the Fugitive Slave Law in 1850 he realized that it would be necessary to step outside the bounds of constitutional law in order to oppose that immoral measure. A "higher law" than the Constitution must prevail in such cases, and he willingly and openly urged a defiant civil disobedience and practiced it himself. For him, the sacredness of individual moral conscience would always be infinitely more important than any institution, including the government of the United States. Even at this time, however, he would have preferred that the system correct itself, using the means available to it. He was bitterly disappointed when Massachusetts Chief Justice Lemuel Shaw refused to challenge the federal statute in the several opportunities provided to him. He consistently maintained that both legal tradition and human nature dictate that "you cannot enact a false thing to be true and a wrong thing to be right."

Emerson lived to see what he considered to be the "second American

Revolution" correct the one glaring deficiency of the first, the cata-
strophic compromise with slavery. The Civil War represented the triumph of principle in a society that had become mired in a corrupt
materialistic skepticism. He was optimistic that the war had redeemed
America from the sinful corruption of the institution of slavery, and
he looked forward to a glorious flowering of the American ideal in the
post–Civil War period. In one of his last speeches, "Fortune of the Republic" (1878), he described the triumph of the liberal spirit in America
in the following terms: "The genius of the country has marked out our
true policy,—opportunity. Opportunity of civil rights, of education, of
personal power, and not less of wealth; doors wide open. If I could have
it,—free trade with all the world without toll or custom-houses, invitation as we now make every nation, to every race and skin, white men,
red men, yellow men, black men; hospitality of fair field and equal laws
to all" (*W* 11:541).

In the light of this, it is profoundly ironic that the image of Emerson that would emerge in the closing decades of the nineteenth century would be quite the opposite of the liberal, activist reformer and
moralist that he truly was. As noted in chapter 1, the Holmes biography in 1884 was undoubtedly influential in creating a very conservative
view of Emerson, but the times themselves reinforced this inclination.
In the waning years of the nineteenth century the concept of rugged
individualism, reinforced by Darwinian science and Herbert Spencer's
social philosophy, came increasingly to dominate American consciousness. By this time Emerson's reputation as a great American thinker was
firmly established, and many individuals looked to Emersonian philosophy for an understanding of, and justification for, what seemed to be
inevitable developments in American society. Unfortunately, to many,
Emerson's early essays like "Self-Reliance," and later ones like "Power"
and "Wealth," from *Conduct of Life* (1860), as well as longer works like
Representative Men (1850), seemed to endorse the deeds of self-made
entrepreneurs like Andrew Carnegie, John D. Rockefeller, J. P. Morgan,
and others. As a result, Emerson's words were often invoked to justify
what Emerson himself would have considered blatant corruptions of the
American spirit.

Conclusion

A typical example of this tendency appears in the pronouncements and preachings of the Right Reverend William Lawrence, Methodist bishop of Massachusetts. In his 1901 essay "The Relation of Wealth to Morals" Bishop Lawrence makes the following statement: " 'Man,' says Emerson, 'is born to be rich. He is thoroughly related, and is tempted out by his appetites and fancies to the conquest of this and that piece of Nature, until he finds his well-being in the use of the planet, and of more planets than his own.' " To this the bishop adds his own observation that "man draws to himself material wealth as surely, as naturally, and as necessarily as the oak draws the elements into itself from the earth," and therefore, "in the long run, it is only to the man of morality that wealth comes." Reinforced by his invocation of Emersonian philosophy, the Reverend Lawrence concludes with the assertion that "Godliness is in league with riches."[1]

Because of perversions such as this, as the historian Daniel Aaron points out, in some quarters Emerson came to occupy the role of "seer of laissez-faire capitalism and the rampant individual." Aaron also notes that even though "Emerson . . . never intended his exhortations to justify the practices of the 'Robber Barons,' " his political philosophy seemed to do just that. "Strongly individualistic, it also spoke for equality of opportunity in economic and political affairs, and it lent support to the belief in laissez-faire and the necessity of the minimized state."[2] Other scholars have also drawn attention to this development and have noted, for example, that "Emerson's essay 'Self-Reliance' . . . provided another ideal justification for what the strong man was going to do anyhow, willy-nilly. And the gentle Emerson, who had grandly declared, 'Let man stand erect, go forth and possess the universe,' lived on into the time when Diamond Jim Brady and Jim Fisk took his advice quite literally and exhibited the success of his doctrine to a pitch appallingly beyond his wildest dreams."[3]

Perry Miller also points out that despite Emerson's early reputation as a revolutionary, "in the course of time, his preaching of individualism, especially 'self-reliance,' came to seem not at all dangerous, but rather the proper code for a young businessman with get-up and go." Miller adds that Emerson's "essay 'Napoleon' in *Representative Men*, . . . is in substance his love letter to the entrepreneurs, to the practical men who brushed aside the 'old legislation' and were building railroads."[4] One of the most prominent spokespersons for this view of Emerson at the turn of the century was Charles W. Eliot, president of Harvard University. President Eliot's commentary on Emerson, celebrating the centenary of his birth, was by far the most widely publicized of the time. It was delivered as part of the Emerson Centennial exercises in Boston, sponsored by the American Unitarian Association, on 24 May 1903. The address was delivered at Symphony Hall and was reported and substantially reproduced in many places, including virtually all of the major newspapers in New York and Boston.[5] In his presentation President Eliot presents an image of Emerson that might be described as a cross between a conservative Boston Brahmin and a captain of industry.

Among other things, Eliot suggests that contemporary American efforts to colonize Cuba and the Philippines would be applauded by Emerson because he believed in education as "the only sure means of permanent and progressive reform," and since "the Cubans are to be raised in the scale of civilization and public happiness," and "the Filipinos, too, are to be developed after the American fashion; . . . we send them 1,000 teachers of English."

Regarding rampant racism in the South, Eliot suggests that through education "the Southern States can be rescued from the persistent poison of slavery . . . after forty years of failure with political methods." The particular type of education that Eliot has in mind, however, focuses on "manual training schools" and, he says, the education of men by manual labor "was a favorite doctrine with Emerson," and Emerson "saw clearly that manual labor might be made to develop not only good mental qualities but good moral qualities."

President Eliot also addressed the question of the distribution of wealth within American society. At a time when American labor, responding to decades of exploitation by the captains of industry, was demanding a minimum wage and improved working conditions, President Eliot indicates that Emerson's position on such questions was clear. "It is interesting, at the state of industrial warfare which the world has now reached, to observe how Emerson, sixty years ago, discerned clearly the

Conclusion

absurdity of paying all sorts of services at one rate, now a favorite notion with some labor unions." According to Eliot, such misinformed egalitarianism would not be appreciated by the great bard, and he notes that Emerson himself had observed that "even when all labor is temporarily paid at one rate, differences in possessions will instantly arise: 'In one hand the dime became an eagle as it fell, and in another hand a copper cent. For the whole value of the dime is in knowing what to do with it.' " Eliot concludes his point with a statement that clearly underscores his own conservative attitude toward the major social problems of the time. He asserts flatly and firmly that "Emerson was never deceived by a specious philanthropy or by claims of equality which find no support in the nature of things."[6]

One might add as a footnote that nowhere in his lengthy memorial address does President Eliot allude to Emerson's extensive efforts as a social reformer or his active participation in the abolition movement. In fact, Eliot states bluntly that "although a prophet and inspirer of reform, Emerson was not a reformer. He was but a halting supporter of the reforms of his day; and the eager experimenters and combatants in actual reforms found him a disappointing sort of sympathizer. . . . When it came to action . . . he was surprisingly conservative." He also notes that Emerson "was intimate with many of the leading abolitionists; but no one has described more vividly their grave intellectual and social defects." For Eliot, Emerson was clearly only a theoretical reformer who "laid down principles which, when applied, would inevitably lead to progress and reform; but he took little part in the imperfect step-by-step process of actual reforming." Finally, he suggests that Emerson "probably would have been an ineffective worker in any field of reform." To reinforce this conservative image of his subject Eliot adds the totally erroneous statement that, despite his well-known religious radicalism, Emerson "attended church on Sundays all his life with uncommon regularity." Not surprisingly, at the conclusion of his memorial address Eliot notes that in his youth he was not fond of Emerson's thinking because it seemed too idealistic. But in his later years he has come to discover a "practical" element in Emerson that places the bard in a new and, apparently, more satisfactory light.

The image of Emerson as an idealist and active social reformer was not entirely lost, however. The Emerson Memorial School, which was held simultaneously in Concord and Boston 13–31 July 1903, was probably the most ambitious effort to set the record straight regarding Emerson's sentiments and activities as a social reformer and abolitionist.[7] The memorial was sponsored by the Free Religious Association of America, of which Emerson was a cofounder and longtime vice president. It consisted of some thirty lectures spread over the two weeks of the gathering. The committee that organized the series included such well-known social activists as Franklin Sanborn and Moorfield Storey. Not surprisingly, many of the talks centered on Emerson's reform activities, and included Julia Ward Howe's "A Century from the Birth of Emerson"; Franklin B. Sanborn's "Emerson and the Concord School of Philosophy"; Francis E. Abbot's "Emerson the Anti-imperialist or Prophet of the Natural Rights of Man"; William M. Salter's "Emerson's Aim and Method in Social Reform"; William Lloyd Garrison II's "Emerson and the Anti-slavery Movement"; and Moorfield Storey's "Emerson and the Civil War." The presentations most significant in projecting an image of Emerson as a reformer and abolitionist were those of Abbot, Garrison, and Storey.

Dr. Francis E. Abbot, who was one of the founders, with Emerson, of the Free Religious Association and a former editor of the *Index*, spoke directly of Emerson's career as an agitator. His concern, as one newspaper put it, was to rebut "certain criticisms recently made upon Emerson as having taught a different sort of equality than appears in the Declaration of Independence."[8] Dr. Abbot spoke at some length about Emerson's service in the antislavery cause, stressing that "his [Emerson's] conception of Americanism was entirely in accord with the teachings of Jefferson and Lincoln, in urging at all times an equal freedom under law for all," and that this was a significant contrast to "the Jefferson Davis concept of a purely white man's rule." Additionally, in an obvious reference to commentaries such as Eliot's regarding the relationship of Emersonian philosophy to the social problems of the present age, he adds emphatically, "Nowhere does he [Emerson] do aught but condemn the modern concept of moral law that grows indignant at restrictions on the game of exploiting other men."

Conclusion

The presentation of William Lloyd Garrison II offered, in the words of one newspaper account, "a remarkable consideration of the way in which a scholar and a man of letters so notably gentle and retiring as Emerson should nevertheless be inseparably linked in history with the aggressive opponents of American slavery."[9] Garrison's lecture provides some interesting insights into the relationships among noted abolitionists, based upon his personal experience in his father's household, and suggests that a lack of personal intimacy did not mean a lack of involvement with the cause, as some critics had maintained was the case with Emerson. The newspaper account indicates that "Mr. Garrison noted the interesting fact that several of the prominent men associated with closely in history for their connection with the anti-slavery movement seldom met: Phillips, Garrison, and Parker held neighborhood and household intimacy; Edmund Quincy was familiar; but Whittier, Mr. Garrison remembers at his father's house only once." The reporter then quotes Garrison. "Lowell [a most active Boston abolitionist] I never saw at an anti-slavery meeting or in [an] anti-slavery household, I never knew him in companionship with my father." Of Emerson, Garrison says, "I think my father spent but a single night under his roof." While useful for personal reminiscences, Garrison's presentation is less than complete in indicating the length and depth of Emerson's abolition service. Undoubtedly this was due to the fact that his specific knowledge of such activities on Emerson's part was largely limited to the biographical resources available at the time, which were, as noted in chapter 1, less than all-encompassing in this regard.[10]

The presentation of Moorfield Storey, on the other hand, is much more effective in dealing with the specifics of Emerson's thought on the questions of slavery, abolition, and human rights. One major reason for this is that Storey had the advantage of quoting directly from Emerson's famous "lost journal," *WO Liberty*, which he had borrowed for this purpose from the Emerson family, and which would remain thereafter unaccounted for among his papers until 1966.[11]

Moorfield Storey was a longtime friend of the Emerson family. He had been a classmate of Edward Waldo Emerson at Harvard and later collaborated with him on a biography of the venerable Ebenezer Rockwood Hoar of Concord.[12] Storey came to know Ralph Waldo Emerson as a result of this association, and at this time, the early 1860s, Emerson was deeply involved in the abolition movement and its aftermath. Storey's own abolitionist heritage was significant. As one biographer points out, his mother was "an outright abolitionist," and the two acquaintances of his father whom Storey claimed most influenced him, after Emerson, were James Russell Lowell, who once served on the *National Anti-slavery Standard* and in other abolitionist capacities, and Charles Sumner, senator from Massachusetts and one of the Senate's most outspoken opponents of slavery.[13] Storey served as Sumner's personal secretary from 1867 to 1869.

After rising to prominence as a successful Boston attorney and eventually becoming president of the American Bar Association in 1896, Storey began to turn his attention to America's pressing social problems. In 1898 he became president of the Massachusetts Reform Club, in 1905 vice president of the National Civil Service Reform Association, and, also in 1905, president of the Anti-imperialist League. Storey's longtime battle for the rights of the Negro, which he considered to be the legacy of the abolitionists he admired, culminated with his election in 1910 as the first president of the National Association for the Advancement of Colored People.[14]

Given his interests in social reform, his friendship with the Emerson family, and his respect for the abolitionist tradition, it is not surprising that Storey should be most interested in maintaining the image of Emerson as an active social reformer with a strong interest in human rights. Storey's address describes Emerson as a poet-reformer. In this capacity "it was possible for him [Emerson] to make his position absolutely clear, to stand ready as a citizen to bear his testimony against slavery whenever occasion demanded, but not to abandon the other work of his life for the purpose of leading the anti-slavery crusade."[15] Storey recognized that much had been made of Emerson's lack of personal sympathy with some individual abolitionists and that this criticism had been extrapolated by some commentators to include the cause itself. In response to this, after taking note of representative comments by Emerson in this regard, Storey states, "But great injustice would be done to Emerson if it were supposed that such words as these expressed his real attitude towards the opponents of slavery." While Emerson could "appreciate their weaknesses" and could "point out their faults," he respected the abolitionists' efforts and their cause, and he once referred to them as individuals "who see the faults and stains of our social order, and who pray and strive incessantly to right the wrong." At another point he quotes from "The Young American" (1844) Emerson's dictum that we must not "throw stumbling blocks in the way of the abolitionist [and] the philanthropist as the organs of influence and opinion are swift to do." He concludes this aspect of his presentation with the assertion that while Emerson at times adopted an "attitude of semi-humorous criticism" toward them, he felt a "real respect towards the anti-slavery leaders."

At other points in his talk Storey alludes to Emerson's earliest associations with the abolition movement in the 1830s and his later alliance and friendship with Charles Sumner. Sumner was most zealous in the cause of freedom and "impatient of apathy or indifference" in the matter, and "in Emerson he found a thoroughly congenial soul; . . . the absolute sympathy that existed between them is proof that Sumner recognized in Emerson as intense a love of freedom as his own."

Storey's lengthy address notes several other aspects of Emerson's thinking on the need to abolish slavery and assert human rights, and the methodology to be employed in reaching these goals, drawing freely from Emerson's journal to support his points. As might be expected, Storey's account of Emerson's commitment to the basic integrity of all individuals and his consequent vigorous opposition to all efforts to enslave and exploit others was directly related to his own concern with contemporary social problems in America, especially racism. Thus at one point Storey notes Emerson's hopeful belief that the very qualities of benevolence, docility, and industriousness that led to the exploitation of the Negro race in the nineteenth century, "in a more moral age will not only defend their independence but will give them a rank among nations." Recognizing the sad truth that twentieth-century America was manifestly *not* moving toward the fulfillment of this dream, Storey is led to exclaim: "How full of inspiration are these words to every lover of freedom and justice! How ineffably sad it is to read them now and to reflect as we listen to the cries of the mob at Wilmington and Evansville and read of the horrors committed in Luzon that ours is a less moral age, and that punishment waits upon our sins as it did of our fathers."[16]

Overall, Storey's address was quite successful in identifying Emerson's strong commitment to the abolition cause and his equally strong belief in the sacredness of the individual and the natural rights, such as freedom and self-determination, that accrue from this belief. Indeed, in this respect the entire Memorial School series was similarly successful. In a commentary in the *Springfield Republican* in July, Franklin Sanborn noted that Storey's presentation contributed significantly to the public's understanding of Emerson because the speaker "had the advantage of access to the private journals of Emerson, and quoted freely therefrom," and hence "was able to do more than rehearse well known opinions."[17] Clearly, Emerson's ideas were "much in advance of those which the educated men of the country in general held at that time." Without referring directly to the proper Boston Brahmins, Sanborn notes that while "the scholarly class in America have usually followed the multitude and not led them, the exceptions [are] Emerson, Parker, Thoreau, Wendell Phillips and Lowell."[18]

Unfortunately, despite such efforts to preserve the legacy of Emerson's campaign for social justice, the works and writings of men like Higginson, Sanborn, and Storey for the most part died with them, their words entombed in the dusty volumes of nineteenth-century newspapers and long-forgotten periodicals. The result is that the image of the serenely disengaged Emerson remains very much with us today.[19] Nevertheless, there are undoubtedly those who, having been stimulated and excited by Emerson as undergraduates, still read the "American Scholar" and the 1844 "Emancipation in the British West Indies" address as moving statements of a pure American idealism. It was this idealism, stimulated by a genuine love for mankind and commitment to human virtue, that fueled Emerson's long and inevitable campaign against slavery, and remains alive and well in his words today.

Notes

Chapter 1. Abolition and the Biographers

1. As Larry Gara has noted in his essay "Who Was an Abolitionist," there has been much disagreement as to the specific definition of this term over the years. For the purposes of this study the term *abolitionist* will refer to one who either belonged to or substantially supported an organized effort to abolish slavery in the United States, either immediately or gradually, through moral suasion, agitation, or political action. See *The Antislavery Vanguard: New Essays on the Abolitionists*, ed. Martin Duberman (Princeton: Princeton University Press, 1965), pp. 32–51.

2. George Willis Cooke, *Ralph Waldo Emerson: His Life, Writings, and Philosophy* (Boston: James R. Osgood, 1881), p. 132.

3. Ibid., p. 28.

4. Ibid., p. 143.

5. Moncure Daniel Conway, *Emerson at Home and Abroad* (Boston: James R. Osgood, 1882), p. 299.

6. Ibid. Actually, Channing, one of the most famous scholars of his day, published his controversial work *Slavery* in 1835, two years before Emerson's first public address on the topic.

7. London: Simpkin, Marshall and Company, 1882.

8. Ibid., p. 95.

9. Ibid., p. 96.

10. Ibid., pp. 187, 189.

11. Ralph Rusk, *The Life of Ralph Waldo Emerson* (New York: Charles Scribner's Sons, 1949), p. 500. See also Emerson's "Remarks at the Meeting for Organizing the Free Religious Association" (*W* 11:477–81).

12. Edwin D. Mead, "Emerson and Theodore Parker," *Index*, August 17, 24, 1882, pp. 78–80, 90–92.

13. Moncure Daniel Conway, "Ralph Waldo Emerson," *Fortnightly Review* (London), 1 June 1882, p. 767.

14. Oliver Wendell Holmes, *Ralph Waldo Emerson* (Boston: Houghton Mifflin, 1884), p. 304.

15. Anonymous, "Holmes' Emerson," *Nation*, vol. 40, 29 January 1885, pp. 99–

100. Although the review was published anonymously, the author is probably T. W. Higginson.

16. *Index*, 12 February 1885, p. 386.

17. Tilden G. Edelstein, *Strange Enthusiasm: A Life of Thomas Wentworth Higginson* (New Haven: Yale University Press, 1968), pp. 3, 241; R. W. Emerson to T. W. Higginson, 25 September 1854, printed in *American Literature* 33 (May 1961), p. 168.

18. *Index*, 27 August 1885, p. 101.

19. *Index*, 19 November 1885, pp. 248–49.

20. *Index*, 17 December 1885, p. 297.

21. Ibid.

22. Holmes Memoranda Book, Houghton Library, Harvard University.

23. Oliver Wendell Holmes, Sr., Papers, Library of Congress.

24. Holmes, *Ralph Waldo Emerson*, p. 181.

25. Ibid., pp. 211, 304.

26. Holmes Memoranda Book, Houghton Library, Harvard University.

27. Ellen Tucker Emerson, *The Life of Lidian Jackson Emerson*, ed. Delores Bird Carpenter (Boston: Twayne Publishers, 1980), p. xxxviii. For an interesting and detailed discussion of the evolution of Cabot's role as Emerson's biographer see Nancy Craig Simmons, "Philosophical Biographer: James Elliot Cabot and *A Memoir of Ralph Waldo Emerson*," in *Studies in the American Renaissance, 1987*, ed. Joel Myerson (Charlottesville: University Press of Virginia, 1987), pp. 365–92.

28. E. R. Hoar to J. E. Cabot, 13 September 1887, MS, Schlesinger Library, Radcliffe College. Three years earlier Hoar had written to Holmes regarding his biography, "I do not yet believe that you have got hold of all there was in Emerson, any more than I thought in his lifetime that he understood all there was in you. Indeed, 'much meditating on these things,' I incline to think that a perfect sympathy is only possible in disciple and admirer—pure and simple—who has no separate gift or quality of his own." Quoted in *Life and Letters of Oliver Wendell Holmes*, 2 vols., ed. John T. Morse, Jr. (Cambridge: Riverside Press, 1896), 2:64.

29. Edith Emerson Forbes to J. E. Cabot, 7 November 1887; Ellen Emerson to J. E. Cabot, 7 November 1887; both manuscripts at Schlesinger Library, Radcliffe College.

30. "Cabot's *Memoir of Ralph Waldo Emerson*," *Nation*, 15 September 1887, p. 214. This review also appeared on the same day in the *Evening Post* (Boston).

31. Lewis O. Bradshaw, "Cabot's Life of Emerson," *New Englander and Yale Review* (January 1888), p. 7.

32. T. W. Higginson, "Emerson as the Reformer," *Boston Advertiser*, 25 May 1903.

33. Nancy Craig Simmons presents an interesting exchange of letters between John Jay Chapman and Cabot that points up the latter's comparatively conservative view of Emerson. Chapman had sent part 1 of his lengthy *Atlantic* article "Emerson Sixty Years Later" to Cabot for his critique, noting in his letter, "Of course I cant expect you to see much in it and some of it is a criticism of a hostile sort directed against new England" [*sic*]. In his response Cabot indicated that he was in general agreement with Chapman's image of Emerson, but he does note, "You do not remark upon what seems to me to be the most remarkable instance of a comparative failure in keeping his [Emerson's] balance,—as to the Slavery question, just at the beginning of the War. He gets a little shrill in his denunciations,—there is a falsetto note, very uncharacteristic, showing that he is voicing the thoughts of other people, not his own." Obviously, judging from the strong and positive emphasis that Chapman later placed on Emerson's abolitionism in part 2 of his article, he disagreed totally with Cabot's opinion on the matter, and he chose instead to characterize Emerson's pronouncements on the topic as expressing a proper "ferocity," not the "falsetto" voice Cabot had suggested. The difference between the two views is striking. As Simmons notes, "Stressing continuity, tradition, and the values on which the society was founded, in the *Memoir*, Cabot depicted Emerson as a conservative, in the root sense of the word, absolving him of any stigma of radicalism." On the other hand, "what Chapman admired in Emerson was the opposite of conservatism; the seer and prophet represented a 'protest against the tyranny of democracy; an attack on the vice of the age, moral cowardice'" (p. 185). The dates of Chapman's and Cabot's letters are 4 November 1896 and 14 January 1897, respectively. "Speaking of Emerson: Two Unpublished Letters Exchanged Between John Jay Chapman and James Elliot Cabot," *Harvard Library Bulletin* 31 (1983), pp. 181–87.

34. Conway died in 1907, Sanborn in 1917, Higginson in 1911, and Peabody in 1894. All, at one time or another, wrote about Emerson's abolition activities.

35. George Edward Woodberry, *Ralph Waldo Emerson* (London: Macmillan, 1907), p. 71.

36. O. W. Firkins, *Ralph Waldo Emerson* (Boston: Houghton Mifflin, 1915), p. 131.

37. Rusk, *Life of Emerson*, pp. 308, 366, 389.

38. Robert Burkholder and Joel Myerson, *Emerson: An Annotated Secondary Bibliography* (Pittsburgh: University of Pittsburgh Press, 1985), p. 531. Konvitz and Whicher, eds. *Emerson: A Collection of Critical Essays* (Englewood Cliffs: Prentice-Hall, 1962), p. 184.

39. Stephen Whicher, *Freedom and Fate: An Inner Life of Ralph Waldo Emerson* (Philadelphia: University of Pennsylvania Press, 1953), p. vii.

40. Ibid., p. 76.

41. Ibid., pp. 79–82.

42. Ibid., pp. 28–29.

43. Gay Wilson Allen, *Waldo Emerson: A Biography* (New York: Viking Press, 1981), pp. viii, xiii, 424, 584.

44. John McAleer, *Ralph Waldo Emerson: Days of Encounter* (Boston: Little, Brown, 1984), p. 518.

Chapter 2. Early Concerns

1. S. N. Dickinson, ed., *The Boston Almanac for the Year 1849* (Boston: B. B. Mussey), p. 65. Because black children were often ridiculed and mistreated in public schools in Boston in the late eighteenth century, segregated schools were considered desirable. Blacks under the direction of Negro leaders like Prince Hall petitioned the city in 1787 for the establishment of a separate black school. The petition was rejected, and the black community founded its own "African School," which was financed privately until it was taken over by the city in 1820. By the 1840s Boston's all-black schools had become instruments for racial segregation. When Negro leaders in the city protested against this situation and the poor quality of instruction in black schools, a five-man subcommittee of the Boston Primary School Committee studied the situation and recommended that the segregation policy continue because, in their opinion, racial distinction, which was created by God, "is founded deep in the physical, mental, and moral natures of the two races," and hence, if the schools were desegregated, colored students would diminish the performance of whites, while the whites would undoubtedly "vex and insult the colored children" and drive them from school. The subcommittee also expressed a concern with the horror of intermarriage and the need for Negro independence. Negro leaders rejected the subcommittee's findings and actively petitioned to end segregation in 1844, 1845, 1846, and 1849. Interestingly enough, the Smith Grammar School was often at the center of this ongoing controversy because black leaders charged its white principal, Abner Forbes, with cruelty, incompetence, and a demeaning attitude toward his Negro students. Eventually, a boycott of the Smith School was organized from 1844 to 1849. Despite the appointment of a black principal, Thomas Paul, in 1849, the situation remained unimproved. Garrisonians joined in the fray, and in 1850 Robert Morris and Charles Sumner, soon to be a U.S. senator, argued the case for desegregation of the schools before the Massachusetts Supreme Court. In April 1850 the court decided that each school system in the state could decide for itself on the question of segregation. Black leaders were unsatisfied with this decision and continued to agitate the cause, with the help of Wendell Phillips and others. Finally, after yet another round of petitions in 1854 and 1855, the Massachusetts legislature was persuaded to act, and on 28 April 1855 the gover-

nor signed into law a measure prohibiting all distinctions of color and religion in admitting children to Massachusetts public schools. Black schools remained open as an alternative for those who wished them, and black leaders decided to maintain their boycott of them, with telling effect. So few Negro students attended them that in the fall of 1855 the Boston School Committee decided to close or integrate them all, including the Smith School, which throughout the decade remained in the center of the storm. See Carleton Mabee, "A Negro Boycott to Integrate Boston Schools," *New England Quarterly* 41 (1968), pp. 341–61; James Oliver Horton, "Generations of Protest: Black Families and Social Reform in Ante-bellum Boston," *New England Quarterly* 49 (1976), pp. 242–56; and Donald M. Jacobs, "William Lloyd Garrison's *Liberator* and Boston's Blacks 1830–1865," *New England Quarterly* 44 (1971), pp. 259–77.

2. C. C. Burleigh (?) to Samuel J. May (?), 3 April 1835, MS, Boston Public Library. The manuscript is inscribed across the top, "C. C. Burleigh to S. J. May." The internal evidence of the letter amply reinforces this assignation; however, since the handwriting of the inscription is different from that of the main body of the letter, and since the manuscript is not otherwise signed, the index notation at the library includes a question mark after each name. There can be no doubt regarding the propriety of the assignation. Charles Burleigh became an agent and lecturer for the Middlesex County Anti-slavery Society in 1835 (the year this letter was written) at the urging of the Reverend Samuel May. Concord was a popular meeting place for that society. Samuel May would probably have been known to Mary Emerson, as the letter indicates, since he was a longtime friend of Emerson, a Unitarian minister, and had been allowed by Emerson to deliver an antislavery address from his Second Church pulpit in 1831.

3. MS records of the Middlesex County Anti-slavery Society, Concord Free Public Library, Concord, Mass.

4. *Concord Freeman*, 7 February 1835, p. 2.

5. MS records of the Middlesex County Anti-slavery Society; the account was also published in the *Concord Freeman*, 28 January 1837.

6. Ralph Rusk, *The Life of Ralph Waldo Emerson* (New York: Charles Scribner's Sons, 1949), p. 228. See also *LL* 43.

7. Charles and Waldo had been living together in the Old Manse with their mother in 1834; shortly after moving into his new home in Concord the following year, Ralph Waldo began renovations to provide living quarters for Charles and his betrothed, Elizabeth Hoar. After Charles's death Waldo noted in his journal, "Besides my direct debt to him of how many valued thoughts,—through what orbits of speculation have we not travelled together, so that it would not be possible for either of us to say, This is my thought, that is yours" (*JMN* 5:151).

8. Charles Emerson, "Lecture on Slavery," MS, Houghton Library, Harvard University.

9. R. W. Emerson would also refer to Touissant enthusiastically in his famous "Emancipation in the British West Indies" speech on 1 August 1844.

10. Franklin Sanborn, "The Women of Concord," *Critic*, May 1906, p. 409.

11. Joan Trumbull, "Concord and the Negro" (M.A. thesis, Vassar College, 1944), p. 31. It was Mrs. Brooks who persuaded Emerson to write his letter to Van Buren on behalf of the Cherokees in 1838 (Sanborn, "Women of Concord," p. 410). She also joined forces with Lidian and the Thoreau women to bring an end to Emerson's seven years of silence on the topic of slavery with his "Emancipation in the British West Indies" speech (F. B. Sanborn, *The Personality of Emerson* [Boston: Charles E. Goodspeed, 1903], p. 14); she was also instrumental in persuading Emerson, for the first time in his career as a lecturer, to boycott the New Bedford Lyceum in 1845 because of its policy of racial discrimination. Mary Merrick Brooks was the wife of Concord's notable Squire Nathan Brooks, one of the town's leading citizens, and served for a time as the president of the Concord Women's Anti-slavery Society. When Ann Weston Warren was visiting the towns of Middlesex County in the fall of 1841 to encourage support for local antislavery fairs (which were the special interest of her sister, Maria Chapman, a leading light in the Boston Female Anti-slavery Society), she visited Mrs. Brooks at her home. In a letter to her cousin Deborah Weston she described that visit and said of Mrs. Brooks, "I like her more & more & I *never* saw a woman more truly independent & conscientious. She is very lively and good tempered, & perfectly fearless—what the transcendentalists might hail as 'the truest of women'—She has but one want: she is no further literary than a thorough knowledge of everything connected with Anti Slavery or Non Resistance makes her so and as she is so companionable in everything else, I miss this knowledge of books. We spent the first evening abusing ministers and telling our own experiences." Letter printed by Thomas Blanding, *Concord Saunterer* 17, no. 3 (1984), p. 8.

12. Ellen Tucker Emerson, *The Life of Lidian Jackson Emerson*, ed. Delores Bird Carpenter (Boston: Twayne Publishers, 1980), pp. 64, 83–84.

13. W. S. Robinson, *"Warrington" Pen Portraits: A Collection of Personal and Political Reminiscences from 1848 to 1876* (Boston: n.p., 1877), pp. 19–71.

14. For a discussion of Furness and Emerson regarding the slavery issue see my "Emerson and Furness: Two Gentlemen of Abolition," *American Transcendental Quarterly* 41 (Winter 1979), pp. 17–32.

15. MS, Boston Public Library, 5 December 1835.

16. Martineau, *Autobiography*, quoted by Edward Emerson in W 11:573.

17. Martineau, *Retrospect of Western Travel*, 3 vols. (London: Saunders and Otley, 1838), 3:229.

18. Walter Harding, *Emerson's Library* (Charlottesville: University Press of Virginia, 1967), p. 37.

19. Quoted in Adapa Rao, *Emerson and Social Reform* (India: Arnold-Heinemann Publishers, 1980), p. 73.

20. Douglas Stange reports that many conservative Unitarians believed that "there were masters, 'high-minded, humane and religious men,' who treated their slaves with uniform kindness and consideration. The North should be considerate to these southern masters. . . . Much injustice [they felt] had been shown the South. Many planters were in a quandary when they saw freedom did 'the colored man no good.'" See "Abolitionism as Treason: The Unitarian Elite Defends Law, Order, and the Union," *Harvard Library Bulletin* 28 (April 1980), p. 154.

21. Arthur C. McGiffert, Jr., ed., *Young Emerson Speaks: Unpublished Discourses on Many Subjects* (Port Washington, N.Y.: Kennikat Press, 1938), p. 5.

22. Rusk, *Life of Emerson*, p. 153. For specific references to slavery in Emerson's early sermons see McGiffert, *Young Emerson Speaks*, p. 256.

23. *JMN* 12:152. The idea that blacks were racially inferior but spiritually equal was common even among strident abolitionists. Ellis Gray Loring wrote to Emerson shortly after Emerson's speech on emancipation in the West Indies on 1 August 1844 and congratulated him on the talk, adding, "The negro may be inferior, but a man's a man, for a' that" (E. G. Loring to R. W. Emerson, 22 August 1844, MS, Houghton Library, Harvard University). Other abolitionists attempted to refute the assertion of racial inferiority by pointing to such capable black leaders as Touissant. Furthermore, various studies attempted to establish the fact of physiological equality. For example, an article in the *Concord Freeman* (29 April 1837) refers to a work by Frederick Tiedemann, M.D., *On the Brain of the Negro, Compared with that of the European and Ourang Outang*, which concluded that "no perceptible difference exists either in the average weight or the average size of the brain of the negro and that of the European . . . nor does the negro brain exhibit any greater resemblance to that of the ourang-outang than does the brain of the European."

24. Leonard Richard, *"Gentlemen of Property and Standing": Anti-abolition Mobs in Jacksonian America* (New York: Oxford University Press, 1970), p. 12.

25. *The Early Lectures of Ralph Waldo Emerson.* Vol. 2, *1836–38*, ed. Stephen E. Whicher and Robert Spiller (Cambridge: Harvard University Press, 1959), p. 176.

26. *Yeoman's Gazette*, 9 December 1837, p. 2. In his "Address to the Citizens of Boston," which was written in response to the aldermen's refusal to allow the use of Faneuil Hall for a meeting to express "public sentiment in regard to the late ferocious assault on the liberty of the press at Alton," Channing asked, "Is there no part of our country, where a voice of power shall be lifted up in defense of rights incomparably more precious than the temporary interests which have often crowded Faneuil Hall to suffocation? Is the whole country to sleep? An event has occurred, which ought to thrill the hearts of this people as the heart

of one man. A martyr has fallen among us to the freedom of the press. A citizen has been *murdered* in defense of the right of free discussion."

27. Emerson, *Early Lectures*, 2:327; see also the essay "Heroism" in Emerson's *Works* 2:245–64.

28. James Elliot Cabot, *A Memoir of Ralph Waldo Emerson*, 2 vols. (Boston: Houghton Mifflin, 1887), 2:425, 426.

29. Ibid., p. 426.

Chapter 3. The Silent Years

1. Daniel Walker Howe, *The Unitarian Conscience: Harvard Moral Philosophy, 1805–1861* (Cambridge: Harvard University Press, 1970), pp. 155, 278. See also Donald Stange, *Patterns of Antislavery Among American Unitarians, 1831–1860* (Madison, N.J.: Fairleigh Dickinson University Press, 1977), pp. 74–84.

2. Ibid., p. 277.

3. P. 15; copies of these and other printed reports of the Boston Female Antislavery Society are held by the Boston Athenaeum.

4. Howe, *Unitarian Conscience*, p. 270.

5. Lydia Maria Child maintained that it was the reading of her 1833 work *Appeal for that Class of Americans Called Africans* that moved Channing to speak out on slavery. See Ethel K. Ware, "Lydia Maria Child and Anti-slavery," *Boston Public Library Quarterly* 3, no. 4 (October 1951), p. 251. Douglas Stange suggests that "Mrs. Child, Garrison, and Samuel J. May had all prodded Channing to speak out in public. The publication of his volume *Slavery* in 1835 must be considered, at least partially, the fruit of this pressure." See *Patterns of Antislavery*, p. 77.

6. William Ellery Channing, *The Works*, 6 vols. (Boston: James Munroe, 1848), 2:107, 115, 11. These statements must have been especially shocking to Channing's parishioners because, at the time, he was very closely associated with the "aristocratic" movers in the business community, a situation that once led Maria Chapman to remark that Channing "had been selected by a set of money-making men as their representative for piety." Quoted by Stange, *Patterns of Antislavery*, p. 77.

7. Channing, *Works*, 2:172.

8. MS, Boston Public Library, 9 October 1843.

9. Howe, *Unitarian Conscience*, p. 293.

10. Ibid., p. 281.

11. Channing, *Works*, 6:59, 70.

12. "Who Was an Abolitionist," in *The Antislavery Vanguard*, ed. Martin Duberman (Princeton: Princeton University Press, 1965), p. 37.

13. Channing, *Works*, 6:68.

14. Ibid., p. 419.

15. Merton Dillon, *The Abolitionists: The Growth of a Dissenting Minority* (New York: W. W. Norton, 1974), p. 122.

16. MS, Houghton Library, Harvard University, 16 May 1854.

17. Albert Bushnell Hart, *Slavery and Abolition, 1831–1841* (New York: Harper and Brothers, 1906), p. 198.

18. James S. Gibbons to Caroline Weston, 14 August 1842, MS, Boston Public Library. James Sloan Gibbons (1810–92) was a New York businessman with a Quaker background. He played a prominent part in the work of the American Anti-slavery Society and was one of the chief supporters of the *National Anti-slavery Standard*. Caroline Weston (1808–82) was the younger sister of the better-known Maria Weston Chapman. She was an active abolitionist and one of the leaders in the Boston Female Anti-slavery Society.

19. Maria Weston Chapman, Notes, 1876(?), MS, Boston Public Library. Maria Chapman has been described as the "soul" of the Boston Female Anti-slavery Society, editing its annual reports from 1836 to 1840. (Emerson was known to have a copy of the 1836 report in his library. Walter Harding, *Emerson's Library* [Charlottesville: University Press of Virginia, 1967], p. 37.) She worked very closely with William Lloyd Garrison. Chapman's apparent ire in these remarks undoubtedly derives, at least in part, from the fact that the famous Boston antiabolition riot of 1835, which began at a meeting of the Boston Female Anti-slavery Society and culminated with Garrison being dragged through the streets of Boston by a howling mob, was blamed on the women. Conservative Unitarian Sidney Willard, at that time editor of the *Christian Register*, maintained that the women should not have publicized their meeting, and that the "gentler sex [should] . . . seek information at home, and lend their influence in a more private way." See Albert Bushnell Hart, *Slavery and Abolition*, pp. 246–49; and Douglas Stange, "Abolitionism as Treason: The Unitarian Elite Defends Law, Order, and the Union," *Harvard Library Bulletin* 28 (April 1980), p. 166.

20. Although Stange asserts that with the death of Channing and Henry Ware, "philosophical abolition" died also, he does suggest in a footnote, correctly I think, that "vestiges of 'abolitionism as a philosophy' continued to appear in the antislavery attitudes of men like Ralph Waldo Emerson" (*Patterns of Antislavery*, pp. 31, 247).

Arthur M. Schlesinger makes essentially the same connection in his work *The American as Reformer* (Cambridge: Harvard University Press, 1950): "One antislavery school consisted of men like Emerson and William Ellery Channing, who believed that all reform must begin with the individual, that you must remake souls before you remake institutions" (p. 32).

David Robinson argues persuasively throughout his study *Apostle of Culture: Emerson as Preacher and Lecturer* (Philadelphia: University of Pennsylvania Press, 1982) for the continuity of the development of Emerson's career, especially through his consistent emphasis on "self-culture" as essential for both social reform and personal development. As he notes, "the appeal of Emerson's career has thus centered around his leaving the ministry, because that gesture affirms the rejection of authority that not only was a central part of his message, but is in many ways our national mythos. That this view of Emerson's career must be qualified we can conclude from the continuities of both form— sermon to lecture to essay—and content—the pursuit of self-culture—that his journals and lectures reveal" (p. 184). Robinson also presents a very detailed and informed discussion of the relationship of the idea of "self-culture" to reform, and the transcendental movement in particular, in "The Political Odyssey of William Henry Channing," *American Quarterly* 34, no. 2 (Summer 1982), pp. 165–84.

In his work *William Ellery Channing: An Intellectual Portrait* (Boston: Beacon Press, 1955) David P. Edgell sees Channing and Emerson as nearly identical in their views on reform, and he criticizes both accordingly. "Underneath the superficial differences between Channing and Emerson in their responses to specific issues lay a fundamental unity. This common foundation made them relatively immune to reform, as the word is usually interpreted. Emerson could talk complacently of the poor, and Channing think that the hardest portion of slavery was the moral degradation. Both of them, speaking from their Olympian detachment and from the coldness of their own natures, did not thoroughly sympathize with the intensely practical problems of those who were literally hungry or whose bodies were so prostrated with mistreatment that they could not think of being men" (p. 135). While Edgell is generally accurate in identifying the early similarities between Emerson and Channing, he fails to take into account the remarkable evolution of Emerson's views on social reform generally, and abolitionism in particular. Emerson's 1844 "Emancipation in the British West Indies" speech was a great step forward for him and represented a significant break with Channing's philosophy. Interestingly enough, even Edgell notes that "the addresses given by Channing and Emerson on the anniversaries of emancipation in the West Indies possess surprisingly little in common" (p. 133).

21. Douglas C. Stange, "From Treason to Antislavery Patriotism: Unitarian Conservatives and the Fugitive Slave Law," *Harvard Library Bulletin* 25 (October 1977), p. 476.

An interesting insight into abolition vulgarity is provided by the following letter from Martha Coffin Wright to her sister, Lucretia Mott, dated 6 February 1852. The discussion concerns Abby Foster (1810–87), a well-known and spirited abolitionist who had recently given a lecture in the Universalist church in

Auburn, New York, which was considered to be highly offensive by the church fathers. The letter states in part:

> After what Mrs. Foster said they would not open it [the Universalist church] nor should she ever speak in the basement again, for there were things that she said, not fit to be said anywhere—even he, could not look on the audience without blushing. The church would have been opened for Miss Holly or Mr May or any decent speaker on AntiSlavery, just as readily as it was for Mr Parker. I did not attempt to defend the coarseness which is as revolting to my taste as to his, but told him as there were all sorts of minds to influence, there must be different instrumentality. I told him what I said to Mrs. F. The substance of it was, that while I didn't care how severely she rebuked the pious indifference of our people, I thought less swearing at them would be better, that it was not well for children to listen to such words. I thought Mr May's kindly manner would have more influence. She defended herself very ably, insisting that people would listen with pleasure to gentle words and go and forget them, but these very things that I complained of, were the ones that remained, made a deep impression, made the hearers very angry it was true, and were therefore remembered, and she must say that where S. J. May and Lucretia Mott had made one convert, she and her husband had made ten.

Interestingly enough, Emerson was also lecturing in Auburn at the time, and he arranged to visit Mrs. Wright, who apparently was less than impressed. She notes in the same letter in speaking of Emerson, "He spoke of visiting Mrs G. and seemed to know that she was one of us. I was not so much attracted towards him as toward Theodore Parker.—Didn't feel that peculiar reverence and admiration for him but listened nevertheless with great interest to one so renowned" (MS, Sophia Smith Collection, Smith College).

22. Edmund Quincy to Caroline Weston, 9 February 1841, MS, Boston Public Library. Edmund Quincy (1808–77) was a Harvard graduate and the second son of Josiah Quincy, former president of Harvard. He joined the Massachusetts Anti-slavery Society in 1837, shocking his aristocratic peers, and eventually became vice president of the American Anti-slavery Society and was associated with several prominent antislavery publications.

23. MS, Boston Public Library, 10 February 1840.

24. Draft article on Emerson, 1844, MS, Boston Public Library.

25. For comments on specific works see chap. 10 of this volume.

26. *Strange Cults and Utopias of 19th-Century America* (1870; reprint, New York: Dover Publications, 1966), p. 104.

27. *Brook Farm* (1899; reprint, Secaucus, N.J.: Citadel Press, 1973), p. 122.

28. G. Curtis to Almira Barlow, 25 November 1853, MS, Houghton Library, Harvard University.

29. *The Early Lectures of Ralph Waldo Emerson*, vol. 2, ed. Stephen Whicher et al. (Cambridge: Harvard University Press, 1964), p. 299.

30. MS, Houghton Library, Harvard University, 16 March 1838.

31. In a letter in February 1835 Emerson told Lidian, "I am born a poet, of a low class without doubt yet a poet. That is my nature & vocation. My singing be sure is very 'husky,' & is for the most part in prose. Still I am a poet in the sense of a perceiver & dear lover of the harmonies that are in the soul & in matter, & specially of the correspondences between these & those" (*L* 1:435).

32. *New England Quarterly* 12 (March 1939), pp. 52–57.

33. David Robinson, in *Apostle of Culture*, indicates the importance of Emerson's concept of "self-culture" in his early career. The application of this concept to Emerson's antislavery crusade is manifest throughout the present study.

34. The *Concord Freeman* reported this meeting on 28 April 1838. The *Yeoman's Gazette* had been reporting extensively on "The Plunder of the Cherokees" on 21 and 28 April 1838, and in the latter edition included a report on the meeting in Concord at which Emerson spoke.

35. Eleanor Tilton, "Emerson's Lecture Schedules—1837–1838—Revised," *Harvard Library Bulletin* 21 (1973), p. 390.

36. Gay Wilson Allen, *Waldo Emerson: A Biography* (New York: Viking Press, 1981), p. 321.

37. MS, Boston Public Library, 30 August 1838.

38. MS, Boston Public Library, 25 January 1839.

39. Harriet Martineau, *Retrospect of Western Travel*, 3 vols. (London: Saunders and Otley, 1838), 3:229.

40. Joel Myerson, "Convers Francis and Emerson," *American Literature* 50 (1978), p. 28.

41. Robert Burkholder, "Emerson, Kneeland, and the Divinity School Address," *American Literature* 58 (1986), pp. 1–14.

42. Ibid., p. 12.

43. George Willis Cooke, *Ralph Waldo Emerson: His Life, Writings, and Philosophy* (Boston: James R. Osgood, 1881), p. 28.

44. Quoted by Howe in *Unitarian Conscience*, pp. 275–76.

45. Henry Steele Commager, *Theodore Parker: Yankee Crusader* (Boston: Beacon Press, 1947), pp. 12, 107.

46. Joel Myerson, *The New England Transcendentalists and the Dial* (Madison, N.J.: Fairleigh Dickinson University Press, 1980), p. 28.

47. MS, Boston Public Library, 10 February 1840.

48. Perry Miller, *The Transcendentalists* (Cambridge: Harvard University Press, 1950), p. 124.

49. MS, Houghton Library, Harvard University, 29 November 1853.

50. Gibbons to Caroline Weston, 14 August 1842, MS, Boston Public Library.

51. MS, Boston Public Library, 9 October 1843. For more on abolition and Unitarians see Stange, *Patterns of Antislavery*.

52. See *JMN* 7:200, 204, 219; *JMN* 8:8, 120; *JMN* 9:120, 247, 392, 427.

53. Gerald Sorin notes, "The great limiting factor for abolitionist growth was racism—a racism that knew no sectional or ideological boundaries. A belief in the inferiority of the black pervaded the consciousness of white America; abolitionists themselves did not escape it entirely." See *Abolitionism: A New Perspective* (New York: Praeger, 1972), p. 37.

54. In a letter to her sister Lidian states, "We did not hear Mr. Garrison when he was in Concord or rather I did not—Mr. E heard a few words from him at an anti-slavery meeting. He gave no Lecture." Letter to Lucy Jackson Brown, 14 May 1839, Houghton Library, Harvard University. See also *L* 3:195; *JMN* 5:32.

55. Emerson notes in a letter to Samuel Ward mailed from Philadelphia, "I have seen Lucretia Mott who is a noble woman" (26 January 1843, MS, Houghton Library, Harvard University). For Phillips see *JMN* 9:136–37; and *Letters from Ralph Waldo Emerson to a Friend*, ed. Charles Eliot Norton (1899; reprint, Port Washington, N.Y.: Kennikat Press, 1971), p. 60. Phillips occasionally visited Emerson's home, as early as 1838. On at least one occasion he was accompanied by Dr. Channing and "made a long call" (*LL* 76).

56. Mary Merrick Brooks indicates in a letter to Wendell Phillips in 1844 that an abolition "convention and tea-party" would be held in Concord and that while "Emerson will not be here, being absent lecturing in Pennsylvania," he did write "a note from New York which will be good to be read at our party" (31 March 1844 [?], MS, Houghton Library, Harvard University).

57. Walter Harding, *The Days of Henry Thoreau: A Biography* (New York: Alfred A. Knopf, 1965), p. 176.

58. M. M. Brooks to W. Phillips, 4 November 1843, MS, Houghton Library, Harvard University.

59. Allen, *Waldo Emerson*, p. 424.

60. *Dial* 4 (1843), p. 134.

61. Dillon, *Abolitionists*, p. 149.

62. Channing, *Works*, 6:380.

63. Undoubtedly one of the reasons that so many critics over the years have drawn inaccurate conclusions about Emerson's philosophy of reform is that they tend to consult almost exclusively these early essays and addresses, which were all written while Emerson was still under the influence of Channing and, more important, before his conversion to overt abolitionism in 1844.

64. Arthur C. McGiffert, Jr., ed., *Young Emerson Speaks: Unpublished Discourses on Many Subjects* (Port Washington, N.Y.: Kennikat Press, 1938), p. 5.

65. Ibid., p. 198.

66. Robert E. Spiller and Wallace E. Williams, eds., *The Early Lectures of Ralph Waldo Emerson*, vol. 3 (Cambridge: Belknap Press, 1972), p. 109.

67. Ibid., pp. 114–15. The "tender American girl" here is Emerson's wife Lidian; see *JMN* 5:382. Emerson would later form a more realistic opinion on the terrors of the middle passage. See *JMN* 5:440.

68. Emerson, *Early Lectures*, 3:371.

69. Joseph Slater, "Two Sources for Emerson's First Address on West Indian Emancipation," *ESQ* 44 (1966), pp. 97–100.

70. Ibid., p. 97.

71. Ibid., p. 99.

72. Harding, *Days of Henry Thoreau*, pp. 174–75.

73. This passage is interesting in two respects. First, it demonstrates clearly that, despite several scholarly assertions to the contrary, Emerson understood quite well man's inherent capacity for evil. Second, Emerson's journal comments at the time indicate that it was he himself who once thought that "the planter does not want slaves; give him a machine that will provide him with as much money as the slaves yield, & he will thankfully let them go" (*JMN* 9:127). The statement was recorded before his research for this address and suggests again the significance of the influence of that research upon him.

74. Emerson might have read about Touissant as early as 1836 in a lengthy biographical article in the *Concord Freeman* (11 June), which begins with the statement that "the friends of liberty are continually told that the Africans are an *inferior race*. If this were true, it would be no reason for enslaving them. But it is not. The world may safely be challenged to produce a nobler character than that of Touissant L'Overture—the George Washington of St. Domingo." Additionally, as noted in chapter 2, Charles Emerson had mentioned Touissant in his antislavery address in 1835.

75. As is clear from the discussion of this speech in chapter 4, which includes excerpts from Emerson's correspondence with Ellis Gray Loring, much was added to the presentation before its printing. However, the detailed outline of the speech, which appeared initially in the *New York Tribune* and was reprinted in the *Liberator* on 16 August, as well as the report of the presentation from a correspondent in Concord published in the *Liberator* on 23 August, make it clear that the information Emerson added was largely factual in nature and concerned the four points he raised in his letter to Loring.

76. MS, 4 August 1844, Archives of the Paulist Fathers, New York City.

Chapter 4. Confusion and Commitment

1. Emerson learned of such pre-Darwinian evolutionary theories earlier from Lyell's *Principles of Geology*, 2 vols. (London: 1830–32), which he withdrew

from the Boston Athenaeum in 1836 and later purchased (see *JMN* 5:83; Walter Harding, *Emerson's Library* [Charlottesville: University Press of Virginia, 1967], p. 177). Such ideas were undoubtedly reinforced by his reading in the mid-1840s of Robert Chambers's *Vestiges of the Natural History of Creation* (New York: Wiley and Putman, 1845), which speaks at length of the progressive development of races and, according to Emerson, contributed the phrase "arrested development" to the language (see *JMN* 9:211, 233; Harding, *Emerson's Library*, p. 54). Also, Edward Emerson points out that "Mr. Emerson had read Lyell and heard of Lamarck's teaching through him and others" (*W* 5:335). During his second trip to England (1847–48) Emerson had the opportunity to meet and hear Charles Lyell and other scientists. On one occasion he attended a meeting of the Geological Society of London, where he heard what he considered to be the best debate of his entire trip (see Ralph Rusk, *The Life of Ralph Waldo Emerson* [New York: Charles Scribner's Sons, 1949], p. 345).

Another influence on Emerson's thought regarding the idea of evolutionary development came with his reading of Andrew Jackson Downing's *The Fruits and Fruit Trees of America* (New York: Wiley and Putnam, 1846). Edward Emerson felt that this work, and especially an "account of the theory and successful experiments in the amelioration of fruits, by Dr. Van Mons, professor at Louvain in the Netherlands" contained in it, was a significant influence on Emerson, and that "all through Mr. Emerson's work crop out allusions to this hopeful theory of Amelioration, to him symbolic" (*W* 5:336). Edward goes on to provide a brief synopsis of Van Mons's theory, which, because it will be helpful to an understanding of Emerson's thought regarding social reform throughout the 1840s, deserves to be quoted in its entirety.

This theory, full of parables, might be thus stated in very condensed form:—

The aim of nature in the wild fruit-tree is only to produce a vigorous tree, and perfect seeds for continuing the species. The object of culture is to subdue excess of vegetation, lessen coarseness of tree, reduce size of seeds, and increase the pulp of the fruit.

There is always a tendency of improved fruits to return by seeds to the wild state, especially seeds borne by old fruit-trees, yet they never quite return.

But the seeds of a young tree of a good sort, being itself in a state of amelioration, have the least tendency to retrograde, and are most likely to produce improved sorts.

There is a limit to perfection in fruits. When this is reached, the next generation will more probably produce bad fruit than if raised from seeds of an indifferent sort in the course of amelioration. Seeds of the oldest food fruits usually produce inferior sorts; those from *recent varieties* of bad fruit, if reproduced uninterruptedly under good conditions for several generations, will certainly yield good fruit.

Edward concludes his discussion of this idea with the statement that Van Mons's teachings and works "should be credited a share in strengthening Mr. Emerson's faith in Compensation and in Ascension" (W 5:336–37).

Emerson's journals in the mid to late 1840s contain several references to Van Mons, and in his last antislavery speech of the decade Emerson refers to the end of the slave system as an inevitable result of social progress, "like the amelioration in the pear-tree, or apple-tree, so well known to botanists" (see *JMN* 10:85, 98, 103, 156). For further discussion of this topic see Joseph Warren Beech, "Emerson and Evolution," *University of Toronto Quarterly* 3 (July 1934), pp. 474–97.

2. *Liberator*, 16, 17 August 1844; Joel Myerson, *Ralph Waldo Emerson: A Descriptive Bibliography* (Pittsburgh: University of Pittsburgh Press, 1982), pp. 106, 144–49; W. J. Potter, "Emerson and the Abolitionists," *Index*, 3 December 1885.

3. M. M. Emerson to R. W. Emerson, 1 August 1844, MS, Houghton Library, Harvard University. See also George Tolman, *Mary Moody Emerson* (Cambridge: n.p., 1929), pp. 27–28.

4. M. M. Brooks to R. W. Emerson, 17 October 1844, MS, Houghton Library, Harvard University.

5. J. G. Whittier to R. W. Emerson, 12 September 1844. *The Letters of John Greenleaf Whittier*, 3 vols., ed. John B. Pickard (Cambridge: Harvard University Press, 1975), 1:648. Emerson declined Whittier's request, indicating that he was pressed for time as a result of the preparation of the proof sheets for the London edition of the second series of *Essays*. However, after pointing out that he had not "the sort of skill that is useful in meetings for debate," and consequently "should be likely to waste other people's time" or his own, Emerson goes on to state, "I delight to know that such meetings are holden; & the spirit which they indicate, & which, I doubt not, they spread, saves & dignifies the ground we tread on." He adds, "Since you are disposed to give so friendly a hearing to opinions of mine, I am almost ready to promise you as soon as I am free of this present coil of writing, my thought on the best way of befriending the slave & ending slavery. We will see" (L 3:260–61). The records show several letters over the next thirty years between Emerson and Whittier indicating the friendship that developed between the two.

6. Maria Weston Chapman, MS, draft article on Emerson, 1844, MS, Boston Public Library.

7. 22 August 1844, MS, Houghton Library, Harvard University. For information on the Somerset case see Albert Bushnell Hart, *Slavery and Abolition: 1831–1841* (New York: Harper and Brothers, 1906), p. 52.

8. Dated Monday night, 26 August, no year, MS, New York Public Library, Astor, Lenox, and Tilden Foundations, Rare Books and Manuscripts Division, Lee Kohms Collection. The internal evidence clearly indicates that the year is 1844. Additionally, 26 August was a Monday that year.

9. Reprinted in Whittier's *Letters*, 1:649. A similar feeling of abolitionist frustration prior to Emerson's August 1844 address is expressed by Lydia Maria Child in a letter to Ellis Gray Loring dated 21 February 1843.

Last Sunday Emerson and J. R. Lowell, and Page were here. Emerson has been very cordial and hearty—gave me tickets for the course, and sent word he wanted to come and see me. I should never have thought of asking him, if he had'nt proposed it himself; for I supposed he would consider it a bore. John and I go to the lectures and find them refreshing as a glass of soda-water; but, as usual, not *satisfactory*. He gave, in one of the lectures, such a glowing and graceful picture of Southern manners and character, that I might have supposed he considered arbitrary power one of the most beneficial influences on man. I should not have quarrelled with this, had he made the least allusion to any *bad* effects. Speaking of the deficiencies between our professions and our practice, as a people, he did not *allude* to slavery. I cannot think that this is manly and true; for the subject *must* occur to him. However, the lectures are a prodigious treat to me, though they are evidently adapted more to the *popular* taste than those he delivered in Cambridge and Boston.

Patricia G. Holland and Milton Meltzer, eds., *The Collected Correspondence of Lydia Maria Child, 1817–1880, Microfiche Edition* (Millwood, N.Y.: Kraus Microfilm, 1980).

10. Emerson notes in his journal, "Now when at any time I take part in a public debate, I wish on my return home to be shampooed & in all other ways aired & purified" (*JMN* 9:71).

11. In preparing his 1 August address, Emerson utilized, and apparently was quite familiar with, Thomas Clarkson's *The History of the Rise, Progress, and Accomplishment of the Abolition of the African Slave Trade by the British Parliament* (1808), and a lesser-known work, *Emancipation in the West Indies: A Six Months' Tour in Antigua, Barbadoes, and Jamaica in the Year 1837*, by James Thome and J. Horace Kimball. Emerson also subscribed to the abolitionist publication *Herald of Freedom* in 1844, and he owned *A Collection from the Newspaper Writings of Nathaniel Peabody Rogers* (Concord, N.H., 1847) written by the one-time editor of the *Herald* (see *JMN* 9:28). The *Liberator* and the *National Anti-slavery Standard* were household reading at the Emersons', which is, no

doubt, a reflection of Lidian's interests as well as Ralph Waldo's. Additionally, a manuscript note by Wendell Phillips in 1847 refers to Thomas Madiou's *Histoire d'Haiti, 1492–1803*, 2 vols. (Port au Prince, 1847) and contains the parenthetical statement, "R. W. Emerson has copy" (MS, Boston Public Library). Emerson also read Arthur Helps, *The Conquerors of the New World and Their Bondmen*, 2 vols. (London: 1848) and would use information from this work in his 1849 emancipation address (see *JMN* 11:77).

12. R. W. Emerson to W. E. Channing, 17 December 1844. No MS found. Text from the *New York Daily Tribune*, 20 December 1844, p. 2. Listed in *L* 3:271. There are echoes of this letter also in Franklin Sanborn, *The Personality of Emerson* (Boston: Charles Goodspeed, 1903), pp. 125–26. As late as 1856 Emerson was moved to speak at length about this incident in his memorial address "Samuel Hoar" (*W* 10:437ff.).

In a letter to Emerson dated 22 December 1844 (MS, Houghton Library, Harvard University), his brother William states, "We are glad of the information you gave us about the departure of Mr Hoar from Charlestown. I thought Greeley's judgement too hasty, & told him so. I chanced to see him again on Friday, the same day on which a letter I suppose to be yours appeared in the Tribune." William notes that Greeley continued to maintain "the old absurdity that Mr. Hoar should have remained until he was expelled by actual physical force." He closes with an expression of his "deep sorrow for this heinous violation of the manifest rights of the free states," and rejoices that Hoar and his daughter are now "both safe in the old Bay State." Emerson had written to William on 17 December that "Mr. Hoar has returned home & gave me this morning a narrative of his visit to Charlestown, which showed him to me in the most honorable light. He seems to have behaved with the utmost firmness & only came away when it would have been the part of a mule not of a man to remain" (*L* 3:272).

13. From this point forward South Carolina would remain for Emerson "a symbol of the exotic decadence which he associated with the whole South." See Linda Prior, "Ralph Waldo Emerson and South Carolina," *South Carolina Historical Magazine* (1978), 79 (4), p. 257.

14. *L* 3:275; Rusk, *Life of Emerson*, p. 306; James Elliot Cabot, *A Memoir of Ralph Waldo Emerson*, 2 vols. (Boston: Houghton Mifflin, 1887), 2:575.

15. A. W. Weston notes in a letter to the "Misses Weston" that Samuel May "represents Emerson as much stirred up by the Hoar matter" (23 January 1845, MS, Boston Public Library).

16. Quoted by Francis B. Dedmond, "George William Curtis to Christopher Pearse Cranch: Three Unpublished Letters from Concord," *Concord Saunterer* 12, no. 4 (1977), p. 6.

17. Walter Harding, *The Days of Henry Thoreau* (New York: Alfred A. Knopf,

1965), p. 176; *The Writings of Henry David Thoreau, Reform Papers,* ed. Wendell Glick (Princeton: Princeton University Press, 1973), pp. 59–62.

18. *L* 3:279; Charles Eliot Norton, ed., *Letters from Ralph Waldo Emerson to a Friend: 1838–1853* (1899; reprint, Port Washington, N.Y.: Kennikat Press, 1971), p. 60.

19. Thoreau, *Reform Papers,* p. 56. For further discussion of the popularity of the *Herald of Freedom* in Concord and the Rogers controversy see Wendell Glick, "Thoreau and the 'Herald of Freedom,'" *New England Quarterly* 22 (1949), pp. 193–204. For a discussion of Thoreau's abolitionism at this time see Glick's *Thoreau and Radical Abolitionism: A Study of the Native Background of Thoreau's Social Philosophy* (Ph.D. diss., Northwestern University, 1950).

20. For a transcription of this speech and an excellent discussion of the circumstances of its delivery see Louis Ruchames, "Emerson's Second West India Emancipation Address," *New England Quarterly* 28 (September 1955), pp. 383–88. For fragments of the speech in Emerson's journals see *JMN* 9:100, 123, 195.

21. R. W. Emerson to Robert Adams, 1 November 1845, MS, Ralph Waldo Emerson Collection, Clifton Waller Barrett Library, University of Virginia. I am indebted to Prof. Eleanor Tilton for this information.

22. Cabot, *Memoir of Emerson,* 2:576–77.

23. Whittier, *Letters,* 1:663–64.

24. Oliver Wendell Holmes, *Ralph Waldo Emerson* (Boston: Houghton Mifflin, 1884), p. 67.

25. Cabot, *Memoir of Emerson,* 1:215.

26. Carl Bode, *The American Lyceum* (Carbondale: Southern Illinois University Press, 1956), p. 21.

27. *Liberator,* 28 November 1845, p. 2.

28. Harding, *Days of Henry Thoreau,* p. 343.

29. *Liberator,* 16 January 1846.

30. Benjamin Rodman to R. W. Emerson, n.d., MS, Houghton Library, Harvard University.

31. Caroline Weston to Wendell Phillips, 2 November 1845, MS, Houghton Library, Harvard University.

32. M. M. Brooks to C. Weston, 19 November 1845, MS, Boston Public Library.

33. *Liberator,* 16 January 1846.

34. M. M. Brooks to C. Weston, 24 November 1845, MS, Boston Public Library.

35. M. M. Brooks to R. W. Emerson, 29 December 1845, MS, Houghton Library, Harvard University.

36. Daniel Ricketson to R. W. Emerson, 29 December 1845, MS, Houghton Library, Harvard University. The development of events in New Bedford was followed closely by the *Liberator.* A complete account of the rejection of David

Ruggles, "a colored man," for membership at the October meeting of the Lyceum is described, along with a statement of "The Protest" (including a list of its signers) in the 28 November 1845 issue. Following this, on 5 December another article appeared that emphasizes the prejudicial nature of the lyceum's membership policy and describes "the generous and noble refusal of Messrs. Ralph Waldo Emerson and Charles Sumner, Esq. to lecture before the Lyceum." The article states that "the slave, whose distant chain in the Carolinas is fastened to this single link of prejudice against color . . . will bless them for it." Yet another account, signed by "D. R." (undoubtedly Ricketson) appeared in the 19 December issue. This article noted the reluctance of the officers of the lyceum to read "the letters received by the committee on lectures, from Messrs. Ralph Waldo Emerson and Charles Sumner, declining to lecture before the Lyceum, on account of the exclusion of persons of color." And it ends with a bitter commentary on the "pro slavery sentiments of the group," indicating further the depth of the divisiveness the incident caused.

37. In addition to the *Liberator*'s account, the *New York Daily Tribune* ran a front-page item on 9 December 1845, which indicted the "illiberal prejudice against people of color" recently evinced by the citizens of New Bedford. The short article describes the efforts at exclusion made by the lyceum and then states, "We rejoice to hear that, in consequence of these measures, R. W. Emerson and Charles Sumner, who were engaged as lecturers, have declined addressing an audience whose test of merit, or right to the privileges of a citizen consists not in intelligence or good character, but the color of the skin."

38. Benjamin Rodman to R. W. Emerson, 25 October 1846, MS, Houghton Library, Harvard University.

39. William Charvat, *Emerson's American Lecture Engagements: A Chronological List* (New York: New York Public Library, 1961), pp. 21–22. These lectures and others were later shaped into the work *Representative Men* (1850).

40. John L. Thomas, *The Liberator: William Lloyd Garrison* (Boston: Little, Brown, 1963), p. 328.

41. M. M. Brooks to M. W. Chapman, 23 February 1846, MS, Boston Public Library.

42. M. M. Brooks to Lidian Emerson, February 1846, MS, Houghton Library, Harvard University.

43. M. M. Brooks to R. W. Emerson, February 1846, MS, Houghton Library, Harvard University.

44. While Emerson's concern about the negativity of "no Union with slaveholders" may have prevented him from signing Mrs. Brooks's petition in this instance, Emerson did sign his name to several other petitions during the 1830s and 1840s. Among these are: a petition sent to the U.S. House of Representa-

tives and the Senate in October 1837 to protest the annexation of Texas; two petitions to the Massachusetts legislature in 1840, the first protesting the admission of Florida to the Union as a slave state, the second protesting the imposition of the "gag rule" on antislavery petitions in the U.S. House. Another was sent in February 1844 to the Massachusetts legislature in support of its resolve against the admission of Texas into the Union. In this latter case the name of R. Waldo Emerson headed a list of 263 citizens of Concord. (I am indebted to Prof. Robert Gross for this information.) Interestingly, in 1834 Emerson expressed in his journal his aversion to signing a temperance petition because he felt that such collective action might "deprive my example of all its value by abdicating my freedom on that point" (*JMN* 4:354). Obviously, the significant political developments that occurred later in the 1830s and 1840s would bring about a substantial change in this and other aspects of his thinking on social reform issues.

45. Henry I. Bowditch, "Did Mr. Emerson Sympathize with the Abolitionists?" *Index*, 19 November 1885, p. 248.

46. *Liberator*, 5 June 1846.

47. MS, Berg Collection, New York Public Library.

48. Louis Ruchames, "Two Forgotten Addresses by Ralph Waldo Emerson," *American Literature* 28 (January 1957), pp. 425–33.

49. Harding, *Days of Henry Thoreau*, pp. 174–75.

50. Ibid., p. 201.

51. Emerson expressed basically this same idea in a letter Cabot reproduces in *Memoir of Emerson* (pp. 453–54) and dates conjecturally "about 1840." Also, Emerson had expressed a similar commitment to a belief in the basic goodness of man as the substratum of social reform in his address "New England Reformers," which was delivered in March 1844. "Nothing shall warp me from the belief that every man is a lover of truth. There is no pure lie, no pure malignity in nature. The entertainment of the proposition of depravity is the last profligacy and profanation. There is no scepticism, no atheism, but that. Could it be received into common belief, suicide would unpeople the planet" (*W* 3:278). Last, it should be noted that in the earlier "standard" edition of Emerson's *Journals* (1909–14) Edward Emerson changed the original "*this* prison" to "*the* prison," thus suggesting to later scholars that Emerson meant literally that going to prison is a suicide, rather than a metaphorical prison suggested by the moral exclusiveness and rigidity of the reformer who sees most of mankind as depraved and irredeemable. *The Journals of Ralph Waldo Emerson*, ed. Edward Emerson and Waldo Emerson Forbes, 10 vols. (Boston: Houghton Mifflin, 1909–14), 7:223.

52. Odell Shepard, ed., *The Journals of Bronson Alcott* (Boston: Little, Brown, 1938), p. 183.

53. Quoted in Bill Ledbetter, "Charles Sumner: Political Activist for the New England Transcendentalists," *Historian* 44, no. 3 (May 1982), p. 351.

54. *Address of the Committee Appointed by a Public Meeting Held at Faneuil Hall, September 24, 1846 for the Purpose of Considering the Recent Case of Kidnapping from Our Soil, and of Taking Measures to Prevent the Recurrence of Similar Outrages* (Boston: White and Potter, 1846). Quoted in Francis B. Dedmond, "A Fugitive Emerson Letter," *American Transcendental Quarterly* 41 (Winter 1979), pp. 13–15.

55. Ibid., p. 14.

56. Henry Steele Commager, *Theodore Parker: Yankee Crusader* (Boston: Beacon Press, 1960), p. 218.

57. Ibid., p. 133. In the Editor's Address to the first issue of the *Review* Emerson noted that "a journal that would meet the real wants of this time must have a courage and power sufficient to solve the problems which the great groping society around us, stupid with perplexity, is dumbly exploring." Among these he included "slavery, in some sort the special enigma of the time" (*W* 11:390–91).

58. S. G. Howe to R. W. Emerson (circular letter), 14 September 1846, MS, Houghton Library, Harvard University.

59. This letter by Emerson is reproduced in several places, including Dedmond, "Fugitive Letter"; *The Life and Correspondence of Henry Ingersoll Bowditch*, 2 vols. (Boston: Houghton Mifflin, 1902), 1:182–83; *The Uncollected Writings of Ralph Waldo Emerson* (1912; reprint Port Washington, N.Y.: Kennikat Press, 1971), pp. 206–7; and, of course, the original committee report.

60. See *Representative Men* (1850); *W* 4:4ff.

61. R. W. Emerson to Mr. John Heraud, 31[?] January 1847, MS, Houghton Library, Harvard University. This draft differs from the letter as actually sent (*L* 3:369–70); the final copy omits the reference to abolition. (I am indebted to Prof. Eleanor Tilton for this material and documentation.)

62. Emerson expressed some of these same ideas in a letter to S. G. Ward, 25 March 1847. See *L* 3:386–87.

63. Emerson would find ample support for this concern in his reading of Chambers's *Vestiges of the Natural History of Creation*, where the author states in the context of a discussion of "arrested development" that while other races are obviously inferior to the Caucasian, this is not caused by inherent deficiency but instead is "simply the result of so many advances and retrogressions in the developing power of the human mothers, these advances and retrogressions being, as we have formally seen, the inevitable effect of external conditions in nutrition, hardship, etc." (p. 309). Emerson said of this book in 1845 that "everything in this Vestiges of Creation is good except the theology, which is civil, timid, & dull" (*JMN* 9:211). In his Editor's Address to the first issue of the *Massachusetts Quarterly Review* Emerson referred to "the author of the Vestiges

of Creation" as one of the "great interpreters" of natural science (W 11:391). Also, in his 1844 emancipation address Emerson had noted when speaking of the wretched condition of the slaves that "the prizes of society, the trumpet of fame, the privileges of learning, of culture, of religion, the decencies and joys of marriage, honor, obedience, personal authority and a perpetual melioration into a finer civility,—these were for all, but not for them." However, with the removal of the arbitrary barrier of slavery, "it now appears that the negro race is, more than any other, susceptible of rapid civilization" (W 11:102, 141). Phillip Nicoloff contends that this statement indicates Emerson's belief in the ultimate extinction of blacks. *Emerson on Race and History* (New York: Columbia University Press, 1961), p. 126.

64. Myerson, *Emerson Bibliography*, p. 210; Charvat, *Lecture Engagements*, pp. 23–24.

65. Quoted in Rusk, *Life of Emerson*, p. 360.

66. In his letter Garrison points out that Theodore Parker had also been asked to speak on 3 August and adds, "Like him, you exercise a strong influence over many minds in this country, which are not yet sufficiently committed to the side of the slave; like him you are not afraid publicly and pointedly to testify against the enslavement of three millions of our countrymen." Walter Merrill, ed., *The Letters of William Lloyd Garrison*, vol. 3 (Cambridge: Harvard University Press, 1973), p. 640.

67. See Louis Ruchames, "Two Forgotten Addresses by Ralph Waldo Emerson," *American Literature* 28 (1956), pp. 425–33.

68. For echoes of this presentation in the journals see *JMN* 11:15, 77, 161.

Chapter 5. Counterattack

1. Ellen Tucker Emerson, *The Life of Lidian Jackson Emerson*, ed. Delores Bird Carpenter (Boston: Twayne Publishers, 1980), p. 115.

2. John L. Thomas, *The Liberator: William Lloyd Garrison* (Boston: Little, Brown, 1963), p. 362.

3. John Jay Chapman, *William Lloyd Garrison* (New York: Moffat, Yard, 1913), p. 200.

4. *The Letters of William Lloyd Garrison*, vol. 4., ed. Walter Merrill and Louis Ruchames (Cambridge: Belknap Press of Harvard University Press, 1979), p. 7.

5. *Nation*, 6 February 1896, pp. 114–15.

6. Merton Dillon, *The Abolitionists: The Growth of a Dissenting Minority* (New York: W. W. Norton, 1974), p. 176.

7. Quoted by Thomas Blanding, in "Thoreau's Local Lectures in 1849 and 1850," *Concord Saunterer* 13, no. 3 (1984), p. 21.

8. Dillon, *Abolitionists*, p. 179.

9. Henry Steele Commager, *Theodore Parker* (Boston: Beacon Press, 1947), p. 214.

10. Ibid.

11. Ralph Rusk, *The Life of Ralph Waldo Emerson* (New York: Charles Scribner's Sons, 1949), p. 366.

12. MS, Houghton Library, Harvard University, 29 September 1850.

13. Peter M. Bergman, *The Chronological History of the Negro in America* (New York: Harper and Row, 1969), p. 197.

14. *Der Diwan von Mohammed Schemseddin Hafis* (Stuttgart and Tubingen, 1812–13); and *Geschichte der Schonen Redekunste Persiens mit einer Bluthenlese aus zweihundert persischen Dictern* (Vienna, 1818).

15. Frederic Carpenter, *Emerson and Asia* (Cambridge: Harvard University Press, 1930), p. 171.

16. See Carpenter, *Emerson and Asia*, p. 193; Arthur Cristy, *The Orient in American Transcendentalism* (1932; reprint, New York: Octagon Books, 1963), p. 123.

17. In his preface to the *Gulistan* Emerson describes Saadi in terms that suggest many of his own values as an artist.

> Saadi, though he has not the Lyric flights of Hafiz, has wit, practical sense, and just moral sentiments. . . . He is the poet of friendship, love, self-devotion, and serenity. There is a uniform force in his page, and, conspicuously, a tone of cheerfulness, which has almost made his name a synonym for this grace. The word *Saadi* means *fortunate*. In him the trait is no result of levity, much less of convivial habit, but first of a happy nature, to which victory is habitual, easily shedding mishaps, with sensibility to pleasure, and with resources against pain. But it also results from the habitual perception of the beneficent laws that control the world. He inspires in the reader a good hope.

The Gulistan or Rose Garden, Preface by R. W. Emerson (Boston: Ticknor and Fields, 1865), pp. vii–viii.

18. Emerson lectured on Plato and other "Representative Men" several times in 1845 and 1846. See William Charvat, *Emerson's American Lecture Engagements: A Chronological List* (New York: New York Public Library, 1961), pp. 21–22.

19. Published in *The Genius and Character of Emerson: Lectures at the Concord School of Philosophy*, ed. F. B. Sanborn (Boston: James R. Osgood, 1884), p. 373.

20. *The Liberty Bell*, by Friends of Freedom (Boston: National Anti-slavery

Bazaar, 1851 [issued in 1850]). Though never reprinted by Emerson, the poems, transcribed with some errors, appeared in 1912 in *Uncollected Writings: Essays, Addresses, Poems, Reviews and Letters*, by Ralph Waldo Emerson, ed. Charles Bigelow (reprint, Port Washington, N.Y.: Kennikat Press, 1971). Fragments of the poems were used by Emerson in his essay "Persian Poetry," which appeared in the *Atlantic Monthly Magazine* 11 (April 1858), pp. 724–34. This essay was later included in *Letters and Social Aims* (Boston: James R. Osgood, 1876), which now appears as vol. 4 in *The Complete Works of Ralph Waldo Emerson* (Boston: Houghton Mifflin, 1904). James D. Yohannan published two informative articles on Emerson and Persian poetry, "Emerson's Translations of Persian Poetry from German Sources," *American Literature* 14 (1943), pp. 407–20; and "The Influence of Persian Poetry upon Emerson's Work," *American Literature* 15 (1943), pp. 25–41. However, neither of these deals specifically with the *Liberty Bell* submissions.

The *Liberty Bell* has been described as the "chief of American antislavery gift books." It was published irregularly in Boston from 1839 to 1857. The leading force behind the *Liberty Bell* was Maria Weston Chapman and her two sisters Anne Warren Weston and Caroline Weston, who were all very active in Boston antislavery circles. Regarding the content of the annual, one commentator notes that "all kinds of writing were desirable, so long as the point was right. *The Liberty Bell* to Mrs. Chapman's mind was not so much a repository of excellent pieces of prose and verse as a yearly testimonial to Abolitionist principles. . . . The contents of the books themselves show that persuasiveness rather than literary quality was the editorial determinant." Ralph Thompson, *American Literary Annuals & Gift Books: 1825–1865* (New York: H. W. Wilson, 1936), pp. 82, 86. Other contributors to the 1851 issue included Harriet Martineau, Wendell Phillips, Theodore Parker, and Emerson's lifelong friend William Henry Furness.

21. Commager, *Theodore Parker*, pp. 215–16; Thomas, *Liberator*, pp. 377–78.

22. Lawrence Friedman, *Gregarious Saints: Self and Community in American Abolitionism, 1830–1870* (Cambridge: Cambridge University Press, 1982), p. 243.

23. Thomas, *Liberator*, p. 379.

24. Townsend Scudder, *Concord: American Town* (Boston: Little, Brown, 1947), p. 208.

25. MS, Concord Free Public Library.

26. John Hope Franklin, *From Slavery to Freedom: A History of Negro Americans* (New York: Alfred A. Knopf, 1967), p. 266.

27. Dillon, *Abolitionists*, pp. 182–83.

28. Scudder, *Concord*, p. 208; Commager, *Theodore Parker*, p. 220.

29. Bergman, *Chronological History*, pp. 178, 208.

30. Commager, *Theodore Parker*, pp. 220–22; Thomas, *Liberator*, pp. 380–81.

31. R. W. Emerson to Emily Mervine Drury, 14 April 1851. Letter published by B. D. Simison, *Modern Language Notes* 55 (June 1940), p. 427.

32. MS, Houghton Library, Harvard University, 9 April 1851.

33. MS, Houghton Library, Harvard University.

34. According to one witness to Emerson's presentation in Cambridge, this pungent statement brought forth from the college audience an "uproar," which "for a minute, was tremendous." S. S. H., "Emerson on Daniel Webster," *Unity* 9, no. 11 (1 August 1882), p. 223.

35. MS, Houghton Library, Harvard University, 7 May 1851.

36. For Garrison's attitude toward political action see Dillon, *Abolitionists*, p. 122; and Gerald Sorin, *Abolitionism: A New Perspective* (New York: Praeger, 1972), pp. 82–83.

37. R. W. E. to Emily Drury, 14 May 1851, MS, Ralph Waldo Emerson Collection, Clifton Waller Barrett Library, University of Virginia; listed in *L* 4:250. (I am indebted to Prof. Eleanor Tilton for this information.)

38. Ellen Emerson, *Lidian*, p. 39.

39. Joel Myerson, *The New England Transcendentalists and the Dial* (Rutherford, N.J.: Fairleigh Dickinson University Press, 1980), p. 34.

40. Dillon, *Abolitionists*, pp. 167–68.

41. John G. Palfrey, *Papers on the Slave Power, First Published in the "Boston Whig"* (Boston: Merrill, Cobb, n.d.), pp. 81–82.

42. MS, Houghton Library, Harvard University, 9 May 1851.

43. See n. 37.

44. R. W. E. to Ainsworth Spofford, 23 May 1851. Letter published by C. C. Hollis in *New England Quarterly* 38 (1965), p. 73.

45. The anarchial element in Emerson's position would indeed be noted and emphasized, but not for some fifty years. In an article entitled "Emerson the Anarchist" (*Arena* [April 1907], pp. 400–404), Bolton Hall would note: "Now that intense sense of unity is what made Emerson an anarchist. . . . The method adopted by the abolitionists was to mitigate the iniquity of slave laws until they could be repealed. . . . The best way to repeal a bad law, the hardest blow that can be struck at a legalized iniquity, is to evade it, to do as they did in slavery days,—steal away the slaves by night; persistently to do these things which are absolutely illegal, without regard to conventional conscience or rights of property, evading iniquitous laws and thus saving our suffering brethren from their sins. It is by such evasions of the law that we have practically repealed Prohibition, and by which we are now repealing taxation of personal property and the tariff."

46. MS, Houghton Library, Harvard University, December 1883.

47. According to Prof. Eleanor Tilton, Emerson gave this speech at least nine times.

48. David Donald, *Charles Sumner and the Coming of the Civil War* (New York: Alfred A. Knopf, 1960), p. 202.

49. MS, Houghton Library, Harvard University, 22 July 1851.

50. MS, Houghton Library, Harvard University, 25 July 1851.

51. R. W. E. to Adeline Roberts, 27 August 1851, MS, Essex Institute, Salem, Massachusetts.

52. MS, Boston Public Library, 26 August 1851.

53. MS, Houghton Library, Harvard University, 17 November 1851.

54. This speech was not published until it appeared in the centenary edition of Emerson's *Works*. See Joel Myerson, *Ralph Waldo Emerson: A Descriptive Bibliography* (Pittsburgh: University of Pittsburgh Press, 1982), p. 387.

55. See n. 44.

56. Thomas, *Liberator*, p. 381; Dillon, *Abolitionists*, pp. 186–87.

57. W. H. Furness to (?), 4 October 1851, MS, Boston Public Library.

58. See *JMN* 11:xxiii.

59. MS, Ainsworth Spofford Papers, Library of Congress, 15 March 1852.

60. Edward Wagenknecht, *Ralph Waldo Emerson: Portrait of a Balanced Soul* (New York: Oxford University Press, 1974), pp. 198–99.

61. During this period Emerson was invited by the Massachusetts Anti-slavery Society to speak again at the annual celebration of emancipation in the British West Indies in August 1852 (S. May to R. W. E., 23 July 1852, MS, Houghton Library, Harvard University); by Wendell Phillips and others to speak to a convention in Boston in April called by the vigilance committee of that city to commemorate the rendition of Thomas Sims (W. Phillips to R. W. E., 24 March 1852, MS, Houghton Library, Harvard University); by Adeline Roberts of the Salem Female Anti-slavery Society to address that group in August 1852 (MS, Essex Institute, Salem, 2 August 1852); and by Lucretia Mott to make a presentation at the Pennsylvania Anti-slavery Fair in November. Mrs. Mott states in her letter: "The abolitionists of Philadelphia were disappointed, last winter, in their expectation of hearing your lecture, in this city, upon this subject. The Executive Committee of the Pennsylvania Antislavery Society, who were obliged to forgo, at that time, the services which you so kindly promised, will be equally gratified to receive them in the way we propose" (MS, Houghton Library, Harvard University, 25 November 1852).

62. Nathalia Wright, "Ralph Waldo Emerson and Horatio Greenough," *Harvard Library Bulletin* 12, no. 1 (Winter 1958), p. 98.

63. Horatio Greenough, *The Travels, Observations, and Experiences of a Yankee Stonecutter* (New York: G. P. Putnam, 1852; reprint, Scholars Facsimiles and Reprints, 1958), pp. 74–75.

64. Quoted in Wright, "Emerson and Greenough," pp. 102–4.

65. Ibid., p. 106.

66. Greenough, *Travels*, p. 82.

67. Quoted in Wright, "Emerson and Greenough," p. 107.

68. Ibid., p. 109.

69. Ibid., p. 110.

70. Ibid., p. 111.

71. See, for example, *JMN* 13:35, 54, 197–98, 286.

72. Philip Nicoloff, *Emerson on Race and History: An Examination of English Traits* (New York: Columbia University Press, 1961), p. 126.

73. Ibid., pp. 127–28.

74. Ibid., p. 124.

75. Thomas Carlyle, *Critical and Miscellaneous Essays*, vol. 4 (London: Chapman and Hall, 1899; reprint, New York: AMS Press, 1969), p. 349.

76. Ibid., p. 350.

77. Ibid., p. 379.

78. Rusk, *Life of Emerson*, p. 392.

79. Gay Wilson Allen, *Waldo Emerson: A Biography* (New York: Viking Press, 1981), p. 573.

80. Nicoloff, *English Traits*, p. 123.

81. J. C. Nott and George R. Gliddon, *Types of Mankind, or Ethnological Researches* (Philadelphia: Lippincott, Grambo, 1854).

82. Ibid., pp. 95–96.

83. Dillon, *Abolitionists*, p. 192.

84. Eleanor Tilton, *Amiable Autocrat: A Biography of Dr. Oliver Wendell Holmes* (New York: Henry Schuman, 1947), p. 227.

85. Quoted in Douglas Stange, *Patterns of Antislavery Among American Unitarians, 1831–1860* (Rutherford, N.J.: Fairleigh Dickinson University Press, 1977), p. 163.

86. Ibid., p. 164.

87. Sorin, *Abolitionism*, p. 37. See also Howard R. Floan, *The South in Northern Eyes: 1831–1861* (Austin: University of Texas Press, 1958; reprint, New York: Haskell House, 1973) for a discussion of this question.

Chapter 6. The Struggle Intensifies

1. Ralph H. Orth et al., eds. *The Poetry Notebooks of R. W. Emerson* (Columbia: University of Missouri Press, 1986), p. 796.

2. Ellen Tucker Emerson, *The Life of Lidian Jackson Emerson*, ed. Delores Bird Carpenter (Boston: Twayne Publishers, 1980), p. 130.

3. Merton Dillon, *The Abolitionists: The Growth of a Dissenting Minority* (New York: W. W. Norton, 1974), p. 193.

4. Letter to R. D. Webb, MS, Boston Public Library, 5 March 1854.

5. Reprinted in *Transcendental Log*, ed. Kenneth Walter Cameron (Hartford: Transcendental Books, 1973), pp. 83–84.

6. Ibid., pp. 82–83.

7. *Records of a Lifelong Friendship: Ralph Waldo Emerson and William Henry Furness*, ed. H. Furness (Boston: Houghton Mifflin, 1910), pp. 92–93.

8. For a fine account of the journal's background see Patricia Barber (Holland), "Ralph Waldo Emerson's Antislavery Notebook, WO Liberty" (Ph.D. diss., University of Massachusetts); and John C. Broderick, "Emerson and Moorfield Storey: A Lost Journal Found," *American Literature* 38 (May 1966), pp. 177–86.

9. See Barber, "Emerson's Antislavery Notebook," pp. xv–xvi.

10. Henry Steele Commager, *Theodore Parker* (Boston: Beacon Press, 1947), p. 232.

11. Ibid., p. 233.

12. John L. Thomas, *The Liberator: William Lloyd Garrison* (Boston: Little, Brown, 1963), p. 386; Commager, *Theodore Parker*, p. 236; Odell Shepard, *Pedlar's Progress: The Life of Bronson Alcott* (Boston: Little, Brown, 1937), p. 444; Harold Schwartz, "Fugitive Slave Days in Boston," *New England Quarterly* 27 (1954), pp. 204ff.

13. Gerald Sorin, *Abolitionism: A New Perspective* (New York: Praeger, 1972), p. 108.

14. Schwartz, "Fugitive Slave Days," p. 207.

15. Ellen Emerson, *Lidian*, p. 125.

16. Walter Harding, *The Days of Henry Thoreau* (New York: Alfred A. Knopf, 1962), p. 318.

17. Oliver Wendell Holmes, *Ralph Waldo Emerson* (Boston: Houghton Mifflin, 1884), p. 236.

18. Bill Ledbetter, "Charles Sumner: Political Activist for the New England Transcendentalists," *Historian* 44, no. 3 (May 1982), pp. 347–63.

19. David Donald, *Charles Sumner and the Rights of Man* (New York: Alfred A. Knopf, 1970), pp. 573–74.

20. Thomas, *Abolitionists*, p. 386; Schwartz, "Fugitive Slave Days," pp. 210–11.

21. MS, Houghton Library, Harvard University, 22 June 1854.

22. The editors of vol. 14 of the *Journals and Miscellaneous Notebooks of Ralph Waldo Emerson* suggest that "in the winter of 1854–1855 Emerson had tried the experiment of touring with one or two lectures, 'American Slavery,' and his 1851 address on the Fugitive Slave Law; in the winter of 1855–1856 he returned to his usual pattern of a variety of lectures" (p. x), but the evidence for this is not clear. However, Emerson did certainly repeat his antislavery speeches several times in his continuing effort to educate the public on the issue.

23. R. W. E. to T. W. Higginson, 25 September 1854. Letter published by William White, *American Literature* 33 (May 1961), p. 168.

24. William Charvat, *Emerson's American Lecture Engagements: A Chronological List* (New York: New York Public Library, 1961), p. 30.

25. Oliver Johnson to W. Phillips, 7 September 1854, MS, Houghton Library, Harvard University. Johnson lists Emerson with Sumner, S. P. Chase, and C. M. Clay as "already invited." He also asks Phillips's opinion "as to inviting Thoreau to be one of our lecturers."

26. R. W. E. to Oliver Johnson, 12 November 1854, MS, Mills College Library. (I am indebted to Prof. Eleanor Tilton for this information.)

27. Charvat, *Lecture Engagements*, p. 30.

28. Quoted in Rollo G. Silver's "Mr. Emerson Appeals to Boston," *American Book Collector* 6 (May–June 1935), p. 209. The article also contains a transcription of the speech that appeared in the *Boston Daily Evening Traveller*, 26 January 1855. All subsequent quotations from the speech are from this source, which reflects the speech as it was actually given. There is a complete manuscript for the presentation at the Houghton Library, Harvard University.

29. MS, Houghton Library, Harvard University, "American Slavery."

30. Joel Myerson, "Convers Francis and Emerson," *American Literature* 50 (March 1978), p. 34.

31. MS, Houghton Library, Harvard University, 28 January 1855.

32. Samuel May invited Emerson to lecture on slavery "in Syracuse this winter" (MS, Houghton Library, Harvard University, 23 November 1854). Later, he wrote to confirm the date of this address, asking Emerson to specify either 24 or 25 February (MS, Houghton Library, Harvard University, 20 January 1855). Charvat notes that they finally settled on 25 February for the performance (p. 30). Higginson wrote to Emerson from Worcester, Mass., on 25 September 1854 asking him "to read the discourse that shall be written, on any night that it suits you after it is read in Boston" which is undoubtedly a reference to "American Slavery" (see n. 26). Charvat lists the Worcester address as "26 (?) Jan" (p. 30), and Emerson did write to Higginson in October to state, "I am content that you shall hold me to the 26 January, as you proposed for my lecture" (*L* 4:473). He probably also presented the speech to the Ladies' Anti-slavery Society in Rochester on 21 February (Charvat, *Lecture Engagements*, p. 30). It is possible that Emerson repeated the speech on other occasions also, and it may be this frequent repetition of the antislavery theme that he refers to in a letter to Lidian mailed from Syracuse, 27 February 1855, where he says, "I have met with an unusual share of annoyances in these days & failed of four promised lectures all which will not urge me to repeat this winter experiment" (*L* 4:497). This could also be the "experiment" referred to in n. 22 above.

33. Commager, *Theodore Parker*, p. 243.

34. MS, Houghton Library, Harvard University.

35. J. M. Winkley, "A Reminiscence of Emerson," *Practical Ideals* (Boston), May 1903, speaks of Emerson's public display of support for Parker at the time of his prosecution.

36. Furness, *Records*, p. 106.

37. For Emerson's labors in preparing *English Traits* see Myerson, *Emerson Bibliography*, p. 242.

38. Furness, *Records*, p. 109.

39. MS, Houghton Library, Harvard University, 29 September 1855.

Chapter 7. The Battle Lines Are Drawn

1. Townsend Scudder, *Concord: American Town* (Boston: Little, Brown, 1947), p. 212.

2. *The Letters of William Lloyd Garrison*, 6 vols., ed. Walter S. Merrill and Louis Ruchames (Cambridge: Belknap Press of Harvard University Press, 1971–81), 4:390.

3. Frank Preston Stearns, *The Life and Public Services of George Luther Stearns* (Philadelphia: J. B. Lippincott, 1907), pp. 108–9.

4. Eleanor Tilton, *Amiable Autocrat: A Biography of Dr. Oliver Wendell Holmes* (New York: Henry Schuman, 1947), p. 226.

5. Ibid., p. 224.

6. Quoted in ibid., p. 227.

7. This part of Emerson's response to Holmes is included with that quoted earlier in draft form. Rusk says of this section, "What follows is on a separate sheet of a different size and may possibly be a fragment of a separate letter, though I think not" (*L* 5:18). In light of the internal evidence and the Holmes letter quoted by Tilton, I think it likely that two letters are in fact represented in the draft that Rusk presents, and I have dealt with them as such.

8. David Donald, *Charles Sumner and the Coming of the Civil War* (New York: Alfred A. Knopf, 1960), p. 282–88.

9. MS, Concord Free Public Library, 10 June 1856.

10. Franklin Sanborn, *The Personality of Emerson* (Boston: Charles E. Goodspeed, 1903), p. 86.

11. For a reproduction of this letter and a discussion of it, see Francis B. Dedmond, "Men of Concord Petition the Governor," *Concord Saunterer* 15, no. 4 (1982), pp. 1–6.

12. MS, Houghton Library, Harvard University, 6 September 1856.

13. MS, Houghton Library, Harvard University, 13 August 1856.

14. MS, Rare Book Dept., Cornell University Library, 26 September 1856. (I am indebted to Prof. Eleanor Tilton for this information.)

15. MS, Houghton Library, Harvard University, 16 August 1856.

16. *Letters of William Lloyd Garrison*, 4:413–14.

17. MS, New York Public Library, Astor, Lenox, and Tilden Foundations, Rare Books and Manuscripts Division, Gilbert H. Montgomery and Amy Angell Collier Montague Collection, 5 December 1856. In the *Liberator*, 10 December 1858, the following item appears: "Portrait of Ralph Waldo Emerson, C. H. Brainard, of this city, has just published a very admirable and life-like portrait of Mr. Emerson, after the style of Theodore Parker, Wendell Phillips, Charles Sumner, Henry Wilson, W. H. Seward, &c, &c."

18. For Concord's Frémont Club see *LL* 1:120.

19. Ibid., 1:125.

20. MS, Houghton Library, Harvard University, 3 April 1857.

21. Scudder, *Concord*, p. 213.

22. MS, Library of Congress, 28 April 1857.

23. G. L. Stearns to John Brown, 6 May 1857, MS, Library of Congress. Stearns says, "Col. Carter has agreed to furnish you with the revolvers and now waits your direction to send them."

24. John W. Clarkson, Jr., "Mentions of Emerson and Thoreau in the Letters of Franklin Benjamin Sanborn," *Studies in the American Renaissance, 1978*, ed. Joel Myerson (Boston: G. K. Hall, 1978), pp. 389–90. See also Otto J. Scott, *The Secret Six: John Brown and the Abolitionist Movement* (New York: Times Books, 1979).

25. F. B. Sanborn, *Recollections of Seventy Years*, 2 vols. (Boston: Richard G. Badger, Gorham Press, 1909), 1:104.

26. Scudder, *Concord*, p. 213; Sanborn, *Seventy Years*, 1:108.

27. George S. Merriam, *The Negro and the Nation* (1906; reprint, New York: Negro University Press, 1969), pp. 147–48; John Hope Franklin, *From Slavery to Freedom* (New York: Alfred A. Knopf, 1947), p. 268.

28. *The Journal of Charlotte Forten: A Free Negro in the Slave Era*, ed. Ray Allen Billington (New York: W. W. Norton, 1955), p. 113.

29. James Elliot Cabot, *A Memoir of Ralph Waldo Emerson*, 2 vols. (Boston: Houghton Mifflin, 1887), 2:596.

30. Boston: William L. Kent, 1858. The author was responding to "Mr. Ralph Waldo Emerson as Lecturer," which appeared in *Radicalism in Religion, Philosophy, and Social Life. Four Papers from the Boston Courier for 1858* (Boston: Little, Brown, 1858), pp. 23–37.

31. *The Revival of Religion Which We Need. Sermon, Delivered at Music Hall, on Sunday, April 11, 1858* (Boston: William L. Kent, 1858), p. 14.

32. Letter to Sarah Blake Shaw, 17 April 1858, MS, Houghton Library.

33. MS, Concord Free Public Library.

34. MS, Sophia Smith Collection, Smith College, 27 January 1859.

35. S. J. May to Richard D. Webb, 8 February 1859, MS, Boston Public Library.

36. Quoted in Sanborn, *Seventy Years*, p. 164.

37. Walter Harding, "Thoreau in Emerson's Account Books," *Thoreau Society Bulletin* no. 159 (Spring 1982), p. 3.

38. Gerald Sorin, *Abolitionism: A New Perspective* (New York: Praeger, 1972), p. 96.

39. Scudder, *Concord*, pp. 218–19.

40. Sanborn, *Seventy Years*, 1:188.

41. MS, Houghton Library, 22 October 1859.

42. MS, Concord Free Public Library, 22 October 1859.

43. Sanborn, *Seventy Years*, 1:194.

44. Ibid., 1:196.

45. Quoted in Sanborn, *Seventy Years*, 1:201.

46. Sanborn, *Personality*, p. 88.

47. Quoted by Edward Emerson in *W* 10:460.

48. Sanborn, *Seventy Years*, 1:201.

49. Cabot, *Memoir of Emerson*, 2:597.

50. Ibid., 2:596. For a discussion of the controversy generated by Emerson's "glorious like the cross" remark, see John McAleer, *Ralph Waldo Emerson: Days of Encounter* (Boston: Little, Brown, 1984), pp. 532–33.

51. MS, Concord Free Public Library, 14 November 1859.

52. Unidentified newspaper clipping reprinted in *Transcendental Log*, ed. Kenneth Walter Cameron (Hartford: Transcendental Books, 1973), pp. 137–38.

53. Sanborn, *Seventy Years*, 1:204–5.

54. Cameron, *Transcendental Log*, p. 138.

55. See n. 37.

56. *Boston Post*, 2 December 1859.

57. MS, Concord Free Public Library, 25 November 1859.

58. *Lydia Maria Child: Selected Letters, 1817–1880*, ed. Milton Meltzer and Patricia G. Holland (Amherst: University of Massachusetts Press, 1982), pp. 331–32.

59. Michael Meyer, "Discord in Concord on the Day of John Brown's Hanging," *Thoreau Society Bulletin* no. 146 (Winter 1979), pp. 1–3.

60. Sanborn, *Seventy Years*, 1:202.

61. Meyer, "Discord in Concord," p. 2.

62. Ibid.

63. "John Shepard Keyes' Unpublished Account of the Exercises in Memory of John Brown, Concord, Massachusetts, December 2, 1859," *Thoreau Society Bulletin* no. 143 (Spring 1978), p. 4.

64. Reprinted in Cameron, *Transcendental Log*, p. 138.

65. F. P. Stearns, *Life of G. L. Stearns*, p. 204.

66. Meyer, "Discord in Concord," p. 2.

67. Ibid.

68. L. M. Child to David Lee Child, 5 December 1859; Patricia G. Holland and Milton Meltzer, eds. *The Collected Correspondence of Lydia Maria Child, 1817–1880*, microfiche edition (Millwood, N.Y.: Kraus Microfilm, 1980).

69. Ibid., 17 December 1859; see *Liberator*, 31 December 1859.

70. MS, Houghton Library, Harvard University, 10 December 1859.

71. MS, Houghton Library, Harvard University, 12 December 1859.

72. MS, Houghton Library, Harvard University, 13 December 1859.

73. MS, Houghton Library, Harvard University, 14 December 1859.

74. MS, Houghton Library, Harvard University, 30 December 1859.

Chapter 8. Conflict and Victory

1. Otto J. Scott, *The Secret Six: John Brown and the Abolitionist Movement* (New York: Times Books, 1979), p. 312.

2. Townsend Scudder, *Concord: American Town* (Boston: Little, Brown, 1947), p. 223.

3. MS, Houghton Library, Harvard University, 24 February 1860.

4. Memorial article on William Henry Furness, *Boston Journal*, 31 January 1896.

5. Unidentified clipping in Furness Class Records, Pusey Library, Harvard University.

6. Joel Myerson, *Ralph Waldo Emerson: A Descriptive Bibliography* (Pittsburgh: University of Pittsburgh Press, 1982), p. 609.

7. MS, Houghton Library, Harvard University, 10 March 1860.

8. MS, Houghton Library, Harvard University, 27 March 1860.

9. *New York Tribune*; reprinted in *Transcendental Log*, ed. Kenneth Walter Cameron (Hartford: Transcendental Books, 1973), pp. 141–42. The account also appeared in the *New York Herald* and the *Liberator*.

10. John W. Clarkson, Jr., "F. B. Sanborn, 1831–1917," *Concord Saunterer* 12, no. 2 (Summer 1977), p. 7.

11. F. B. Sanborn, *Recollections of Seventy Years*, 2 vols. (Boston: Richard G. Badger, 1909), 1:212.

12. MS, Concord Free Public Library, 1–9 April 1860.

13. *Boston Journal*, 5 April 1860. Clipping in "Notes and clippings on History of Concord, compiled by William A. Wheeldon," Concord Free Public Library.

14. *Liberator*, 13 April 1860.

15. Sanborn, *Recollections of Seventy Years*, 1:218.

16. Edwin D. Mead, *Emerson and Theodore Parker* (Boston: American Unitarian Association, 1910). This account also appeared as an article in the *Index*, 17 and 24 August 1882.

17. Franklin Sanborn, "Theodore Parker and R. W. Emerson," *Critic* (September 1906), p. 273.

18. Thomas W. Higginson, "Address of T. W. Higginson, *The Emerson Centenary in Concord*" (printed for the Social Circle of Concord by the Riverside Press, 1903), p. 60.

19. James M. McPherson, *The Struggle for Equality* (Princeton: Princeton University Press, 1964), p. 29.

20. Milton Meltzer and Patricia Holland, eds., *Lydia Maria Child Selected Letters, 1817–1880* (Amherst: University of Massachusetts Press, 1982), p. 372.

21. McPherson, *Struggle*, p. 35.

22. Ibid., p. 41.

23. Merton Dillon, *The Abolitionists: The Growth of a Dissenting Minority* (New York: W. W. Norton, 1974), p. 250.

24. McPherson, *Struggle*, pp. 41–42.

25. MS, Houghton Library, Harvard University, 7 December 1860.

26. McPherson, *Struggle*, p. 43.

27. MS, Houghton Library, Harvard University, 17 December 1860.

28. Child, *Letters*, p. 373.

29. McPherson, *Struggle*, p. 44; Child, *Letters*, pp. 371ff.

30. The notice Emerson refers to is from the *Philadelphia Medical Journal* and is provided by Edward Emerson. It reads, "We listened with great pleasure to the chaste and beautiful lecture of the Boston Essayist. He is tall and literarily thin; and was remarked by a medical friend, the least remarkable man on the stage. As usual in the lectures of our Yankee brethren, a good degree of sensible and well-applied physiology entered into the discussion." *The Journals of Ralph Waldo Emerson*, 10 vols., ed. Edward Waldo Emerson and Waldo Emerson Forbes (Boston: Houghton Mifflin, 1909–1914), 9:163.

31. Lucius M. Sargent, *The Ballad of the Abolition Blunder-Buss* (Boston: For Sale by the Booksellers, 1861). A copy of this book is held by the Concord Free Public Library.

32. MS, Houghton Library, Harvard University, 6 February 1861.

33. Peter M. Bergman, *The Chronological History of the Negro in America* (New York: Harper and Row, 1969), p. 225. Emerson would note in his December 1863 lecture "The Fortune of the Republic" that "an eminent benefactor of the Union in this war has been the Vice President of the Confederacy proclaiming that the theory & policy of his government,—a manifesto hitherto unrebuked, never disowned,—that 'Slavery was the cornerstone of their State.' No public act has served so much at home and abroad, except Emancipation" (MS, Houghton Library, Harvard University).

34. Edward Emerson, in the notes for the essay "Civilization" (W 7:19–34), indicates that "in April, 1861, Mr. Emerson began a course of lectures on Life and Literature at the Meionaon in Boston. He had probably prepared the lecture

on Civilization in much the same form that it is printed here." He then goes on to note that "the lecture, written in less stirring days had to be remodelled for the hour. Mr. Emerson named it 'Civilization at a Pinch!'" This remodeled lecture, says Edward, "with the addition of an earnest appeal to the administration for emancipation of the slaves, was read by him before the Smithsonian Institution at Washington in January, 1862. Under the title there used, 'American Civilization,' it was printed in the *Atlantic Monthly* for April, 1862."

Cabot indicates that the announced Boston lecture was the "Doctrine of Leasts," which was then changed to "Civilization at a Pinch" (James Elliot Cabot, *A Memoir of Ralph Waldo Emerson*, 2 vols. [Boston: Houghton Mifflin, 1887], pp. 599–600), and he quotes a brief portion of the lengthy speech. I have supplemented Cabot's material with quotations drawn from the original manuscript of the lecture, which is catalogued at the Houghton Library, Harvard University, as "Civilization at a Pinch" (23 April 1861). The internal evidence suggests that this is most certainly the lecture that Emerson gave on that date.

35. Emerson might well have had his own household in mind here. In a letter dated 11 May 1861 Lidian wrote to her daughter Edith that "the clothing for the soldiers has taken some of my time; not much, however, as I have done my share and am doing it, as Solomon built the Temple. Marie and the machine have given several days' work to the good cause and she is still basting and 'machining' blue flannel shirts like the Adirondac-costume. She has thrown in her own evening time, of her own accord" (*LL* 210).

36. Concord itself had raised a princely sum of $4,000 by 19 April to outfit its artillery company. See *EL* 242.

37. In a letter to her daughter Edith on 20 April, Lidian says, "Yesterday our Concord artillery, joined by a number of volunteers, left Concord in the [troop] train. There was a great feeling manifested—great enthusiasm for the Cause, and much gratitude and admiration for those who had resolved to risk all for their country. At the Depot they formed a line and after an address by Judge [Ebenezer Rockwood] Hoar, and prayer by Mr [Grindall] Reynolds, there was an affecting scene of leave taking between soldiers and their acquaintances. The nearest friends were of course not there, but in sorrow at home. Many of the soldiers were trying, with working twitching faces, to stop the tears which would come" (*LL* 208–9).

38. For abolitionist views on the Civil War, see McPherson, *Struggle*, pp. 47ff.

39. Cabot, *Memoir of Emerson*, 2:601.

40. Ibid., pp. 604–5.

41. MS, Boston Public Library, 20 May 1861.

42. In his 12 November 1861 lecture "American Nationality" Emerson would reiterate the idea that the South also would benefit from the war. "I cannot be blind to the service which war is doing to the Southern State. I think they have

never, since their first planting, appeared to such advantage as during the last few months. They have waked to energy, to selfhelp, to economy, to valor, to self-knowledge & progress.

"They have dared to consider the conditions & the future of Slavery; have suggested the policies of their emancipating their Slaves, as a war measure. They have put forth, for the first time, their sleepy half-palsied limbs, & as soon as the blood begins to tingle & flow,—it will creep with new life into the moribund extremes of the system, & the white trash will say, we too are men" (MS, Houghton Library, Harvard University).

43. McPherson, *Struggle*, pp. 59–60.

44. Bergman, *History*, pp. 226–27.

45. Child, *Letters*, p. 394.

46. Cabot, *Memoir of Emerson*, 2:783.

47. Child, *Letters*, p. 394; McPherson, *Struggle*, pp. 74–75.

48. MS, Houghton Library, Harvard University, December 1861.

49. McPherson, *Struggle*, pp. 63–64.

50. MS, Houghton Library, Harvard University, 17 January 1862.

51. Frank Preston Stearns, *The Life and Public Services of George Luther Stearns* (Philadelphia: J. B. Lippincott, 1907), p. 280. Emerson himself did not report this statement in his journal account of his meeting with Lincoln, where he recorded almost exclusively the conversations of the other principals. That Emerson felt the need for an element of firmness in leaders when dealing with such matters is suggested in his later journal comment that "President Lincoln should remember that humanity in a ruler does not consist in running hither & thither in a cab to stop the execution of a deserter, but, as Napoleon said, 'justice is the humanity of Kings' " (*JMN* 15:336). Some years later Emerson expressed this sentiment again, in his memorial address on Lincoln.

52. Willie Lee Rose, "Iconoclasm Has Had Its Day: Abolitionists and Freedmen in South Carolina," in *The Antislavery Vanguard: New Essays on the Abolitionists*, ed. Martin Duberman (Princeton: Princeton University Press, 1965), p. 183.

53. MS, Houghton Library, Harvard University, 30 January 1862.

54. A local Washington paper, the *Evening Star* (31 January and 1 February 1862) refers to Emerson's lecture as "Nationality." Cabot gives the title as "American Civilization," *Memoir of Emerson*, 2:786.

55. See *JMN* 15:206 for the clipping of Lincoln's proposal.

56. "Moral Forces," 13 April 1862. Read on Fast Day, appointed by the president of the United States. MS, Houghton Library, Harvard University. See also Cabot, *Memoir of Emerson*, 2:786–87.

57. Walter Harding, *The Days of Henry Thoreau* (New York: Alfred A. Knopf, 1970), p. 451.

58. Letter reprinted in *Concord Saunterer* 12, no. 3 (Fall 1977), pp. 20–21.

59. MS, Boston Public Library, 10 April 1861.

60. Gabrielle Fitzgerald argues persuasively that Emerson frequently felt a tension between the active and the contemplative lives and had generally satisfied himself that the scholar was just as heroic in his intellectual pursuits as those who were given to strenuous physical actions. However, the pressure of the Civil War "smashed through his image of the scholar-hero . . . and for some years the scales were tipped decidedly toward the ideal of forceful action." This, says Fitzgerald, was the context of Emerson's funeral oration and explains its tone of disappointment with Thoreau's apparent failure to be more active at the time. See "A Time of War: The Context of Emerson's 'Thoreau,'" *American Transcendental Quarterly* (Winter 1979), pp. 5–12. This position is reinforced by a recently discovered letter in which Emerson tells his correspondent, who had suggested in an article that Emerson had been disappointed by Thoreau, that the view was erroneous. "Thoreau was a superior genius. I read his books and manuscripts always with a new surprise at the range of his topics and the novelty and depth of his thought. A man of large reading, of quick perception, of great practical courage and ability,—who grew greater every day, and had his short life been prolonged, would have found few equals to the power and wealth of his mind." See George Stewart, "Emerson's Esteem for Thoreau," *Thoreau Society Bulletin* 181 (Fall 1987), p. 6.

61. Ellen Tucker Emerson, *The Life of Lidian Jackson Emerson*, ed. Delores Bird Carpenter (Boston: Twayne Publishers, 1980), p. 146. See also *EL* 1:388. Edward never lost his desire to enlist and serve, and when emancipation did at last become a fact in 1863 both Lidian and Ralph Waldo, reluctantly, gave their permission for him to do so. However, as he was about to go off, Edward was stopped by John Murray Forbes, whose son William would eventually marry Emerson's daughter, Edith. As Ellen relates the story, Forbes told Edward, "I am not half the man I was, since Will went to the war. If Malcolm should go too, I think my usefulness would be ended. You are your Father's only son. I leave it to you to judge whether your Father's services to your country or those that you could offer would be of most value." Edward, in response to this plea, "gave up his heart's desire just as he had at last attained it, and came home to the friends he had just said goodbye to, and told them he would not go" (p. 142).

62. McPherson, *Struggle*, p. 118.

63. David Donald, *Charles Sumner and the Rights of Man* (New York: Alfred A. Knopf, 1970), p. 78.

64. Ibid., p. 81.

65. Quoted in McPherson, *Struggle*, p. 119.

66. Quoted in William H. Hale, *Horace Greeley: Voice of the People* (New York: Harper and Brothers, 1950), p. 263.

67. Kenneth Cameron, "The First Appearance of Emerson's Boston Hymn,"

ESQ 22 (1961), p. 99. See also *The Poetry Notebooks of Ralph Waldo Emerson*, ed. Ralph Orth et al. (Columbia: University of Missouri Press, 1986), pp. 748–49.

68. F. P. Stearns, *Life of G. L. Stearns*, p. 274. Stearns also indicates that Emerson's reading of his poem was so dynamic that "the audience felt something like an electric shock."

69. MS, Houghton Library, Harvard University, 18 February 1863.

70. Nancy Craig Simmons, "Arranging the Sibylline Leaves: James Elliot Cabot's Work as Emerson's Literary Executor," *Studies in the American Renaissance, 1983*, ed. Joel Myerson (Charlottesville: University Press of Virginia, 1983), p. 368.

71. Douglas Stange points out that "many Whites doubted that manliness or heroism was an attribute of the Negro race. Among political abolitionists, with the exception of [Thomas Wentworth] Higginson, it was uniformly believed that blacks lacked aggressiveness." Douglas C. Stange, *Patterns of Antislavery Among American Unitarians, 1831–1860* (Rutherford, N.J.: Fairleigh Dickinson University Press, 1977), p. 162.

72. Bergman, *History*, p. 229.

73. McPherson, *Struggle*, pp. 202–3.

74. Ibid., p. 203.

75. Ibid., p. 123.

76. Ibid., p. 205.

77. Bergman, *History*, p. 231; John Hope Franklin, *From Slavery to Freedom: A History of Negro Americans* (New York: Alfred A. Knopf, 1967), p. 292.

78. Bergman, *History*, p. 233.

79. All quoted in McPherson, *Struggle*, p. 211.

80. In a letter dated 30 July Ellen states, "We are all very sorry that Robert Shaw is killed. What a magnificent attack! But they say nothing was gained" (*EL* 1:311).

81. Scudder, *Concord*, p. 258.

82. Howard Lowry and Ralph Rusk, eds. *Emerson-Clough Letters* (Rocofant Club, 1934; reprint, Hamden, Conn.: Archon Books, 1968), no. 33.

83. Donald, *Charles Sumner*, pp. 107–8.

84. MS, Schlesinger Library, Radcliffe College, 14 August 1863.

85. For Emerson's opinion of Wasson see *JMN* 15:54, 244, 440. Among other things, Emerson held that "Wasson is good company for prince or plowman."

86. MS, Houghton Library, Harvard University. This lecture, which Emerson delivered on several occasions from December 1863 through January 1864, should not be confused with the 1878 work by the same title, which was published as a pamphlet in that year and later incorporated in *Miscellanies*, vol. 11 of the *Works* (1903). The former, which Edward Emerson describes as "the basis of" the 1878 lecture, bears little resemblance to it.

87. In the light of these comments it is interesting to read Emerson's opin-

ion of *Frederick the Great* in his letter to Carlyle on 8 December 1862 where he thanked him for an inscribed copy of the book. This letter, and Carlyle's comments on it, offer an amusing insight into Emerson's mastery of the nuanced statement and the extent to which both men strove to avoid offending one another while holding dramatically different views on important issues. Emerson says, among other things, that "the book was heartily greatful, & square to the author's imperial scale" and "tis sovereignly written, above all literature, dictating to all mortals what they shall accept as fated & final for their salvation." Emerson also adds, "I find . . . that you are very wilful, & have made a covenant with your eyes that they shall not see anything you do not wish they should." He ends his letter with a comment about the war. "Here we read no books. The war is our sole & doleful instructer. All our bright young men go into it, to be misused & sacrificed hitherto by incapable leaders. One lesson they all learn—to hate slavery, *teterrima causa*. But the issue does not yet appear. We must get ourselves morally right." At the outset of his letter Emerson also spoke of the war and indicated that he had been waiting for Lincoln to "emancipate slaves," which he was reluctant to do "until on the heels of a victory, or the semblence of such" (*CEC* 535–36).

Carlyle sent Emerson's letter on to his brother with the following comment, "Emerson's letter will rather disappoint you; nothing in it about the Practical State of America that is not more or less chimerical,—conquering the South, and becoming celestial by emancipating Niggers, and so forth. But I find him entirely sincere: where he says I have made a covenant with my eyes;—not true, I hope, but evidently sincere" (*CEC* 537).

Apparently Emerson's anger with Carlyle cooled considerably with the passage of time. Also, in considering the American situation as it might be viewed by others, he was prepared to admit that the Union's waffling on the slavery issue may have legitimately confused those who otherwise would have been supportive. Hence, an account of Emerson's presentation in the *Cambridge Chronicle* (16 January 1864) indicates that he made the following statement regarding Carlyle when he delivered "Fortune of the Republic" in that town: "We can afford to pass by the needless insult from the pen of Carlyle, displeasing to those who love him, pleasing to those whose favor he would not like. His merits are so great he can afford an insincere word. Besides he had cause to judge us pretentious and not in earnest. Best of all men in England Carlyle has kept the manly attitude in his time. He has stood ever firm for the people. His errors cannot be measured with this. Admitted into this narrow circle, where very few scholars ever come, he has carried himself erect; made himself a high power; taught all men their duty."

An account in the *Brooklyn Daily Eagle* (22 December 1863) indicates that Emerson was bitter in his attack on England and held, among other things, that "She is fettered too in intellect, her best writers such as Carlyle are shocked at this want of universal sympathy." Other newspaper accounts allude to Emerson's attack on the British, but only these two include references to Carlyle. Later in his journal Emerson notes, "Carlyle is to be defended plainly as a sincere man who is outraged by nothing so much as sentimentalism, or the simulating of reform, & love of nature, & love of truth" (*JMN* 15:77).

88. This article is reproduced in Kenneth Walter Cameron's "Reports of Emerson's Lectures in 1864," *American Transcendental Quarterly* 17 (1973), p. 45.

89. MS, Houghton Library, Harvard University, 7 January 1864. Tilden G. Edelstein, *Strange Enthusiasm: A Life of Thomas Wentworth Higginson* (New Haven: Yale University Press, 1968), pp. 255ff.

90. Clarence Gohdes, ed., *Uncollected Lectures by Ralph Waldo Emerson* (New York: William Edwin Rudge, 1932), p. 412. See also *JMN* 15:342.

91. McPherson, *Struggle*, pp. 75–76.

92. MS, Houghton Library, Harvard University, 17 September 1864.

93. Kenneth Marc Harris, *Carlyle and Emerson: Their Long Debate* (Cambridge: Harvard University Press, 1978), p. 156.

94. Moncure Conway, "Thomas Carlyle," *Harper's New Monthly Magazine* 62 (May 1881), pp. 908–9.

95. Some critics have indicated that there was a cooling of Emerson's friendship with Carlyle toward the end of their lives. Several explanations of this development have been offered, but given the circumstances described here, it seems certain that differences on the matter of slavery were a large contributing factor. In his study *Emerson's Impact on the British Isles and Canada* (Charlottesville: University Press of Virginia, 1966), William J. Sowder offers the following summary of nineteenth-century British views on the question. "One reason for the break between the two writers was doubtless their divergent views on slavery, which Carlyle 'was not known to disapprove.' Although Britton maintained that Emerson's 'sweetness of temper prevented the constraint [imposed by the slavery question] from ever degenerating into a coolness,' the *Athenaeum* wrote that it was 'a sore trial' for Emerson to read Carlyle's comments on the subject. Had the American been in England during the war, said the *Saturday Review*, 'they would almost certainly have quarrelled, owing to Mr. Carlyle's decided opinion about the proper treatment of "Sambo."' Armstrong speculated that Carlyle's *The Occasional Discourse on the Nigger Question* and *The American Iliad in a Nutshell* must have been difficult for [Emerson] . . . to forgive" (p. 209). See also, Kenneth Marc Harris, *Carlyle and Emerson: Their Long Debate* (Cambridge: Harvard University Press, 1978), p. 156.

96. Ruth Wheeler, *Concord: Climate for Freedom* (Concord, Mass.: Concord Antiquarian Society, 1970), p. 192.

97. W. L. Garrison II to Martha Coffin Wright, 29 November 1864, MS, Sophia Smith Collection, Smith College.

98. Ghodes, *Uncollected Lectures*, p. 6. Emerson also incorporated these

thoughts in his later "Fortune of the Republic," where it was altered slightly, perhaps to address the more specific concerns of post–Civil War America. The later version reads, "The genius of the country has marked out our true policy, —opportunity. Opportunity of civil rights, of education, of personal power, and not less of wealth; doors wide open" etc. (*W* 11:541).

99. Reprinted by Kenneth Walter Cameron, in "Reports of Emerson's Lectures," pp. 41–45.

100. Ghodes, *Uncollected Lectures*, pp. 40–41.

Chapter 9. Reconstruction and Other Struggles

1. Ellen Emerson to Haven, 2 February 1865, MS, Houghton Library, Harvard University.

2. This idea was not unique to Emerson. Four days later Wendell Phillips delivered a eulogy for Lincoln where he maintained that the assassination was providential because "the nation needed a sterner hand for the work God gives it to do." Quoted in "The Blagden Papers: A Description and Select Listing," prep. Suzanne N. H. Courrier, *Perspectives in American History* 12 (1979), p. 149.

3. David Donald, *Charles Sumner and the Coming of the Civil War* (New York: Alfred A. Knopf, 1970), pp. 61, 255ff.; John Hope Franklin, *From Slavery to Freedom* (New York: Alfred A. Knopf, 1967), pp. 302–3.

4. MS, Houghton Library, Harvard University, 20 April 1865.

5. Joel Myerson, *Ralph Waldo Emerson: A Descriptive Bibliography* (Pittsburgh: University of Pittsburgh Press, 1982), p. 614.

6. Peter M. Bergman, *A Chronological History of the Negro in America* (New York: Harper and Row, 1969), p. 243.

7. James M. McPherson, *The Struggle for Equality* (Princeton: Princeton University Press, 1964), p. 332.

8. Ibid., p. 321.

9. MS, Sophia Smith Collection, Smith College, 5 November 1865.

10. MS, Houghton Library, Harvard University, 7 December 1865.

11. McPherson, *Struggle*, pp. 339–40.

12. MS, Houghton Library, Harvard University, 23 February 1866.

13. Unidentified newspaper clipping reproduced in Kenneth Walter Cameron, ed., *Transcendental Log* (Hartford: Transcendental Books, 1973), p. 170.

14. Anon. "The Johnson Party," *Atlantic Monthly*, September 1866, pp. 374, 375.

15. David Donald, *Charles Sumner and the Rights of Man* (New York: Alfred A. Knopf, 1970), p. 285.

16. Ibid.

17. Ralph Rusk, *The Life of Ralph Waldo Emerson* (New York: Charles Scribner's Sons, 1949), p. 435.

18. *Every Saturday*, 21 September 1867; reprinted in *Emerson Among His Contemporaries*, Kenneth Walter Cameron, ed. (Hartford: Transcendental Books, 1967), p. 120.

19. "The Thirty-Fourth National Anti-Slavery Subscription Anniversary," *New York Daily Tribune*, 13 January 1868. Reprinted in Cameron, *Transcendental Log*, pp. 184–85.

20. McPherson, *Struggle*, p. 430.

21. MS, Houghton Library, Harvard University, June 1870.

22. John B. Pickard, ed., *The Letters of John Greenleaf Whittier*, 3 vols. (Cambridge: Belknap Press of Harvard University Press, 1975), 3:233–34.

23. MS, Houghton Library, Harvard University, 9 November 1870 (?).

24. Franklin, *Slavery*, p. 308.

25. "What Books to Read, by Ralph Waldo Emerson: An Address Delivered Before the Law Students of Howard University," unidentified clipping reproduced in Cameron, *Transcendental Log*, p. 255.

26. Donald, *Rights*, p. 587. This statement was also noted prominently in *A Memorial of Charles Sumner*, which was "printed by order of the Legislature" of Massachusetts (Boston: 1874), p. 12.

27. Rusk, *Life of Emerson*, p. 490.

28. Ellen Tucker Emerson, *The Life of Lidian Jackson Emerson*, ed. Delores Bird Carpenter (Boston: Twayne Publishing, 1980), p. 172.

29. W. L. Garrison II notes in a letter to his wife that "Father had a good time in Concord, although the meetings were small. Mr. Emerson attended in the evening." He adds, "The Centennial was productive of feuds. Father freed his mind about Concord, Lexington & Bunker Hill. He was entertained delightfully at the Alcotts" (MS, Sophia Smith Collection, Smith College, 21 May 1875). Garrison may not have planned to attend the gathering initially. He turned down an invitation to attend the Centennial Anniversary of the Pennsylvania Society for the Abolition of Slavery on 14 April. In a letter to that group, dated 5 March, he indicated that his poor health would not permit him to attend (*The Letters of William Lloyd Garrison*, 6 vols., ed. Walter M. Merrill and Louis Ruchames [Cambridge: Belknap Press of Harvard University Press, 1971–81] 6:38). Similarly, he sent a letter to the Concord Committee of Invitation (which included E. R. Hoar, George Heywood, and Emerson) on 12 April 1875 which indicated that "circumstances . . . will prevent my attendance at the celebration." He goes on in the letter to praise the heroes of the Revolution, and then adds the following:

> It is an easy matter to celebrate the deeds of such, and to be proud of them as ancestors. To make the occasion worthy of us, there should be drawn from it an admonitory lesson to chasten our exultation,—lessons of justice not yet enforced, of equal rights still denied, of national unity not yet at-

tained. The Declaration of Independence still remains to be carried out in its fundamental principles and self-evident truths. True, the atrocious system of chattel slavery has been abolished, and its victims nominally admitted to citizenship; but they still need to have their rights protected, and to be put in possession of all those privileges and immunities which are accorded even to aliens and foreigners on our soil. Moreover, in persistently denying to one half of our population (solely on the ground of sex) all political power, all representation in legislative and municipal assemblies, all voice in the enactment and administration of the laws, and classifying them in an opprobrious manner, we are trampling under foot our own heaven-attested declaration that "governments derive their just powers from the consent of the governed," and in imitation of the mother country under George the Third, imposing taxation, but denying the right of representation. This great injustice must be removed.

The tone of this statement by Garrison may serve to explain his son's statement about "feuds." This letter is published in its entirety in *Proceedings at the Centennial Celebration of Concord Fight, April 19, 1875* (Concord: Published by the Town, 1876).

30. Rusk, *Life of Emerson*, p. 487.

31. MS, Boston Public Library, 1 May 1876.

32. MS, Houghton Library, Harvard University, 3 March 1870.

33. Phillips to L. Emerson, 26 July 1876, MS, Houghton Library, Harvard University. Lidian was most concerned throughout this period with the treatment of American Indians. She notes the following in a letter to Ellen and Waldo, dated 28 April 1873, regarding recent Indian affairs: "But our white savages whose mouths have been shut in some measure by the process of the 'peace policy'—are now in full cry for the extermination of all the Indian tribes. Sherman who twelve or more years since wrote an official letter, saying that the Indian men, *women & children* !!! must all, doubtless be exterminated begins his savage war now" (*LL* 309).

34. MS, Houghton Library, Harvard University, 16 September 1876. See also *L* 6:297.

35. Robin W. Winks, "'A Sacred Animosity': Abolitionism in Canada," in *The Antislavery Vanguard: New Essays on the Abolitionists*, ed. Martin Duberman (Princeton: Princeton University Press, 1965), p. 311.

36. MS, Houghton Library, Harvard University, 12 August 1875.

37. MS, Houghton Library, Harvard University, 13 January 1878.

38. MS, Houghton Library, Harvard University, 19 January 1878.

39. Alexander Milton Ross, *Memoirs of a Reformer* (Toronto: Hunter, Rose, 1893), p. 169.

40. Ibid., p. 171.

41. MS, Houghton Library, Harvard University, 11 March 1879.

42. Nancy Craig Simmons, "Arranging the Sibylline Leaves: James Elliot Cabot's Work as Emerson's Executor," *Studies in the American Renaissance, 1983*, Joel Myerson (Charlottesville: University Press of Virginia, 1983), pp. 356ff.

43. Because it is difficult to say with certainty what role the aged Emerson played in selecting the lecture materials gathered together to create this presentation, a close analysis of the work seems unjustifiable. However, the *tone* of the address definitely represents Emerson's own feeling. (For a history of its editing, see the Simmons article noted in n. 42.)

44. James McPherson, *The Abolition Legacy: From Reconstruction to the NAACP* (Princeton: Princeton University Press, 1975), p. 102.

45. MS, Sophia Smith Collection, Smith College, 15 May 1879.

46. Lidian survived for another decade. When she passed away, her friends and family remembered her as a loving mother and wife, and also as a vigilant crusader for human rights. Her tombstone inscription reads, in part, "Love and care for her husband and children was her first earthly interest, but with overflowing compassion her heart went out to the sick, the slave, the dumb creatures. She remembered those that are in bonds as bound with them, their sufferings were hers and to solace them was her constant effort" (Drafts of inscription for tombstone of Mrs. Lidian Emerson; letter from Edith to Ellen about epitaph, 1898, MS, Houghton Library, Harvard University). At first, Edward suggested deleting the biblical reference to "those in bonds," a phrase made famous by abolition women. However, his sisters, who had so often participated with their mother and other women of Concord in antislavery efforts, insisted, and it remained. One can only speculate as to the true influence of Lidian in encouraging her famous husband to take an active interest in the plight of the slaves, especially in the early years. However, Ellen provides an interesting insight when, three years after her mother's death, she reports that one evening Franklin Sanborn, Lizzy Weir, and herself were discussing Ralph Waldo's tendency to think original thoughts and not to quote others. "'Yet you often hear the thoughts of others in what he says,' said Mr. Sanborn. 'Yes,' said Lizzy, 'don't you think sometimes he says things he learned from Mrs. Emerson?' 'Often!' said Mr. Sanborn decidedly. When Lizzy said this I remembered Mrs. Nathan Brooks's remark, 'Mr. Emerson wouldn't be the man he is if it weren't for Mrs. Emerson. People have no idea how much he owes to his wife'" (Ellen Emerson to Edith, 1 June 1895, MS, Houghton Library, Harvard University). As far as Emerson's abolition campaign was concerned, Mrs. Brooks would certainly be the one to know.

Chapter 10. Conclusion

1. Published originally in *World's Work* (January 1901), pp. 286–92. Reprinted in *Democracy and the Gospel of Wealth*, ed. Gail Kennedy (Boston: D. C. Heath, 1949), pp. 68–76.

2. Daniel Aaron, "Emerson and the Progressive Tradition," from *Men of Good Hope* (1951; reprinted in *Emerson: A Collection of Critical Essays*, ed. Milton R. Konvitz and Stephen E. Whicher [Englewood Cliffs, N.J.: Prentice-Hall, 1962], pp. 86, 94).

3. "The New Consciousness: 1861–1914," in *American Literature: The Makers and the Making*, 2 vols., ed. Cleanth Brooks, R. W. B. Lewis, and Robert Penn Warren (New York: St. Martin's Press, 1973), 2:1206.

4. Perry Miller, *The Responsibility of Mind in a Civilization of Machines*, ed. John Crowell and Stanford J. Searl, Jr. (Amherst: University of Massachusetts Press, 1979), pp. 172, 205.

5. For example, see *New York Times*, *New York Tribune*, *New York Herald*, *Boston Daily Advertiser*, *Boston Daily Globe*, *Boston Post*, *Boston Morning Journal*, and *Boston Herald*, all on 25 May 1903. The quotations used here are from the *New York Times* account. The speech was also reprinted in *Four American Leaders* (Boston: American Unitarian Association, 1906), pp. 75–126, and *Charles W. Eliot: The Man and His Beliefs*, 2 vols., ed. William Allan Neilson (New York: Harper and Brothers, 1926).

6. It is interesting to note that in a 1910 essay that condemns the evil effects of trade unionism in America, Eliot says of the concept of a minimum wage, "Now a true democracy means endless variety of capacity freely developed and appropriately rewarded. Uniformity of wages ignores the diversity of local conditions as well as of personal capacity, obstructs the ambitious workman, cuts off from steady employment those who cannot really earn the minimum wage and interferes seriously with the workman's prospect of improving his lot. It is high time it should be generally understood that trades unionism in important respects works against the very best effects of democracy" (*Charles W. Eliot, the Man and His Beliefs*, 1:268).

7. Descriptive pamphlet in Moorfield Storey Papers, Library of Congress. See also John Broderick, "Emerson and Moorfield Storey: A Lost Journal Found," *American Literature* (May 1966), pp. 177–86.

8. *Boston Evening Transcript*, 22 July 1903.

9. "Emerson and Anti-Slavery," *Springfield Republican*, 30 July 1903.

10. Garrison says in a letter to his daughter, "This year the 100th birthday of Ralph Waldo Emerson is to be celebrated and there are to be many tributes in his honor. I have been invited to speak at Concord in one of them, taking for my theme his connection with the Anti-Slavery Movement, so I am reading up

the Emerson biographies and writings" (W. L. Garrison II to Eleanor Garrison, 1 April 1903, MS, Sophia Smith Collection, Smith College).

11. See n. 7.

12. Moorfield Storey and Edward W. Emerson, *Ebenezer Rockwood Hoar: A Memoir* (Boston: Houghton Mifflin, 1911).

13. William B. Hixson, Jr., *Moorfield Storey and the Abolitionist Tradition* (New York: Oxford University Press, 1972), p. 192; also, Bill Ledbetter, "Charles Sumner: Political Activist for the New England Transcendentalists," *The Historian, A Journal of History* (May 1982), pp. 347–63.

14. McPherson, *The Abolition Legacy: From Reconstruction to the NAACP* (Princeton: Princeton University Press, 1975), p. 335; Hixson, *Storey*, pp. 42–43.

15. Moorfield Storey, "Emerson and the Civil War," MS, Concord Free Public Library, Concord, Massachusetts. All quotations are from this manuscript.

16. Wilmington and Evansville were scenes of violent race riots and lynchings. Luzon, in the Philippines, was the scene of bloody battles involving U.S. troops and native forces. Storey's quotation from Emerson comes from his speech "The Emancipation Proclamation" (W 11: 326). Storey would echo these sentiments some years later in a speech given at the unveiling of the Emerson statue in Concord where he stated in part: "No ceremony to-day would be worthy of Mr. Emerson that was not simple, for he was always simple,—'as the greatest only are in his simplicity sublime.' No eulogy is needed nor would it be in place. We cannot but feel that he is present and that any word of praise would be unwelcome. Yet we could well wish that he were indeed here, for 'in these distempered days' we would fain turn again to him, who, in the words of Lowell during the years that preceded the Civil War 'constantly kept burning the beacon of an ideal life above our lower region of turmoil' and whose confidence in the sure triumph of right—as he phrased it in the 'God-way,'—is sorely needed now" (Address delivered at Concord, 23 May 1914, at the unveiling of a statue of Ralph Waldo Emerson). A print copy of this presentation is included in the Moorfield Storey Papers, Library of Congress.

17. Clipping in the Moorfield Storey Scrapbook, Library of Congress.

18. Sanborn had noted in an earlier address, "Emerson and Concord Town," that Concord was known for its "opposition to human slavery," and that "it was usually only a small minority, headed by Emerson, who gave Concord this present reputation" (*Springfield Republican*, 16 July 1903). Also, Sanborn speaks at some length, largely in the form of personal reminiscences, of Emerson's abolition activities from the 1850s on in his study *The Personality of Emerson*, also published in the centennial year (Boston: Charles E. Goodspeed).

19. For example, Arthur M. Schlesinger, Jr., in his influential *Age of Jackson* (New York: Little, Brown, 1945), states that the transcendentalists "from their book-lined studies or their shady walks in cool Concord woods, . . . found

the hullabaloo of party politics unedifying and vulgar." Schlesinger goes on to state that "for the typical transcendentalists the flinching from politics perhaps expressed a failure they were seeking to erect into a virtue. The exigencies of responsibility were exhausting: much better to demand perfection and indignantly reject the half a loaf, than wear out body and spirit in vain grapplings with overmastering reality." According to Schlesinger, for transcendentalists like Emerson, "the headlong escape into perfection left responsibility far behind for a magic domain where mystic sentiment and gnomic utterance exorcised the rude intrusions of the world" (p. 382). Emerson, in particular, evinced these presumed shortcomings of the transcendentalists in dealing with the major concerns of society. "Politics" was "his greatest failure." Emerson "would not succumb to verbal panaceas, neither would he make the ultimate moral effort of Thoreau and cast off all obligation to society. Instead he lingered indecisively, accepting without enthusiasm certain relations to government but never confronting directly the implications of acceptance" (p. 384).

Fourteen years later, Stanley Elkins would echo Schlesinger's views in his well-known study *Slavery: A Problem in American Institutional and Intellectual Life* (New York: Grosset and Dunlap, 1959). In his study Elkins depicts the transcendentalists, and Emerson in particular, as almost totally detached from the everyday affairs of society. He states flatly that "the thinkers of Concord, who in the later thirties and forties would create an intellectual attitude at least coherent enough to be given a name—"Transcendentalism"—were men without connections. . . . They took next to no part in politics at all" (p. 147).

George Frederickson reinforces this notion of absolute antiinstitutionalism and aloofness when speaking of Emerson as a social thinker in his influential work *The Inner Civil War: Northern Intellectuals and the Crisis of the Union* (New York: Harper and Row, 1965). The view of Emerson as a recluse is so persistent in Frederickson's study that despite the fact that several biographers point out that Emerson was always a concerned and active citizen of Concord, Frederickson insists, on the contrary, that "the former hermit . . . had always shunned social commitments and public activity, even to the point . . . of avoiding town affairs in the village of Concord," and it was not until the war that Emerson became an "influential and active citizen" (pp. 178–79).

In the next decade Paul Boller rectified, somewhat, this decidedly lopsided view of Emerson's social existence in his *American Transcendentalism; 1830–1860* (New York: G. P. Putnam's Sons, 1974). Boller does take note of Emerson's numerous reform concerns, even while stressing Emerson's general dissatisfaction with most organized reformers, a position Boller supports, like earlier scholars, with references to early lectures like "Man the Reformer" (1841). This emphasis, however, leads him in turn to suggest that, despite his oft-articulated social concerns, Emerson was "primarily a man of letters, not a social activist"

(p. 102), and that "until 1850 . . . Emerson was decidedly lukewarm about the antislavery movement" (p. 106) for a variety of reasons.

Five years later, Taylor Stoehr, in his *Nay-saying in Concord; Emerson, Alcott, and Thoreau* (Hamden, Conn.: Archon Books, 1979), would offer further insights into the complexity of Emerson's thinking about abolition, but he furthers the impression that the transcendentalists overall, and Emerson in particular, were far removed from the major social reform movements of their day. He states, for example, that "compared to the communitists and other reformers, the transcendentalists are like a band of monks sitting cross-legged on the floor, indistinguishable in their chant" (p. 19). For Stoehr, the transcendentalists, at least as represented by his three subjects, remained largely aloof from the dusty affairs of the world. In fact, he suggests that they transcended them. "The truth is that Emerson, Alcott, and Thoreau, rather than say aye or nay, were more likely to abstain entirely. Theirs was the most conservative attitude of all, neither approving nor rejecting but simply awaiting the outcome—as their Eastern philosophers would say it, standing out of the way. The universe could be trusted to unfold without taking a vote" (p. 20).

The position that Anne Rose takes in her study *Transcendentalism as a Social Movement, 1830–1850* (New Haven: Yale University Press, 1981) is even more insistent than Stoehr's in its emphasis on transcendental aloofness from public affairs. She asserts that "of the original transcendentalists . . . only Emerson publicly opposed slavery with any regularity, but the same philosophical bent which made him a powerful speaker ran against the grain of the most important development of the decade, antislavery politics" (p. 219–20). In Rose's view, not only was Emerson generally disengaged from the more painful elements of the abolition crusade, but she seems to echo Elkins when she says of Emerson, "There was an abstraction in his approach to slavery which made his occasional musings on agencies of abolition—providence, commercial progress, purchase, disunion—comparatively desultory" (p. 219).

Finally, even a president of Yale University, A. Bartlett Giamatti, in an address entitled "Power, Politics and a Sense of History" (*The University and the Public Interest* [New York: Atheneum, 1981]), once stated that "with extraordinary literary skills at a crucial moment in our nation's life, it is Emerson who freed our politics and our politicians from any sense of restraint by extolling self-generated, unaffiliated power as the best foot to place in the small of the back of the man in front of you." According to Mr. Giamatti, "Emerson is as sweet as barbed wire, and his sentimentality as accommodating as a brick," and he leaves the distinct impression that Emerson cared but little for the have-nots of his society.

Index

Index

Index

Index

Index

Index

Index

Index

Breinigsville, PA USA
06 May 2010
237477BV00001B/59/P